Géneros de Gente in Early Colonial Mexico

A book in the Latin American and Caribbean
Arts and Culture publication initiative.
Latin American and Caribbean Arts and Culture is
supported by the Andrew W. Mellon Foundation.

GÉNEROS DE GENTE IN EARLY COLONIAL MEXICO
Defining Racial Difference

Robert C. Schwaller

UNIVERSITY OF OKLAHOMA PRESS : NORMAN

Library of Congress Cataloging-in-Publication Data

Names: Schwaller, Robert C., 1981– author.
Title: Géneros de gente in early colonial Mexico : defining racial difference / Robert C. Schwaller.
Description: Norman, OK : University of Oklahoma Press, [2016] | Includes bibliographical references and index.
Identifiers: LCCN 2016007549 | ISBN 978-0-8061-5487-9 (hardcover : alk. paper)
Subjects: LCSH: Mexico—Race relations—History—16th century. | Mexico—Race relations—History—17th century. | Mestizaje—Mexico—History | Ethnicity—Mexico—History. | Race discrimination—Mexico—History | Racially mixed people—Mexico—History—16th century. | Racially mixed people—Mexico—History—17th century. | Blacks—Race identity—Mexico. | Mestizos—Race identity—Mexico. | Mexico—History—Spanish colony, 1540–1810
Classification: LCC F1392.A1 S39 2016 | DDC 305.80097209/031—dc23
LC record available at http://lccn.loc.gov/2016007549

The paper in this book meets the guidelines for permanence and durability of the Committee on Production Guidelines for Book Longevity of the Council on Library Resources, Inc. ∞

Copyright © 2016 by the University of Oklahoma Press, Norman, Publishing Division of the University. Manufactured in the U.S.A.

All rights reserved. No part of this publication may be reproduced, stored in a retrieval system, or transmitted, in any form or by any means, electronic, mechanical, photocopying, recording, or otherwise—except as permitted under Section 107 or 108 of the United States Copyright Act—without the prior written permission of the University of Oklahoma Press. To request permission to reproduce selections from this book, write to Permissions, University of Oklahoma Press, 2800 Venture Drive, Norman, OK 73069, or email rights.oupress@ou.edu.

*In loving memory of Henry and Juliette Schwaller,
dueños de la Villa de Flores*

Contents

List of Illustrations	ix
List of Tables	xi
Acknowledgments	xiii
Introduction	3
Part I. Ideology and Law	
Chapter 1. Defining Difference in Iberia and the Americas	17
Chapter 2. Shaping Society	50
Part II. Lived Experience	
Chapter 3. Tacit *Españoles*	87
Chapter 4. Afro-indigenous *Mulatos*	111
Chapter 5. Marriage	147
Chapter 6. Occupation	185
Conclusion	223
Notes	229
Bibliography	263
Index	277

Illustrations

FIGURES

1. Castilian semantic domains of difference   19
2. Schema of *géneros de gente*   31
3. Depiction of Nahua disciplinary techniques   128

MAPS

Cartography by Erin Greb

1. Sixteenth-century Mexico City and Tlatelolco   153
2. Northern New Spain   155

Tables

3.1. Tacit *españoles* of sixteenth-century New Spain	92
4.1. Afro-indigenous marriage pairings, Santa Veracruz, 1576–1581	120
4.2. Afro-indigenous marriage pairings, Santa Veracruz, 1626–1631	121
4.3. Afro-indigenous marriage pairings, Guanajuato, 1605–1615	122
4.4. Afro-indigenous marriage pairings, Guanajuato, 1631–1641	123
5.1. Cohen's Kappa for Santa Veracruz and Guanajuato	156
5.2. Marriages, Santa Veracruz, 1576–1581	157
5.3. Conditional Kappas, Santa Veracruz, 1576–1581	157
5.4. Marriages, Guanajuato, 1605–1615	158
5.5. Conditional Kappas, Guanajuato, 1605–1615	158
5.6. Marriages, Santa Veracruz, 1626–1631	160
5.7. Conditional Kappas, Santa Veracruz, 1626–1631	160
5.8. Marriages, Guanajuato, 1631–1641	161
5.9. Conditional Kappas, Guanajuato, 1631–1641	161
6.1. *Mestizo* and *mulato* occupations, 1555–1657	190
6.2. *Mestiza* and *mulata* occupations, 1564–1598	191
6.3. Property held by *mulato* defendants	215
6.4. Property held by *mestizo* defendants	216

Acknowledgments

Every book has a history all its own. The seed of this book was planted long before I was born. In 1938, after taking Spanish classes at the University of Kansas, my grandfather Henry Schwaller decided to go on a road trip to Mexico to test his new language skills. I can only imagine the world that he entered. He traveled through a country still recovering from decades of civil war and revolution, only ten years removed from the Cristero Rebellion and only months after President Lázaro Cárdenas expropriated the foreign oil industry. The journey must have been thrilling, because the young Kansan fell in love with Mexico—its people, cultures, and history. After World War II, Henry began to bring his family to Mexico for long winter vacations. My grandmother Juliette fell in love too and came to see the mild winters as a respite from the bitter cold of the Great Plains. It was on one of these vacations in 1953 that my father, John F. Schwaller, first experienced Mexico. As my grandparents, father, and uncle continued to travel south for warmer winters, they saw the nation bloom and develop. Mexico City grew from a small colonial city to a megalopolis. In the late 1970s, as my father completed his dissertation research in Mexico City, Henry and Juliette decided to extend their stays and began to investigate places where they could retire. Eventually they settled on Cuernavaca, "City of Eternal Spring." I joined the family tradition and celebrated my first birthday in Cuauhnáhuac. By my third birthday, my grandparents would own a home there. In their home, often over winter vacations, I became enchanted with Mexico.

This book, like ones written by my father, owes its genesis and its completion to Henry and Juliette's love for Mexico. Their profound love for the Mexican people, cultures, and history has inspired at least two generations of historians and lives on in these pages.

While this book grows out of a long family history, no work of scholarship comes to fruition without immense help from mentors, colleagues, and friends. I am deeply grateful for all the great minds and kind hearts that have helped me as I developed this project. I am deeply grateful to the History Department at the Pennsylvania State University for guiding me as I took my first steps as a young historian. I am indebted to the mentorship of Matthew Restall. His encouragement and insights have helped me to find my way as a scholar. Over the years, his friendship has been a source of strength in the good times and the difficult ones. I am also extremely grateful for the other members of my graduate committee: Russell Lohse, Anthony Kay, and Kenneth Hirth. Their contributions to earlier versions of this research have greatly influenced the shape of this book. This project would not exist without the guidance and support of Ben Vinson III. The questions that first prompted my research into race in colonial Mexico stirred as Ben directed me in an independent study on the *sistema de castas*. Little did I know in the fall of 2003 that one day a book—this one—would be the result of that class.

Since leaving Penn State, I have been supported by numerous other colleagues and friends. I am very grateful for my time at the University of North Carolina at Charlotte. The year I spent in the Department of History there proved invaluable to me as I entered the world of professional academics. In my short time there, I benefited from a campus rich in Latin Americanist colleagues, and I am especially thankful for having had the opportunity to receive advice, counsel, and support from Jürgen Buchenau, Jerry Dávila, and Lyman Johnson.

Through an amazing confluence of luck, providence, encouragement, and hard work, in the fall of 2011 I joined the faculty of the University of Kansas. This institution has educated at least three generations of my family. My grandparents, Henry and Juliette, met just off the campus on the downslope of Mount Oread. Both my father and my uncle attended KU, as did my cousins Henry and Jennifer. My son, Fritz, is the fifth generation of my family to live in Lawrence, Kansas.

Besides having deep family ties to KU, I am blessed by numerous colleagues who have proven invaluable as this book took shape. From the moment I arrived on campus, Elizabeth Kuznesof has been a mentor, advocate, and guide. She has helped me grow as a scholar and researcher. Over dinners and tapas, Gregory Cushman and Santa Arias have provided me with hours of enlightening conversation. Their advice and encouragement has helped me navigate grant applications, annual reviews, committee assignments, and book contracts. I am also thankful to be part of a campus community rich in Latin Americanists from all over the disciplinary map. In my time here I have benefited from numerous colloquium discussions, seminar presentations, and excellent conversations. My thanks go out to Melissa Birch, Veronica Garibotto, Peter Haney, John Hoopes, Jill Kuhnheim, Ruben Flores, Pat Manning, Brent Metz, and Tony Rosenthal. My colleagues in the history department have provided a nurturing home where I have been able to grow as a scholar and educator. I am grateful to one and all, but special thanks go to Marie Brown, Luis Corteguera, Adrian Finucane, Megan Greene, Sarah Gregg, Jonathan Hagel, Sheyda Jahanbani, Paul Kelton, Elizabeth MacGonagle, Marta Vicente, and Nathan Wood for their support and companionship.

I am also indebted to numerous other colleagues, many of whom I have met as my research into race in colonial Mexico developed. My memories of the Archivo General de la Nación will always be shared with Richard Conway, Mark Lentz, Jemima Mieville, Tatiana Seijas, Jon Truitt, and Margarita Vargas. Similarly, I cannot pass the threshold of the Archivo General de Indias, in Seville, without remembering the numerous conversations and *cafés con leche* shared with Brad Benton, John Chuchiack, Magdalena Díaz, Ann Eller, Juan Jose Ponce-Vásquez, Allyson Poska, Elena Schnieder, and David Wheat. As I have shared my research through papers and presentations, I have been lucky to find critical minds full of useful comments and sage advice. For the many ways that they have helped me grow as a scholar, I thank Michael Francis, Kris Lane, Amara Solari, and Yanna Yannakakis. For decades of friendship, going back to when I was still in diapers, I must thank Francisco Morales, José Hernández Palomo, and María-Antónia Colomar.

The many years of research that helped me produce this book were supported by numerous grants and fellowships. This journey began with a James Scobie Pre-Dissertation Award from the Conference on Latin American History. I am grateful for additional support from Pennsylvania State University through a Sparks Dissertation

Fellowship and an Institute of Arts and Humanities Dissertation Release. I am deeply honored to have spent a year researching in Seville as Fulbright Research Fellow. The University of Kansas has generously supported my ongoing research and the conclusion of this project with a New Faculty General Research Fund Grant and a Craig Anthony Arnold Faculty Research Stipend.

As this book developed, some of my research was published. An earlier justification for the use of the term *géneros de gente* appeared in "'For Honor and Defence': Race and the Right to Bear Arms in Early Colonial Mexico," *Colonial Latin American Review* 21, no. 2 (2012): 239–66. Part of chapter 4 appeared in an earlier form as "'Mulata, Hija de Negro y India': Afro-Indigenous *Mulatos* in Early Colonial Mexico," *Journal of Social History* 44, no. 3 (2011): 885–910. I thank the editors for permission to reprint and expand upon these articles.

Finally, I must thank my family for their unwavering support and great sacrifices. This book honors Henry and Juliette Schwaller and Mary Taylor, even though they have left this world. I am deeply grateful for my parents, John and Anne. Not only did I first learn about Latin America traveling in their company, they have worked tirelessly to help support me as a son, scholar, and parent. They have read endless drafts and offered sage counsel at every turn. I must thank my maternal grandfather, Bramts (Bob Taylor), for always asking the question that catches me off guard. His quick mind and unique view of the world have challenged me throughout this process. For my brother, Will, I am thankful for an always-open ear and well-measured advice.

My greatest thanks goes to my wife, Rachel Beckley, who has been beside me as this book has evolved. She has given of her time over and over to help make it come to fruition. She is a colleague, a companion, a spouse, a partner in parenting, an advisor, and a friend. I could not have completed this book without her unwavering assistance and support. I can never repay the hours that she has put in to help me. I must also thank my in-laws, Joe and Deb Beckley, for their support and encouragement. They have learned far more about colonial Mexico than they thought they ever would, but they have also inspired me to grow in ways impossible to enumerate. My final thanks goes to the newest member of our family, Fritz. Although he has only been part of the family for a short time, he has been a light in the darkness and occasionally the source of a scream too. His boundless energy, overwhelming joy, and inquisitive nature have helped sustain my work and warmed my heart. To everyone who has enriched this work and touched my life, named or unnamed, I offer profound thanks.

Lawrence, Kansas
August 2015

Géneros de Gente in Early Colonial Mexico

Introduction

On December 19, 1554, the members of Tenochtitlan's indigenous *cabildo* (city council) wrote to their sovereign, Emperor Charles V of Spain. In their letter, they voiced concerns that the developing colonial order was stripping them of their rights and threatening their ability to govern the community. Specifically, the *cabildo* complained that the creation of two *alcadías mayores* (local magistracies) would impinge on the rights of the *cabildo* to administer justice within its jurisdiction. In response, the council members asked the emperor to support the decision of his viceroy, Don Luis de Velasco, to designate the two officials "protectors," not *alcaldes mayores.* The letter asked that the officials be charged "to save us from any Spaniard, *mestizo,* black, or *mulato* afflicting us in the marketplace, on the roads, in the canals, or in our homes."[1] The *cabildo* went on to implore the crown "to order [the protectors] to take great care with their task, for the Spaniards, *mestizos,* blacks, and *mulatos* do greatly harm us." The general pleading and supplicatory tone of this letter was not unique.

Almost immediately after the Spanish conquest, native communities—both those allied with the Spanish and those defeated in battle—recognized the power of the Spanish monarch and used petitions and memorials to further their communities' interests within the nascent colonial system. This strategy, which bore similarities to pre-Colombian imperialism, resonated well within the colonial order because it emphasized the traditional role of the Castilian monarch as mediator and judge. And, in so far as royal interests favored the perpetuation of a loyal indigenous elite and the survival of indigenous subjects as laborers and tribute payers, the monarchy was disposed to ameliorate policies that harmed these conquered subjects. Nevertheless, the specific damages claimed by the nobility of Tenochtitlan highlight other facets of the developing colonial order.

The charges leveled against "*mestizos,* blacks, and *mulatos*" cannot be overlooked. The emphatic condemnation of these particular groups highlights that within thirty years of the conquest—just over one generation—the colonial order included Spaniards, indigenous peoples, Africans, and individuals born of mixed ancestry, called *mestizos* and *mulatos*. Not only had these groups quickly become part of the fabric of New Spain, as early as the 1550s their presence was sufficiently large that the indigenous elite felt dismayed by their impact on the social, economic, and cultural order.

Importantly, such a view was not limited to the native inhabitants of New Spain. Two years before the members of the *cabildo* composed their missive, Fray Nicolas de Witte, an Augustinian friar, penned a strong warning to the emperor lamenting the moral decay of the region. Fray Nicolas charged, "The people are no less bellicose than they were in the past, more malicious than ever, less virtuous than ever, and of less conscience than ever." He blamed this radical change in morals on the changing demographics of the developing society. In particular, he leveled his ire against the "*gente baja y ruin*" (lowborn and base people) who, with slaves, "have caused the largest riots, most tyrannous uprisings, and the most cruelty that one can imagine in this land." Most importantly, he lamented that New Spain had become a land "that engenders and populates itself with a mixture of a people so evil. It is clear that this land is full of *mestizos,* who are born with a very bad disposition; it is full of *negros* and *negras* from whom are born the slaves; it is full of *negros* who marry *indias* from whom are born the *mulatos;* it is full of *mestizos* who marry *indias* from whom are born a diverse breed without number. From all these mixtures are born other diverse mixtures none good."[2] Fray Nicolas's diatribe expresses a vehement opposition to interethnic unions. To this clergyman, new groups like *mestizos* and *mulatos,* born of evil "mixtures," were causing the downfall of New Spain's social and political order. In his understanding, these groups not only inherited the base and dangerous characteristics of their progenitors but also engendered innumerable other mixtures, each of which further threatened the stability of New Spain.

During the sixteenth century, the Spanish monarchy responded to such complaints by enacting laws to limit interactions between indigenous groups and other members of society. Other laws sought to limit marriages and unions between Africans and indigenous persons as well as circumscribe the social and economic positions of *mestizos* and *mulatos*. Nevertheless, all these efforts would fail to undermine the progression outlined by Fray Nicolas. Interethnic unions continued to occur and the "diverse mixtures" of society grew even more complex. Although this process began with three founding groups (*españoles, indios,* and *negros*), by the middle of the sixteenth century colonial society contained a variety of new groups, including *mestizos, mulatos, castizos,* and *moriscos*.

Scholars of race in colonial Spanish America have referred to these categories of difference as the *sistema de castas* or *sociedad de castas*.[3] Recently scholars have argued that colonial subjects used the concept of *calidad* (quality) to describe these groupings.[4] Unfortunately, the terms *casta* and *calidad* are themselves products of the evolving discourse of difference. In the sixteenth century neither *casta* nor *calidad* had become synonymous with the range of difference embodied by *españoles, indios, negros, mestizos,* and *mulatos*. For example, in his letter, Fray Nicolas used the term *casta* to describe the offspring of *mestizos* and *indias* as "*una casta diversa sin numero.*" Importantly, the sense of his meaning corresponds to the notion of breed or lineage, the common sixteenth-century understanding.[5] He did not use the plural *castas* to collectively describe all the "diverse mixtures" of the social order. Nor did he use *casta* to reference the existing categories of *mestizo, mulato, negro,* or *indio*. Instead, for Fray Nicolas the Castilian term *casta* served to reference those born of a particular lineage (children of *mestizo* men and *india* women) that did not yet have a specific name. The prevailing use of *casta* and *calidad* in scholarly literature stems from the fact that most studies on the development of race in colonial Mexico have examined the seventeenth and eighteenth centuries. By that time, the meanings of *casta* and *calidad* had evolved to encompass the various categories of difference that divided colonial society.[6]

Even though the concepts of *casta* and *calidad* had yet to develop, sixteenth-century Iberians did develop a framework for understanding the growing diversity within their society. During the early colonial period, the phrase *géneros de gente* (types of people) came to encapsulate the belief that colonial society was made up of different kinds of people. Chapter 1 will examine how Iberians' Old World cultural framework preconditioned them to see a social order composed of various types of people. Eventually the concept of *géneros de gente* would be subsumed by the later concept of *castas* and a *sociedad de castas*. The chapters that follow highlight the gradual development of a framework of difference that initially viewed society as a pluralistic mix of diverse types of people.

Although this book describes the evolution of race, the categories of difference under analysis were not yet "races." Consequently, I have avoided using the term "race" except in order to draw specific parallels with later concepts and beliefs. Nevertheless, during the sixteenth century, categories of difference had begun to undergo a process of racialization.[7] Individual terms of difference encoded particular cultural, social, and at times physical stereotypes. In perpetuating these linkages such terms served to naturalize difference and entrench prejudice in racial ways. By the late seventeenth century, what had initially developed as *géneros de gente* would more closely model modern notions of race as Iberian thought began to view the differences inherent in such categories as natural qualities.[8] Yet in order to understand the nature and function of later notions of race we must delve into the origins of such thought. This work serves as a bridge that connects medieval Iberian notions of difference to the unique societies forged in the Americas.

Géneros de Gente in Early Colonial Mexico traces this process in two ways. First, this work analyzes the ideological and legal development of *géneros de gente*. Second, an examination of early colonial *mestizos* and *mulatos* helps to illustrate how individuals of mixed ancestry experienced life within the colonial order. Together these two strands of analysis illustrate that the process by which colonial categories of difference were created, defined, and appropriated into law was complex and historically constituted. The stereotypes and legal restrictions imposed on various *géneros de gente* grew out of the conjuncture between previous notions of difference and new social, economic, and cultural encounters in the Americas. Although historical encounters within the colonial order produced abstract racial stereotypes and codified legal restrictions, the specific experiences of colonial subjects were not monolithic but rather mediated by a matrix of factors tied to their person and lifestyle. Any individual's social, cultural, and economic relationships could reinforce or undercut abstract stereotypes and restrictions. As a result, individuals ascribed to the same *género* could lead very different lives. Because of this variety, many individuals of mixed ancestry were able to live in ways that openly rejected or violated *género* stereotypes or legal prohibitions or both. Even as the colonial order established a system of governance that entrenched racial difference, colonial subjects' social networks, cultural affinities, occupation, and residence could mediate their racial existence.

The dual focus of this study mirrors two historiographical trajectories exploring race in Spanish America. First, a large body of scholarship has focused on the structure and organization of the *sistema de castas*. The issue of structure has been examined primarily through quantitative methodologies. Parish records, ecclesiastical censuses, and tax records have helped uncover the relationship between ascribed category, occupation, marriage, and occasionally residence. The great debate has focused on whether the *sistema de castas* reflected a late medieval "estate" division of society or if these categories comprised an early manifestation of a class-ranked society.[9] While the estate model emphasized continuities with the corporate social organization that predominated in late medieval Iberia, the class model emphasized the increasingly strong relationship between occupation and ascribed socio-racial category. This research has been invaluable in demonstrating the complex web of factors that become incorporated into socio-racial categories.[10] More recent works have examined the importance of cultural preconceptions in shaping colonial stereotypes.[11]

Second, scholars have examined the ways in which colonial subjects have experienced race, especially the ways in which individuals and groups could mediate and negotiate their categorizations. In general, Afro-Mexicans have received the most attention. Research into social place and ascription have relied much more on qualitative documents, including *cofradía* records, criminal cases, militia rosters, and

Inquisition cases. These sources have allowed scholars to uncover the processes by which slaves negotiated their experience of slavery and the mechanisms they used to form and maintain families.[12] Regional studies on African and African-descended groups have emphasized that the experience of slavery, community, and family formation varied depending on local demography, economics, and social structures.[13] Institutional studies have shown that *casta* labels could facilitate the creation of corporate identities. *Cofradia* membership and militia service provided Afro-Mexicans social spaces for the creation and maintenance of community.[14] Moreover, these corporate bodies allowed *mulatos*, *negros*, and *pardos* to negotiate collectively for increased rights and privileges or for the redress of grievances. Witchcraft and popular medicine have been revealed as occupations that afforded Afro-Mexicans opportunities for social interaction and economic advancement.[15] Finally, the relationship between Africans and native populations has seen increased analysis. Although typically described as antagonistic by Spanish sources, African-indigenous interaction could be as much amicable as conflictive, and indigenous communities often provided Africans and Afro-Mexicans an alternative location for the creation and maintenance of families.[16]

Géneros de Gente in Early Colonial Mexico adds to both fields of inquiry by extending our knowledge of these processes backward into the sixteenth century. This work supports the idea that *géneros de gente* evolved from a society divided along corporate lines and argues that its origins lie in Iberian conceptualizations of difference. By noting the complex ethnic and religious past of Iberia, this study emphasizes that in the Americas Iberians were preconditioned to seek out and define categories of difference in order to organize and govern a pluralistic society. Yet, importantly, the abstract stereotypes and legal restrictions born from this process cannot be understood without examining the lived experience of colonial subjects. The analysis of early colonial *mestizos* and *mulatos* complicates our understanding of *géneros de gente* by illustrating that these terms were not rigid categories. Each one was mutable in a variety of ways. The variability found within the sixteenth-century uses of the terms *mestizo* and *mulato* speaks to the contextual nature of ascription even in the earliest manifestation of socio-racial categorization. In colonial Mexico—

and likely throughout Spanish America—the language of difference and the ascription of socio-racial epithets were never based on a single criterion but rather represented a holistic valuation based on multiple facets of an individual's physical traits and culturally significant attributes.

By exploring the formation of ideology and law alongside that of social position and lived experience, this book reconciles two distinct debates over the history of race in colonial Mexico. The intersection of these two frameworks provides a window into the strengths and weaknesses of early Spanish imperialism. Most crucially, this study shows that although colonial elites and the monarchy were able to create and disseminate an ideology of difference and incorporate that ideology into law, the ability of the colonial state to enact and regulate those laws was limited. Despite attempts to prevent the rise of groups of mixed ancestry, social, economic, and cultural forces conspired to facilitate such growth. Additionally, once present in society, individuals of mixed ancestry were able to achieve levels of social mobility and success incongruent with their juridical station. This disjuncture helps illustrate that despite being an "empire of law," the state's ability to enforce its laws was limited by the degree to which the populace—including secular and religious officials—accepted and adhered to them. Moreover, the comparison between the idealized legal code and the actualized experience of colonial subjects speaks to Brian Owensby's recent charge to embrace a more nuanced view of law in Latin America that recognizes that law "is best seen in terms of the complex, open-ended interplay between recognized legal principles and the words and actions of all who took part in legal proceedings."[17] The disjuncture between the juridical and ideological and the social and quotidian highlights the fact that colonial constructions of difference, the basis for later understandings of race, were from the outset dynamic and ever-shifting. Most importantly, the processes that gave rise to colonial notions of racial difference resulted from the interrelationship between quotidian social relations and the developing colonial state. A close examination of the historical contingencies that constituted this evolution exposes the early modern antecedents to modern conceptions of race. In doing so, *Géneros de Gente in Early Colonial Mexico* contributes to a growing body of evidence that highlights the role of Spanish colonial encounters in shaping modern Western civilization.[18]

The sources used to examine this process come from colonial-era documentation preserved in Mexico and Spain. Most of the material used in this study is housed in the Archivo General de la Nación (AGN) of Mexico and the Archivo General de Indias (AGI) in Seville, Spain. In conducting archival research, the aim of this study was to search for documents that could provide a window into the underlying beliefs influencing the ascription of socio-racial labels. Consequently, many of the sources consulted were chosen for their ability to provide qualitative information about colonial subjects. Ideally such documents can help construct a "thick description" of colonial perceptions of difference as well as convey the richness of individuals' particular experiences.[19] Although the documents usually do not render a scene as clearly as one experienced via the eyes or ears of the ethnographer, archival material can provide very candid views into the everyday life of individuals and allow the cultural historian to construct a detailed inscription of cultural phenomena otherwise lost to the past. Additionally, this study draws from the work of James Lockhart and other historians of the New Philology, which has focused on the close linguistic analysis of colonial-era, native-language documents.[20] Key to these works was the textual analysis of particular native words and concepts that help us better understand colonial indigenous society. *Géneros de Gente in Early Colonial Mexico* draws from the New Philology in a tangential manner. Although primarily concerned with Spanish-language sources and the cultural perceptions conveyed by those texts, this work is ultimately a study in historical cultural linguistics. It focuses on the detailed analysis of a small set of words and associated beliefs created within the framework of Iberian culture and articulated in the Castilian language.[21] To that end, it likewise engages in philological analysis by attempting to delineate the semantic domains that shaped the perception of difference in early colonial New Spain.

Scholarship on the African diaspora has also influenced the direction and methodology of this study. Ben Vinson has charged scholars to explore the "space in-between, among, and through various racial existences."[22] This call demands that scholars of race search for complexity and mutability wherever they might be found. *Géneros de Gente in Early Colonial Mexico* has incorporated this goal into its dual focus on the origins and lived experience of *géneros de gente*. This comparison highlights that discriminatory and prejudicial terms did not completely circumscribe the lives of those being defined. In seeking to highlight the permeability, contextuality, and fixedness of colonial labels, this research broadens our understanding of the variability inherent in racial language. This approach furthers our understanding of the African diaspora by exploring the similarities and differences between individuals of African ancestry and other colonial subjects bounded by the nascent racial categories of the early colonial period.

The organization of this study reflects its varied documentary sources and multiple findings. Part 1 explores the Iberian notions of difference and their transformation into *géneros de gente* in the New World. Chapter 1 focuses on the evolution of Iberian notions of difference into colonial *géneros de gente*. Before venturing to the New World, Iberians lived in a diverse society. This variability manifested itself in a society composed of numerous corporate groups defined socially and juridically. As Iberians colonized the Americas and described the diverse population of their new kingdoms, these older notions of difference were reconstituted within new *géneros de gente*. Chapter 2 adds to our structural understanding of sixteenth-century *géneros de gente* by tracing the juridical history of socio-racial labels. This chapter provides a diachronic assessment of the forces that led to the entrenchment of *géneros de gente* into colonial legal codes during the sixteenth century. Most importantly, legal norms evolved recursively as particular local circumstances influenced royal policies. In turn, those policies and juridical responses entrenched stereotypes and contributed to evolving conceptions of difference. As local conditions changed or did not, this process repeated and could incorporate new, locally conditioned notions of difference into the ideological and juridical order.

Part 2 moves away from the ideological and juridical and examines the quotidian experiences of individuals labeled *mestizo* and *mulato*. By focusing on the two most common *género* categories for individuals of mixed ancestry, these four chapters uncover the diversity of lived experiences found within two *géneros de gente*. In exposing this diversity they illustrate how social and cultural forces within early colonial society differentially affected individuals of mixed ancestry. Chapter 3 examines the existence of a unique sixteenth-century group, one I have termed "tacit *españoles*." These individuals, often born to elite conquest-era Spaniards by native women, lived lives very much like their Spanish contemporaries. Such individuals reveal the strong social and cultural basis for ascription along the *español-indio* spectrum.

Chapter 4 turns to early colonial *mulatos* and highlights the presence of Afro-indigenous *mulatos*. These individuals represented a unique subset of New Spain's *mulatos*. An examination of qualitative and quantitative evidence suggests that Afro-indigenous *mulatos* may have accounted for as many as half of New Spain's *mulatos* during the sixteenth century. These individuals manifested strong multigenerational ties to indigenous kin that were often based in their acculturation to indigenous ways of life. Additionally, this chapter highlights the different factors that contributed to *mulato* and *mestizo* ascription. Although both relied heavily on social and cultural attributes, they did so in different ways.

Chapter 5 examines the relationship between *género* and marriage. Parish marriage registers from the late sixteenth and early seventeenth century, provide a window into early colonial endogamy and exogamy. By comparing parish records with individual lives preserved within Inquisition cases, this chapter illustrates the ways that *mestizos* and *mulatos* experienced marriage. In doing so, it reveals that social networks, economic relationships, and cultural affinities played a large role in facilitating marriages for individuals of mixed ancestry. The marriage choices of *mestizos* and *mulatos* invite a reconsideration of our understanding of endogamy and exogamy. Even when marrying spouses from other *géneros*, marriages frequently grew out of strong social and cultural affinities that transcended the boundaries of nascent categories of difference.

Chapter 6 turns to the occupations of *mestizos* and *mulatos*. Although juridical codes imposed real limits on advancement for individuals of these *géneros*, the range of occupations and economic positions held by men of these *géneros* varied considerably. As with marriage, varied social networks, kinship ties, residence, and cultural affinities contributed to diverse experiences of work. On the whole, the economic development of the colony encouraged both mobility and entrepreneurial choices by non-Spaniards. The need for labor in rural areas drew *mestizos* and *mulatos* into spaces that allowed them to interact with indigenous and Hispanic individuals. This exploration of ways of work reveals that by the end of the sixteenth century, *mestizos* and *mulatos* had already come to represent an important middle layer of the colonial work force.

Overall, the comparison drawn between part 1 and part 2 reveals the complex origin of New Spain's *géneros de gente*. While Spaniards created these categories of difference, their stereotypes and legal meanings evolved over time. Events on the ground shaped the ways that the monarchy responded to colonists' fears and complaints about the growing diversity within society. Royal legislation appropriated and perpetuated popular stereotypes. As new conflicts prompted further legislation, the legal code continued to evolve. Yet, even as the body of law came to entrench difference, the lived experience of individuals remained rooted in their particular contexts. Kinship, social networks, residence, and acculturation could all influence the racial experience of *mestizos* and *mulatos*. The diversity found among individuals of mixed ancestry provides a more complex picture of how difference came to be defined. In doing so, it reveals important tensions within Spanish colonialism and the developing social order.

NOTE ON LANGUAGE AND TRANSLATION

Given the nuance of categories of difference, I have tried to be as specific and consistent as possible throughout the text. Because the terms being examined had not yet become known as races or castes (*castas*), I have avoided the use of those terms unless drawing attention to the continuities or disjunctures between sixteenth-century *géneros de gente* and later permutations of difference. I have chosen to italicize colonial categories of difference throughout this study in order to emphasize that notions of difference were embodied in specific Castilian terms. The linguistic meanings of *mulato* in sixteenth-century Mexico may share similarities with the later English construction of "mulatto," but the two terms are not equivalent. Similarly, the cultural significance of *negro* to an *español* was not necessarily the same as our understanding of the English terms "black" or "Negro." I have also used the gendered endings for *géneros de gente* (e.g., *indias* for indigenous women) when appropriate. Unless otherwise noted, the translations that appear in this text are mine. In some instances, I have included the original Spanish transcription in the endnotes to complement my rendering. When included, transcriptions appear as in the original. When discussing individuals and places in the chapters that follow, I have modernized archaic spellings of proper names and included accents where necessary.

Part I

Ideology and Law

CHAPTER 1

DEFINING DIFFERENCE IN IBERIA AND THE AMERICAS

> The *españoles* of this land grow and multiply greatly, but in addition to the *españoles* born here and those that come from those kingdoms [Castile and Aragon], there are many *mulatos* and *mestizos*, people very poorly inclined but bold and capable of any shameful thing, and it is advisable that Your Majesty plant and sustain noble people here in your service to defend against them and the inconveniences that ruinous people might cause.
>
> *Letter from various conquistadors and early settlers to King Philip II, 1564*

The search for difference in the New World cannot begin without understanding the ways in which Europeans, particularly Iberians, differentiated the members of their own societies.[1] How they viewed the world in which they lived shaped and preconditioned the lands that they would come to conquer and colonize. While the Americas may have represented a vast unknown landscape populated by diverse and unique peoples, conquistadors and settlers could conceptualize the unknown and unexpected only through the cultural framework that structured their understanding of human difference. The search for Spanish American racial distinctions therefore begins in early modern Iberia in the kingdoms of Castile and Aragon.

Although scholars and laypeople alike typically categorize the conquests of the late fifteenth century as Spanish, the Iberian men and women who participated in these ventures had only recently begun to use the word *españoles* (Spaniards) to describe themselves and their nation. In fact, even our use of the name "Spain" to describe the state undertaking colonial expansion belies the fact that no political entity called *España* existed during the fifteenth and sixteenth centuries. In 1474, the dynastic marriage of Ferdinand of Aragon and Isabel of Castile united the two largest Iberian kingdoms and started the process that would form the future state of Spain. Nevertheless, in the fifteenth century the subjects over whom Ferdinand and Isabel ruled were immensely heterogeneous.

As descendants of Phoenicians, Celts, Romans, Vandals, Visigoths, Berbers, and Arabs, the subjects of Ferdinand and Isabel manifested almost every possible human variety of skin, hair, and eye color. They spoke any number of languages—Arabic, Basque, Castilian, Catalan, Galego, Ladino, and Valencian—and practiced at least three different faiths, Christianity, Judaism, and Islam. Moreover, unlike other parts of Europe, the kingdoms of Castile and Aragon never developed fully articulated feudal societies. While there was a distinction between nobility, commoners, and the church, corporate associations and unique political arrangements mediated the relationships between individuals within society.[2] As Teofilo Ruiz has argued, the complex social order of early modern Iberia grew out of "social filiations" that were tied to "privilege, tax-exemption and power."[3]

When Iberians expanded into the Atlantic world, their conception of the social order mediated the ways in which they constructed difference among the new peoples they encountered. Importantly, just as earlier notions of difference were rooted in culture and society, so too would their new understandings of difference take shape via the complex interaction between cultural belief and social interactions. This chapter argues that prior to Atlantic expansion, Castilians had developed a complex set of categories to define and describe their contemporaries. The pluralistic nature of this framework predisposed Iberians to incorporate the new groups of people they encountered into a social order that anticipated diversity. In the Americas, new categories were imbued with certain stereotypical attributes, each shaped by its own particular historical development.

To illustrate the unfolding of this process, this chapter is divided into two parts. The first highlights the pluralistic nature of medieval Iberian society and argues that social difference could be mapped into three semantic domains: socioeconomic, ethno-religious, and

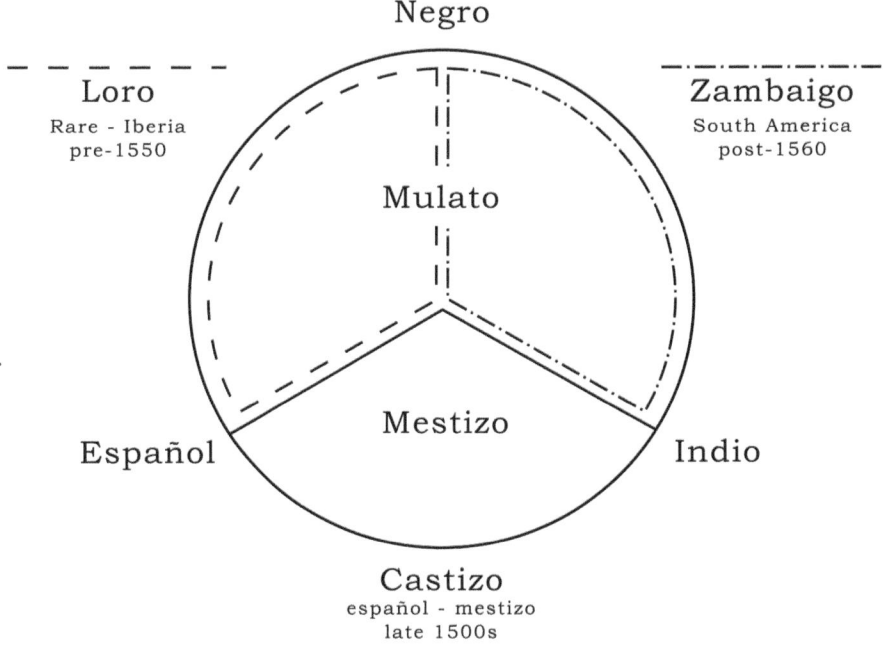

Figure 1. Castilian semantic domains of difference

ethno-geographical (see figure 1). These domains represent a useful means of understanding the matrix of social difference that individuals in Iberia used to define and contextualize their contemporaries. The second part of this chapter traces the evolution of the primary New World categories of socio-racial difference and argues that these colonial notions of difference were formed through interplay between Iberian preconceptions and the particular historical forces that brought Iberians into contact with new groups of people.

IBERIAN ANTECEDENTS

Socioeconomic Terms

Categories of socioeconomic difference represented some of the clearest markers of an individual's overall social position and served as a catchall for political and economic status. These categories were not directly tied to any modern class model of society but tended to elide social status with general economic position. Socioeconomic categories served to define all individuals, from the wealthiest noble to the poorest peasant or slave. Importantly these terms were not just markers of wealth and status, they also conveyed moral valuations that privileged those with higher status.

The highest rungs of the socioeconomic hierarchy were held by individuals who could lay claim to hereditary titles of nobility such as "duke," "marquess," or "count." With title frequently came land and seigniorial privilege.[4] The financial benefits of those privileges led their contemporaries to call them *los ricos hombres* (the rich men). Below this elite group were the *hidalgos* (petty nobility). The men and women that constituted the untitled nobility could vary in their wealth and status. Membership in this level of nobility was based the complex interrelation between lineage, privilege, and lifestyle.[5] In general, members of the petty nobility could trace their lineage to a titled forbear, held privileges granted by the monarch, and were publicly reputed to lead noble lives. Yet the vagaries of membership ensured that entrance into the noble ranks was possible for the upwardly mobile. Conversely, individuals with diminishing resources and social capital could see their claim to nobility contested by their contemporaries.

Below the nobility were the commoners. Like the nobility, the common classes manifested a range of socioeconomic diversity. The greatest division between commoners existed between those who held some form of privilege or tax exemption and those who did not. Most commoners were required to pay a head tax called the *pecho*, and because of this they were known as *pecheros*. The exempt, *los francos*, tended to work in professions privileged by the state, such as mint workers, textile producers, and servants of religious institutions. Just as entrance into the petty nobility was possible for those of some means, the acquisition of exempt status represented a viable strategy for upward mobility among non-nobles.[6]

Importantly these divisions not only represented markers of increasing or decreasing wealth and social status, they carried with them moral valuations tied to their relative position in the socioeconomic hierarchy. Those at the top of the hierarchy viewed the majority of the population as lacking honor, social grace, and personal virtue. From this perspective commoners could be glossed with the term *gente común* (commoners), *gente baja* (low-born people), *gente vil* (vile people), or *gente perdida* (lost people).⁷ All four terms, in order of increasing disdain, could be used to reflect the condescension that elites had of those below them. At the opposite end of the spectrum, those with noble titles or claim to exemptions and prerogatives could be glossed under the terms *gente honrada* (honored people), *de buenas costumbres* (well-mannered), or *de buena vida y fama* (renowned).⁸ Within this framework, one's place on the socioeconomic hierarchy implied a certain moral character. The tendency to imbue social difference with moral value would continue in the creation of new categories in the Atlantic world.

Ethno-religious Terms

As a result of the almost eight centuries of conflict and cohabitation between Christians, Jews, and Muslims, religion and religious categories of difference played a crucial role in ascribing to an individual a place in the social world. The basic terms for describing a person's religious place in society were *cristiano, judío,* and *moro*. Through the centuries many Jews and Muslims living in Christian kingdoms converted to Christianity. The need to describe these newly converted Christians led to the creation of several other terms of difference. Generically, converts were called *cristianos nuevos* (New Christians) to distinguish them those whose families had always been Christian—*cristianos viejos* (Old Christians).⁹ Beyond that basic distinction the terms *converso* and *morisco* were used to describe converted Jews and Muslims respectively. Importantly, these terms were not limited to individuals who converted. These categories became multigenerational markers used to describe individuals whose ancestors had converted previously. This tendency to elide lineage with religious ancestry was made manifest through two ethno-religious concepts central to Iberian thought: *casta* and *raza*.

In the Americas, by the mid-seventeenth and eighteenth centuries, the term *casta* would come to refer to individuals with some degree of mixed ancestry. Yet four centuries earlier this term referred not to mixed ancestry but rather to untainted lineage. During the late medieval period *casta* was used to define a particular type, and was used for both animals and humans. In Covarrubias's 1611 dictionary, *casta* was defined as "representing noble lineage," and it could be applied to plants, animals, and people to describe purity in breeding or ancestry.[10] This Iberian root would enter the English language via its use by the Portuguese to describe the social divisions, *castas*, found in India during the sixteenth century—the caste system.[11]

Closely related to *casta* was the term *raza*. More so than *casta*, *raza* defined an individual's religious lineage. Covarrubias gives three definitions for the word: "*Raza:* the breed of purebred horses, those that are branded so that they are known. *Raza*, in cloth, the thread which is different than the rest. Seems to have been almost like *reaza* because *aza*, in Tuscan, means thread, and the *raza* of cloth is similar. *Raza*, in that of lineages, is taken to be the bad part, such as having *raza* of Moors or Jews."[12] The first definition is directly tied to *casta* and its implication of pure, unblemished lineage, a purebred horse. The second definition suggests the notion that *raza* referred to something unlike the rest, a thread that stands out. The third definition shares several aspects with the previous two: the inherent notion of lineage or descent and that of pejorative difference.

At their core, these terms reflect the blending of cultural categories with genealogical ones. Religious belief and practice came to be seen as an attribute that could be passed down from generation to generation. In Iberia this confusion was institutionalized through the belief in *limpieza de sangre* (purity of blood). This phrase encapsulated the view that religious impurity, specifically descent from Jews, Muslims, and heretics, was transmitted from generation to generation. Broadly speaking, the emphasis on *limpieza de sangre* evolved as a means to circumscribe the social and economic advancement of New Christians.

From the late fourteenth century through the sixteenth century, various religious and secular institutions passed ordinances that required individuals to prove their *limpeza de sangre*.[13] The existence of these statutes and of the hardened distinction between *cristianos nuevos* and *cristianos viejos*, mandated that individuals wishing to hold secular or religious posts, take religious orders, receive university degrees, or enter guilds provide a *probanza de limpieza de sangre*, or proof of blood purity.[14] These *probanzas* used both written documentation such as censuses, tax records, and birth and marriage registers, as well as oral testimony from community members to determine an individual's religious lineage.[15] According to María Elena Martínez, the oral component of these examinations helped shape the way that Iberians began to view their contemporaries. The increasing emphasis on genealogy and its relationship to religious difference increased the salience of those differences and led individuals to see the world through that prism. In other words, even though only some institutions required *limpieza de sangre,* the need to prove an individual's blood purity through *publica voz y fama* (public reputation) placed the issue of genealogy and ancestry into the realm of communal discourse.[16] The increased salience of religious descent in the sixteenth and seventeenth centuries helped transpose the conception of genealogical purity (or taint) onto the diverse new society developing in the Americas.[17]

Ethno-geographic Terms

The complex political history of Iberia also helped spur the development of categories that defined individuals based upon their place of birth and residence. The two most important terms used to describe ethno-geographic diversity were *naturaleza* and *vecinidad.* The former described one's place of birth, one's natal home, while the latter referred to formal membership (citizenship, in modern terms) within a corporate community. Tamar Herzog has explored the complex evolution of both terms and their uses in Iberia and Latin America from the sixteenth to the eighteenth century. She argues that these terms were essential to defining individuals' positions as members of communities and as bearers of specific rights and privileges.[18] Due to the varied history of conquest, reconquest, and incorporation, different political jurisdictions and cities had different legal systems and particular privileges vis-à-vis the monarchy. Consequently, residents and natives of different parts of Iberia could lay claim to a diverse array of rights depending on their *naturaleza* and *vecinidad.*

Intricately tied to the maintenance of power and authority within a complex and heterogeneous empire, *naturaleza* served as shorthand for defining difference between the disparate regions of the Spanish kingdoms. *Naturaleza* in a given community was required in order to hold appointments to certain public offices or benefices.[19] In legal proceedings witnesses were identified by their names and *naturalezas*. For vassals of Castile and Aragon the mention of community of origin and kingdom were all that was necessary to define one's *naturaleza*.

On the other hand, foreigners living within these kingdoms were very often described by their *nación* (nation) of origin rather than by their natal community. Terms such as *catalán, portugués, genovés, piamontés, milanés,* and *veneciano* were used to describe various individuals from areas outside Castile.[20] Additionally, sixteenth-century Inquisition cases from Mexico record the use of terms such as *vizcaíno, flamenco* (to refer to the Dutch), *francés, inglés,* and *alemán*.[21] These national terms served to localize non-Castilian *naturalezas*. Whether based in an Iberian locality or a *nación*, these terms played a vital role in establishing an individual's social identity.

During the fifteenth century, as the Portuguese slave trade began to bring more and more African slaves to the Iberian peninsula, residents there began to incorporate African *naciones* into their schema of difference. Sub-Saharan African slaves were collectively grouped under the Castilian term *negro*. This somatic marker reflected their distinct phenotypical appearance as well as differentiated them from other slaves, in particular *esclavos blancos*.[22] Despite the glossing of all sub-Saharans as *negros*, Iberians did recognize distinctions among these slaves. For example, slave records from Valencia include references to categories including *jalof, bañul, beafer, berbesi, calabres,* and *sapi*.[23] Similar documentation from Andalusia lists terms such as *jalof, manicongo, iburon, capi,* and *jolongo*.[24] Iberians integrated these terms into their matrix of difference as new *naciones*. In some cases, slaves received the label of the geographic region that they came from. For example, *guinea, cabo verde,* and *terranova* referred to specific regions of the West African coastline stretching from modern-day Gambia to the Bight of Benin.[25] In general, the phrases *negro de* (*negro* from) or *negro de tierra de* (*negro* from the land of) preceded the ethnic marker or general region.[26] In other cases, the ethnic name or region served as a surname (for example, "Juan Angola").

In practice, Iberians used African ethnic and regional labels similarly to their use of national labels from Europe and the circum-Mediterranean region. In both cases, these terms helped to localize an individual from a distant region within a known ethno-geographic category. Both European and African *naciones* could be applied as surnames. Yet the use of these African *naciones* differed from the use of European national labels in an important way. While European *naciones* frequently took the adjectival form, African *naciones* did not. For example, "Juan Genovese" uses the adjectival reference for Genoa, while "Juan Angola" simply uses the ethno-geographic label. At one level this suggests greater familiarity with other European groups. Longer association would have led to clear distinctions between European *naciones* and the development of adjectival forms for those groups. The more recent exposure to Africa allowed for the introduction of *naciones* but not their conversion into adjectives. Additionally, the lack of an adjectival form may suggest doubt in the veracity or applicability of a specific ethnic marker to slaves. The European explorers and traders were aware that African slavery involved the capture of individuals from other ethnic groups. The common use of *de* or *de tierra de* may indicate that Iberians understood that African *naciones* could refer to regions of sale and not necessarily to regions of birth.

More so than *naturaleza*, an individual's *vecinidad* marked one's primary location of residence. Individuals acquired *vecinidad* through residence and continuous participation in a specific community.[27] Generally, the status of being a *vecino* was defined through informal means, although formal procedures could be used if an individual's status was contested.[28] *Vecino* status generally implied access to the rights and privileges of the community as well as responsibilities, including the requirement to pay taxes, maintain residence, and serve in local militias.[29] The social status afforded *vecinos* reflected a commonly accepted social marker that worked in conjunction with an individual's *naturaleza* and socioeconomic status. Importantly, while one's birthplace determined one's *naturaleza*, an individual acquired *vecindad* during his or her life. In this regard, the acquisition of *vecindad* represented an important marker of social standing, one that might mitigate other less mutable markers of difference.

DEFINING DIFFERENCE IN EARLY SPANISH AMERICA

The diversity of socioeconomic, ethno-religious, and ethno-geographic terms in early modern Iberia created a matrix of difference in which individuals could be defined by various aspects of their lifestyle, lineage, and outward appearance. When explorers, traders, and conquistadors from Iberia began to encounter new groups in the Atlantic world, they sought to define and categorize them through the lens of their own cultural beliefs and understandings.[30] Consequently, the Iberian framework of difference would form the basis for their conceptualizations of the human groups they encountered or who came into existence as a result of those interactions. Importantly, this transfer was not perfect. The categories of difference devised by Iberians could not be mapped perfectly onto the people they encountered. Yet the experience of living within a pluralistic society containing multivalent categories of difference intimately shaped the evolving language of difference in the Americas.

During the sixteenth century, five main categories came to define the bulk of colonial subjects: *español, indio, negro, mestizo,* and *mulato.* Each of these terms would be inscribed with beliefs originating in the earlier matrix of difference. The formative triad of *españoles, indios,* and *negros* encapsulated ethno-geographic difference most clearly, as each term implied a distinct linage from diverse parts of the globe. Terms of mixed ancestry, *mestizo* and *mulato,* would likewise encode ethno-geographic distinctions, with the added twist that such individuals were perceived as having an amalgamation of characteristics originating in their parent lineages. Conceptions of religious difference would similarly be inscribed into colonial terms. In the Americas, most *españoles* could lay claim to being *cristianos viejos* while Africans and Native Americans would be marked as perpetual *cristianos nuevos.* Categories of mixed ancestry embodied differential perceptions of religious purity, as *mestizos* were perceived as being closer to *cristianos viejos* than were *mulatos*. In the Americas, socioeconomic differences were also transferred in a modified way. In the colonial context, all Spaniards could claim privileges generally reserved to Iberian *hidalgos* while the burden of tribute converted *indios, negros,* and *mulatos* into the *pecheros* of the New World. Importantly, the social construction of these new categories occurred over time as Iberians encountered new peoples and began to render them within their existing frameworks of understanding.

Géneros de Gente

Over the course of the sixteenth century, the diverse array of individuals that comprised colonial society came to be seen as a collection of *géneros de gente,* or "types of people." Scholars have not previously used the phrase *géneros de gente* to refer to the new categories of difference that would come to define race in Spanish America. The lack of previous scholarly emphasis may be due to the fact that the phrase *géneros de gente* was not a formal, legal encapsulation of racial, or ethnic, variety. Rather, the phrase embodied a general Iberian perception of a diverse society. The most common term used by most scholars to describe these groups has been *castas*. However, as mentioned above, this usage is anachronistic for the sixteenth century.[31] At no point in the sixteenth century was *casta* used to describe these new categories of people, nor was its plural, *castas,* synonymous with these groups collectively.[32]

Some scholars utilize the terms *calidad* and *calidades* (quality, qualities) to describe the spectrum of new categories of difference.[33] While *calidad* is less problematic than *casta* for the sixteenth century, *calidad* tended to emphasize distinctions along the socioeconomic spectrum and the conflation of wealth with political privilege and social status. Scholars who favor *calidad* as the salient marker of difference view the categories of *español, indio, negro, mestizo,* and *mulato* as each embodying different levels of quality. While certainly true in a general sense, the use of *calidad* as an umbrella term for the colonial hierarchy of socio-racial difference overlooks the fact that differences in *calidad* could be found within any one of the included categories and could vary depending on a specific individual's perceived social circumstances.

In official documentation, *calidad* was used as a means of judging an individual's merit for the purposes of appointments to bureaucratic or ecclesiastical posts and the conferral of privileges. Consequently, even among *españoles* there would be noticeable differences in *calidad.* For example, a 1528 *real cédula* (royal edict) stipulated that any person soliciting the crown for rewards of merit or bestowal of privileges submit a petition which demonstrated the *"calidad y condición"* of their person and documented any services rendered to the crown.[34] This use of *calidad* implies a highly subjective and fluid measure of quality based largely in the socioeconomic position of an individual and in that person's previous demonstrations of service and honor, which might be influenced by ethno-religious lineage or natal community.[35] The sixteenth-century meanings of *calidad* and *casta* preclude them from describing the system of socio-racial terms as they developed in the sixteenth century.

Géneros de gente on the other hand does capture the sixteenth-century understanding of a society divided between different types of persons.[36] Iberians expected a pluralistic society composed of various categories of persons. I use the phrase *géneros de gente* as a collective reference for all socio-racial labels of the sixteenth century, in particular *español, indio, negro, mulato,* and *mestizo*. While I feel that *géneros de gente* best conveys the sixteenth-century understanding of a diverse, pluralistic social order, this phrase was not codified in any formal way. I have chosen to adopt it because its use as a collective gloss for categories of difference has been preserved in a variety of colonial documents produced by diverse individuals. Despite not being a legal phrase, sixteenth-century subjects would recognize the diversity implied by the label *géneros de gente*.

The use of the terms *género* and *gente* to describe social diversity in colonial documentation began sometime during the middle of the sixteenth century. An early example can be found in a 1552 *real cédula* limiting the use of slaves in personal entourages. This order noted that many enslaved retainers caused great disruptions and offenses against "all *género*[s] of persons."[37] In 1573, Alonso Pérez de Arza, a swordsmith and *vecino* of Mexico City, shared with the crown his fears concerning the use of weapons by *negros, indios,* and *mulatos*. He feared that because "every day this *género de gente* grows" there would be more and more uprisings, disruptions, and rebellions so long as no efforts were made to curtail the possession of weapons.[38] In 1576, Cristóbal Ramírez de Cartagena, a judge in the Audiencia of Lima, warned the king of the difficulty in using *negros, mulatos, mestizos,* and *zambaigos* in lieu of *indios* in that kingdom's industries. He confessed, "I tell Your Majesty the truth, I know that none of the *géneros de gente* I have named are suitable [for such work] unless, over them, there is great caution and oversight."[39] In 1601, the crown sought to minimize the deaths of native miners by mandating that mining work be done by "*negros* or other *géneros de gente.*"[40] The viceroy was also ordered to limit the use of *indios* in other mining activities and to seek ways of providing miners with "*negros* or other *género* of labor."[41] In 1604, Diego Martínez, a *vecino* of Mexico City, wrote a long memorial to the crown in which he suggested many possible changes to the collection of tribute in New Spain. He argued that "other *géneros de gente* who pay tribute, like the *mulatos* and *mulatas*, *negros*, *chichimecos*, and *chinos*," be forced to relocate to known settlements and neighborhoods so their tribute burden could be more accurately assessed and collected.[42] Similarly in 1606, António Rodríguez de Robles submitted a list of suggestions for improving the government of New Spain. He noted that, "Today in New Spain there are between fifty and sixty thousand *negros* and *mulatos* and *mestizos*, and it is this *género de gente* that conforming to reason should be made to labor in the mines and remove the ore from within them, and of all fifty thousand men of this *género* there are not to be found fifty men who have ventured to bring from the depths of the mines a single arroba of ore."[43] According to Antonio Rodríguez Robles, not only were these other *géneros de gente* unwilling to work in the mines, their labor would be too expensive and make mining less profitable. Therefore, he suggested that the *indios* be reserved for mining but relieved of other burdens. Rodríguez went on to add that sugar mills should "purchase *negros*, or hire *españoles*, or another *género de gente* or not run a mill off of the lives of the *indios*."[44] These recorded uses of *género de gente* suggest that this phrase resonated during the sixteenth and early seventeenth century as a short gloss that encapsulated the variability of colonial subjects.

Additional evidence for the development of this sixteenth-century expression of social diversity can be seen in literary works. For example, Miguel de Cervantes used almost identical phrasing to denote social diversity in his famous novel *El ingenioso hidalgo don Quijote de la Mancha.* At one point Cervantes describes women, children, and clerics as "*estos tres géneros de gente.*" In a later passage, the title character Don Quixote argues that he has been charged to serve "*todo género de gente.*"[45] The use of this phrase by Cervantes speaks to its utility in describing a complex, pluralistic society. While the social divisions of Iberia differed from their New World counterparts, both groups could speak of a society composed of *géneros de gente.*

In addition to being a versatile phrase for describing any number of social groups, the use of *género* with *gente* also allowed contemporaries to describe social groups using dynamic groupings. For example, Pérez de Arza's statement combined *negros, indios,* and *mulatos* as a single *género* capable of endangering society. On the other hand, Diego Martínez considered these groups to be separate *géneros,* each subject to paying tribute. This flexibility added to the phrase's utility by allowing it to selectively identify and isolate one or more groups within the diverse social order.

Further evidence of this versatility can be seen in Sebastián de Covarrubias Horozco's 1611 definition: "*Género:* Commonly in Castilian it signifies sex as in masculine or feminine, or for what is called species as in 'There is a *género* of sheep with six horns.' It can refer to a condition: 'There is a *género* of men that are tend toward evil.' As a type: 'It is a wicked *género* of trick to hit someone.'"[46] This definition illustrates the ability of *género* to define categories both broadly or narrowly. While not implicitly tied to race, the phrase *géneros de gente* expresses the early modern notion that society was composed of various types of people. In the pages that follow I have chosen to use *géneros de gente* as a collective description of the categories under study and *género* to describe individual groups. While I recognize that sixteenth-century society contained *géneros* other than *españoles, indios, negros, mulatos,* and *mestizos,* this phrase most closely encapsulates how contemporaries discussed such groups. Moreover, the fact that this phrase was not exclusively used for socio-racial categories helps differentiate it, and the cultural framework of the sixteenth century, from the later transformations in socio-racial difference that viewed these groups as *castas* and *calidades.* The remainder of this chapter will briefly sketch the process by which the *géneros* of *negro, indio, español, mulato,* and *mestizo* came to be imbued with social meaning.

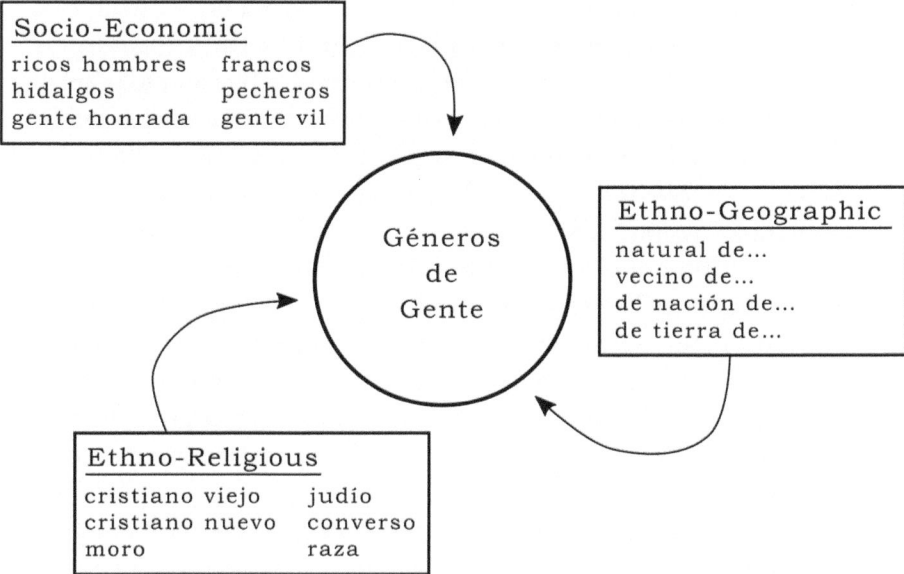

Figure 2. Schema of *géneros de gente*

Negro

Of the *géneros* common to sixteenth-century society, the category of *negro* experienced the longest period of development. Importantly, the Iberian experience with Africans predated the discovery of the Americas. In the American context, older Iberian attitudes were transferred largely intact from the Old World. The primary social meaning of *negro* was based in three interrelated historical processes: the cultural encounter and interchange between Christians and Muslims, the rise of a trans-Saharan and later transatlantic slave trade, and intellectual attempts to explain the perceived physical and cultural traits of sub-Saharan Africans.

Beginning in the eighth century, Christian Iberians came to form opinions of sub-Saharan Africans through contact with Muslims on the peninsula. Christian inhabitants labeled their Muslim neighbors as *moros*. In general, the most salient difference between *moro* and *cristiano* was religion. From the seventh through the fifteenth centuries, there existed a limited degree of religious toleration allowing religious minorities to live in Christian and Muslim kingdoms.[47] During this period, Christian encounters with Iberian and North African *moros* were complex and varied, alternating between conflict and tolerance. The completion of the Reconquest in the late fifteenth century brought about a shift in the historical memory of a religiously and ethnically diverse Iberia. *Moros* had by 1492 become the antithesis of *cristianos*, a long-standing foe finally vanquished by the pious Catholic Monarchs in fulfillment of divine Providence. Although the *moro* was defined primarily by religion, Christian Iberians began to conflate phenotypical differences with cultural ones. Since most *moros* were of North African descent, they tended to have darker skin than Christians of the Iberian Peninsula. This attribution helped precondition Christian Iberians to viewing somatic differences as markers of cultural and moral difference.[48]

The use of physical difference to define persons of non-Christian descent only increased as Christian Iberians came into greater contact with darker-skinned Africans. The initial arrival of sub-Saharan Africans in the Iberian Peninsula occurred via extensive trade networks connecting Iberia and North Africa to sub-Saharan Africa. From the twelfth to the sixteenth century as many as two million sub-Saharan Africans were transported north across the desert to be sold as slaves in the circum-Mediterranean.[49] Just as Christians in Iberia had begun to use somatic difference to denigrate North African Muslims, the trans-Saharan trade led Muslims in Iberia and North Africa to begin to differentiate slaves based on color.[50] In the Muslim world, "blacks" (*abid*) were tasked with more onerous and degrading tasks than other slaves and servants. As more and more sub-Saharan slaves passed through the Muslim world into Christian Iberia, Muslim prejudice against "black" slaves was appropriated by Christians and augmented by their existing somatic prejudices. By virtue of this connection, Christian Iberians came to view sub-Saharan Africans as servile and barbarous, a people fit for enslavement and subjugation. In general, both Christians and Muslims viewed sub-Saharan Africans as less intelligent, prone to childish expressions of joy and levity as well as barbarous violence.[51]

To explain these differences, scholars from both faiths turned to scripture and premodern notions of climate and environment. The scriptural basis for sub-Saharans' physical and psychological differences can be traced to the biblical account of the "Sons of Noah," Genesis 9:24–27.[52] For scholars of the Abrahamic religions, these verses helped link the postdiluvian dispersal of Noah's heirs to the contemporary distribution of human groups. The central issue under consideration was tracing modern populations back to Noah's sons: Ham, Shem, and Japheth. By the end of the fifteenth century a general consensus had arisen that connected Japheth to Europeans, Shem to the Semitic nations of the Middle East, and Ham to Africans.[53]

Importantly, in the biblical account, the descendants of Noah's son Ham were cursed to be the slaves of the descendants of Japheth and Shem. The rise of sub-Saharan African slavery had helped link the peoples of that region to slavery. The enslavement of Africans by the descendants of Shem (North African Muslims) and Japheth (Christian Europeans) appeared to fulfill the biblical curse imposed on the descendants of Ham.[54] In this regard, the religious story of Ham served to explain and justify the rise of sub-Saharan African slavery.

For the slave-buyers of the circum-Mediterranean, the practice of slavery among sub-Saharan kingdoms led to the a priori conclusion that, as a people, *negros* were less than human and innately preconditioned for enslavement and servitude.[55] The biblical narrative helped explain the relationship between the enslaved and those who purchased them while at the same time justifying their continued subjugation. Finally, although the biblical account did not apply any stereotypes to the descendants of Ham, in the popular imagination "the curse of Ham" served to explain the blackness of Africans. In both Christian and Muslim sources, black skin came to be associated with the curse of slavery.[56] The shared textual tradition of Christianity and Islam and the close relationship between Iberian scholars of both faiths helped propagate these anti-black stereotypes across political and religious boundaries.

Yet not all scholars situated the perceived physical and psychological traits of Africans within the realm of religion. As early as the fourteenth century, Ibn Khaldun, an Islamic scholar and traveler, rejected the religious explanation for sub-Saharan blackness. Instead he attributed the physical and psychological characteristics of Africans to environmental causes. Ibn Khaldun saw the hot climate as the primary factor in determining a people's appearance and temperament. According to his argument, the apparent joy and levity of blacks could be traced to the effect of heat upon their temperament.[57] Furthermore, the heat of their native lands caused their blacker skin, just as the cold of northern climates caused residents there to have whiter skin.[58] Despite differing in his explanation of Africans' physical and psychological traits, Ibn Khaldun agreed that their "animalistic" nature made them natural slaves.[59] Importantly, these understandings of climate and environment did not fully account for how the movement of people from one environmental zone to another might change their physical or mental attributes.

As a result of centuries of contact with Iberia, North Africa, and sub-Saharan Africa, Iberians developed strong negative prejudices against individuals categorized as *negros*. These prejudices cannot be divorced from slavery. Sub-Saharans entered the circum-Mediterranean primarily as slaves. The low status of slaves led Christians and Muslims to view such people negatively. These prejudices were institutionalized and popularized through religion and medieval science. For some, *negros* were a people condemned to slavery as the cursed descendants of Ham. For others, they were an animal-like people said to be burned by the sun. Either formulation considered their natural condition best suited for slavery and domination.

Indio

In 1492, Columbus and his crew, believing they were somewhere in the Indies, then conceived of as the Far East, labeled all Native Americans *indios*. Although the belief that the new lands were part of Asia quickly disappeared, the term *indio* remained in use to describe the indigenous inhabitants of the Americas. Additionally, the term *natural* came to be used synonymously with *indio* throughout the colonial era. Sometimes glossed in the depreciatory Western sense of "native" or "natives," the term initially served as shorthand for the phrase *natural de la tierra*. Based in the idea of *naturaleza*, early Iberians viewed indigenous peoples as "natives of the land." Although American-born *españoles, negros, mestizos,* and *mulatos* would eventually be "native" to the Americas, this phrase remained tied to Native Americans. In the first decades of conquest, the social perception of *indios* was shaped by the tension between conquistadors' and missionaries' hopeful expectations for these new people and the difficult realities of conquest and conversion.

In general, early explorers, conquistadors, and missionaries viewed the inhabitants of the Americas through the lens of their own expectations. Native Americans were seen as ideal trading partners, a new peasantry, or ideal converts. For example, Christopher Columbus described some of the first Caribbean peoples he encountered as, "very well made, with formidable bodies and good faces. Their hair was thick much like horses' tails and short . . . and they were the color of the Canary Islanders, neither black nor white. . . . They were to a one of good size and appearance, well made."[60] This passage expresses Columbus's initial fascination with native peoples and their physical attributes. Although Columbus hoped to establish trading posts rather than conquer, his focus on the physical abilities of the natives sought to reassure his royal patrons that the inhabitants of these lands would be productive laborers.

Similarly, Columbus sought to inform Ferdinand and Isabel about native religion and their capacity to accept Christianity. Columbus noted, "They do not follow any sect [as in Islam or Judaism] at all, and I believe that very quickly they will become Christians because they are quite intelligent."[61] This view was not without bias; indeed, Columbus did not recognize an indigenous religion at all. Importantly, Columbus's cultural blindness toward indigenous religion was rooted in the hope that the people he encountered would quickly convert. This hope was rooted in the politics of European overseas expansion. During the fifteenth century, the papacy supported Portuguese claims to territories in Africa so long as the Portuguese monarchy spread the Christian faith.[62] Columbus recognized that papal recognition of Spanish claims to new land would require similar missionary efforts.

Even after the initial settlement of the Caribbean, optimistic views of *indios* were a common feature of encounters with new Native American groups. In his first letter to Emperor Charles V, Hernán Cortés praised the inhabitants of Mexico's gulf coast. "The people of this land, who inhabit [the coast] from the island of Cozumel and the point of Yucatán to where we are now, are a people of medium stature with well-proportioned bodies and faces. . . . And the clothes they wear cover their genitals and over their bodies [they wear] thin, painted tunics."[63] Like Columbus, Cortés emphasized the positive physical attributes of the *indios* he encountered. Additionally, the mention of clothing that covered one's genitals portrayed the *indios* he encountered as more civilized than those elsewhere. As Cortés and his men traveled through Mesoamerican cities, they praised the monumental architecture and urban organization that they experienced. Upon seeing Mexico-Tenochtitlan, Cortés compared the Mexica capital to Seville and Cordoba. He described its residents in glowing terms. "The people of this city pay much greater attention to their manners and mode of dress than those in other provinces and cities because the Lord Moctezuma is always present. . . . Within the city there is always great order and courtesy in all things. . . . In the daily life of the people of this city there is a great similarity to life in Spain especially in the well-ordered manner of things. Considering that these people are barbarians and so distant from the knowledge of God and contact with other nations with reason it is an admirable thing to see."[64] The favorable account provided by Cortés reflected his own hopes of conquering such a populous and developed region, as well as his desire to convey the scale and scope of his efforts to his emperor.

For their part, early missionaries reported similarly positive descriptions of the *indios* they encountered. In the 1530s, Fray Toribio de Benavente (Motolinía), one of the first twelve Franciscans in New Spain, wrote a lengthy account of the native population. His view of the natives mirrored early secular accounts. "The people are naturally timid and very reserved, [and] they seem as if they were born to serve. . . . Of this stock one can say that they are alien to our manners . . . these *indios* and all the animals of this land are naturally docile . . . but capable of all virtues and very able for any trade or art and of great memory and sound understanding."[65] Conquistador and missionary alike viewed the docility of natives as an ideal quality, one that hopefully implied an easy conquest and quick conversion. Furthermore, Motolinía's description perpetuates the belief that the environment and climate imbued its human and animal inhabitants with a timid nature. Nevertheless, Motolinía emphasized that *indios* had admirable qualities, including their intellectual aptitude. He felt that God had bestowed upon these people their particular skills in learning and intellect. "He who teaches man science is the same one who granted these *indios naturales* great intellect and ability to learn all the sciences, arts, and trade that they have learned, because all of these have been learned so quickly, that even the trades that in Castile take many years to teach, here only by watching them done many natives have become masters. They [*indios*] have active, reserved, and peaceful intellects, not boastful or wasted ones like those of other nations."[66] Motolinía's experiences led him to esteem the admirable traits of the native population and to see a hopeful future for them as productive, Christian subjects of the monarchy.

Despite the positive accounts of many early explorers, conquistadors, and missionaries, the realities of conquest, conversion, and governance quickly diminished the perception of *indios*. The belief that *indios* were naturally "passive" and "docile" helped contribute to their consolidation within *encomiendas*. This Iberian institution granted a conquistador the right to collect tribute and labor from a specific group of *indios*. Originally used to reward military service during the Reconquista (reconquest of the Iberian Peninsula, eighth century through fifteenth century), this medieval institution became the primary mechanism for administering *indios* and extracting wealth from their communities. Those natives that did not demonstrate such submission were branded "cannibals" and decimated and enslaved.[67] During the course of the first several decades of rule, disease, warfare, and harsh demands took their toll, and the native population quickly diminished.

The quick population collapse of Native Americans led to two shifts in the perception of *indios*. First, the massive depopulation caused by European disease led many, both laity and religious, to view the natives as being weak and physically inferior. Although they recognized the effects of disease, they were unaware of the vast differences in immunity between Europeans and natives. Consequently, native deaths were seen as reflecting weak bodies. Laments over the weakness of *indios* replaced the earlier praise of their "stature" and "formidable" bodies. Writing in 1582, the archbishop of Mexico, Pedro Moya de Contreras, observed, "The *indio* is so miserable and of such weak constitution that removing him from his environment is death."[68]

Second, the massive depopulation increased tensions between missionaries and conquistadors. Missionaries including Antonio Montesinos and Bartolomé de las Casas urged the monarchy to remove *indios* from the control of conquistadors and place them under the sole oversight of the Church.[69] The arbitration of this conflict led to the enactment of paternalistic royal legislation designed to protect natives from abuse. Ostensibly, royal policy sought to insure the temporal and spiritual welfare of their native subjects. Yet these efforts resulted in the creation of a colonial order based in "dual republics," one Spanish, the other *indio*. This dual system defined a unique legal space in which native persons received certain protections and rights at the expense of various obligations and responsibilities not required of *españoles*. By the 1540s, royal legislation explicitly stated that *indios* were free vassals of the realm and should be treated as such. Native enslavement had been banned, natives were to live in their own self-governing communities, they were to have access to the legal system, they were to be paid wages for any labor they provided, and their religious education was to be undertaken by clerics trained in native languages.[70] At the same time that the crown sought to protect its native vassals, the burdens placed on *indios* clearly set them apart from Spanish subjects. As conquered people, *indios* were required to pay tribute and provide labor. Although the tribute and labor requirement went through many changes in its application, tribute and labor always remained mandatory for natives and their communities. In its attempts to protect *indio* subjects, the monarchy permanently entrenched the idea that *indios* were necessarily distinct and inferior to Europeans. In constructing a unique legal space for native persons, the crown perpetuated the view that *indios* needed special protection.[71]

Even though missionaries strove to defend *indios* from the abuses of conquistadors and settlers, they faced difficulties in achieving clear and lasting conversions. As hopes of rapid conversions dwindled, negative views of natives' mental and moral capabilities became more widespread. Writing in the 1530s, Motolinía's high praise for *indios'* capacity to learn reflected the hopes of early missionaries. Unfortunately, although great efforts were made to baptize hundreds of thousands of native subjects, language barriers and limited numbers of clergy prevented missionaries from adequately catechizing their new flock. By the middle of the sixteenth century, frequent examples of indigenous apostasy and idolatry began to appear.[72] In response, some missionaries learned native languages in the hopes of bridging the cultural divide and more fully planting the Christian faith. Others advocated for campaigns of extirpation to seek out and eradicate the remnants of preconquest indigenous belief.[73] In either case, indigenous idolatry and heterodoxy persisted. Unable to recognize the shortcomings of their own efforts, missionaries began to blame the failure of conversion on the mental and psychological capabilities of *indios*. By the end of the sixteenth century, royal cosmographer Juan López de Velasco cataloged the many failings that *indios* had come to embody. "The majority are without charity one to another, despicable in their sins and passions . . . easy to trick, but inconstant, of little faith, liars . . . and so disordered and depraved in their understanding and use of reason that the devil had tricked them into eating one another."[74] López de Velasco's pathetic description of the *indios'* capacity reflects almost a century of disappointment and disillusionment. Despite the hopes of conquistadors, missionaries, and settlers, native peoples did not submit easily to Spanish control and religious conversion. They actively worked to retain their traditions and cultural patterns. While this process of negotiation and conflict ultimately created a unique political and cultural space for *indios*, it also helped to forge a view of *indios* that cast them as physically weak, mentally inferior, and prone to vice and sin. As with the category of *negro*, the stereotypes encompassed by the term *indios* evolved through the interplay between Old World beliefs and expectations and the particular circumstances that shaped the historical encounter between Iberians and Native Americans.

Español

Of the three parent categories of colonial society, that of *español* took the longest to develop. During the reign of Ferdinand and Isabel no single term was used to describe the early European population of the Americas. In these early decades, if a term was required to encompass all Europeans in the Americas the most common choice was *cristianos*. The use of this word evolved naturally from early modern Iberian experience in the Reconquest. Iberians had already become accustomed to describing individuals and groups based on ethno-religious origins, while the term "European" had not yet come into popular usage in western Europe. Rather, at the beginning of the sixteenth century, Europe was still envisioned by its inhabitants as "Christendom."[75] So far as a common identity could be attributed to Europeans, they viewed themselves collectively as Christians. This shared Christian identity did not subsume other national identities such as Castilian, Catalan, Flemish, French, and Portuguese. In most cases, the common Christian identity served as a counterpoint to non-European, non-Christian others. Within medieval Europe, Christians existed in contrast to the remaining non-Christian "barbarians."[76] In the Americas, *cristiano* represented a logical category that contrasted easily with the non-Christian *indio*. Moreover, this formulation recognized the presence and participation of numerous non-Iberians in the early conquest and colonization campaigns of the Catholic Monarchs and later the Habsburgs.[77]

The use of *cristiano* as a generic gloss for "European" or "Iberian" continued into the first several decades of the sixteenth century. During this time, royal policy furthered the link between Christianity and conquistadors and settlers. As early as 1501, royal orders given to Fray Nicolás de Ovando prohibited the immigration of any Muslims, Jews, heretics, *reconciliados*, or new converts other than slaves born in the power of Christians.[78] This policy limited immigration to Old Christians but did not place any limits on other European *naciones*. The royal emphasis on Christianity over *nación* or *naturaleza* recognized that a notable minority of early conquistadors came from areas outside Castile and Aragon and at the same time drew a stark contrast between the conquistadors and the indigenous population.

Beginning in the 1520s, the term *español* began to be used simultaneously with *cristiano*. In 1525, the crown upheld the right of *indios* to marry Europeans and noted that many *caciques* (native lords) desired that their children be allowed to marry "*cristianos y cristianas españoles*" and that this would lead to peace and well-being between "*cristianos y indios*."[79] Similarly, in 1527, the crown ordered slave owners to oversee the marriages of their African slaves. In this *real provisión* (royal provision) the crown referred to the European population as *"cristianos españoles."*[80] Five years later, the crown ordered that *indios* with the requisite capacity and ability should be allowed to live in self-governing *pueblos* in a similar manner to *"cristianos españoles."*[81] The following year, 1533, the crown ordered that all "children of *españoles* born by *indias"* be sent to *"pueblos de cristianos."*[82]

The inclusion of *español* most likely served several purposes. First, by the 1530s at least two generations of native people would have been born as Christians in the Caribbean. Although the dichotomy between *indios* and *cristianos* certainly remained salient, *español* and *indio* both represented ethno-geographic categories.[83] Second, during the first half of the sixteenth century the crown began to prohibit the immigration of Europeans born outside of Castile and Aragon to the Indies.[84] This shift led to a slightly more homogeneous European-born population drawn from the kingdoms of Castile and Aragon. While the political state had yet to be named España, the persons living within those kingdoms could be jointly called *españoles,* a derivative of the Latin geographical designation Hispania.[85] During the course of the sixteenth century, the rapid growth of the Habsburg dynastic state increased Iberians' awareness of their shared cultural history and traditions.[86] As the residents of Castile and Aragon began to view themselves in opposition to other imperial subjects, the ethno-geographic label *español* became a clearer marker of national identity than the broader religious category of *cristiano.*

Despite its broad application to persons of Castilian and Aragonese descent, the category of *español* was not monolithic. During the course of the sixteenth century, a new term came to differentiate American-born *españoles* from those of European birth. The term *criollo* (creole) began to be applied to American-born *españoles.* Importantly, the term *criollo* was not initially devised as a means of describing American-born Europeans. Rather, it first entered the lexicon to describe American-born slaves of African ancestry. Most likely derived from *criar* (to raise, as in a child or livestock), this term differentiated between recently arrived African slaves, *bozales,* from those born in the Americas.[87] By the end of the sixteenth century, this slave-specific use had broadened as the term *criollo* could be applied to both individuals of European and African descent born in the Americas. In the 1570s the royal cosmographer, López de Velasco, noted that the American-born children of *españoles* were called *criollos*.[88] In 1609, Inca Garcilaso de la Vega explicitly linked the original application of *criollo* to American-born slaves with its later adoption among *españoles*:

> The children of Spaniards born there [the Americas] are called *criollos* and *criollas*; this means they were born in the Indies. It is a name invented by the *negros* as can be seen by this work. Among them [*negros*] it means "one born in the Indies." They invented it in order to differentiate between those that come from over here [the Old World], born in Guinea, from those that are born there [the Americas], because they hold those born in the homeland with higher esteem and of higher quality than their children who were born in foreign lands, and the parents are offended if they are called *criollos*. The Spaniards for similar reasons have introduced this name into their language in order to name those born there [the Americas]. In this manner, the Spaniard and Guinean born there [the Americas] are called creoles.[89]

Modern etymology supports Garcilaso's claim that African slaves may have participated in the derivation of *criollo* from the Latinate *criar*.[90] More significantly, Garcilaso's definition emphasizes the deprecatory nature of the term. American-born *criollos* were considered less than their Old World parents.

In response, *españoles* resident in the Americas developed their own terms to disparage European-born arrivals. By the end of the sixteenth century, term *chapetón* entered popular parlance to describe those who had recently arrived from Spain, often with few financial resources.[91] In the seventeenth century, the term *cachupín*, later *gachupín*, would be used by American-born *españoles* to deride those of European birth.[92] By the nineteenth century, the political and economic disparity between *gachupínes* and *criollos* helped fuel Latin American independence movements. Finally, by the late colonial period, the term *peninsular* would be coined as a more neutral descriptor for *españoles* born on the Iberian Peninsula.[93]

Although the rivalry between American-born and European-born *españoles* was rooted in the competition for offices, privileges, and power within colonial society, during the sixteenth century the term *criollo* conveyed inferiority based on notions of climate and geography. In his treatise, López de Velasco noted that *criollos* could be differentiated from their European-born parents in size and color; they were larger and darker than *peninsulars*. According to his understanding these changes could be attributed to different astral influences and climatic conditions.[94] López de Velasco feared that the cumulative effect of this new environment on *españoles* would render them phenotypically identical to native persons: "In many years, even if the *españoles* do not mix themselves with natives, they will return to being like them."[95]

López de Velasco believed that the effects of climate and geography did not just affect outward attributes. The temperament and mental faculties of *criollos* had degenerated from those of their parents. He noted, "And not only in physical qualities are they different, but those of the spirit often follow those of the body, and changing [the body, the qualities of spirit] change as well, or because many unquiet and lost spirits have passed into those provinces, the dealings and interactions have become depraved, and give more emphasis to those with less virtue, and as a result in those parts there have always been and are [now] many scandals and unrest among men."[96] This belief was firmly rooted in the same understandings of human difference that had been used to explain Africans' perceived barbarity and blackness. These early modern beliefs stemmed from long-standing conceptualizations of human difference based in the writings of classical authors.

Medieval writers had promoted the belief that climate and geography shaped both the physical and mental traits of human groups.[97] Inherent in these conceptions, and still present until the end of the sixteenth century, was the belief that a specific climate not only determined the appearance and qualities of its native inhabitants but that it could similarly affect anyone who entered or resided there for a period of time. López de Velasco's views are important in this regard as he felt that although the New World minimally affected European immigrants, their offspring, *criollos*, were far more altered as a result of being raised in such a climate.

As the *criollo* population of the Americas grew, American-born scholars developed contrasting theories that sought to vindicate the increasingly prejudicial views of European intellectuals concerning American-born Europeans.[98] Jorge Cañizares-Esguerra has argued that in the seventeenth century scholarly debate on both sides of the Atlantic altered the way in which intellectuals explained physical and psychological difference. Significantly by this time, all observers recognized that *criollos* had neither degenerated into *indios*, nor had *negros* whitened in the cooler climates of Iberia and the Americas. In order to explain this lack of change, Iberian- and American-born scholars began to argue that the separate human groups, *españoles*, *negros*, and *indios*, had "essential" traits that determined their primary physical and psychological characteristics.[99] Although scholars continued to discuss the impact of climate, environment, and astrology on the bodies of colonial subjects, the effects of those forces diminished in the face of a growing consensus that these different groups had "essential" or "natural" traits.[100] Importantly, although these scholars sought to explain differences between *españoles* and *indios*, with an occasional mention of *negros*, none of their works attempted to analyze the "essential" nature of mixed groups. Rather, this strand of scholarship focused entirely on the essential, natural qualities of the founding populations of colonial Spanish America and not the additional *géneros de gente* that were produced within that developing society.[101] Importantly, these scholarly debates over the essential nature of *indios*, *españoles*, and *negros* illustrate that not until the mid-seventeenth century did a fully racialized view of difference, based in perceived essential or natural differences, become common in Iberian thought.

People in the Middle: *Loro, Mulato, Zambaigo, Mestizo*

As unions between the founding groups created individuals of mixed ancestry in the Iberian Peninsula and the Americas, new terms arose to define and differentiate these new *géneros*. Unlike *indio* and *negro*, these new categories were not subject to the same degree of intellectual debate as the parent groups from which they were descended. While scholars seeking to understand the ever-widening world and its people debated the origins and nature of Africans and Native

Americans, individuals of mixed ancestry rarely received the same degree of intensive analysis. Nevertheless, these groups came to be conceptualized in a variety of ways. In general, categories of mixed ancestry represented amalgamations of the parent lineages. The elitist and prejudicial nature of Iberian definitions of difference tended to place upon these categories the negative valuations of parent groups while limiting the attribution of any positive characteristics.

The earliest manifestation of this process began as a means to describe the offspring of Christian Iberians with enslaved Africans. Two terms, *mulato* and *loro*, entered Castilian during the fifteenth century to describe such individuals. Of these two, *loro* is the more problematic but also more limited in its duration. The first usage of *loro* appears to have been as a reference to color. As early as the tenth century some livestock were referred to as being *loro* in color. Most likely a derivation of the Latin *laurus* (laurel), this ascription referred to an intermediate shade of dusky brown similar to the color of laurel leaves.[102]

By the thirteenth century, some slaves in Iberia had begun to be designated *loros*. In the fifteenth century, slaves not labeled as black (*negro*) or white (*blanco, berberisco*) tended to be labeled *loros*, if labeled at all.[103] At this time *loro* may have marked either phenotype or ancestry, the children born of Christian-Muslim unions. Nevertheless, early-sixteenth-century examples suggest that *loro* primary served as a phenotypical reference. Some writers described Canary Islanders, Native Americans, and subcontinental Indians as being *loro* in color.[104] In these documents, *loro* served as a color reference describing the phenotype of these newly discovered peoples. This usage did not last long as new peoples came to be known as *canarios* or *indios*.[105] During the course of the sixteenth century, *loro* fell into disuse in Iberia.

Coinciding with the decreased usage of *loro*, the term *mulato* came to be the primary term used to describe individuals of mixed-African ancestry in the Americas. The etymology and early usage of *mulato* is complex. There are two possible derivations for the term. The first, and the one most often cited in the colonial period, links the term *mulato* to the word *mula*, meaning mule. In the seventeenth century, Covarrubias defined *mulato* as "one who is the child of a *negra* and a white man, or the reverse, and because it is an odd mixture it is compared to the nature of a mule."[106] The negative connotation enshrined in this definition certainly reflected the popular opinion of such individuals. Like the mule to the horse, the hybrid *mulato* was of a lesser nature than its Spanish forbear.[107]

An alternate explanation traces *mulato* to the Arabic term *muwallad*. In modern Arabic, *muwallad* can be used to refer to individuals of mixed ancestry. In medieval Portuguese, the term *malado*—a derivative of *muwallad*—was used to describe servants or other individuals bound by obligations to serve. In describing the history of slavery, the nineteenth-century historian José António Saco argued that the term *malado* described individuals of mixed Christian-Muslim descent and may have had linguistic ties to the later *mulato*.[108] These Arabic-derived terms were used most frequently during the late medieval period in the context of domestic slavery. It is possible that both linguistic traditions might have contributed to the evolution of *mulato*. The closeness of *mulato* to Iberian Arabic terminology describing hybridity and subservience may have melded with Latinate terms for animal hybrids and provided additional semantic grounding to the new term *mulato*.[109] While Arabic terms may have helped forge the new term *mulato*, Castilian dictionaries from the sixteenth and seventeenth century did not preserve that meaning. Rather, the popular conception of *mulato* remained tied to degenerative hybridity—Afro-Hispanic individuals who were innately inferior to their Castilian parents.

In the Americas, the term *mulato* retained its connection to hybrid people but did not remain fixed to solely African-European individuals. At some point during the middle of the sixteenth century, the meaning of *mulato* broadened in the Americas. *Mulato* came to describe both the mix between Africans and Castilians as well as the mix between Africans and Native Americans. The precise dating of this transition is unclear, but references from the mid sixteenth century onward suggest that quotidian usage had incorporated this new meaning within decades of the conquest.[110]

Mulato was not the only early colonial label applied to individuals of mixed African-indigenous ancestry. López de Velasco also noted that the term *zambaigo* was used in some colonial settings to refer specifically to Afro-indigenous *mulatos*. In other contexts, *zambo* described similar individuals. According to Covarrubias's dictionary, *zambo* meant "knock-kneed," "one that strides outward, the opposite of bowlegged [*estevado*]."[111] More recent etymology posits that *zambo* was likely a Mozarabic derivation from the Latin *strambus,* meaning bowlegged, while *zambaigo* may be an elision of *zambo* and *hijo.*[112] Despite describing opposing traits, both link individuals of African descent to physical traits of the legs. Although *zambaigo* entered the lexicon during the sixteenth century, it was not used in New Spain. Its incorporation into royal legislation stems from its local development in other parts of the Americas.[113] In New Spain, *mulato* quickly became the only term used to describe anyone of presumed African descent during the sixteenth and early seventeenth centuries. Chapter 4 will further examine the homogenizing nature of the term *mulato* and explore the diversity of individuals to which it was applied.

Almost immediately after Europeans entered the Americas, unions between conquistadors and native women, forced and consensual, prompted the creation of a new category, *mestizo.* The development of this term took several decades. Initially, individuals of European-indigenous ancestry were categorized by their predominate cultural affiliation. Children born of native women but recognized and raised by their European parents were often called *españoles* or *cristianos.* Similarly, children raised by indigenous parents, mostly *indias,* were called *indios.*[114] By the 1530s, greater differentiation became important. *Cédulas* from the 1530s referred to these European-indigenous persons as "children of *españoles* and *indias."*[115] By the 1550s, *mestizo* had entered common usage.[116] Covarrubias defined *mestizo* as "that which is engendered from different species of animal: from the verb *misceo,* meaning to mix."[117] As this definition indicates, this term referenced both mixture and animal hybrids. Nevertheless, the application of *mestizo* was never uniform.

As scholars have pointed out, the tendency to apply the term *mestizo* to an individual remained rooted in concepts of culture and status.[118] Many children born of *indias* to prominent Spaniards could avoid the ascription of the term *mestizo* by virtue of their familial ties and adoption of Spanish cultural norms. On the other hand *mestizos* born to less-prominent Spaniards or Hispanicized persons with connections to both indigenous and Spanish culture were more readily termed *mestizos.* By the middle of the sixteenth century, the term *mestizo* had become pejorative in law. Popularly, *mestizos* were seen as wastrels and vagabonds. The cultural and social underpinnings to the ascription of the *mestizo* category created a discrepancy among European-indigenous persons. During the sixteenth century, many individuals born of *españoles* and *indios* avoided categorization due to status and familial ties while others became subject to this discriminatory and limiting label. As the social order became more developed and Spanish elites sought to further restrict claims to *español* status, the term *castizo* was developed. This category, rarely used in the sixteenth century, could be ascribed to the offspring of a Spaniard with a *mestizo*. On the whole, categorization of European-indigenous individuals involved more subjectivity than other ascriptions, the subject of chapter 3.

The process by which Iberians defined differences between human beings cannot be divorced from the cultural traditions of the Iberian Peninsula and the particular historical interactions that occurred between Iberians and those with whom they came into contact. Most importantly, by the fifteenth century, Iberians had become conditioned to define difference in polyvalent terms. Individuals within their society could be described by various terms that together helped situate them within a complex social matrix that encompassed ethno-geographic, ethno-religious, and socioeconomic difference. Shaped by this cultural tradition, Iberians were predisposed to construct a similarly diverse social order in regions that they conquered and colonized. In this regard the colonial notion of a society divided between *géneros de gente* reflects the continuation of an older Iberian mind-set.

Just as the older mode of defining difference had been shaped by social interaction and cultural beliefs, the new categories of Spanish America became imbued with meaning through the interactions between Iberians and those they encountered. Importantly, although difference in Iberia was measured along several different axes, the new *géneros de gente* of the Americas tended to elide earlier domains of difference into a single term. New *géneros de gente* simultaneously encapsulated ethno-geographic, ethno-religious, and socioeconomic differences and stereotypes. In this way, sixteenth-century *géneros de gente* began to embody differences that were more racial in character than those that came before. Yet, importantly, they were not yet races in any modern sense. Only when seventeenth-century scholars began to ascribe "essential" or "natural" attributes to these groups did they begin to approximate the modern notion of races.

While it would be wrong to equate sixteenth-century *géneros de gente* with races, these terms represent an important developmental stage along the path to modern notions of race. Certainly, different *géneros* had been imbued with particular attributes, but the source of those differences varied. Premodern notions of climate and geography played a large role, as did religious understandings of human diversity and the importance of lineage in perpetuating particular moral and physical qualities. Unlike later notions of scientific racism based in Darwinian theories of evolution, the role of lineage was not understood in wholly scientific or biological terms. Lineage for Iberians was more than just genetics. One's lineage defined more than physical attributes or mental capacities. Lineage represented a conduit that conveyed honor, purity, and morality from one generation to the next. Thus, although *géneros de gente* reveal certain incipient racial attitudes they do not constitute races.

Nevertheless, the social and cultural stereotypes embodied by *géneros de gente* did lead to institutionalized discrimination. These terms entered into legal discourse and became entrenched in to the fabric of Spanish American law. The following chapter shifts its focus from the social beliefs and cultural assumptions that produced these categories of difference and traces the process by which *géneros de gente* and their stereotypes were appropriated into the colonial legal system. The incorporation of *géneros de gente* into the legal system reveals a recursive historical process within which stereotypes and prejudices continued to evolve as colonial officials appropriated and mobilized *género* categories in their efforts to effectively govern a diverse overseas empire.

CHAPTER 2

Shaping Society

> [T]his land is so full of *negros* and *mestizos*, they exceed by a large margin the number of *españoles* and all of them wish to buy their freedom with the lives of their masters.
>
> *Viceroy Luis de Velasco (the elder), 1553*

> Many are the free *negros, mulatos,* and *mestizos* who live in this land, for the bad weed always grows and one cannot trust in them, what is possible is to have them as subjects and to suffer them where they can be punished but not in *pueblos de indios* where they will have more freedom and can take more excess without punishment.
>
> *Viceroy Luis de Velasco (the younger), 1608*

The monarchs of Castile and Aragon did not create the social categories that defined the populations over which they ruled. The historical progression of Iberian expansion produced the *géneros de gente* that populated Spanish America. Yet Spanish monarchs did enact legislation that appropriated such categories and endowed each with certain legal rights, responsibilities, or obligations. This process involved the participation of many individuals. Local elites, conquistadors, settlers, and bureaucrats created and gave meaning to categories of difference. Through petitions, letters, complaints, and reports those elites educated the monarch and his councils about the *géneros de gente* of the Americas. When the king and his ministers responded to local concerns by enacting legislation, they perpetuated and entrenched *género* categories within colonial legal codes. This recursive process transformed popularly constituted social categories of difference into juridical categories capable of regulation and enforcement by the legal system.

This chapter argues that the legal framework defining and circumscribing the new *géneros* of the Americas, especially those of mixed ancestry, developed through an organic and recursive process. As colonists and settlers wrote to the king about their developing social order they mobilized new categories of difference. When royal legislation responded to specific local problems, real or imagined, in the Americas, it appropriated the colonists' language of difference. As new issues or fears arose, additional legislation entered the legal landscape, complimenting or limiting previous laws and further elaborating the juridical place of colonial *géneros de gente*. This process entrenched *género* categories within a complex, ever-evolving legal code shaped by specific social, cultural, and economic relationships on the ground.

FEATURES OF SPANISH JURISPRUDENCE

The relationship between royal legislation and society in the Americas can only be explained as part of the historical construction of Spanish American jurisprudence and government. After their discovery, the Americas were initially incorporated into the kingdom of Castile and by virtue of annexation made part of the jurisdiction and legal framework of that kingdom.[1] Over the course of the first three decades of colonial rule, the importance of the Indies became more apparent, and the crown sought to more firmly establish its control over the governance of these possessions.[2] This process entailed the creation of overseas governmental entities and institutions separate from those of Castile and the creation of a separate body of law and jurisprudence, called *derecho indiano*.

Constructing administrative and judicial institutions took decades, but by the end of the 1520s the crown had established a basic model that was repeated as needed. Although initial *capitulaciónes* (agreements) with conquistadors allowed leaders like Cortés and Pizarro to govern in the wake of conquest, the crown quickly recognized that entrepreneurial conquerors did not make good officials. Consequently Spanish monarchs systematically appointed professional administrators and trained jurists to succeed its conquistador-governors. Shortly after regions were conquered, the crown established high courts, *audiencias*. Early *audiencias* were established in Santo Domingo (1511), Mexico City (1527), Panama City (1538), Santiago de Guatemala (1542), and Lima (1542). These courts oversaw judicial appeals and other matters pertaining to jurisprudence. In each region, governors oversaw the administrative aspects of government, and a host of lesser officials presided over local issues of justice and government. In 1535, the crown appointed Antonio de Mendoza viceroy of New Spain; his duties were to oversee provincial governors and provide more stable, reliable governance. In 1544, a viceroy was appointed to oversee the newly conquered regions of Peru, although a civil war sparked by the new royal policies resulted in political instability for several years. The creation of viceroyalties finalized the basic structure of secular governance used in Spanish America until the eighteenth century. The growth of a Spanish American bureaucracy with unique institutions led to the creation of the Real y Supremo Consejo de Indias (Royal and Supreme Council of the Indies) in 1524. This council separated the institutional oversight of the Americas from the governance of Castile.[3] By the 1530s, the development of Spanish American institutions and governing bodies helped to create the uniquely American legal sphere that would come to be known as *derecho indiano*.

Before examining how *derecho indiano* incorporated categories of *genéros de gente*, four salient features of Spanish law should be noted. First, medieval philosophies concerning the role of the monarch in governance strongly influenced production, scope, and content of royal legislation. Specifically, Castilians viewed the monarch as a "natural lord" whose authority to govern was granted via divine sanction, hereditary rule, and the body politic.[4] The primary duty of the monarch was to serve as chief judge and mediator of society. To this end it was the duty of the monarch to establish *buen gobierno* (good governance) and *buen policía* (good order) for his subjects. The monarch was duty-bound to dispense justice and maintain a virtuous society.[5] Yet the Iberian concept of justice should not be confused with modern notions of justice. The legal principles of early modern Castile linked justice to status, including notions of *calidad*. In this regard, justice did not necessarily mean equal treatment. In dispensing justice, the king or his ministers had to weigh the relevance of social difference and legal privileges when considering the merits of conflicting parties. Even though status mediated the enactment of justice, the legal system recognized that even the lowliest subjects had rights and that the law should protect the weak and needy.[6] In the ideal realm, the need to protect the weak and needy counterbalanced the tendency of justice to favor those with status. The complexity of determining justice made the concept of *buen gobierno* a fertile battleground for conflicting demands by colonial subjects. Consequently, in seeking to uphold justice and facilitate *buen gobierno*, royal policy rarely dealt with abstractions. Rather, policy-making and lawmaking focused on negotiating the conflicts and competing claims of royal subjects.

A second essential feature of Spanish law was its interest in the religious and spiritual life of the crown's subjects. Pope Alexander VI's support of Spanish claims to the Americas necessitated state intervention into the spiritual life of Native Americans and other residents of the Indies. According to several bulls issued in 1493, the papacy recognized the Spanish claims to the Indies provided that the monarchy oversaw the conversion and evangelization of the indigenous population.[7] To this end, Spanish monarchs regularly enacted legislation intended to better the ecclesiastical needs of its American territories. Royal laws mandated the spread of Christianity and promoted the spiritual education of the populace. The necessity of religious instruction for natives was emphasized almost immediately in royal instructions to early Caribbean governors and was reiterated frequently in instructions to later viceroys.[8] In legislation regulating matters of spiritual and religious life, the crown sought to construct an idealized religious landscape very much in contrast to secular legislation that was characterized by pragmatism and particular attention to specific problems and conflicts. Consequently religious legislation tended to accentuate the differences between theory and praxis, law and reality.[9]

Third, early modern Castilian legislation in Iberia and the Americas tended to be casuist.[10] Most royal laws and policies were issued in order to rectify or correct a particular problem or issue. Only rarely did the monarchy issue expansive general legislation.[11] For contemporary jurists, casuistry represented the means by which *buen gobierno* could be achieved.[12] The emphasis on the particular insured that rulers responded to the changing circumstances of subjects. This process created a body of legislation in which each constituent law responded to a particular historical circumstance. Consequently laws issued in response to similar problems could differ significantly depending on the particular circumstances that prompted a royal response. At the same time, existing laws established precedents that could be used by officials and magistrates operating within their jurisdictions.

Fourth, the legal system sought uniformity and a consistent *vida juridical* (juridical life) across all jurisdictions. In order to overcome the particularity of casuist laws, the legal system acknowledged the principle of analogy in the implementation of policy and application of law across the Americas.[13] When royal legislation was made in response to a particular problem in one jurisdiction of the Indies it could be held as valid in other areas where similar problems existed. Insofar as a particular policy had relevance in a general sense it was to be construed as being valid for all similar cases. In the application of analogy, jurists had to weigh how the particular context of a case influenced its general application. An excellent example of this can be seen in a 1581 case between Sebastián, a native of the Indian subcontinent, and several Portuguese men who captured and enslaved him.[14] In this case, the royal *fiscal* (prosecutor) successfully argued that royal laws issued between 1532 and 1570 consistently prohibited the enslavement of *indios*. Even though these laws were issued in response to the enslavement of Native Americans, the term *indio* also applied to the inhabitants of India. Consequently, the *fiscal* argued that, as an *indio*, Sebastián could not be enslaved. The court agreed—the *vida juridical* formed by the collective legislation concerning *indios* clearly prohibited their enslavement in any Spanish territory. This aspect is most important for understanding royal policy toward *genéros de gente*. Casuist legislation produced a multitude of laws that responded to particular problems or issues involving *genéros de gente* across the various jurisdictions of the Americas. To fully understand the evolution of a royal policy toward *genéros de gente* in the Americas, all relevant legislation must be examined with the understanding that individual laws at the time were not seen as being limited to the particular case. The entire body of relevant casuist law shaped the *vida juridical* of *genéros de gente* in the Americas.

The plethora of casuist legislation led to a variety of attempts at codifying *derecho indiano*. Beginning in the 1570s, the Council of the Indies sought to compile all relevant legislation pertaining to the spiritual and temporal government of the Indies.[15] Although the process took over twenty years, in 1596 the Cedulario Indiano (also known as the Cedulario de Encinas) collected legislation relevant for general application across the Indies.[16] This process was repeated again in 1680 with the creation of the Recopilación de Leyes de Las Indias.[17] Both the Cedulario Indiano and the Recopilación recognized that although most royal legislation was issued in response to a particular case, laws with general application needed to be preserved and codified so they could be uniformly applied across the Indies.

This peculiar nature of the construction of *derecho indiano* worked against general and comprehensive legislation that explicitly defined the juridical place of *genéros de gente*. Instead royal policy must be understood as evolving from the particular historical circumstances that created conflicts, real or imagined, between colonial *genéros*. The crown never sought to specifically define any socio-racial term or delineate a specific legal hierarchy of categories. Insofar as a commonly recognized hierarchy existed, broad social and cultural values mediated the relative status of a particular term or category. Legislation grew out of popular views, and, in constructing a *vida jurídical*, colonial laws codified popular stereotypes. For example, no law ever stipulated that a *mestizo* should be seen as having a higher *calidad* than a *mulato*. While one could construct a hierarchy by comparing which *géneros* benefited from the most privileges and which faced the most restrictions, such a construction would be an extrapolation from the colonial legal code and strictly speaking not an aspect of it.[18] The crown and its ministers did not specify such a hierarchy. The absence of a clear legal hierarchy reinforces the reality that Spanish racial legislation evolved out of particular historical conflicts between colonial subjects.

CREATING TWO REPUBLICS

One of the earliest moral and political debates spurred by Spanish conquests centered on the legal, social, and economic place of indigenous people. Spanish conquistadors and settlers argued that *indios* should rightfully be subjugated under the control of *encomenderos*. Early missionaries and clergy countered this claim and advocated for the freedom of *indios*. Some even hoped that the crown might remove secular Spaniards from any position of authority over *indios* and allow the Church sole purview over these neophytes to the faith. As arbiter, the crown chose a middle ground. The monarchy allowed Spanish conquistadors and settlers to retain authority over native people's labor and tribute but to prevent excess exploitation added new restrictions on the relationship between Spaniards and *indios*. The cumulative effect of these policies was to create a system of two *repúblicas* (republics), one indigenous and the other Spanish.

The two republics did not come into existence at once. Instead, over time, royal legislation, including the Laws of Burgos (1512) and the New Laws (1542), slowly established that native communities were to be the exclusive preserve of indigenous subjects.[19] In effect, the developing legal code sought to maintain the geographic and spatial separation of *indios* from other colonial subjects. Although Spaniards could be granted *encomiendas* or native laborers through the *repartimiento de indios*, they were not to live within native communities. In 1550, the crown reiterated that even if Spaniards had the right to labor or tribute from native communities, they were not under any circumstances to reside in those communities because, "In addition to collecting the tributes, they take their food the result of which is many crimes and bad examples that result from these visits to the *pueblos*."[20] For the monarchy, the two-republic system functioned as a means of maximizing native productivity by limiting abuses by other *géneros de gente*. In so doing, the legal protection of the *indios* further perpetuated stereotypes that they were weak and unable to protect themselves. In the eyes of the monarch, "because the *indios* are a timid people the *españoles* do as they wish to them without [the *indios*] daring to complain." While legislation attempted to prevent harm, the legal framework that created the two-republic system entrenched indigenous inferiority into the legal code.

Nonetheless, the binary created between Spanish and indigenous spheres did not define a separate republic for *negros, mulatos,* or *mestizos*. Instead social convention and the law included these other *géneros de gente* within the *república de españoles*. As these groups grew in number, legislation began to address concerns that their presence within indigenous communities was detrimental to the *república de indios*. In 1541, the crown responded to complaints that the *negros* of Peru's *encomenderos* had caused numerous problems in *pueblos de indios*, including drunkenness, robberies, and "many other damages."[21] In response, the monarch prohibited any *negro* from entering a *pueblo de indios*. Similar prohibitions against *negros* entering or living in *pueblos de indios* were repeated in subsequent decades. By the last quarter of the sixteenth century, the prohibition expanded to include individuals of mixed ancestry. In 1578, a *cédula* declared that *mestizos, mulatos*, and *negros* were "so universally inclined to evil" that they should not be allowed to even be in the company of natives because "they treat them poorly and they take advantage of them and teach them bad customs and laziness and errors."[22] A similar *cédula* from 1586 went further in denouncing these interlopers:

> There are many *negros, mulatos*, and *mestizos*, and people of other mixtures, and every day the number grows. The majority are born out of wedlock and do not know their parents, and all of them are raised in vice and freedom without work or profession. They eat and drink without restraint and they are raised with the *indios* and *indias* and they get drunk [with the *indios*] and practice witchcraft [with them] and they do not go to mass or listen to sermons. As a result they do not know the things relevant to Our Holy Catholic Faith. From being raised this way many damages and inconveniences will result.[23]

Although damning in its critique of *negros, mulatos*, and *mestizos*, this *cédula* did not address the underlying problem that *mulatos* and *mestizos* lived among the *indios* because they had been born in their *pueblos*. Even though these orders attempted to solve particular local problems, they reinforced the abstraction of the two-republic model. The social problems that the crown sought to remedy arose precisely because the lived reality of colonial life did not conform to the legal expectation of a *república de españoles* distinct from a *república de indios*.

In 1589, the crown wrote to the viceroy of Peru and provided specific directives for dealing with the confusion caused by individuals of mixed indigenous ancestry living in their natal communities. "In what touches upon the *mestizos* and *zambaigos*, those that are children of *indias*, and born among them, that they should inherit their [parents] homes and property, it appears to us a difficult thing to remove them from their parents."[24] However, of free *negros* and *mulatos*, the crown was adamant that they should be expelled from any native community. Spaniards and their enslaved *negros* and *mulatos* could reside near native communities. However, if either Spaniard or slave harassed the native inhabitants or damaged their lands, they were to be expelled. While clearly allowing some persons of mixed indigenous ancestry to live in native communities, this policy was far from clear in its application. The wording implied that *mestizos* and *zambaigos* could live in their natal communities but that their right had to be based on a claim of inheritance. Did this clause allow the illegitimate child of a Spaniard and native woman—or an African and native woman—to live in a community? While protecting the inheritance of these individuals, the law would seemingly destroy any nuclear family—if it existed—by expelling a nonindigenous parent from the community in which one had created a family and held a sense of community. Despite its increasingly poor correlation with the lived realities of colonial life, the two-republic model would remain the legal basis for the colonial order.

SIXTEENTH-CENTURY SLAVE POLICY

Royal legislation regulating African slaves played an important role in establishing the juridical place of all individuals of African descent during the colonial period. In particular, the evolution of royal policy toward African slaves demonstrates a preoccupation with issues of social control and the possibility of rebellion. These fears were consistently reinforced by the reality that as soon as enslaved Africans entered the Americas they began to engage in various forms of resistance and revolt.[25] Concurrently, by the middle of the sixteenth century, royal policy had facilitated the rise of the transatlantic slave trade to the Americas and linked the status of slavery to African ancestry. Royal policy regarding slavery demonstrates a tension between permitting and profiting from African slavery while simultaneously working to prevent rebellion and revolt.

In 1521, Diego Colón, viceroy and governor of Hispaniola, issued the first comprehensive legislation regulating enslaved persons in the Americas. In late December of that year, a number of African slaves began an insurrection that led to the deaths of several Spaniards and the flight of slaves into the mountains.[26] In the wake of this violent rejection of captivity, secular officials on the island sought to more rigidly control the enslaved population. The ordinances passed on January 6, 1522, sought to recapture existing runaway slaves and prevent future uprisings and runaways.[27]

The physical control of slaves featured prominently in these comprehensive regulations. No slave was to have any offensive or defensive weapons, and a slave could only carry a small knife for personal use. No slave was to travel more than two leagues from his or her owner's home or estate without being accompanied or carrying written authorization. Slaves were not to be rented out or allowed to work for anyone but their owners without the express consent of the authorities. These provisions demonstrate a belief that slaves' mobility played a role in facilitating their rebellion and flight. In addition, the provisions made owners more directly responsible for overseeing their slaves' movements. Owners were to report runaways within ten days or face a financial penalty, and a tax was levied to support the enforcement of the new provisions. Owners found guilty of being delinquent in their oversight duties could be fined and have their slaves taken away. The penalties established for slaves caught violating the new provisions or running away were severe. The first instance merited whipping, the second resulted in the amputation of a foot, and the third meant death. The focus on restricting Africans' movement and limiting their access to weapons would remain a prominent feature of legislation for centuries.

These ordinances provide an important window into the complex relationship between ethnicity and slavery in these early decades. Throughout the provisions the phrase "*negros* and *esclavos*" appears, as does the phrase "*esclavos negros, blancos,* and *canarios.*" The mandating of ordinances for regulating *negros* and *esclavos* demonstrates that the regulations were meant to apply to anyone who was enslaved but also to all sub-Saharan Africans, *negros*, regardless of slave status.[28] Although unstated, the colonial government may have feared free *negros* joining with their enslaved counterparts. Simultaneously, the inclusion of "*esclavos negros, blancos,* and *canarios*" illustrates the ethnic variation among slaves toiling on early Hispaniola, a diversity that mirrored that of slaves in Iberia.[29]

In response to the insurrection of 1521 and other early acts of slave revolt, the crown began to implement slave importation policies that would result in an increasingly African-born slave population. Reports sent to the Council of the Indies by settlers on Hispaniola argued that Hispanicized slaves, *ladinos*, were more likely to engage in insurrection and plots to escape bondage than those who came directly from Africa, *bozales*. In response to these growing complaints, in 1526 the crown prohibited the importation of *negros ladinos* to limit the spread of the "bad customs that they have" and their tendency to rebel and flee. At the same time, the monarchy expressed a clear preference for *bozales* because the settlers perceived them to be more controllable. Specifically, the royal order noted that "the *bozales* are those that serve and are pacific and obedient and the others, *ladinos* [are] those who disobey and incite [the rest] to flee and rise up and cause other crimes."[30] The prohibition on importing *negros ladinos* encouraged greater reliance on the nascent transatlantic slave trade.

Prior to 1520, most slaves living in Spanish America had been transported to the Americas by their owners or in small-scale shipments from Iberia to America.[31] After 1530, royal orders increased the oversight on all private slave imports from Iberia, making it more burdensome for private individuals to transport slaves of any ethnicity to the Americas. On February 2, 1530, the crown mandated that no one could import "male or female slaves [be they] *blancos, negros, loros,* or *mulatos,* without our express license."[32] Any unlicensed slave who was "*berberisco,* of the *casta* of *Moros* or *Judios,* or *mulato*" was to be returned directly to Iberia and a one-thousand-peso fine imposed on the owner. This order required that slave owners wishing to transport slaves to the Americas apply for and receive authorization before leaving Spain. The inclusion of *mulatos* and *loros* in this restricted list paralleled the previous 1526 restriction of *negros ladinos*. Most enslaved *mulatos* and *loros* were likely Hispanicized by virtue of their parentage and life in Iberia and were consequently perceived as being a threat to social stability. The blanket restrictions on importing enslaved *blancos, negros, mulatos,* and *loros* was repeated again in 1531, 1550, and 1552.[33] The increasing oversight of private slave importation to the Americas from Iberia mirrored the establishment of new mechanisms for the mass importation of sub-Saharan Africans to the Americas.

In 1518, soon after ascending to the throne, Charles I granted *asientos* (royal trade monopolies) to Don Jorge de Portugal and Lorenzo de Gouvenot that authorized their importation of four hundred and four thousand slaves respectively.[34] The slaves were to be transported directly from Africa to the Americas. These shipments radically increased the number of slaves being transported to Spanish America. This new system of importation streamlined the collection of royal duties on slaves while addressing the colonists' demands for slaves, especially their interest in *bozales*. In 1528, just prior to the increased restrictions on private slave importation, an exclusive *asiento* granted Heinrich Ehinger and Hieronymus Seiller the right to import four thousand slaves over a four-year period.[35] From 1532 until 1580, the crown responded to colonists' demands for slaves by granting licenses that authorized a trader to transport a fixed number of slaves to a specific region.[36] Between 1580 and 1640, the union of Spain and Portugal under Phillip II facilitated a return to an exclusive *asiento* system.[37] By the last quarter of the sixteenth century, mass importation under the *asiento* system helped to bring in African laborers just as the indigenous population of the Americas reached its nadir, while increasing the revenue generated by the slave trade itself.

By the second half of the sixteenth century, the changes in royal slave trade policy had altered the demographics of slavery and more closely linked slavery to African ancestry. The diversity of slaves seen in early Hispaniola gradually gave way to an enslaved population of almost exclusively African descent. During the first half of the century, indigenous slaves, whether from the Canaries or Native Americans, decreased in number through overwork, disease, and the prohibition against indigenous enslavement. Although indigenous slaves could be taken from groups that opposed continued Spanish conquests and colonization, the relative number of indigenous slaves taken after the 1540s paled in comparison to African slave imports, especially in the developing colonial centers of Peru and Mexico.[38] By the end of the century, Africans and those of African descent had become the predominant slaves in Spanish America. Through these shifts, royal policy served to reinforce the already existent Iberian association between Africans and slavery and reinforced the stereotypes that Africans were suited for slavery because of their presumed bestial mental and physical traits.[39]

As royal policy facilitated increased volume in the transatlantic slave trade, fears of rebellion continued to shape royal policy. Over the course of the sixteenth century, the accelerating slave imports began to exceed Spanish immigration to the Americas. In 1556, Don Luis de Velasco, viceroy of New Spain, urged the crown to reduce the pace of African slave imports, fearing that they would cause public disorder.[40] Even though settlers had initially viewed *bozales* as less rebellious to Spanish owners, Velasco's letter does not perpetuate these earlier views. Over the next few decades, the pace of imports did not slow. As early as 1570, African slaves outnumbered Spanish residents of Mexico City.[41] By 1593, the same would occur in the city of Lima.[42] As the slave trade boomed between 1590 and 1640, the African population would continue to outpace Spanish residents.[43] Even while the number of Africans increased, Spanish slave owners' use of slaves posed its own problem for social control.

In the conquests of the Caribbean and mainland, Spanish conquistadors had armed their African slaves and servants to help bolster the number of armed combatants.[44] Some of these black conquistadors received their freedom and settled as colonists. Many continued to carry arms for their protection and as status symbols recognizing their service.[45] For freed *negros* and former black conquistadors swords represented status symbols that demonstrated their previous service and elevated their social position.[46] Additionally, masters allowed their slaves and servants to carry arms while working in rural areas or areas in which banditry or hostile indigenous raids threatened Spanish interests.[47] Throughout the Americas, Spaniards regularly allowed Africans, both enslaved and free, to carry swords and other weapons.

Even royal officials took to traveling with armed African slaves to insure their safety and demonstrate their status.[48]

During the course of the sixteenth century, Spanish settlers fueled a paradoxical process. Their collective demands for African slave labor led the crown to authorize the importation of an ever-increasing number of slaves, a category of people they considered bestial and savage. At the same time, individual Spanish slave owners regularly allowed their African slaves or freed African and Afro-descended servants to carry weapons in order to protect Spaniards and their interests. Despite the overwhelming emphasis on social control of *negros*, Spanish policy never fully dealt with this paradox by attempting a thorough reassessment of the interrelationship between the slave trade, slave owners' use of slaves, and mechanisms of slave control. Instead the casuist nature of royal policy responded to specific moments in which the tension between these practices necessitated a direct response.

One such moment came in 1535 when Sebastián Rodríguez, a representative of the town of Veracruz, complained that armed *negros* in that city frequently caused social affronts and instigated crimes.[49] In response, the crown mandated that no *negro* was to have or carry any weapon. Any *negro* found in violation was to receive fifty lashes, and any Spaniard convicted of giving a *negro* a weapon was to receive a penalty of three thousand *maravedíes*.

The royal order proved prescient. In September 1537, a group of *negros* attempted a rebellion in Mexico City. According to the report sent by Viceroy Antonio de Mendoza, a group of *negros* had elected a king and set about organizing themselves into squads.[50] Mendoza believed that the *negros* hoped to gain the support of the native population and take over Mexico City and some nearby mines. The plot was leaked by a *negro*, and Mendoza was able to round up the supposed ringleaders before any of their plans were set in motion. Interestingly, Mendoza does not mention any weapons found or other arms to be used in the uprising. However, in its wake Mendoza issued ordinances to help protect against future attacks.[51] Within two weeks, Mendoza had prohibited the sale or gift of any form of weapon to *negros*, *moriscos*, and *indios* under penalty of death to both the slave and whomever gave the weapon. He also prohibited the gathering of more than three *negro* or *morisco* slaves of different owners under penalty of one hundred lashes. Finally, the orders imposed a curfew on *negros* and *moriscos*, prohibiting them from traveling after dusk without their owners. The penalty for violation was to be six pesos or one hundred lashes but death if the slave was found with a weapon after dark. Two years later, the *cabildo* of Veracruz issued a local set of ordinances that took similar steps to control their *negro* population. Their orders also required that slave owners report all slaves to the authorities within three days of entering the city's jurisdiction.[52] Despite the severity of these laws, they did not put an end to African rebellion or resistance, real or imagined.

In the years that followed, laws regulating *negros*, free and enslaved, were issued by both local communities and the monarchy. In 1551, the crown confirmed a set of ordinances passed by the city of Lima.[53] One ordinance expressly prohibited any "*negro* . . . *loro*, [and] *berberisco*, either free or enslaved," from carrying any type of weapon at any time in any place. Only the armed slaves of magistrates were exempted. The following year, the monarchy issued its own order that throughout the kingdom of Peru *negros* be prohibited from carrying swords, dirks, or daggers because the "liberty" with which they had done so had resulted in the deaths of *indios* and other inconveniences.[54] In 1552, the crown even questioned the practice of arming slaves as personal retainers. According to that order, "while their masters are at Mass or conducting business, the *negros* go through the pueblos and with their weapons offend many people, and in such manner Spaniards have been killed and *indios* maimed. And because they are slaves of powerful people, they are protected from punishment, and those that are aggrieved by these [crimes] remain unable to attain justice."[55] In response, the Audiencia of New Spain was charged to review all licenses that authorized Spaniards to travel with armed *negros* and revoke those that were unnecessary. These orders illustrate the tension caused by Spanish subjects' paradoxical attitudes towards *negros*. At the individual level, Spaniards saw *negros* as auxiliaries, extensions of their interests, and in that capacity carrying weapons could be beneficial. In contrast, when someone else's *negro* caused problems, then restrictions needed to be imposed in order to prevent catastrophe.

Consequently, Spanish laws concerning *negros* and their attitudes expressed a clear and persistent contradiction. As a *género*, *negros* were perceived of as dangerous, barbaric, and prone to violence. Yet Spaniards needed African labor, and individual Spaniards tended to view their slaves as auxiliaries, trusting them to protect Spanish lives and interests. This paradox coupled with casuistry of Spanish laws insured that in the abstract *negros*, enslaved and free, would continue to be seen as dangerous and in need of regulation, often with severe penalties. At the same time, individual Spaniards frequently allowed their *negros* to carry weapons, and local and regional governments looked to free *negros* and *mulatos* as military auxiliaries. The tension between law and practice was not limited to *negros*. As individuals of mixed African ancestry grew in number, similar paradoxes developed as the crown sought to regulate their position in society.

INTERETHNIC UNIONS AND MARRIAGE

From the earliest years of conquest, many Spaniards had entered into sexual relationships with indigenous women, often by force but other times with consent. The crown quickly recognized that the abduction and sexual violation of native women endangered alliances with Native Americans and could result in rebellion and continued armed conflict. Additionally, the sexual violation of indigenous women or enslaved women represented a moral lapse that violated Christian ethics and could inhibit the spread of Christianity among conquered *indios* and enslaved *negros*. In responding to these early instances of sexual assault, the Spanish monarchy approached the issue of interethnic sexual unions and Christian marriage pragmatically. In general, the crown only favored interethnic unions and marriages when they benefited the long-term stability of their American possessions and did not impede the growing partition between a *república de indios* and a *república de españoles*.

The crown issued its first regulations on Spanish and indigenous unions in the 1501 instructions sent to Fray Nicolás de Ovando. As governor of the Indies, Ovando was ordered to return any *indias* taken without consent to their families. Notably the instructions explicitly allowed for consensual unions, ones made "by choice and not by force."[56] Although this allowed for Spanish-indigenous unions, the order did not seek to promote Spanish-indigenous unions. Rather, this policy represented a pragmatic solution that sought to prevent colonists from engaging in politically and spiritually harmful acts while allowing for politically beneficial, consensual unions.

Over the next decade royal policy would continue to reflect this pragmatism. In 1514, a royal order reiterated that European residents on Hispaniola could marry native peoples without penalty or hindrance. By this point, the crown viewed these marriages as "useful and beneficial to the service of God and [the crown] and convenient for the populating of the island."[57] The prospect of augmenting the population through Spanish-*india* unions had become politically expedient. In 1525, the crown again recognized the utility of marriages contracted between Spaniards and native elites. In an order sent to Darién (Panama), Emperor Charles V wrote, "I am informed that many of the *indios principales* and *caciques* of this land want to marry their sons and daughters to *cristianos y cristianas españoles* and that the *españoles* [wish to do the same] with the *indios* . . . from this God our Lord would be well served and from which much fortune and peace [would come] to the land and the tranquility [of it] and its governance of *cristianos* and *indios*."[58] This order illustrates that early royal policy saw Spanish-indigenous marriages as one means to more easily achieve conversion and peaceful government. By recognizing that the individuals involved needed to act out of their own free will, the crown honored the Church's prerequisites for marriage without actively encouraging interethnic unions.[59] Nevertheless, the eventual exclusion of Spaniards from *pueblos de indios* placed greater limits on this tacit acceptance of Spanish-indigenous unions. The prohibition of *españoles* from indigenous communities made all interactions, including marriage or informal unions, illicit in those spaces. In contrast, Spanish-indigenous interaction within the *república de españoles* remained legal and unregulated.

While Spanish-indigenous unions were allowed by royal legislation, the crown always attempted to prevent interethnic unions involving Africans. Nevertheless, the crown did see marriage as a tool for keeping the *negro* population separate and distinct from native peoples and for preventing slave revolt and resistance. In this regard, royal policy toward African slave marriages represents a continuation of policies that sought to control slaves and prevent rebellion.

In 1527, a royal order remarked that Hispaniola had received many African slaves and the Christian (European) population was too small to safely control these captives. The emperor worried that this situation could incite an uprising, lead to slave runaways, or in other ways cause harm and inconveniences to the colony. Consequently, the order concluded that marriages between slaves represented the best solution for ensuring a peaceful slave population. According to the emperor, "the love that [*negros*] will have for their wives and children and the order brought by marriage will cause great tranquility among them and will prevent other sins and inconveniences which would otherwise persist."[60] Moreover, the crown mandated that in the future all private individuals who held or were granted licenses to import slaves to Hispaniola be required to bring an equal number of males and females and see that their slaves marry other slaves. Any slaves already present in the colony were to be married within fifteen months.

This policy toward African marriage created its own paradox. Just as with Spanish-native marriages, the crown insisted that slaves be allowed to exercise their free will in choosing a spouse. Yet owners were mandated to ensure that *negro* slaves only married other *negros* and that slave marriages occur within a specified time. Even though the crown favored endogamous marriage among African slaves, its own stipulations implicitly allowed for exogamy through the emphasis on free will. Moreover, the royal ideal of endogamous African marriages placed the burden of enforcement and coercion on slave owners. As with the policies concerning slave control, the success of such a policy regarding African marriage could only succeed if individual Spanish slave owners' interests led them to act in accordance with the mandates of the crown.

Over the next several decades the crown reiterated its desire to circumscribe African unions and marriages. In 1541, a *cédula* ordered Governor Pizarro to ensure that *negros* only married *negras*.[61] The crown had received reports that African slaves in Peru had taken a diverse number of native women, some by choice, others against their will. Fearful that the abduction or seduction of *indias* by *negros* could antagonize the native population, Pizarro was ordered to insure that male and female African slaves only marry each other. The crown continued to promote endogamy among *negros* by forcing slaves to marry each other. In promoting such marriages, the crown idealized the benefits of Christian marriage by assuming that African men would eschew illicit sexual unions with other women after marriage. As with the order of 1527, it relied on the compliance of *encomenderos*, the same individuals that allowed their slaves to travel to indigenous communities on their behalf.

The issue of intermarriage cannot be separated from the rise of the two-republic system. The crown based its protection of a *república de indios* on the perceived aggravation, damage, and inconveniences caused by non-*indios* living in indigenous communities. As the 1541 order illustrates, informal unions and sexual violence caused by these interlopers were perceived to be harmful and inconvenient to royal interests. Even though most decrees that prohibited non-*indios* from entering *pueblos de indios* lacked direct references to sexual assault, informal unions, or marriage, the intent of these policies was to isolate *indios* from *negros, mulatos, mestizos,* and *españoles*. Impeding interethnic marriage and informal unions was inherent to that separation. In this way, the establishment of the two-republic model furthered royal attempts at limiting marriages and unions between *indios* and other *géneros de gente*, at least those that occurred in *pueblos de indios*. Crucially, these overlapping policies made no provision for *indios* that resided in Spanish settlements. Although *pueblos de indios* were to be the exclusive preserve of native people, Spanish settlements did not prohibit the presence of *indios*. Consequently, royal efforts had almost no effect on limiting marriages and unions that occurred within the *república de españoles*.

Taken together, royal policy toward interethnic marriage illustrates various tensions. Especially in the immediate aftermath of conquest, sexual assault of native women by Spaniards and Africans threatened political stability, while consensual marriages between Spaniards and native elites promoted political stability and encouraged population growth. Likewise, endogamous marriages between enslaved Africans could foster a more peaceful slave population and minimize revolt, while prevailing stereotypes of Africans as violent and dangerous led to their perpetual exclusion of *negros* from indigenous communities. Over time, the legal division of society into two republics attempted to further limit all interactions between *indios* and other *géneros*. Yet the presence of *indios* within the *república de españoles* undermined the idealized separation of Spanish and indigenous spheres.

Furthermore, the implementation of such policies required enforcement by colonial officials and acceptance by colonial subjects. The clerics who performed the marriages represented the most substantial impediment to the enactment of royal interethnic marriage policy. As Patricia Seed has noted, during the sixteenth and seventeenth century clergy placed a great deal of emphasis on the sacramental requirement of free will.[62] Consequently, royal efforts to limit marriage choices of particular *géneros* faced strong doctrinal opposition by the very individuals charged with performing marriages. Moreover, the attempts to limit *negros* from marrying or interacting with *indios* required Spanish slave owners and masters to stop using slaves as representatives or agents in indigenous communities. Such a change went against the established patterns of economic exploitation. Similarly, the presence of *mestizos, mulatos, negros,* and *españoles* in *pueblos de indios* reflected the complex social, economic, and familial ties that traversed the legal barrier between the *república de indios* and the *república de españoles*. The frequent need to repeat such prohibitions attests to the lack of compliance by subjects in the Americas.

HIJOS DE ESPAÑOLES Y INDIAS

Royal policy toward the children born of European-indigenous unions developed throughout the sixteenth century, changing in response to evolving social and demographic conditions. Through this process, the legal position of such individuals, especially those labeled *mestizo*, diminished over time. Initially, policy toward *mestizos* viewed them as extensions of their *español* parents who could fill important social and economic roles. As the *español* population increased via immigration and natural growth, the crown began to circumscribe the legal position of *mestizos*. Even after losing some legal rights, *mestizos* still retained important privileges that distinguished them from other non-Spanish *géneros.*

Despite early legislation dealing with Spanish-indigenous unions, the offspring of those unions did not receive specific attention from the crown until the early 1530s. The earliest usage of the term *mestizo* that I have found comes from an Inquisition case from 1539.[63] Most early references to individuals of mixed indigenous-European ancestry described those persons as "children of *españoles* and *indias.*" In eschewing the application of a new term, this phrase suggests an attempt to avoid disparaging these individuals because of their non-European mothers. In some cases, the mother's role was even more subdued through the use of the phrase "child of an *español* born by an *india.*" This construction depicts the indigenous woman as merely a vessel that bore a European child. The early view of European-indigenous individuals initially rejected the creation of a categorical distinction by tacitly considering them Europeans born of the wombs of native women.

The first decree responding to the presence of these individuals was promulgated in 1533. This order responded to reports of "children of *españoles* born by *indias*" wandering lost among the *indios,* dying of starvation or being sacrificed.[64] The crown ordered the Audiencia of Mexico to collect these children and have them sent to Spanish towns or entrusted to *encomenderos* so that they could be educated. This paternalistic attitude toward the offspring of Spaniards and *indias* continued over the course of the next several decades. In 1550, the crown asked the viceroy of Mexico to provide information as to the utility of a school to educate *"mestizos* and lost girls."[65] In fact, such as school already existed. Three years earlier, the *cabildo* of Mexico City, acting on its own initiative, authorized the creation of "a center for *mestizos,* children of unknown parents."[66] In addition a school for young *mestizas* was founded to house, support, and indoctrinate these young women.[67]

One other important aspect of this early move to collect and support *mestizos* is the correlation between the label *mestizo* and perceived illegitimacy. These early orders implied that, when born to their native mothers, *mestizos* existed outside of Spanish society. While Spaniards may have fathered these children, those men were "unknown" and left their offspring to be raised in native pueblos, where they were "lost." The construction of *mestizo* as both illegitimate and orphaned by the Spanish parent created a discrepancy wherein publicly recognized, albeit often illegitimate, children of Spaniards and native people could avoid the stigmatizing label of *mestizo*. These socially prominent individuals continued to be called *hijos de español e india* (children of a Spaniard and an *india*) or *hijos naturales* (natural children), the term for illegitimate offspring.[68] This trend marked a social, legal, and linguistic division by which Spanish elites tacitly accepted some individuals of Spanish-indigenous ancestry as fellow *españoles* while labeling others *mestizo* and subjecting them to the developing legal and social stigmas attached to that *género*.

Although the label *mestizo* implied illegitimacy, initially the crown did allow *mestizos* some prerogatives due to their Spanish heritage. During the 1550s, the crown issued several decrees that allowed *mestizos* and their *india* parents to travel freely between the Americas and Spain without prior royal license.[69] This privilege was never extended to other non-Spanish groups. Also, unlike other non-Spanish individuals, in 1549, *mestizos* who were either *vecinos* or the legitimate sons of *vecinos* were allowed to manage native laborers through the institutions of *encomienda* or *repartimiento*.[70] In 1538, the crown sought to better foster a stable social order by ordering officials in the colony to persuade and admonish all *encomenderos* to marry or lose their grants and to give preference to married men in all future *encomienda* or *repartimiento* grants.[71] The following year, marriage was made mandatory, and *encomenderos* had three years to marry or they would be stripped of their grants.[72] This policy led many *encomenderos* to formalize previously informal unions with native, African, *mestiza*, or *mulata* women. In light of the *encomenderos'* reaction, the 1549 extension of privileges to legitimate *mestizos* can be interpreted as a means of appeasing *encomenderos* and entrepreneurial *vecinos* who feared that their *mestizo* children might be prohibited from inheriting or managing their estates. Later generations of *encomenderos* who were more likely to find Spanish wives did not face similar issues. Furthermore, after the mid sixteenth century, royal orders did not mention the incongruous situation of legitimate *mestizos*, effectively promoting the broader stereotype of *mestizos* as illegitimate.

Nonetheless, the close association between *mestizos* and their *español* forebears did set them apart from other *géneros*. One notable privilege held by *mestizos* was the right to bear arms. From the earliest decades of the colonial period, the crown had consistently enjoined Africans and *indios* from carrying weapons.[73] In contrast, the issue of *mestizo* arms ownership did not receive royal attention during the first half of the sixteenth century. In December 1566, the crown reprimanded the Audiencia of Peru for issuing arms licenses to *indios*, *mestizos*, and *mulatos* and ordered that those licenses be revoked.[74] Although the reprimand noted an existing royal prohibition against *mestizos* carrying arms, no such order has been located. Seven months prior, in April 1566, a plot involving Don Martín Cortés, the son of Hernán Cortés and his indigenous translator Doña Marina, threatened the royal government of New Spain.[75] Only months later, before the Audiencia of Peru received the reprimand, another plot involving *mestizos* threatened that kingdom. In early January 1567, a group of discontented creoles, including a number of *mestizos*, hatched a plot to assassinate the president of the Audiencia and take over Lima and Cuzco. The plot failed after a member confessed the plan to an Augustinian friar.[76] In February 1567, Licenciado Lope García de Castro, president of the Audiencia, reported on the government's investigation into the "mutiny of the *mestizos*" and warned, "There are so many *mestizos* in these kingdoms and they are born every hour. It is necessary Your Majesty send a *cédula* stating that no *mestizo* or *mulato* be allowed to carry any weapon or own a harquebus under penalty of death. This is a *gente* that as time goes by will be very dangerous and pernicious to this land."[77] In December 1568, the crown responded to García de Castro's request but remitted the issue to the newly appointed viceroy of Peru, Don Francisco de Toledo.[78]

After spending several years in the viceroyalty, in 1572 Toledo provided his own opinion of *mestizos* and the right to bear arms.[79] In his letter to the crown, Toledo captured the social and cultural paradox that *mestizos* posed to royal authorities. On the one hand, *mestizos* were dangerous because they were a "Hispanicized people" (*gente españolada*) skilled in the use of arms and horsemanship and "inclined to evil," capable of leading a perilous rebellion. On the other, *mestizos* were "the children of free women and Spanish fathers such that by no right, divine or human, does it appear that they are incapable of the honor, dignity, and privileges that are due to their fathers."[80] When Toledo attempted to implement the crown's ban of 1566, many *mestizos* sought exceptions for being the children of conquistadors or *encomenderos* or for having served in conquests and pacifications.[81] Toledo warned the crown that a complete prohibition would be taken as an affront by *mestizos* and their families and could serve as the impetus for a rebellion. Cognizant of the local sentiment, Toledo implemented a modified ban on arms in 1572. This new policy expressly prohibited *mulatos* and *zambaigos* from carrying arms but allowed *mestizos* to solicit a license from the viceroy. The viceroy stipulated that to receive a license *mestizos* had to live in Spanish settlements, maintain their own homes, and be employed.[82] In 1573, the king confirmed Toledo's new policy, effectively expanding it to all Spanish territories.[83]

The process by which *mestizos* secured a right to bear arms illustrates the complex relationship between their social position and the legal system. On the one hand, stereotypes portrayed them as illegitimate, dangerous, and disloyal. Some prominent *mestizos* fed these stereotypes by participating in conspiratorial plots and rebellions, while common *mestizos* harassed indigenous communities or wandered about as vagabonds.[84] Nevertheless, when legislation threatened to restrict the rights of all *mestizos*, their response (and the response of their families) highlighted the reality that many *mestizos* lived with and were supported by their Spanish families. In the eyes of these families, such a restriction tainted the honor of the entire family, not just their *mestizo* kin. Toledo's compromise sought to balance the abstract negative stereotype of *mestizos* with the pragmatic reality that providing a privilege to socially prominent *mestizos* secured their loyalty and that of their families.

The association between *mestizos* and *españoles* did not always prove beneficial. While some *mestizo* men would eventually gain the right to bear arms as a demonstration of their honor and status, society and the law held *mestizas* to a higher standard of female honor. In 1548, the crown chastised the Audiencia of Peru for not prosecuting and punishing *mestizas* who committed adultery against *españoles*.[85] The king ordered that in future cases *mestizas* be prosecuted and punished similarly to *españolas* in accordance with the laws of the kingdom.

The content of the order does not specify in what ways authorities were lax in these cases. Religious and secular authorities may have felt that *mestizas* were inherently unable to maintain the Spanish ideals of female honor or, conversely, that *españoles* cuckolded by *mestiza* wives were less deserving of redress. Whatever the cause, the royal order rejected the notion that *mestizas* married to *españoles* should be held to lower standard than *españolas*. Nevertheless, this order did not apply to *mestizas* who committed adultery against spouses of other *géneros*. Thus, while the crown sought to hold *mestizas* to a higher standard, it only did so for those *mestizas* who had married well and whose dalliances might dishonor Spanish men.

While *mestizos* held a slightly privileged position during the first half of the sixteenth century, by the 1560s the changing social order of the colonies led to a shift in royal legislation against *mestizos*. This process resulted in the loss of early privileges and a greater tendency to group *mestizos* in with the *géneros de gente* of African descent. In particular, the 1570s saw major attempts to restrict *mestizo* privileges. In 1576, the crown ordered that no *mestizo* was to be granted a commission to serve as an *escribano* (scrivener). The wording of this order reveals that colonial elites' increasingly negative stereotypes of *mestizos* led them to demand restrictions on the occupations those individuals could hold. According to the reports received by the crown, *mestizo escribanos* "harm and vex all persons with whom they work."[86] Similarly, in 1578 the crown ordered that *mestizos* never be given responsibilities over natives because often they harmed the *indios* rather than helped them.[87] The same year, reports from the colonies led to *mestizos* being barred from ordination. The crown feared that they were not "virtuous, elevated persons sufficient in the qualities required for the priesthood."[88]

In 1582, further communication between colonial residents and the monarchy led to a clarification of the prohibition against *mestizo* ordination. While *mestizos* born of a native and a Spaniard were prohibited, the child of a *mestizo* and a Spaniard was not.[89] The distinction between a child of an *español* and an *india* and that of an *español* and a *mestiza* mirrors attitudes toward the gradual, generational redemption of impurities of blood by Jews, Muslims, and heretics.[90] Importantly, this law did not give a categorical name to the children of *mestizos* and Spaniards, even though the term *castizo* was beginning to be used within the colony. The cumulative effect of these policies was to erode the marginal privileges enjoyed by first- and second-generation *mestizos*. By the last quarter of the sixteenth century, the view that *hijos de españoles e indias* should be near-equals to their Spanish parents had shifted such that individuals ascribed the *género* of *mestizo* had become dangers to the social order.

HIJOS DE NEGROS Y INDIAS Y ESPAÑOLES Y NEGRAS

Although individuals of mixed African descent were present in the Americas from the earliest voyages of exploration and conquest, most legislation concerning *mulatos* grouped them with other individuals of African descent or with *mestizos*. As these individuals were descendants of *negros*, royal legislation aimed at them frequently focused on physical control and the perceived need to control violent subjects. As early as 1530, owners of enslaved *mulatos*, the children of Europeans and Africans, had to apply for a royal license to be transported to the Americas. However, no explicit provisions were made concerning the travel of free *mulatos*. In 1566, the crown included *mulatos* among those banned from carrying weapons, with *negros, loros,* and *berberiscos*.[91] In 1573, royal confirmation of Viceroy Toledo's arms policy added *zambaigos* to the list of Afro-descendants prohibited from carrying weapons.[92] Unlike *mestizos*, the arms restriction against *mulatos* made no exemption for those born of *españoles* or who led respectable lives. However, in practice, some viceroys of New Spain did issue arms licenses to *mulatos* and *negros* even if royal policy did not authorize such grants.[93]

During the 1570s, the numerical growth of a free population of African descent would spur new debates about their place in the colonial order. By this period, individuals of partial African descent had come to account for a sizable portion of the non-indigenous colonial population. Around 1570, New Spain may have had as many as six thousand *mulato* residents, either African-European or African-indigenous, while the Spanish population numbered around fifteen thousand and enslaved Africans probably numbered about the same.

Anecdotal evidence suggests that many individuals of partial African descent were African-indigenous rather than African-European. The increasing numbers of *hijos de negros e indias* (children of *negros* and *indias*) held financial implications for the governing of the colonies. Sometime prior to 1572, the Audiencia of Guatemala sought royal guidance on how to apply tribute burdens to these partially indigenous *mulatos*. The Audiencia asked, "If some free *negros* or enslaved [*negros*] marry *indias* and have children, and these children claim to be exempt from personal *tribute* saying that they are not *indios*, should they pay or not"?[94] The question had significant ramifications. On one hand, if these Afro-indigenous individuals were excluded from tribute burdens, the crown would indirectly favor African-indigenous unions as a means by which indigenous parents might free their children from tribute obligations.[95] On the other hand, broadening tribute to include the children born of mixed African-indigenous unions would lead to increased revenue from a growing segment of the population. Consequently in 1572 and 1573, the crown ordered the Audiencia of Guatemala to consider the children of *negros* and *indias* tributaries.[96] Neither letter applied a *género* label to the children of *negros* and *indias*. This exchange illustrates the pragmatism of royal policy toward individuals of mixed ancestry. Although previous legislation went to great lengths to prevent African-indigenous unions, after a significant number of such unions occurred, the crown enacted a response that generated royal revenues from these explicitly undesirable social groups.

By 1574, this policy was expanded and sent to all jurisdictions of the empire. In reformulating the policy and applying across all of the Americas, the crown chose to lump *mulatos* and free *negros* together. This new legislation stipulated that "all the free *negros* and *negras*, *mulatos*, and *mulatas* that are in the Indies shall pay tribute to His Majesty."[97] By choosing to simply use the phrase *mulatos y mulatas* this order did not impose any difference between individuals of African-European descent and those of African-indigenous descent, considering them equals for the purposes of taxation. The inclusion of free blacks further increased revenue by taxing another growing segment of the population. However, in combining *mulatos* and *negros*, the crown shifted the ideological basis for tribute. In the initial query of the Audiencia of Guatemala, the question of Afro-indigenous tribute linked it to tribute obligations of *indios* as conquered subjects. The new policy of 1574 did not mention *indios*. Instead the new tribute policy based itself on a connection to slavery and represented a perpetual tax on freedom. In effect the policy required that free people of African descent pay the crown for the opportunity of living in the New World.[98]

This change was not received well by some individuals of African descent. In 1583, Juan Bautista de Cardona, self-described as a *"mulato, son of a cavallero español* (Spanish nobleman)," sought exemption from these new tribute levies.[99] According to a petition presented before the *corregidor* (local magistrate) of Mexico City, Juan Bautista provided evidence that he had been born in Iberia to Gaspar Rubio de Cardona, a *vecino* of Valencia, and Catalina Martín, *de color morena*. Moreover, his father was a *caballero* (nobleman) in the kingdom of Valencia. For his part Juan Bautista claimed that he demonstrated through his person and actions that he was of the *calidad* of his father and a "an honorable person regarded as good and virtuous." As further demonstration of his personal qualities and abilities, Juan Bautista presented evidence that he had served the crown as a soldier in Malta during its 1565 siege by the Ottomans, had helped build the stronghold of Bernia in Valencia, and had helped put down the 1568 *morisco* rebellion in the Alpujarra mountains of Granada. Finally, prior to arriving in Mexico, Juan Bautista had lived in Madrid where he had worked as a tailor often in the service of *"cavalleros y personas principales"* (noblemen and principal persons). What most concerned Juan Bautista was that this new legislation was an affront to his status as the son of a *caballero*. He expressed a deep conviction that his noble lineage and his service to the king should be taken into account in the application of the new tribute policy.

The legal arguments he presented were of dubious success. Given the clarity of the 1574 order to extend tribute to all individuals of African descent, Juan Bautista could not directly refute the claim that he should pay tribute. Instead he argued that the tribute was really only being collected from *negros libres* and therefore, due to his service and status as the *mulato* son of a *caballero*, he should be exempted. As evidence, he presented a royal order from 1578 issued to Tierra Firme (Panama) that authorized a temporary cessation of tribute collection for *negros libres* due to their financial hardships in that region. Juan Bautista used this relief as evidence that "this tribute is collected only from free *negros* and not *mulatos.*"[100] This legal strategy relied on a manipulation of the tension between casuistry and analogy inherent in *derecho indiano*. The 1578 *cédula* was clearly intended to provide minor financial relief to poor subjects in Tierra Firme. That it was only applied to *negros libres* most likely reflected their socioeconomic position as tributaries in the region. *Mulatos* there may have been better off financially and less in need of favor. Juan Bautista's attempt to use this *cédula* as proof that only *negros libres* should pay tribute rested on a tenuous legal manipulation. Although the document does not record a definitive finding in Madrid, presumably the Council of the Indies saw through his strategy. As of its initial review by the council, Juan Bautista was still pursuing his case.

Importantly, the experience of Juan Bautista illustrates the difference in the political influence of *mulatos* and *mestizos.* When new laws threatened to limit *mestizos'* right to bear arms, they and their *español* relatives successfully moderated the policy. In contrast, the application of tribute to free *mulatos* and *negros* did not generate an equivalent movement. Individual *mulatos* could mobilize rationales similar to those of *mestizos* for being excluded from the general policy. In 1600, Juan Quesada de Figueroa, the *fiscal* of the Audiencia of New Spain, wrote to the king complaining that *mulatos* there had inundated the court with petitions for tribute exemptions on the grounds that they were the children of *españoles*.[101] In order to stop the flood of requests, Quesada asked that the king order "all this *género de gente* pay without distinction of being the children of *negros* or *blancos.*" As Quesada's response illustrates, *mulatos* did not have the social connections to effectively pressure colonial officials or overcome the negative stereotypes that produced the new policy. Despite the protests by Juan Bautista and others, royal legislation would not recognize any difference within the category of *mulato.* Nevertheless, in the sixteenth century and beyond, some *mulatos* and others of African descent were given tribute exemptions for military service.[102] While these grants offered relief from tribute payments to individuals or corporate groups for specific reasons, they did not attempt to undermine or modify the general policy established in 1574.

As with *mestizos*, restrictions on *mulatos* and *negros* could be gendered. In 1571, the king ordered that no *negra* or *mulata* be allowed to wear gold, pearls, or silk.[103] Under no circumstances were *negras* and *mulatas* to wear "Canton crape mantles or those of any fabric except shawls that only reach to just below the waist." Any woman wearing gold jewels, silk dresses or capes would lose those items. As with the imposition of tribute, this prohibition highlights the growing economic resources of free people of color in the colonies. The issuance of this law demonstrates that in at least some Spanish communities *negras* and *mulatas* had sufficient resources to adorn themselves like *españolas*. The prohibition granted one exception to the ban. *Negras* and *mulatas* married to *españoles* were to be allowed to wear gold earrings with pearls, a necklace, and velvet hems on their skirts. Although this exception allowed some *negras* and *mulatas* to wear items of status, it did so in order that those women might reflect the honor of their spouses. Just as with the prosecution of adulterous *mestizas*, the central issue in allowing some *negras* and *mulatas* access to precious clothing and jewelry was the maintenance of Spanish male honor. Unless connected to a Spanish husband, lavishly dressed *negras* and *mulatas* represented a dangerous deviation from the expected socioeconomic order.

On the whole, royal policy toward *mulatos* and other free persons of African descent continued to deal with issues of control and rebellion. Limitations on carrying weapons included them alongside enslaved Africans. Yet their freedom posed new problems. As free people of color achieved economic success, their financial prosperity put them at odds with their perceived social standing. The imposition of tribute allowed the royal treasury to benefit from that prosperity while marking *mulatos* and *negros* as the descendants of slaves whose freedom indebted them perpetually to the king.

THE PROBLEM OF VAGABONDS

During the sixteenth century, the mobility and fluidity of the developing colonial order bred a major social problem that included individuals of all *géneros*. The search for quick wealth, lucrative employment, and a better life led men and women of every *género* to travel widely.

The ease by which individuals could travel to and within Spanish colonies led many elites to complain about vagabonds living unconnected to particular communities or employers.[104] As early as 1550, Viceroy Velasco (the elder) wrote to the crown complaining that many single Spaniards arrived in the colony uninterested in making a living from the land and instead wandered the land. Velasco feared that the increasing number of single, listless men would not only harm native peoples but could "cause unrest in the land and a conflict that would be hard to remedy."[105] To this end he suggested that the crown stop granting licenses to immigrate to the colony. Importantly, Velasco understood that the problem of vagabondage was not limited to *españoles* hoping to make it rich. He also favored a policy of pressing *mestizos* into service and sending them as soldiers to fight in Europe. Initially the crown responded by reiterating the importance of separating Spaniards and *indios* into separate *repúblicas*. While consistently favored by the crown, this policy was difficult to enforce. To complicate matters, individuals of mixed ancestry soon joined the growing numbers of transients. Keenly aware of this fact, Velasco warned, "The *mestizos* grow rapidly and all are inclined to wickedness and are prone to all kinds of evil deeds . . . the *mestizos* wander among the *indios* and as they are half [*indio*] they are taken in and hidden and given food and from this the *indios* acquire bad customs and are treated poorly."[106] To better combat the parasitic nature of these vagabonds, the crown sought to integrate them more fully as functional members of the colony.

In 1558, the crown ordered Velasco to round up any vagabonds, be they *españoles, mestizos,* or *indios,* and have them resettled into newly founded communities.[107] This order was envisioned as working alongside the two-republic system and in conjunction with it. According to the *cédula,* Spaniards and *mestizos* were to be resettled together while *indios* were to be placed in separate communities. The location of these new settlements was to be determined by the viceroy, and each community was to have lands for farming and livestock. The crown was even generous enough to authorize royal funding to help purchase initial quantities of seed and breeding stock for the settlers. Ideally this order would have helped reduce the number of vagabonds and provided additional security and increased trade through the creation of new cities. Nevertheless, the complexities involved in executing such a policy undoubtedly prevented its implementation.

While the programs of new settlement would continue to be proposed over the course of the century, royal policies towards vagabonds and jobless wanderers would quickly shift to more manageable plans.[108] A royal order from 1563 returned to the problem of Spanish vagabonds living parasitically off native communities.[109] Reiterating the "damage and aggravation" caused by Spaniards in native communities, the crown ordered that no "unmarried *español* vagabonds" could live in native communities and that otherwise any such person should face "grave penalties." The king also ordered that the authorities should mandate that such vagabonds be compelled to find employment, learn trades, or be forced to find some means by which to support themselves financially.

In 1569, the crown extended this plan to control non-Spanish vagabonds. In an order directed toward the Nuevo Reino de Granada, the king mandated that all *mestizos* be compelled to work, taught trades, become farmers, or be exiled.[110] As in previous orders, the crown was responding to the perceived harm that the lax lifestyle of these *mestizos* could bring about. In 1577, this policy was extended yet again to include free *negros* and *mulatos.* As free persons, *negros* and *mulatos* could travel freely in search of work and communities. This mobility tended to hinder attempts to collect the newly imposed tribute burden.[111] The order lamented that tribute could not be collected because *negros* and *mulatos* were "people that do not have a residence or known home."[112] In order to enforce their tribute obligations and insure that they had permanent stable work, the king stipulated that these free-colored individuals work for Spaniards and that a register of their names and the names of their employers be maintained by the local magistrate. Moreover, they were not to be allowed to change employers or residence without a license. If they did leave, they were to be arrested and returned, by force if necessary, to their employer of record.

The continuing problem of vagabonds had reached new levels toward the end of the sixteenth century. In the late 1590s, the viceroys of both New Spain and Peru received specific instructions concerning this social ill and its relation to other policy issues, namely the separation of *repúblicas*. Upon being appointed viceroy of Peru in 1595,

Don Luis de Velasco (the younger) was ordered to closely watch over "the unmarried vagabonds, *españoles, mestizos, mulatos,* and *zambaigos,* that live among the [*indios*]."[113] He was to "castigate their excesses with rigor and without leniency, and ensure that those who have trades are employed in them, and those that do not practice their trade or do not know a trade learn one, or serve masters, or find some other manner of supporting themselves." Additionally, he was to insure that the religious authorities in the colony oversaw the problem so that they could prevent or rectify the problems caused by those that "live freely and licentiously." Those individuals who refused to rectify their behavior and continued to pose a problem were to be exiled or sent as soldiers to Chile or other such campaigns.

The evolution of policies designed to curb vagabondage illustrate a social problem that transcended *género* categories. Nevertheless, in seeking to rectify the dangerous mobility of colonial subjects, the policies created to castigate vagabonds dealt with individuals according their *género*. Spanish vagabonds faced the least legal compulsion, while the law imposed greater and more specific punishments on *mestizos* and free people of color categorized as vagabonds. This differential approach to vagabondage highlights the way in which *género* influenced the regulation of a common problem. Men and women of all *géneros* were vagabonds, yet the developing stereotypes mapped onto those *géneros* shaped how colonists and the monarch reacted to the same illicit activity.

This chapter has shown that royal legislation incorporated *género* categories into the legal system as it sought to mediate the social, cultural, and economic conflicts that arose between colonial subjects. Most colonial legislation did not create restrictions a priori. Rather, local circumstances prompted colonial subjects or bureaucrats to share their experiences and problems with the monarchy. Based on these reports, the crown issued legislation designed to rectify specific problems. In response, local officials and subjects implemented, or in some cases ignored, the new royal policy. This cycle continued as problems, old and new, real or imagined, prompted new legislation and enforcement. Laws regulating *géneros de gente* came into existence because the monarchy responded to specific concerns of its subjects in the

Americas. Yet, as the legal code itself demonstrates, the issuance of a law did not always lead to compliance. Instead local circumstances always mediated the application and enforcement of the law.

The following chapters turn to the lived experiences of individuals of mixed ancestry. Importantly, the complex relationships that mediated the creation of *género* stereotypes and created a prejudicial and discriminatory legal system also operated at the level of the individual. Despite the prejudices and legal restrictions mapped onto the various *géneros de gente,* within each *género* there existed a diversity of lived experiences that belie the homogeneous stereotypes perpetuated by law and social discourse. Throughout the sixteenth century, social, cultural, and economic positioning mediated individuals' experience of their *género*. In their variety, they attest to the disjuncture that existed between abstract stereotypes and quotidian relations.

Part II

Lived Experience

CHAPTER 3

Tacit *Españoles*

> Of the *mestizos* I do not worry as much. Even though among them there are many who lead ruinous lives and have bad customs, they are in the end the children of *españoles*. They are all raised by their fathers and after four or five years they leave the power of the *indias* [their mothers] and always continue on the side of the *españoles* because that is the part of themselves that they most honor.
>
> *Viceroy Martín Enríquez, 1574*

During the first half-century after the conquest, the initial conquistador-settlers of New Spain sought to consolidate their economic and political position within the kingdom. Even a cursory examination of the voluminous documentation produced by this generation evidences their profound desire to shape the colony's development in order to privilege their position and interests. *Probanzas de merito y servicio* (proofs of merit), *informaciones de servicio y parte* (information concerning service), and *cartas de buen gobierno* (letters of good governance) all reflected the vested interest of the early Spanish elite in the continuing development of the colony.[1] These individuals hoped to preserve their *encomienda* grants, receive *ayudas de costa* (financial remuneration), consolidate control in bureaucratic positions, and preserve their elevated status. The promulgation of the New Laws, increased royal control over native tribute and labor, and the arrival of increasing numbers of immigrants and peninsular bureaucrats all threatened the first conquistadors and settlers. Within the context of mid-sixteenth-century development, this chapter takes as its focus a unique set of individuals born of the conquest but intimately connected to this formative phase of social, political, and economic development—children born of Spanish-indigenous parents, raised within Spanish society, and to whom society did not frequently ascribe the *género* of *mestizo*—a group that can be termed "tacit *españoles*."

The previous chapters examined the ideological and juridical evolution of *géneros de gente*, including *mestizo*. To recapitulate this evolution, Spaniards in the Americas coined the term *mestizo* and by the 1530s had begun to ascribe this label to some individuals of European and indigenous ancestry. In general, the application of the term *mestizo* varied according to social and economic factors.[2] Individuals with property or social connections to elite Spaniards were less likely to be labeled *mestizo*, while individuals with stronger ties to indigenous society and of lower economic position were more frequently referred to as *mestizos*. Yet individuals of mixed ancestry who were wholly integrated into indigenous life and community were likely to be called *indios*. Thus, the ascription of *mestizo* constituted a highly subjective act that often weighed cultural and social factors alongside known ancestry.

Among those individuals of European and indigenous ancestry, one of the most unique subsets is that of tacit *españoles*. The phrase "tacit *españoles*" emphasizes that most contemporaries accepted them as *españoles*. Although most individuals examined here were never ascribed the category of *español*, they were not generally categorized as *mestizos* even when their mixed parentage was known. This knowing silence in *género* ascription effectively acknowledged them as members of the broader *género* of *españoles*. Even though they may have had similar ancestry to commonly reputed *mestizos*, their lives were markedly different in terms of their social, political, and economic standing.

Recent scholarship examining the recognized and supported children born of *españoles* and *indias* has referred to them as *mestizos* or "elite *mestizos*" by virtue of their lineage, even while acknowledging that such labels were rarely ascribed to them by contemporaries.[3] To do so implies that the primary basis of *mestizo* ascription rested in lineage and ancestry. Yet the same research increasingly demonstrates that known ancestry did not trump social and cultural factors, especially the importance of family support. Early colonial society did not ascribe the label *mestizo* to all persons of known or presumed Spanish-indigenous ancestry. Only a particular subset of such individuals received the label. By adopting the label "tacit *españoles*," this study emphasizes the important way that social and cultural position mediated known ancestry in the ascription of *género* categories to individuals of Spanish-indigenous descent.

Universally, tacit *españoles* had close connections with their Spanish parents.[4] They were recognized as their offspring, very often as *"hijos naturales"*—illegitimate but recognized children. Some tacit *españoles* were legitimate offspring of Spanish-indigenous marriages. However, the dynamics of Spanish-indigenous sexual encounters involving elite Spaniards did not generally result in many legitimate *mestizo* children during the sixteenth century.[5] Often these individuals were raised in a Spanish home and raised by a Spanish parent, relative, or close friend. Males in this group often received financial support for training in professions or investment in career opportunities. Females were generally raised like Spanish *doncellas* (virginal young women), with the intention that they be married well, preferably to Spaniards.

As a result of the support and recognition in each case by a Spanish parent, these individuals were rarely labeled *mestizos.* In general, socio-racial terms served as epithets that placed an individual in reference to Spaniards. In sixteenth-century documentation in which non-Spanish *género* labels appeared consistently, the label *español* frequently did not appear.[6] This tendency to omit *español* illustrates how Spanish American society had begun to constitute that term as the norm from which all other *géneros* diverged.[7] Consequently, when contemporaries chose not to ascribe a socio-racial label to an individual the omission implied that the individual was considered an *español*. The incorporation of some individuals of mixed Spanish-indigenous ancestry into the category of *español* reflects these individuals' integration within Spanish society and the social deference given them by virtue of their Spanish parents' status.[8]

The reality that individuals of Spanish-indigenous ancestry could be ascribed the *géneros* of *español, mestizo,* or *indio* suggests that the basis of *género* ascription along the Spanish-indigenous spectrum cannot be reduced to ancestry or lineage. In her study on *mestizos* in the kingdom of New Granada, Joanne Rappaport describes the category of *mestizo* as "disappearing" precisely because the social processes involved in ascription allowed some individuals classified as *mestizos* to drop out of that *género* and into another.[9] The findings of this study corroborate Rappaport's view of the ascription of the *mestizo* label. In early New Spain, just as in early New Granada, the ascription of a *género* label to individuals of mixed Spanish-indigenous ancestry resulted from a complex valuation of their social and cultural place in society.

Tracing the forces that influenced such an assignation can be made more difficult because of differential documentary preservation. Those individuals who were seen as *indios* did not leave many clues in colonial documents—at least not ones that would allow for a correlation between mixed ancestry and ascribed *género*. Indigenous communities tended not to single out individuals of mixed ancestry with epithets or labels.[10] In contrast, individuals commonly labeled *mestizos* abound in criminal and legal cases, but often in those contexts there are few direct clues as to why they were perceived of as being *mestizo*. On the other hand, the upwardly mobile drive of tacit *españoles* and their Spanish kin has helped preserve subtle clues about their life and the social contexts that led to their incorporation into the ranks of *españoles*. Like *españoles*, they frequently petitioned the crown for pensions and rewards, and, although these documents could minimize indigenous ancestry, offhand comments and implied admissions frequently provide evidence of mixed European-indigenous ancestry. Thus, an examination of tacit *españoles* can help highlight the factors that contributed to *género* ascription. The lived experience and social context of tacit *españoles* illustrates the mutability of *género* labels and highlights the ways in which social norms worked to undercut the abstract social order embedded in colonial legal codes.

This chapter explores these issues in three ways. First, the lives of several sixteenth-century tacit *españoles* illustrate how social and cultural integration into Spanish society facilitated their acceptance as *españoles*. Second, a discussion of tacit *indios*, a corollary to tacit *españoles*, illustrates how social and cultural positioning could result in the incorporation of some individuals of Spanish-indigenous ancestry within the *república de indios*. Finally, a discussion of tacit *españoles* and colonial society highlights the important role these individuals played in the sixteenth century and how their experiences elucidate our understanding of what it meant to be a *mestizo* or not.

HIJOS DE LOS CONQUISTADORES

In the sixteenth century, most tacit *españoles* were the offspring of the first conquistadors and settlers of the colony.[11] The status acquired by this conquest-era elite afforded their children many advantages. Several examples from the mid-sixteenth century can help illustrate the unique position of tacit *españoles*. The following cases are preserved as *probanzas* written by tacit *españoles* requesting royal favor in light of their merits and those of their parents. For more examples of tacit *españoles,* see table 3.1.

In 1579, María García Pareja wrote to the crown requesting that she be given a grant of two hundred pesos annually for the services rendered by her father, Andrés García, a conquistador who participated in the conquest of Mexico-Tenochtitlan.[12] María noted that in return for his services Andrés had received a grant of two hundred pesos. Nevertheless, after the deaths of her father and her husband, the conquistador Juan Gómez de Almaçan, María found herself impoverished and in need of financial support.[13] To sway the crown to her necessity, María presented evidence of a 1544 grant to Andrés that awarded him and his legitimate children two hundred pesos of income to be paid from tribute revenues. She also included testimony that corroborated her claim to be a legitimate daughter and wife of conquistadors.

According to the material she presented, Andrés García was one of the first conquerors of New Spain. At some point following the conquest of Mexico-Tenochtitlan, Andrés married Luisa, an *india principal* (elite indigenous woman) from Tlaxcala. María García was the legitimate daughter of that union. Eventually María García had married Juan Gómez de Almaçan, conquistador who arrived in Mexico with Pánfilo de Narváez in 1520.[14] The witnesses she presented soundly

Table 3.1
TACIT *ESPAÑOLES* OF SIXTEENTH-CENTURY NEW SPAIN

Name	Date	Parents	Social Details
Alonso Rieros	1540s	Alonso Martín Rieros (conquistador) and Luisa (*india*)	Lived in Mexico City and Puebla; petitioned for right to travel to Spain; supported by Bishop Quiroga (Michoacan)
Hernando de Araçena	1550s	Juan de Araçena (conquistador) and Catalina (*india*)	Lived in Zapotecas; father was given *encomiendas*; sought royal recognition of his claim to be the legitimate heir
Antonio de Leyba	1550s	Juan de Najera (conquistador) and Francisca (*india principal*)	Lived in Mexico; served in conquest of Jalisco; sought *corregimiento* for his service and that of his father
Hernán Pérez de Villanueva	1560s	Diego López de Villanueva (conquistador) and Inés Hernández (*india*)	Lived in Guatemala and Mexico City; father was *encomendero* of several pueblos; sought royal appointment as *escribano*; supported by *vecinos* and conquistadors
Isabel de Montejo	1560s	*Adelantado* Don Francisco de Montejo and Doña Catalina (*india principal*)	Lived in Mexico City; married to Cristóbal Gentil; was close to other Montejo relatives
Diego Montejo	1560–70s	Adelantado Don Francisco de Montejo and an unknown woman (probably *india*)	Lived in Mexico City; was close to other Montejo relatives; contracted marriage with prominent widow in Yucatán
María García Pareja	1570–80s	Andrés García (conquistador) and Luisa (*india principal* from Tlaxcala)	Lived in Mexico City (Tlatelolco); sought remuneration for her father's services; continued ties to Tlaxcalteca
Juan de Montejo	1570–80s	Capitán Franciso de Montejo and an unknown *india*	Lived in Mérida (Yucatán); sought royal pension; well integrated into Yucatecan elite

SOURCES: AGI, Mexico, vols. 95, 96, 97, 100, 104, 107, 117, 280.

supported her claims. These individuals were drawn from the ranks of the colony's oldest conquistador families. Her supporters included Juan Carlos de Bonilla, a conquistador who had arrived in 1523; Juana Hernández, daughter of Diego Hernández, a conquistador of Mexico-Tenochtitlan; Guiomar de Molina, widow of Diego Hernández; Juan Montaño, priest and son of Francisco Montaño, conquistador; and Luís Pérez de Padilla, son of Alonso Pérez, conquistador. In addition to the support of conquistadors and their descendants, María also gathered testimony from two *indias*. These women, Juana María and María Tepi, both gave their testimony in Nahuatl and provided detailed accounts of María García's mother, Luisa. In particular, they noted that the wedding between Andrés and Luisa had occurred in Tlaxcala and that Luisa was a relative of the Tlaxcaltecan leader Maxixcatzin.[15] María Tepi recalled that the wedding was sufficiently important that her husband's kinsmen had ordered him to return to Tlaxcala in order to participate in the festivities.

The testimony also highlights the relationship between the term *mestizo* and individuals of high status. Despite being of known Spanish-indigenous descent, none of the witnesses chose to call María García a *mestiza*. This lapse was not accidental. By 1579, *mestizo* was well entrenched in the vocabulary of the colony. Many of her contemporaries were being so labeled. Rather, María García demonstrates the limits of the term. To her contemporaries, she was not a *mestiza*. She was the legitimate child of a conquistador and an *india principal*. Since its creation, *mestizo* had served to describe illegitimate children. In the early colony the children of Spaniards born by *indias* were almost always out of wedlock. Yet in María's case a Spaniard had married a member of the indigenous nobility, an *india principal,* herself a member of an important indigenous community, Tlaxcala. In the eyes of her contemporaries María García was not one of the many children born of the conquest and left to be raised as foundlings in the new colony. She had important social connections. Her father and husband connected her to the earliest conquistador elite, and her mother's kin bound her to one of the major lineages of Tlaxcala, itself a key ally in the conquest. This position was not lost on her contemporaries. By not labeling her a *mestiza*, despite discussing her Spanish and indigenous parents, the witnesses demonstrated that her *género* was not a simple product of her mixed parentage but rather a complex function of her place in society.

Although her contemporaries did not consider her a *mestiza,* textual evidence suggests that she still had ties to indigenous culture and individuals. Almost all of the witnesses noted that she lived in poverty "among the *indios.*"[16] The claim to poverty was universal in this genre of supplication and not a strong indicator of actual financial status.[17] Several witnesses noted that she lived in the barrio of Santiago Tlatelolco. Given her connections to conquistadors and Spanish society, María likely did not reside in Tlatelolco out of necessity. Even without the support of friends, she could have relied on her daughter Francisca Gómez and her son-in-law Gonzalo de Sosa. Like María, they sought financial remuneration for the conquest services of Juan Gómez de Almaçan, Francisca's father and María's husband.[18] Rather, she may have chosen to live in Tlatelolco because of long-standing social connections to its indigenous residents.

The witnesses in her petition indicate that she had lasting ties with Tlaxcalteca from the conquest period. The two women who provided testimony concerning her parents' wedding lived in Tlatelolco themselves. The fact that María García was able to recruit them as witnesses on her behalf speaks to her continued social ties to other Tlaxcalteca in Mexico City. Additionally, the fact that María Tepi and Juana María both spoke Nahuatl suggests that María García's interaction with them in Tlatelolco was more grounded in indigenous social and cultural norms than Spanish. María García was related to the most elite of Tlaxcaltecan society. Her mother's kinsman, Maxixcatzin, had been *tlatoani* of Ocotelolco, Tlaxcala's most prosperous subdivision. In the initial Tlaxcalan encounter with Cortés, Maxixcatzin, unlike fellow noble Xicotencatl the younger, had been an ardent supporter of an alliance with the newcomers against the Triple Alliance of Tenochtitlan, Tetzcoco, and Tlacopan. The marriage of Andrés García and Doña Luisa typified conquest-era alliances between Spaniards and indigenous elites. These connections were of paramount importance to the creation of the early colonial political order.[19] Consequently, María García visibly manifested this conquest-era alliance. Her life in Tlatelolco and association with the Tlaxcalteca who resided there demonstrates the continued importance of her indigenous ancestry and her complex position in early colonial society. To Spaniards she was a daughter of one of the first conquistadors, and to the Nahua she was the descendant of a Tlaxcalan noble house, but for none of her contemporaries was she a *mestiza*.

Another excellent example of a tacit *española* in early colonial society can be seen in Isabel de Montejo. Our knowledge of Isabel de Montejo has been preserved in a 1562 *probanza* written by her husband Cristóbal Gentil in which he used his marriage to Isabel to support a request for a position in the colonial bureaucracy.[20] The son of Melchior Gentil, *portero* (doorman) for the Audiencia, Cristóbal hoped that his marriage to Isabel de Montejo, the illegitimate daughter of *adelantado* Don Francisco de Montejo would secure him a position as *escribano* or *receptor* (financial administrator) in the government of Mexico City.[21] He claimed that the "*adelantado* Don Francisco de Montejo had as his natural [illegitimate] daughter Isabel de Montejo [born of] an *india principal* named doña Catalina."[22] Moreover, Cristóbal emphasized that Isabel had been treated as if she had been a Spanish daughter. He stated that Montejo had raised her as his daughter "*por casar*" (to be married) by always providing for her needs. This statement reinforces the fact that Isabel was an important social commodity for Don Francisco. Isabel was fit to be married, and her upbringing reflected her status as a member of the conquistador elite, albeit illegitimate and partially indigenous. Cristóbal reinforced his claims to her parentage by pointing out that "in her appearance [literally, "face"] she appears very similar to the *adelantado*." He concluded his mention of Isabel by noting that they had been married publicly in the Mexico City home of Doña Catalina Montejo, the *adelantado*'s legitimate daughter.

To support his case, Cristóbal gathered testimony from other prominent members of Mexico City's Spanish elite. These included a conquistador, many *vecinos*, the *portero* of the Audiencia, and Diego Montejo, another illegitimate child of the *adelantado*.[23] Most witnesses simply affirmed Cristóbal's claims about Isabel's parentage without adding many details. However, several statements elucidate her public perception. Andrés Mexía, a resident in Yucatán, testified that in Mérida he had seen Isabel in the home of the *adelantado*. In that setting, Montejo had referred to Isabel as his daughter and treated her as such. Diego Montejo, her half-brother, likewise reported that Isabel had been born in Montejo's home and openly raised as his daughter. Diego Hermoso and Cristóbal Aznar de Luna went further in describing her position in the Montejo household. They noted that Doña Beatriz, the wife of Montejo, had gone to great lengths to insure that Isabel was raised as an "honest" woman.[24] Other witnesses recalled that after Isabel moved to Mexico City, Doña Catalina, Montejo's legitimate daughter, continued to take care of her. These statements are important because they reinforce Cristóbal Gentil's claim that Isabel was a valuable social commodity and a woman of marriageable status. Thanks to her father's recognition and protection of her, Isabel became incorporated into the extended family that likewise provided her financial support and served to incorporate her into elite Spanish society.

Unlike María García, two of the witnesses in this *probanza* referred to Isabel as a *mestiza*. Both Diego Hermoso and Bartolomé Muñoz, Spanish *vecinos* of Mexico City, referred to her as *"una hija mestiza."* They did not use the phrasing more commonly used in the ascription of the term *mestizo*, which would have used *mestiza* as an epithet immediately following her name, as in "Isabel Montejo *mestiza*."[25] Their choice of wording slightly lessened the deprecatory impact of the term. Their phrasing placed the primary emphasis on her relationship to Montejo while also recognizing her mixed parentage. Moreover, the rest of their statements reinforced her elevated social position and close ties to the Montejo clan.[26] One final aspect of Isabel's social position can be seen in the lack of the honorific *doña*. All other members of her family—her father, uncles, legitimate half-siblings, and even her *india* mother—were given the honorific *don* or *doña*, yet she and her tacit *español* half-brother Diego did not receive the status marker in this *probanza*.[27] The absence of *don* and *doña* in the cases of Diego and Isabel may stem from some combination of their illegitimate birth and mixed parentage. While Isabel's social and familial support helped her to avoid frequent ascription as a *mestiza*, her illegitimate birth still limited her overall social standing.

The experiences of tacit *españoles* provide interesting parallels to those of tacit *españolas*. In general, tacit *españoles*, like their female counterparts, received familial support that helped them maintain prominent positions within society. However, given their gender they could participate more actively in the early colonial bureaucracy. An excellent early example of a tacit *español* can be found in the 1542 *probanza* of Alonso Rieros.[28] According to his petition, Rieros was the son of Alonso Martín Rieros, a conquistador who accompanied Cortés.[29] His petition requested that information be taken so as to verify his identity as a son of a conquistador so that he could travel to Castile. A letter from the bishop of Michoacan, Vasco de Quiroga, accompanied the request. The bishop described Alonso as "a *criado* [servant or dependent], the son of an *español* and *india*."[30] Quiroga praised Alonso Rieros for his service as an interpreter during the Second Audiencia's inquiry into illegal indigenous slavery. The letter also noted that Alonso Rieros was married with children, lived in poverty, and deserved royal favor in return for his services and those of his father.

Alonso Rieros focused on the merits of his father. Alonso Martín Rieros had served with distinction in Cortés's campaigns. In return for this service, Cortés had granted him the *encomienda* of Ocelotepec.[31] Alonso Rieros was born to Alonso Martín Rieros and an *india* named Luisa. Around 1540, the *indios* of Ocelotepec killed Alonso Martín Rieros when he visited the pueblo. His son's petition explained the death by claiming that the *indios* "were not well pacified."[32] Alonso concluded his statements by repeating that his father had accepted him as a natural son and treated him as such. The witness testimony gathered by the petition substantiated Alonso's claims. All three witnesses were *vecinos* of Puebla and included the *alguacil mayor* (constable) of the city. They supported Alonso's claim to be the natural son of a conquistador. Witnesses corroborated the *encomienda* grant and Alonso Martín Riero's unfortunate death at the hands of "incorrigible and bad" *indios* who "rose up and made war."[33] Importantly, none of the witnesses called Alonso Rieros a *mestizo,* although Francisco de Cordina did mention Alonso's mother, "Luisa *india.*"

The *probanza* highlights important aspects of Alonso Rieros's life as an early tacit *español.* Despite his father's untimely death, the community recognized that Alonso had been acknowledged and raised as a son by Alonso Martín Rieros while he lived. The witness testimony confirms this, as does the existence of the petition. Given the early date of this petition, Alonso was born during or soon after the conquest. Had he not been recognized and supported by his father from birth,

Alonso would never have entered the historical record, at least not through a royal petition. Unrecognized children of conquistadors were typically incorporated into indigenous society, where to Spanish eyes they would appear as any other *indio*.[34] His Hispanicization and incorporation into Spanish society demonstrate that his father raised him and that even after his father's death he continued to receive support from other Spaniards. His service to Vasco de Quiroga and incorporation into the early Spanish bureaucracy further marks his acceptance by other Spaniards in the new social order. This participation as a translator also suggests that Alonso's upbringing was not solely dominated by Spanish society. At some point he learned native languages and became an excellent linguist. While we do not know the exact circumstances of his upbringing, his mastery of native languages and his participation in the investigation of native slavery suggests that he was able to maintain some social and cultural ties to indigenous culture. Whether that was via his mother or a result of necessity or opportunity, the evidence is not clear.

Yet, despite his ties to indigenous culture, none of the witnesses in his petition called him a *mestizo*.[35] He clearly had a powerful patron in Bishop Quiroga. He drew his witnesses from the ranks of the Spanish elite in Puebla. Moreover, Alonso's interest in returning to Spain suggests that he was interested in improving his situation. Following the death of his father, Viceroy Mendoza reassigned the *encomienda* of Ocelotepec to Alonso Ruiz, *portero* of the Audiencia.[36] This loss certainly hurt Alonso Rieros's social and economic status. Similar contestations over grants led many early conquistadors and their descendants to travel between the colony and Spain in order to personally petition the crown and the Council of the Indies for restitution. Given these patterns, Alonso's travel plans likely included a trip to the royal court.

The timing of this petition, only two years after his father's death, further supports the supposition that Alonso intended to rectify the loss of the *encomienda* by seeking royal favor. The 1540s were a crucial time for the early recipients of *encomiendas*. The promulgation of the New Laws cast doubt on the long-term profitability of that institution. Alonso, like legitimate children of conquistadores, would have wanted to receive royal recognition of claims to his father's award or at the very least a royal pension that would provide equivalent financial support. Finally, the fact that he could propose such a journey suggests that his financial situation was not as dire as the *probanza* would have suggested. Transatlantic crossings and time at court required substantial financial reserves. Despite his mixed ancestry, Alonso's goals and social status reflect those of countless other children of conquistadors who sought to consolidate conquest-era privileges and advance their position in early colonial society.

During the colony's first century, many new arrivals and children of early conquistadors continued to provide armed service to the crown in attempts to secure lucrative grants and privileges. Many tacit *españoles* likewise saw service to the crown as an ideal means to secure their position within society. In 1552, Antonio de Leyba petitioned the crown asking to be given a *corregimiento* as a reward for the services he and his father had provided.[37] In his petition, he claimed that he was the son of Juan de Najera, a conquistador, who had served the crown by conquering the land with "zeal" and staying to help populate it. Antonio claimed his father had had many children, of which he was one. Like other tacit *españoles,* he acknowledged being a natural son recognized and raised by his father. In his own life, Antonio served on Viceroy Mendoza's expedition to Jalisco during the Mixtón War (1540–42). Unlike common recruits, Antonio had provided his own weapons and horse. Later he had joined the reinforcements being sent to Peru in support of Viceroy Pedro de la Gasca (around 1547). During his services, Antonio had spent much of his own wealth and found himself "at the point of death many times." He concluded by stating that he had always maintained "weapons and horses to serve His Majesty in any occasion like an *hijodealgo* [hidalgo, or nobleman]."[38] Antonio's claim to have served with his own arms demonstrated his status as a prominent member of early colonial society. In 1530, Emperor Charles V had allowed all "conquistadors and settlers" to have weapons for their defense and that of the kingdom. In 1535, the maintenance of arms was made mandatory for all *vecinos* of Mexico.[39]

Antonio chose his witnesses from the ranks of conquistadors and *vecinos*. Andrés Roças, a conquistador, verified Antonio's claims about his father. Andrés had known Juan de Najera in Hispaniola and had traveled with him from that island in order to join the ranks of Cortés's men. Moreover, Andrés knew that Antonio's mother was an *india principal* named Francisca and that Juan had always recognized Antonio as his son. Other witnesses supported Antonio's claims to service in Jalisco. Most stated that Antonio had served with distinction. Juan de Jasso, a *vecino* of Mexico, highlighted Antonio's valor, saying, "He served very well, as a good, valiant soldier, demonstrating this in his service in the war and especially in the expedition of *la barranca* where he served as a valiant man."[40] All the witnesses agreed that Antonio lived like an *hidalgo*, keeping horses and weapons for service to the crown and the protection of the kingdom.

As with other tacit *españoles*, Antonio de Leyba was never directly labeled a *mestizo*. Only two witnesses mentioned that Antonio was the son of an *india principal*. The remaining testimony, including Antonio's own, completely avoids mention of his *india* mother, simply noting that he was a natural son. His claims to service and attentiveness to the duties of conquistadors and settlers reinforced his elevated social position as well as his economic prosperity. Although he spent much in the service of the crown, Antonio had enough to continue to support his station and household. Unlike Alonso Rieros, Antonio never suggested that he was destitute and in need of financial support. Rather, Antonio felt that his service and that of his father warranted an appointment as *corregidor*. The Council of the Indies agreed to a point. They ordered he be given a recommendation for appointment, but ultimately the viceroy would make the decision. The decision to favor Antonio with a recommendation demonstrates recognition, even in Iberia, of the important position of tacit *españoles*.

Moreover, Antonio's recommendation illustrates the interrelationship between popular *género* ascription and the application of colonial legal codes. Had Antonio been publicly labeled a *mestizo*, royal law prohibited appointment as a *corregidor*. By the time of Antonio's petition, the crown had begun to restrict the privileges of *mestizos* in the face of increased competition with Spanish residents and legitimate children of conquistadors. In recommending Antonio for a position the Council of the Indies implicitly acknowledged that Antonio was not a *mestizo* in the eyes of the law, even though the documents attested to his mixed parentage. The council's decision accepted the *género* status ascribed to Antonio by his contemporaries. In part, this process reflects the way in which royal laws appropriated *género* categories without defining them. The legal system entrenched socially constructed and popularly ascribed *géneros* without enumerating separate legal processes for ascribing or adjudicating *género* status. Consequently, in the application of royal laws, officials relied on the ascriptions of contemporaries. Even when the determination of an individual's *género* proved vital to the adjudication of a particular case, royal officials could only construct an individual's legal *género* on the basis of collective social constructions.[41] For men and women like Antonio, the lack of a socially ascribed identity as *mestizo* insured that the legal system did not characterize them as such. In these cases, the absence of ascribed *género* allowed these individuals of Spanish-indigenous ancestry to become *españoles* in the eyes of the law.

The treatment of tacit *españoles* by their contemporaries in New Spain and by royal officials illustrates the precedence placed on their social and cultural position over the circumstances of their parentage. They demonstrate that the ascription of *mestizo* did not simply follow known parentage or ancestry. Spanish society applied the *mestizo* label to individuals perceived as being less than *españoles* by virtue of some combination of social position, cultural practice, illegitimacy, and indigenous ancestry. The attitudes of contemporaries toward tacit *españoles* suggest that when making this complex valuation, concerns over legitimacy and mixed parentage played a less significant role than social and cultural context. In fact, tacit *españoles* demonstrate that sufficiently elevated status and clear integration into the Spanish cultural sphere trumped known mixed ancestry in the ascription of the *mestizo género*. Such an attitude is not surprising. These individuals played key roles in the social order. Tacit *españoles* served as dependents to their fathers or other notable Spaniards, and if necessary they could be legitimated and carry on the family name and inheritance. Spanish families valued tacit *españolas* as social capital that could be used to cement alliances between the early conquest elite. In many cases, even these individuals' ability to speak indigenous languages and serve as intermediaries enhanced their value to their families and the Spanish social order. Given the important place of tacit *españoles* in the social structure of early colonial society, it should not be surprising that the crown supported these men and women through financial rewards and bureaucratic posts. Events like civil war between Almagro and

Pizarro, the outright rebellion sparked by the New Laws in Peru, and the Dávila-Cortés conspiracy made the threat of disaffected conquistadors and settlers quite real. The incorporation of some individuals of Spanish-indigenous ancestry into the *género* of *español* reflects the important role they played in the everyday lives of their Spanish families and their ability to contribute to the stability of the Spanish colonial state.

CACIQUES Y GOBERNADORES

In discussing the individuals above, I chose to call them "tacit *españoles*" because of their privileged position within the Spanish sphere of colonial society. Nevertheless, there did exist another subset of persons born of Spanish-indigenous ancestry who likewise avoided ascription as *mestizos* due to their social and cultural connections to indigenous culture. Unlike tacit *españoles*, individuals of Spanish-indigenous ancestry ascribed the *género* of *indio* fell into two very different social-cultural camps. One set contained those children born out of rape or fleeting unions between Spaniards and non-elite indigenous women, who were born and raised by their *india* mothers within *pueblos de indios*. Society perceived these individuals as *indios* because they lived, worked, and acted like *indios*. Their ancestry would likely have been unknown and unquestioned by anyone outside their natal community. The other set more closely resembled tacit *españoles* because of their membership within the colonial indigenous elite. Many were born from conquest-era marriages similar to the one between Andrés García and Luisa. Yet while their daughter, María García, entered Spanish society, some children born of early strategic Spanish-indigenous marriages remained within the indigenous community where they continued to play roles within the indigenous elite. As with tacit *españoles*, contemporaries likely knew the parents and lineage of these indigenous elites yet chose not to label them *mestizos*. In this regard, this subset of mixed Spanish-indigenous subjects can be labeled "tacit *indios*."

In his study of colonial Cuernavaca, Robert Haskett traces several prominent indigenous families that included individuals of mixed Spanish-indigenous ancestry.[42] In the seventeenth century, the Hinojosa family of Cuernavaca and the Rojas family of nearby Tepoztlan both included prominent members who were known to be of mixed ancestry. Importantly for this discussion, the knowledge of their mixed genealogy rarely played a role in their incorporation into community life. Both families were important within the ruling elite and frequently served as governors and members of their respective *cabildos*. Their incorporation into the elite of these indigenous communities reflects the reality that among indigenous groups, familial and cultural ties trumped genealogy or Castilian *géneros* as defining categories of group membership.

Nevertheless, a sense of community based in shared culture and family did not completely negate the possibility for conflict between these tacit *indios* and their peers. Indigenous elites were well aware of Spanish legal norms and the colonial laws that collectively constructed the *república de indios*. Spanish law prohibited *mestizos* from residing in native communities or serving as leaders of them. Consequently, in moments of conflict, the fact that a claimant to indigenous political office may have been of some Spanish ancestry could be used to delegitimize any claims to power.[43] By explicitly ascribing the *mestizo género* to an individual generally regarded as a tacit *indio*, indigenous elites used the Spanish legal system and Spanish *géneros de gente* to adjudicate internal conflicts. In many cases these claims did not last long, and families like the Hinojosas and the Rojases were able to continue holding office within their communities.

The tacit *indios* of colonial society further attest to the strong social and cultural basis of *género* ascription in colonial New Spain. Most importantly, they demonstrate that individuals of mixed Spanish-indigenous ancestry could be perceived as belonging to a *género* other than *mestizo* or *español*. In the case of tacit *indios*, this perception was based both in communal norms and Spanish "ignorance." Firstly, most colonial indigenous groups based membership on familial ties, residence, and cultural incorporation. As members of known lineages who lived, worked, and socialized within their communities, the tacit *indio* elites of indigenous society acted like every other member of their society. Consequently, except in moments of conflict, they were not likely to be singled out for their ancestry, much less be given a label based in a foreign language and culture. Secondly, because Spanish law constructed such a rigid separation between the *república de españoles* and the *república de indios,* many colonial bureaucrats, curates, and observers were inclined to describe any resident of mixed indigenous ancestry within an indigenous community as an *indio*—unless other factors warranted their mention.⁴⁴ This "blindness" perpetuated the idealized social breakdown of indigenous communities while simultaneously allowing a large number of ethnically mixed, culturally indigenous individuals to avoid inclusion in the category *mestizo* while living their lives as *indios.*

In some cases, tacit *indios* could leverage their Spanish ancestry to their advantage even while maintaining positions of indigenous nobility. Such an example can be seen in the case of Don Juan de Zarate. In 1599, Zarate served as the cacique of the indigenous pueblo of Cuiotepec. Like other caciques and *indios principales,* Zarate sought permission to carry a sword as a marker of his elite social status. Despite the blanket ban on weapon sales to *indios,* indigenous elites had been allowed an exception that let them petition the viceroy or governor for a license to carry weapons, similar to *mestizos.*⁴⁵ Such privileges helped visually reinforce the sovereignty of *indios principales* over their *indio* subjects and further tied indigenous elites to the Spanish monarch.

Zarate's request demonstrated a delicate balancing act of *género* mobilization. Ostensibly he positioned himself as an indigenous lord. The petition records his name and title solely within the context of indigenous lordship: "Don Juan de Zarate cacique and *señor natural* (natural lord)." Yet Zarate complicated his positioning as a tacit *indio* by claiming to be the "grandson of the first conquistadors of this New Spain." He then balanced that claim to Spanish ancestry by emphasizing that "through his mother, doña Juana Sánchez, he enjoys the *cacicazgo* (hereditary estate) of the pueblo."⁴⁶ Finally, he summed up his petition by emphasizing that because of his *cacicazgo* and "for being a *mestizo* he should enjoy the privileges that [they] enjoy in carrying arms for the defense of his person." Although Zarate explicitly included a reference to being a *mestizo,* his rhetoric mobilized that *género* in order to establish his ancestry as a grandson of a conquistador rather than as his primary legal identity. Yet, by self-ascribing as a *mestizo* and a cacique before the viceroy, Zarate ran a risk. Since at least 1576, *mestizos* had been explicitly banned from holding the office of cacique.[47] While Zarate's admission may have helped demonstrate his legal right to bear arms, it ostensibly made him ineligible to hold the position of cacique or to benefit from the *cacicazgo* that he claimed. Nevertheless, such an assertion did not hurt his case: the viceroy issued the license.

This case exposes the complex relationship between the social and legal ramifications of *género* ascription. In the legal realm, Don Juan de Zarate presented himself as an indigenous leader, a cacique and *señor natural*, an individual worthy to bear arms by virtue of his indigenous position. At the same time, his ancestry tied him to the social world of the Spanish. Yet this social and ancestral tie had its own legal ramifications. The descendants of conquistadors and *mestizos* could also claim the right to bear arms. Had Zarate chosen to rely only on his indigenous claims, his Spanish ancestry would likely have never been recorded. Yet he chose to admit that ancestry in order to bolster his case. This choice represents an important difference between tacit *indios* and tacit *españoles*. For tacit *indios*, circumstances could arise in which claiming *español* ancestry would be beneficial, even if it resulted in ascription as *mestizos*.[48] Conversely, tacit *españoles* enjoyed more rights than *mestizos* because of their inclusion into the *género* of *español*. In this case, Zarate's choice to complicate his ascription by claiming rights of *mestizos* suggests that he felt confident that the viceroy would be swayed by such arguments. The law prohibited *mestizos* as caciques because of fears that *mestizos* were likely to abuse their *indio* subjects. So long as no one claimed that Zarate was guilty of such abuse, there would be no reason that the viceroy should dispossess a loyal cacique for admitting some Spanish ancestry.

TACIT *ESPAÑOLES* AND COLONIAL SOCIETY

Tacit *españoles* represented a small fraction of the Spanish-indigenous population of the sixteenth century. These individuals tended to be recognized children of elite Spaniards, conquistadors or early settlers. The social status and support of their fathers placed tacit *españoles* in an elevated position within the colony. They received financial and familial aid in a variety of ways. Like their fathers and fellow children of conquistadors, they sought royal recognition for their services to the crown. Nevertheless, the unique position occupied by tacit *españoles* was one born of the early decades of the kingdom. During the first few generations of colonial rule, tacit *españoles* prospered through their connection to the early conquistador elite and the relatively small Spanish population. As the colony matured, more Spanish arrivals expanded the ranks of Spanish society and began to displace tacit *españoles*. As royal control over the economy and governance of the colony grew, the crown no longer needed to privilege the children of the conquistadors and initial settlers. Along with increased efforts to restrict the social and political access of *mestizos* and other non-Spaniards, this shift led to a reduction in the number of tacit *españoles* by the end of the century. In other words, as their social and political utility diminished, Spanish families and Spanish society at large assimilated fewer such individuals.

Importantly, the gradual diminution of tacit *españoles* was not a simple matter of increased prejudice and social competition. Successful marriages within Spanish society would have helped to place the descendants of tacit *españoles* firmly in the ranks of *españoles*. Tacit *españolas* were particularly important in this regard.[49] The case of María García Pareja provides a clear example of this possibility. She was a tacit *española*, raised by her father and married to a fellow conquistador. During her marriage to Juan Gómez de Almaçan, María gave birth to a daughter, Francisca Gómez. As the daughter and granddaughter of conquistadors, Francisca enjoyed membership within the elite ranks of mid-sixteenth-century society. Yet, unlike her mother, she was not directly tied to a native parent. Moreover, the fact that María García was not commonly regarded as a *mestiza* benefited Francisca as it further removed her from ties to her indigenous relatives. At some point, Francisca married Gonzalo de Sosa, a Spaniard. In 1575, Francisca and Gonzalo sought royal aid in return for the previous service of Juan Gómez de Almaçan. Although unsuccessful in their attempt, the *probanza* preserves Francisca's social status as an *española*. Her initial description presents her only as the legitimate child and legitimate wife of Spanish men: "Francisca Gómez, legitimate wife of Gonzalo de Sosa, *vecina* that I am of this great city of Mexico of this New Spain, legitimate daughter of Juan Gómez de Almaçan, deceased that he be in Glory, *vecino* and conquistador of this city."⁵⁰ Similarly, when Francisca and Gonzalo mention María García's connection to Juan Gómez de Almaçan, they do so simply as "María García Pareja, his legitimate wife." None of the witnesses presented on behalf of Francisca and Gonzalo make any allusions to the mixed ancestry of María García. These include several early conquistadors and witnesses to the wedding of María and Juan. The only clue that the descendants of Juan Gómez de Almaçan had indigenous ancestry can be found in his *probanza* written in 1536, and included with that of Francisca and Gonzalo, in which he mentions his marriage to "a woman, native of this land." Yet none of the witnesses to his *probanza* referred to his wife as an *india* or to his children as *mestizos*. Together these *probanzas* demonstrate that for several generations, Spaniards avoided ascribing the *mestizo* label to the descendants of Juan Gómez de Almaçan. Consequently, by the end of the sixteenth century, his granddaughter was no longer a tacit *española*, for the memory of her indigenous grandmother was long faded. Instead, she and her husband were just another pair of *españoles* seeking remuneration for her forebear's service.

As this case shows, marriages between tacit *españolas* and Spanish men would have led to the gradual incorporation of socially prominent and upwardly mobile individuals into the category of *español*. In later centuries, similar phenomena have been called "passing."⁵¹ In the late seventeenth and eighteenth centuries, "passing" can describe how socially and economically successful individuals succeeded in moving up the socio-racial hierarchy. But the eventual disappearance of tacit *españoles* differs from later mechanisms of passing in several ways.⁵² Firstly, tacit *españoles* were already subsumed within the social world of *españoles*. Despite being of known mixed ancestry, in not being ascribed the label of *mestizo* they already lived as *españoles*. This initial social position allowed their descendants—born of unions with other *españoles*—to further distance themselves from the increasingly pejorative label *mestizo* and be fully incorporated as *españoles*. *Probanzas* like those examined here suggest that those seeking royal favor carefully measured references to their indigenous ancestors. Similarly, witnesses, drawn from their Spanish friends and acquaintances, contributed to the obfuscation or omission of indigenous ancestry by following the rhetorical strategy of the supplicants. Rarely did witnesses go beyond what the supplicants asserted, and even more rarely did witnesses ascribe *género* labels other than what witnesses claimed. This process became more pronounced over time. While some early-sixteenth-century tacit *españoles* included references to indigenous parents if that could connect them to *indios principales*, later descendants avoided even those connections.

Secondly, the multigenerational nature of this process also differentiates it from the later phenomenon of passing. By the late colonial period, passing generally occurred during one's life. An individual's descendants might also succeed in passing, but the process essentially related to an individual's life and changing social perception of that individual. In contrast to passing, the sublimation of tacit *españoles* into the ranks of *españoles* reflected a multigenerational process wherein the first generation of Spanish-indigenous children avoided the ascription of the category *mestizo* that in turn allowed their descendants born of further unions with Spaniards to completely remove themselves from the European-indigenous spectrum.

Several scholars have argued that the incorporation of tacit *españoles* and their descendants into the category of *español* brought about the rapid and sizable growth of a *criollo* population in the kingdom.[53] While this argument reflects the overall impression of these sources, such a claim may overstate our ability to track such a process in early colonial society. While most conquest-era elite probably engendered tacit *españoles*, the specific rhetorical strategies of these individuals and the generation as a whole hampers the specific identification of such a process. For the purpose of this study, only individuals who had clear ties to an indigenous parent have been included as tacit *españoles*. Countless other *"hijos naturales"* petitioned the crown for remuneration or benefits. Some of these individuals may have had indigenous parents unattributed in their statements or those of witnesses. Generally, the individuals who constructed these documents avoided presenting any evidence that was not deemed beneficial. Certainly in some of these cases, a Spanish mother of lower social status may have been omitted just as easily as a common *india*.

Moreover, from a terminological point of view, the common usage of *criollo* as a means to distinguish American-born Spaniards from their peninsular counterparts did not become common until the last quarter of the sixteenth century. This shift occurred alongside the gradual disappearance of tacit *españoles*. The adoption of *criollo* and its disparaging connotation toward American-born *españoles* could reflect a suspicion that American-born Spaniards were heavily tainted by indigenous ancestry. Nevertheless, such a claim was not solely tied to a belief that all *criollos* were to some degree descendants of *indios*.[54] Rather the distinction had by the late sixteenth century become important for social and political contestation within the maturing colony. While tacit *españoles* undoubtedly contributed to the growth of *españoles criollos*, a full accounting of their numerical contribution to this Spanish population will remain difficult if not impossible due to the particular rhetorical strategies they and their contemporaries used.

Nevertheless, the examples of this chapter illustrate the ways in which social positioning and family connections could influence the ascription—or not—of the category *mestizo* during the sixteenth century. Individuals of mixed Spanish-indigenous ancestry could be classified as *español*, *mestizo*, or *indio* depending on the various circumstances of their life, including where they lived, who their parents and family were, what language they spoke, and how they dressed. In general, those individuals most commonly labeled *mestizo* were those who lived within Hispanic society, were known to be of mixed European-indigenous ancestry, but lacked strong ties to social elites. Those with strong ties to elites as patrons or parents were most likely to be tacitly accepted as *españoles*. As an individual's Hispanicization or integration into Spanish social networks decreased, and their connection to indigenous culture and society increased, they were more likely to be perceived as *indios*. The reverse held true as well. Some *indios* were subsumed into the category *mestizo* because of their perceived Hispanicization and integration into Spanish rather than indigenous society.[55] Phenotype undoubtedly played a role in these ascriptions. Unfortunately, most sixteenth-century documents lack physical descriptions of people they record. Given the social forces inherent in the ascription of the label *mestizo*, the gradual absorption of tacit *españoles* into the category of *español* required continued intermarriage and social ties to Spanish society. Certainly the descendants of some tacit *españoles* did not fare as well. If tacit *españoles* could not continue their social and familial ties to Spanish society and instead found themselves socializing and forming families with *mestizos, mulatos, negros,* or *indios,* their descendants would likely have been ascribed to another *género de gente.*

Overall, the unique position of tacit *españoles* during the early colonial period reveals the strong role played by social and cultural position in the ascription of *género* categories to individuals located along the Spanish-indigenous spectrum. Yet that spectrum only accounts for some of the individuals born of mixed unions. The next chapter explores those individuals ascribed the *género* of *mulato.* Although such ascription similarly considered social and cultural factors, the attribution of the *mulato* label followed logic distinct from that of *mestizo.* While some individuals of mixed Spanish-indigenous ancestry could seemingly disappear into other *géneros,* the ascription of *mulato* proved more indelible than that of *mestizo.*

CHAPTER 4

AFRO-INDIGENOUS *MULATOS*

> Thus, with such a great sum of *negros* coming every year and the *mulatos* continuing to multiply so much, be watchful Your Majesty, over time what number of people [*negros* and *mulatos*] will there be, and these are the lords of the *indios* because born and raised among them.
>
> Viceroy Martín Enríquez, 1574

By virtue of their *género*, Francisco Jasso and Juana Agustina might seem to have much in common. To their contemporaries both were considered *mulatos*. Nevertheless, their inclusion within the same *género* masked vast differences in genealogy and cultural formation. For his part, Francisco was born sometime around 1570 in the Andalusian town of Teba, located northwest of Málaga.[1] When investigated by the Mexican Inquisition for renouncing God, he declared that he was the son of an *español* and a *mulata*. He was also a slave, which suggests that his mother was a slave and that he was born into that status. Unfortunately for the historian, cases of blasphemy or renouncing God (*reniego*) did not generate as many familial details as bigamy cases. In this case, the inquisitors did not ask Francisco for any genealogical details other than his parents' names. His father was named Pedro García and his mother was named Geronima de Angulo. Nevertheless, his place of birth and declared parentage can tell us a great deal. As the European-born son of a Spaniard and a *mulata* slave—herself likely European-born—Francisco very likely had three *español* grandparents and only a single African one.

On the other hand, Juana Agustina was born around 1576 to an *indio,* Juan Martín, and a *mulata,* Catalina.² Like Francisco, Juana did not declare her mother's parentage. If her mother was Afro-European, Juana would have had two indigenous grandparents, a Spanish grandparent, and an African—or possibly *mulato*—grandparent. If her mother was Afro-indigenous—a distinct possibility given the rural setting— Juana could have had three indigenous grandparents and one African or *mulato* one. In all likelihood, Juana and Francisco were similar only in that they each had one African grandparent. Yet despite such disparate genealogies, both were lumped into the *género* of *mulato.* Although the majority of contemporaries likely did not know the ancestries of Francisco and Juana, comparing individuals with known lineages and ancestries provides a means of gauging the ethnic and cultural diversity of individuals ascribed the *mulato* label.

Moreover, differences in parentage and birthplace provide some clues as to how Juana's and Francisco's upbringings shaped their cultural formation. Raised in rural Andalusia, Francisco worked on a small farming estate (*cortijo*) for a time before being brought to Mexico. He had received some religious instruction and could recite common prayers in Castilian, albeit poorly. Furthermore, his Inquisition testimony suggests some understanding of Iberian cultural and religious traditions outside of Catholic orthodoxy. Ostensibly the case against Francisco revolved around his renouncing God while being held in an *obraje* (textile mill) near Mexico City. Although he admitted to renouncing God, after numerous interviews Francisco confessed that while in Andalusia a man named Diego Hernández had taught him to follow "the laws of Moses." According to Francisco's account, Diego Hernández had been investigated by the Inquisition of Seville for Judaizing but had been released. Francisco admitted to keeping fasts on certain days, dressing in fine clothes on Saturday (to celebrate the Jewish Sabbath), and abstaining from eating pork. Although Francisco eventually admitted to having made up the entire story, the fact that he was able to concoct such a story illustrates how aware he was of the cultural-religious landscape of sixteenth-century Spain. Francisco knew about conversos and could construct a plausible story involving Jewish practices and Inquisition cases. The specificity and detail of Francisco's account speaks to his acculturation within the conflicted religious landscape of Iberia.

In contrast, Juana grew up in a radically different environment after being born in a rural mining community outside of Guadalajara and orphaned at an early age. Martín Cano, an *indio,* and his wife, Mariana, a *mulata,* raised her in their home. These caregivers eventually married her to an *indio* named Juanillo. After a few years her *mulato* uncle collected her and took her to Guadalajara. There she entered the service of several Spanish patrons and was the victim of at least two abductions. Although her case does not specifically contain details of her cultural upbringing, the narrative of her life does allow for some reasonable speculation. For example, both her parents were native to the mining community (Guaxacatlan) in which she was born. Residence in a late-sixteenth-century mining community ensured exposure to individuals of various cultures, ethnicities, and *géneros.* In the early 1570s, Lopéz de Velasco reported that Guaxacatlan had about twenty *españoles* and a hundred slaves.[3] Like most mines in the region, Guaxacatlan probably relied primarily on indigenous labor complemented by slaves, including Africans and *indios* enslaved through warfare.[4] Consequently, Juana's parents lived in a multiethnic and multilingual environment composed of indigenous, Hispanic, and probably African cultural spaces. Juana would have benefited from their experiences and have been exposed to similar diverse cultural and linguistic experiences living in the home of her caretakers, also an *indio-mulata* couple. Later in life, her uncle placed her in a Spanish home working as a *criada* (servant). While Spanish cultural fluency would not have been a prerequisite for such a post, she spent several years serving in a number of Spanish homes. Thus, it would be hard to imagine that by the time of her Inquisition trial she was not reasonably comfortable in Spanish, indigenous, and possibly African cultural spaces.

In this instance and in others, I have chosen to use the general term "indigenous" to describe Juana's cultural fluency. Regrettably, this phrase tends to homogenize an indigenous cultural landscape that included many diverse cultures. Yet in most instances the documents that record the indigenous connections of *mulatos* like Juana do not specify the particular indigenous culture with whom they interacted. For example, Juana's upbringing might have been among Nahuatl speakers who had been transplanted into the northern mining region. However, she might have been exposed to local indigenous groups like the Tecuexe or the Caxcanes. Thus, while it is clear that Juana lived and interacted with indigenous persons in largely indigenous contexts, the details of her case do not allow for a clear identification of the specific indigenous culture with which she was most familiar.

These two examples illustrate that individuals labeled *mulato* could vary in a variety of ways. *Mulatos* in New Spain could have been born in Iberia or in the Americas. They could have been raised by Spaniards or indigenous people or others of African descent. Culturally they were likely Hispanicized to some degree, but many acquired fluency in native languages and cultural practices. The diversity of lived experience among *mulatos* like Francisco and Juana raises many questions concerning this *género* in early New Spain. What commonalities transcended different lineage and cultural formation? Were most Mexican *mulatos* of Afro-European ancestry, of Afro-indigenous ancestry, or of some other combination of lineages? How did lineage and ancestry influence the acculturation of *mulatos*? What factors influenced the ascription of the *mulato* label? Unfortunately, the available documentation does not allow us to completely explore all of these issues, but it does provide telling glimpses into the lives of early colonial *mulatos*.

This chapter broadens our understanding of early colonial New Spain by highlighting the importance of Afro-indigenous *mulatos* within the social order. Although scholars have noted that many *mulatos* in Spanish America had some indigenous ancestry, the unique social and cultural factors that gave rise to these individuals and their impact on sixteenth-century society have not been as examined.[5] This chapter explores these Afro-indigenous *mulatos* and their impact in three ways. First, an analysis of qualitative and quantitative documentation demonstrates that Afro-indigenous *mulatos* likely represented a significant plurality of New Spain's *mulatos* by the end of the sixteenth century. Second, a close reading of Afro-indigenous *mulatos'* lived experiences suggests that they were comfortable moving between Spanish and indigenous cultural spheres. Their connections with indigenous people and communities fostered multigenerational ties with others of indigenous ancestry, which in turn helped perpetuate African-indigenous unions. Third, a comparison between the *géneros* of *mulato* and *mestizo* suggests that the process of ascription differed between the two. In most cases, colonial subjects manifested a greater consensus on who should be labeled a *mulato*. Consequently, despite the diversity of *mulato* experiences, the ascription of *mulato* was less mutable than that of *mestizo* in the sixteenth century.

UNCOVERING AFRO-INDIGENOUS *MULATOS*

The records of the Mexican Inquisition contain numerous cases involving *mulatos* as defendants and witnesses. Within those records I have identified sixty individuals about whom I have substantial personal information suitable for qualitative analysis.[6] The cases in which they appear were investigated between 1545 and 1599, with the bulk of the cases falling between 1566 and 1599. In forty cases, the record indicated the *mulato*'s birthplace. American-born *mulatos* accounted for thirty individuals. Twenty-six were born in Mexico and four in Guatemala.[7] Of the ten European-born *mulatos*, seven were born in the kingdoms of Castile and Aragon and three in the kingdom of Portugal.[8]

From a demographic point of view, birthplace can help us understand the overall diversity within the category of *mulato*. Unlike American-born individuals, those born in the Iberian Peninsula have a smaller range of possible parentage. Specifically, they were unlikely to be born of unions other than those between parents of African and European ancestry.[9] Of the ten Iberian-born *mulatos*, nine declared their parentage. In eight cases, the parents were *españoles* and *negras*, and in the case of Francisco Jasso they were an *español* and a *mulata*. These cases reinforce the commonly held notion that the term *mulato* described the offspring of a European man fathering children with an enslaved or free woman of African descent. In contrast to their Iberian counterparts, American-born *mulatos* demonstrated greater variety in their parentage. Of the thirty known American-born *mulatos*, twelve did not declare their parentage. Nevertheless, the remaining eighteen show a tantalizing trend. Thirteen of the *mulatos* were born of *negros* and *indias*. The remaining five were born of a variety of parent combinations involving one *mulato* parent and a parent from another *género*: *mulato-india, español-mulata, indio-mulata,* and *mulato-mulata*. While this cannot be considered a random sample of colonial *mulatos*, it does hint that *mulatos* of Afro-indigenous ancestry may have predominated over *mulatos* of Afro-European ancestry. In this sample sixteen of eighteen American-born individuals with known parentage could be labeled Afro-indigenous.

Qualitative evidence drawn from early colonial officials and limited quantitative data corroborate the trend found in Inquisition records. Although some of these observations have been cited in the introduction and first chapter, their importance for understanding the growth of New Spain's *mulato* population bears further discussion. As early as 1552, Fray Nicolas de Witte identified *negros* and *indias* as the progenitors of New Spain's *mulatos*:

> What should one think of this land that engenders and populates itself with a mixture of a people so evil. It is clear that this land is full of *mestizos*, who are born with a very bad disposition; it is full of *negros* and *negras* from whom are born the slaves; it is full of *negros* who marry *indias* from whom are born the *mulatos*; it is full of *mestizos* who marry *indias* from whom are born a diverse breed without number. From all these mixtures are born other diverse mixtures none good.[10]

His emphasis on African-indigenous unions to the exclusion of African-European ones is telling. Although Afro-European *mulatos* would have been a familiar sight in mid-sixteenth-century Spanish port cities, Fray Nicolas did not include them in his assessment of New Spain's crucible of ethnic mixing. The emphasis on *negro-india* pairings likely indicates that Fray Nicolas viewed those unions as the primary lineage for the *mulatos* he encountered. Considering his harsh critique of mixing and fears of "diverse mixtures," the inclusion of another axis of interethnic unions would have only bolstered the rhetorical effect of his message. Consequently, the absence of Afro-European unions in his account may suggest that such unions were less prevalent than Afro-indigenous ones.

AFRO-INDIGENOUS *MULATOS*

The phenomenon observed by Fray Nicolas did not abate over time. In 1574, Viceroy Martín Enríquez conveyed his observations on interethnic unions in a missive rich with details:

> The only thing that worsens day to day, and if God and Your Majesty do not remedy it I fear it will be the perdition of this land, is the great growth of the *mulatos*. Of the *mestizos* I do not worry as much. Even though among them there are many who lead ruinous lives and have bad customs, they are in the end the children of *españoles*. They are all raised by their fathers and after four or five years they leave the power of the *indias* [their mothers] and always continue on the side of the *españoles* because that is the part of themselves that they most honor. But the *mulatos*, who are children of *negros*, are always raised with their mothers and from them and their fathers cannot learn very good customs, and as free persons they do what they wish and very few of them apply themselves to trades and almost none of them to cultivating the land, instead they oversee livestock and other occupations in which they can wander with liberty. And it is a thing in which one cannot cease to believe: that all universally have ability and strength; because they [*mulatos*] take advantage so much of *mestizos* as men do with dolls, the [*mestizos*] being children of *españoles*, it would appear that nature would work in this more strongly. They [*mulatos*] always go among the *indios* because that is the part that they have that they most honor, from which *indios* receive great harm.[11]

The viceroy's portrayal of *mestizos* and *mulatos* links both to *indios*. In the case of *mestizos*, he believed that most were drawn toward their Spanish fathers because of pride in that ancestry. In contrast, Enríquez believed that *mulatos* prided their ties to *indios*. As with Fray Nicolas, Enríquez implied that Mexican *mulatos* were primarily born of *negros* and *indias*. While the phrasing of his letter is difficult and circuitous, he reported that *mulatos* were the children of *negros*, and being born free they went among the indios because they were partially indigenous. Although he did not directly label their mothers, their partial indigenous ancestry, free birth, and *negro* fathers implied that their mothers were *indias*. Later in the letter, Viceroy Enríquez went on to describe the social and economic forces contributing to *negro-india* unions:

> Your Majesty will observe that every year a great quantity of *negros* come to this land, and necessarily they have to come because in this land there is no other labor, either for mines or for other things, and the *españoles* do not only use the slaves for absolute necessities here, instead they honor themselves with them [the slaves], and have many pages and footmen, all of whom are *negros,* as in Spain. And the *indias* are a weak people taken advantage of by the *negros* and would rather marry them [the *negros*] than *indios*. No more, no less, the *negros* marry them [*indias*] over other *negras* because they wish their children to be free. Thus, with such a great sum of *negros* coming every year and the *mulatos* continuing to multiply so much, be watchful Your Majesty, over time what number of people [*negros* and *mulatos*] will there be, and these are the lords of the *indios* because born and raised among them. They are a people who would dare to die no matter how many *españoles* there are in the world. Thus, if the *indios* come to be corrupted and they join together with them [*negros* and *mulatos*] I do not know who will be able to resist them.[12]

In this account, Viceroy Enríquez clearly linked the growth of *mulatos* to unions between *negros* and *indias*. He attributed this pairing to the weakness of *indias* in resisting male slaves and to the desire of those slaves to have freeborn children. Enríquez cautioned that these *mulatos* were born and raised among the *indios.*

Further evidence for the Afro-indigenous origins of many *mulatos* can be seen in several proposals made by the viceroy to control these individuals. Viceroy Enríquez proposed that all children born of unions between *negros* and *indias* or *mulatas* be enslaved. To further this suggestion, Enríquez mused that the pope could prohibit marriages between *negros* and *indias* or *mulatas*. He argued that enslaving the children of such unions would have several beneficial results: "Although this would not stop the birth of many *mulatos*, it is a different thing to be a slave or to be free. Similarly, [in their] upbringing, they would be raised with *españoles* and not with liberty as now among the *indios.*

And even if His Holiness did not prohibit the marriages, it would not be much worse, because [currently] *negros* attempt to marry *indias* only so their children are free; the *indias* seeing that their children would not be free would not marry *negros* so frequently."[13] As with Enríquez's previous comments, his proposal noted that most *mulatos* were born and raised among *indios* outside of Hispanic homes. The proposal to enslave the children born of *negros* and *indias* or *mulatas* addressed two social realities. First, women of these two *géneros* were likely the most common free spouses or sexual partners for enslaved *negros*.[14] Second, the *mulatas* in question may have been born of *negro-india* unions and lived with their indigenous mothers. By enslaving the children of such marriages, the viceroy hoped to completely remove individuals of mixed African-indigenous unions from among their *indio* relatives and place them in bondage under Spanish owners. Although the king did not enact these proposals, the frequent prohibition of *mulatos* from *pueblos de indios* corroborates the viceroy's assessment.

About the same time that Viceroy Enríquez wrote his letter, the royal cosmographer, Juan López de Velasco, chronicled the rise of *mulatos* in the Americas. In a section entitled "Of *mestizos, mulatos,* and *zambaigos,*" he wrote, "In addition to these [*mestizos*], there are many *mulatos,* children of *negros* and *indias,* who are called *zambaigos,* who come to be the worst and most vile people of those lands. Of these and the *mestizos,* because of there are so many, some parts come to be in danger of unrest and rebellion. *Mulatos,* children of *españoles* and *negras,* are not as numerous because of the many *indias* that lead ruinous lives."[15] As with the earlier observers, López de Velasco linked *mulatos* to *negro-india* unions. His assertion that some called such individuals *zambaigos* reflected his accumulation of material from across the Americas. No contemporary resident of New Spain used that label, but it was used elsewhere. Unlike the previous accounts, López de Velasco provided an explanation for why Afro-indigenous *mulatos* predominated over Afro-European ones: ruinous *indias*. This explanation raises several questions. Did *indias'* sexual immorality promote the rise of Afro-indigenous *mulatos* because they chose to have children with *negros,* or did their sexual licentiousness draw *españoles* away from unions with *negras*? He may have thought licentious *indias* fostered both possibilities.

Table 4.1
AFRO-INDIGENOUS MARRIAGE PAIRINGS, SANTA VERACRUZ, 1576–1581

Pairing	Marriages
Afro-European and Other	
español-mulata	2
mulato-española	1
negro-mulata*	1
mulato-negra*	5
Total	9
Afro-indigenous	
negro-india	5
mulato-india	3
mulato-mestiza	1
Total	10
Percent Afro-indigenous	52%
Mulato Endogamy	0%

* These pairings could result in Afro-indigenous offspring if the *mulato* partner was Afro-indigenous.

The paucity of quantitative documentation complicates our ability to gauge the size of the early colonial *mulato* population. Nevertheless, extant parish records can provide further evidence for the importance of Afro-indigenous unions during this time. In order to explore interethnic marriage patterns, I examined two parishes, Santa Veracruz in Mexico City and Santa Fe in Guanajuato. Both parishes have extant marital records for the late sixteenth and early seventeenth century. While the next chapter explores the overall marriage trends observed in these two parishes, the registers provide evidence that early colonial marriage patterns contributed to the rise of Afro-indigenous *mulatos*. If marriages are viewed as a rough proxy for future offspring, the marriage patterns in both Mexico City and Guanajuato suggest that *mulatos* of Afro-indigenous ancestry might have accounted for as many as half of all *mulatos* in some early colonial communities. Tables 4.1 through 4.4 present marriages from each parish likely to produce *mulato* children. For this analysis, unions between an individual of African descent (*negro* or *mulato*) and an individual of indigenous

Table 4.2
AFRO-INDIGENOUS MARRIAGE PAIRINGS, SANTA VERACRUZ, 1626–1631

Pairing	Marriages
Afro-European and Other	
español-negra	2
español-mulata	5
negro-mulata*	5
mulato-negra*	5
mulato-mulata*	17
Total	34
Afro-indigenous	
mestizo-negra	1
mestizo-mulata	3
negro-india	8
negro-mestiza	2
mulato-india	2
mulato-mestiza	10
Total	26
Percent Afro-indigenous	43%
Mulato Endogamy	53%

* These pairings could result in Afro-indigenous offspring if the *mulato* partner was Afro-indigenous.

descent (*mestizo* or *indio*) were considered to be Afro-indigenous. Consequently, pairings involving a *mulato* and a *negro* or two *mulatos* were considered "other" even though in many instances the *mulato* partner may have been Afro-indigenous.

In the early periods for each parish, within marriages likely to produce a *mulato* child, Afro-indigenous pairings predominated. In late-sixteenth-century Mexico City, just over half of all marriages likely to produce *mulato* offspring could be considered Afro-indigenous. In the first decades of the seventeenth century, over three quarters of such marriages in Guanajuato were Afro-indigenous. Significantly, in each locality the percentage of marriages that would produce Afro-indigenous offspring decreased over time. Increased *mulato* endogamy influenced this shift in both parishes, a finding examined more fully

Table 4.3
AFRO-INDIGENOUS MARRIAGE PAIRINGS, GUANAJUATO, 1605–1615

Pairing	Marriages
Afro-European and Other	
español-negra	1
negro-mulata*	2
mulato-mulata*	1
Total	4
Afro-indigenous	
mestizo-mulata	1
indio-mulata	5
negro-india	1
mulato-mestiza	1
mulato-india	5
Total	13
Percent Afro-indigenous	76%
Mulato Endogamy	13%

* These pairings could result in Afro-indigenous offspring if the *mulato* partner was Afro-indigenous.

in the next chapter. Even so, the high rate of Afro-indigenous marriage in the early period indicates that many of the *mulatos* marrying in the later period were themselves Afro-indigenous. Moreover, even with increased *mulato* endogamy, Afro-indigenous unions in each parish still accounted for over 40 percent of all unions likely to produce *mulato* children.

The significance of this finding cannot be overlooked. The possibility that roughly half of Mexican *mulatos* may have been of mixed African-indigenous descent in the late sixteenth century illustrates that Africans and native peoples frequently forged close personal connections despite legal attempts to prevent such unions. Moreover, the children born of such unions represent an important subset of colonial subjects because of their exposure to diverse cultural and social contexts. Because the label *mulato* could be applied to individuals from many diverse lineages and cultural backgrounds, the unique lived experiences of Afro-indigenous *mulatos* have remained obscured by

Table 4.4
AFRO-INDIGENOUS MARRIAGE PAIRINGS, GUANAJUATO, 1631–1641

Pairing	Marriages
Afro-European and Other	
negro-mulata[*]	2
mulato-negra[*]	2
mulato-mulata[*]	12
Total	16
Afro-indigenous	
mestizo-mulata	1
indio-mulata	2
negro-india	3
mulato-mestiza	1
mulato-india	15
Total	22
Percent Afro-indigenous	58%
Mulato endogamy	50%

[*] These pairings could result in Afro-indigenous offspring if the *mulato* partner was Afro-indigenous.

the homogenizing nature of their *género* label. Yet a close examination of early Afro-indigenous *mulatos* highlights their distinctive cultural and social position, one that likely helped facilitate cross-cultural interaction within the social order and helped fuel interethnic unions.

AFRO-INDIGENOUS *MULATOS* IN COLONIAL SOCIETY

Afro-indigenous *mulatos* manifested a great degree of cultural fluency and were able to operate within and between Spanish and indigenous cultural spheres. This cultural fluency tended to facilitate multigenerational ties with those of indigenous ancestry, which in turn served to perpetuate African-indigenous pairings well into the colonial period. Over time, the presence of Afro-indigenous *mulatos* in the overall social order perpetuated affinities between those of African ancestry and native peoples. This section examines the lived experiences of a number of Afro-indigenous *mulatos* in order to demonstrate their unique cultural and social position during the early colonial period.

Cultural Fluency

Many Inquisition cases involving Afro-indigenous *mulatos* and *indios* provide evidence that indigenous and African-descended individuals shared a cross-cultural awareness of the other. Most significantly for this analysis, these cases show that the prolonged and profound contact that occurred between Africans, their descendants, and indigenous persons helped Afro-indigenous *mulatos* gain a degree of fluency in native culture.[16] For the purposes of this analysis, cultural fluency has been construed broadly. While linguistic fluency in a native language would indicate a high level of cultural fluency—at least the ability to negotiate largely indigenous spaces and interactions—in other cases cultural fluency might be less tied to the ability to converse as a native speaker and more based in a familiarity with indigenous culture, which might be manifested through particular cultural practices or use of material goods. It is hard to imagine the forces bringing Africans and indigenous persons together and engendering Afro-indigenous *mulatos* not acculturating their descendants to indigenous ways of life. The following cases illustrate the myriad ways in which Afro-indigenous *mulatos* acquired and manifested fluency in indigenous cultures.

An example of this process can be seen in the bigamy case against Juana Ramírez.[17] In 1574, Antón Yaruniga, an African slave and Juana's husband, denounced his *mulata* wife for remarrying. In his denunciation, Antón claimed that he had married Juana, who was then known as María, twenty-three years before in the mining camp of Taxco. Yet, shortly after their marriage, Juana had fled, leaving Antón in Taxco. Eventually, after many years, Antón heard that his wife, now known as Juana, had remarried a *negro* slave owned by Don Francisco Velasco. Initially Juana denied any marriage to Antón. She might have hoped that a denial coupled with a changed name would introduce enough confusion that Antón's claims would be dismissed. That strategy did not work, forcing Juana to present her account of their marriage. She countered Antón's story by claiming that she had been coerced into marriage while still very young. Juana claimed that the *mayordomo* (estate manager) of Antón's owner had gone so far as to clap her in irons and whip her in order to coerce her consent. She confessed that she had not wanted to marry Antón because he was older than she and was too tall. Nevertheless, the *mayordomo* had been able to break her down, after which she and Antón had exchanged vows. For one month, the couple had lived together, sleeping in the same bed and having sexual relations. After a time, Juana had fled and did not see Antón again.

Juana's testimony speaks to a long history of Afro-indigenous interaction, beginning with her mother, Francisca *india*. Francisca was born sometime before 1530 in the community of Texcoco.[18] As a child born during or immediately after the conquest, Francisca would have been exposed to Spanish cultural influence via missionaries and early entrepreneurs seeking to profit from Texcoco's rich natural resources. Nevertheless, in those years Texcoco was one of the most populous indigenous communities in the Valley of Mexico, insuring that Francisca's day-to-day life would have remained grounded in indigenous culture.[19] At some point, Francisca left Texcoco and made her way to Taxco. Juana did not mention what forces had led her mother to the mining region. She or her family may have been mobilized through *encomienda* or *repartimiento* labor. Alternatively, following the disruptions and dislocations of the conquest, Francisca may have sought a life for herself in a burgeoning mining camp. Regardless of what drew her to Taxco, once there she found herself enmeshed in a highly diverse, multicultural community. Unlike her native Texcoco, Taxco was populated by Spaniards and other Europeans of various nationalities, Africans from a host of different ethnic and linguistic groups, and an assortment of native laborers drawn from nearby *altepetl* (Nahua communities).[20] In this context, survival demanded cultural adaptability. Not only did Francisca manage to survive, she was able to find companionship with two African men, Jorge and Francisco. According to Juana and other witnesses, her mother was *amancebada* (in a nonmarital sexual relationship) with Jorge at the time of her birth. Despite having a child by Jorge, sometime later Francisca married Francisco, a *negro biafara*. Although we do not know where Jorge was born, Francisco's *biafara* identity suggests that he was a *bozal* born in Africa. On the surface, Francisca, an *india* born in the Valley of Mexico, and the two men with whom she forged affective relationships initially shared neither culture nor language. Yet the fact that she was *amancebada* with Jorge and later married Francisco suggests that the cultural divide between an *india* and a *negro* was not insurmountable.

While Francisca likely had to work hard to adapt to the cultural demands of the mining camp, her daughter, Juana, was born and raised in this multicultural setting. Although the case is silent on Juana's linguistic abilities, she likely learned at least some Nahuatl from Francisca. At the time of her trial, Juana had two sisters. One of those sisters lived in the community of Tenancingo, while the other sister remained in Taxco. Tenancingo was a rural, indigenous town in which native language and culture predominated.[21] That one of Juana's sisters felt comfortable living in a predominately native community further supports the likelihood that Francisca inculcated her daughters with an awareness of and fluency in Nahua culture and language.

In his testimony, Antón Yaruniga, Juana's first husband, declared that he had arrived from Africa as a young man. He had first met Juana when she was still a child.[22] As a *bozal*, Antón had little familiarity with either indigenous or Spanish culture when he arrived in Taxco. Yet over the years he did acculturate to his multicultural environment. The fact that he denounced Juana suggests that he had learned Spanish and acquired a passing familiarity with Catholicism and Catholic norms. He had come to understand the duties and responsibilities of married spouses and the relevant canon law pertaining to marriage. Finally, he had learned which clerical figures oversaw marriage and allegations of bigamy. As a slave Antón would have needed to find a scribe to transcribe his claims and then mail the denunciation to the Holy Office in Mexico City. Further evidence of his Spanish fluency can be found in his testimony before the tribunal. If witnesses provided testimony in a language other than Castilian, the case documentation typically noted which language the witness used and specified the translator used by the court. During Antón's testimony, no translator was used nor did the notary indicate that his grasp of Castilian was poor.

Over the years, Antón also acquired some familiarity with native culture. According to a slave named Thomás, Antón had accidentally burned Juana's face when he tried to punish her by forcing her to breathe chili smoke.

Evidence of using chili smoke as a punishment can be found in the Codex Mendoza (see figure 3).[23] In that early colonial codex, several images depict parents punishing boys and girls by forcing them to breathe burning chili smoke. The accusation that Antón had used such a punishment on his *mulata* wife suggests that had become familiar with traditional indigenous practices, or at least others believed that he had such knowledge.[24] On the whole, the evidence suggests that Antón underwent a dual acculturation in Taxco, gaining familiarity with both Hispanic and indigenous cultural beliefs and practices.

Some of the conflict evident in the marriage between Antón and Juana may have grown out of cultural differences. Over the course of their marriage she made persistent efforts to escape Antón. While Juana may have simply chafed at being forced into a marriage with an older man she hardly knew, the conflict may suggest deeper differences between the two. According to the testimony, the couple met when Antón was still a *bozal*. As an Afro-indigenous *mulata*, Juana was likely capable of relating to indigenous persons, Spaniards, and *ladino* slaves. However, *bozales* may have posed a problem to her. Unless she had been raised among *bozales* of the same ethnic and linguistic traditions as her future husband, Juana very well may not have had any familiarity with Antón's native language or culture. Such a situation was likely. In the period between her birth (around 1550) and her marriage to Antón (around 1560–65), the slave trade to Spanish America drew heavily from the West Africa (for example, Senegal, Sierra Leone, and Guinea). The cultural-linguistic diversity of West Africa and the varied ports used by slave traders worked together to make the *bozales* of mid-sixteenth-century New Spain a diverse group.[25] Consequently, it is not surprising that despite her broad multicultural fluency Juana may not have had much in common with Antón. Ultimately her reticence to marry likely stemmed from unfamiliarity with her husband— and his culture—as much as from her opposition to outside pressure. In this regard, Juana's case provides evidence of the limits of cultural fluency and the highly contextual nature of such fluency.

Although Juana's linguistic fluency can only be inferred, other cases better illustrate this outward manifestation of native culture by *mulatos*.

Figure 3. Depiction of Nahua disciplinary techniques: Nahua parents punishing their children by holding them in the smoke of burning chilies, as recorded in the Codex Mendoza. Drawing by Joseph T. Beckley, after *Codex Mendoza*, fs. 60. http://codice.manuvo.com/

AFRO-INDIGENOUS *MULATOS* 129

One such case dates from 1559 and provides a short, tantalizing account of the marriage between Francisca de Acosta, a *mulata,* and Antón Sanchez, an enslaved *negro,* also called a *moreno*.[26] The two exchanged vows in a clandestine, pre-Tridentine ceremony on a rural *estancia* (livestock estate) near Oaxaca.[27] Later Francisca would leave that *estancia* and eventually remarry a *mulato* slave on a different estate near Tehuantepec.

The majority of the testimony gathered against Francisca dealt with her initial marriage to Antón. The crux of the case revolved around Francisca's use of Nahuatl in the couple's exchange of vows. According to Martín de San Miguel, a *mulato* servant of the *estancia,* Antón and Francisca arrived on the *estancia* together. One day, before several witnesses, Antón grasped Francisca's hand and proposed that she marry him. According to Martín, Francisca responded to Antón's proposal by recounting that Francisca "said 'yes' she would take him, which she said in the Mexican language [Nahuatl]."[28] Martín Ximénez, a *moreno* slave, gave a clearer account of the exchange. Ximénez recalled that, as he returned from the Mixteca, he encountered Francisca, Antón, and Martín de San Miguel. When he approached the group, Antón asked him to be a witness to their marriage. Ximénez recalled that "[Antón] asked Francisca, 'Señora would you like to marry me?' At this Francisca was silent, and a second time he asked, 'Would you be my wife?' She responded to him in the Mexican language, 'Quema.' This means 'yes.'"[29] Martín Ximénez was correct. In Nahuatl *quema* does mean yes. Despite this tantalizing exchange, the record contains no further testimony about the marriage. Both Ximénez and San Miguel noted that the couple lived together as husband and wife after their exchange. Neither witness provided an explanation for why Francisca would have chosen to reply in Nahuatl or any further clues as to her familiarity with the language and culture. Similarly, inquisitors did not prompt the witnesses for more details. As far as they were concerned, the testimony was sufficient to prove that each party had exchanged consent. The language of the exchange did not matter as long as the prospective spouses understood what each other was saying. For her part, Francisca did not elaborate on her background or parentage. The only additional information she gave was her age, fifteen.

The lack of biographical data makes it impossible to determine if Francisca was born of an African-indigenous union. Nevertheless, this case provides abundant evidence of acculturation by Africans—and Afro-Mexicans—to local indigenous languages. Not only did Francisca speak at least some Nahuatl, Martín Ximénez and Martín de San Miguel, both Afro-Mexican men, understood what she had said. Such knowledge is not surprising given the local context. In the 1540s and 1550s, few Spaniards lived in rural areas. The most frequent Spanish presence would have been clergy assigned to native communities who may have also served the scattered residents of rural estates. Moreover, the residents—often *mestizos, mulatos,* and *negros*—relied heavily on local indigenous communities for supplies and support. The ability of these *mulatos* and *negros* to speak and understand Nahuatl was likely born out of such connections.

Although rural areas tended to foster cross-cultural interaction between Africans and indigenous residents, urban areas also saw such relationships. One such case can be seen in the marriages of Luis Hernández in Mexico City.[30] The Inquisition's investigation into his marriages provides significant evidence of *mulatos'* connection to both Hispanic and indigenous cultures. The case itself revolved around two marriages, one to a *mulata* named Agustina and a later marriage to a *mulata* named Madalena de la Cruz. During the investigation of the case, Luis, Agustina, and Madalena each demonstrated a significant degree of familiarity with Spanish legal and religious norms. Luis's initial claims sought to nullify his first marriage by claiming parental coercion. Agustina countered such assertions by stating that Luis had made repeated proposals as a sign of his willingness to marry her. She also noted that they had lived together for a time following their marriage. As the supposed first wife, Agustina recognized that her best strategy was to provide evidence for the marriage and subsequent cohabitation. Madalena, Luis's second bride, sided with Agustina and petitioned that she be declared free of her marriage to Luis and be awarded financial restitution for the damage he had caused to her reputation. At this point, Luis changed his strategy and began to deny both marriages, retracting his previous statements. He told the court that he was "a young boy, witless, stupid, and incapable."[31] Interestingly, this change in strategy relied on reinforcing Spanish stereotypes of his *género*. As a *mulato*, he was not considered to be as rational or intelligent as a Spaniard. By coupling his youth with the assumption that he lacked sufficient reason to enter into a marriage, Luis sought to extricate himself from both marriages and undermine the charges leveled against him. In the face of this new strategy, Agustina provided further evidence to counter his claims by presenting evidence drawn from her indigenous family.

Agustina solicited testimony from her mother and Luis's mother. The two women, Isabel and Madalena, were described as *indias*. Neither woman spoke Castilian—at least not to the degree required to present testimony in that language—rather, they gave their statements in Nahuatl before a translator. The most damning evidence against Luis came from his own mother, who testified, "About three or so years ago Luis *mulato*, my son, told me, 'I have taken the virginity of Agustina *mulata*, Madalena's daughter, and I want to marry her.'"[32] In response, Isabel had told Luis that he should marry Agustina. Madalena corroborated Isabel's account. Suggestively, unlike Isabel, Madalena did not apply a *género* label to her daughter Agustina. Moreover, neither woman spoke of her child's father. The testimony of the two *india* mothers provides several important clues about Agustina and Luis. Most prominently, the two *mulatos* spent considerable time with their *india* mothers, interactions that included conversations—almost certainly in Nahuatl—about their affective relationships.

None of the testimony clearly identified the fathers of either *mulato*. This lacuna, coupled with the apparent affinity between the *mulato* children and their *india* mothers, suggests that Luis and Agustina resided with their mothers in the barrio of San Pablo and may have spent more of their time with the indigenous residents of that neighborhood. Agustina certainly lived with Madalena *india* because it was in that home that Luis made most of his advances. Luis may have lived with Isabel *india*; however, as a tailor he may have lived with his employer. If he worked for a Spanish tailor, he may have lived in that home. Nevertheless, his affinity to his mother likely meant that he spent time in her home even if he did not reside there. The barrio of San Pablo was a diverse neighborhood. In 1571, the parish contained almost a thousand Spaniards, four thousand *indios*, and an unknown number of *mestizos*, *negros*, and *mulatos* like Agustina and Luis.[33] Within this diverse environment, both *mulatos* were likely to be exposed to and acculturated into Spanish and indigenous cultural practices.

The strategies of these individuals speak to their awareness of legal processes, possibly acquired through their residence in the capital city. Both suspected brides presented petitions to the court in order to sway the tribunal to find in their favor. Agustina was well aware that at the time of her marriage canon law stipulated that the sacrament only required the exchange of consent followed by consummation. Similarly, Madalena's desire for an annulment and financial compensation represented the most typical outcome for second spouses of bigamists. Although Luis's strategy suggests a familiarity with the legal system, he was less adept at mobilizing an effective defense. Rather than complete honesty coupled with contrition and a plea for mercy, Luis vacillated between blaming his parents and claiming incompetence. Most individuals in his position either threw themselves at the mercy of the court or did their best to obfuscate the facts. He did neither effectively.[34] Nevertheless, his attempt to cast doubt on the first marriage by claiming parental interference or blaming his own ignorance does suggest that he knew of legal grounds for discrediting the evidence of his first marriage.

In the end, the court found Luis guilty but did not side with either Agustina or Madalena's petitions. Instead the tribunal ordered that Luis return to married life with Madalena while providing some financial support for Agustina. Despite the fact that the exchange of vows with Agustina occurred before his marriage to Madalena, the court was still dubious of the specific exchange of consent that had occurred. Their ruling suggests that they chose to enforce the marriage contracted under clerical oversight while providing for the suspected first spouse.

These examples present several candid glimpses of how *mulatos* became acculturated to indigenous culture. Importantly, the acquisition of indigenous culture occurred alongside that of Hispanic culture. Similarly, these cases capture how *mulatos* like Juana Ramírez and Luis Hernández could move between predominately Hispanic and indigenous spaces. This mobility helped foster relationships with individuals drawn from a wide array of *géneros de gente*. For a number of

Afro-indigenous *mulatos* these relationships included affective ties with *indios*.

Multigenerational Ties

While cultural fluency contributed to the numerical growth of Afro-indigenous *mulatos* and endowed such individuals with a unique set of cultural traits, once formed Afro-indigenous families tended to perpetuate African-indigenous pairings over subsequent generations. An example of this can be seen in the life of Isabel Díaz. In 1574, her husband, Francisco Granados, a *mulato* sandal maker, denounced Isabel for being married twice.[35] After describing both himself and Isabel as *mulatos*, he noted that she was the daughter of an *india*. The case revolved around the fact that before Isabel met Francisco she had been married to an *indio* shoemaker named Pedro. According to the case testimony, Isabel and Pedro's marriage occurred sometime around 1560. The *indio-mulata* couple had a daughter, labeled a *mulata* by Isabel's employer. After only two months of marriage, Pedro, who Isabel derided as "very crazy," left in the midst of a pregnancy.[36] Later, around 1568, Isabel would enter into a relationship with Francisco Granados. The couple lived *amancebados* for four years before Francisco fell deathly ill. On his deathbed, Francisco asked Isabel to marry, falsely claiming that Pedro had died. The couple married, and Francisco recovered from his illness. Yet Francisco's lie would catch up with the couple. Two years later, their marriage would end when the Inquisition found Isabel guilty of double marriage and convicted Francisco as an accomplice for abetting her crime.

The case against Isabel Díaz provides a window into a multigenerational African-indigenous family. The case does not mention any details about her parents other than their *géneros*. According to her statement, Isabel's father was a *mulato* named Francisco Díaz, and her mother was an *india*. Isabel did not give her mother's name, possibly because she did not know it. As the daughter of a *mulato* and an *india* Isabel represents the second generation of an African-indigenous family. Her marriage to the *indio* shoemaker Pedro García continued that trend. Isabel's daughter, called a *mulata* despite her largely indigenous ancestry, represents the third generation of the family. We do not know the parents of Francisco Granados. If he was Afro-indigenous—a possible scenario—both Isabel's spouses would have perpetuated an Afro-indigenous family.

For his part, Francisco demonstrated his own ties to indigenous persons. As the tribunal proceeded in their investigation of Francisco for abetting Isabel's crime, a woman named Juana Vásquez accused him of being married to at least three other women.[37] Juana claimed that Francisco was married to a *mestiza* named Juana de Castañeda, an *india* from Coyoacan, and another *india* who lived on a rural estate. Regardless of whether those claims were true, the fact that they were made suggests that Juana Vásquez thought they might have been real. Such claims demonstrate that contemporaries perceived Francisco Granados to be a *mulato* who might reasonably marry *indias* and *mestizas*.

Another example of a multigenerational African-indigenous family can be seen in the life of Beatriz Ramírez. The Inquisition case against her provides copious details of her movement within and between Spanish and indigenous social spaces. Beatriz was born in Taxco sometime around 1550. Although she did not name her parents, Beatriz described herself as "having been born free, to an *india* and a *negro*."[38] She was raised on the mining estate of Don Luis de Castilla. In her interviews, she did not mention her childhood in any detail. Nevertheless, given the wealth of the Castilla family, Beatriz likely grew up in a populous camp surrounded by *indios, negros,* and *españoles*.[39] Eventually she left Taxco and headed north. Sometime in the early 1560s, she found herself in the Chichimecas on an *estancia* owned by Gaspar Salvago.

On the *estancia*, she became involved with an *indio* named Diego López. During her interview, Beatriz admitted to having a relationship with Diego, but claimed that she and Diego had never formally been betrothed (*desposado*).[40] Other witnesses provided contradictory evidence. Juan de Medina, a *mestizo* employee of Salvago, remembered that the couple had been *amancebados* but had gone to San Miguel to be married. When he traveled there, the "*indios, negros,* and *mestizos,* and *espanoles*" of San Miguel told him that the couple had indeed been married.[41] Most damning to Beatriz was the testimony of Diego himself. Diego recounted that they had met while working for Salvago and had been married in a rather large ceremony that had included Salvago, two other Spaniards, Juan de Saavedra and Rodrigo Quesada, several *morenos*, and a *mulato* named Miguel Sánchez. After the marriage, they had lived together for two years before Beatriz fled from their home. After leaving the Chichimecas, Beatriz had traveled to Guadalajara, then Puebla, eventually making her way to Antequera.

Once in Antequera, she met a freed *negro* also named Diego López. They were married in Oaxaca but eventually moved back to Mexico City where her new husband found work as a fruit vendor in the plaza. Eventually, however, her past and present collided. In the spring of 1574, Diego López, *negro*, denounced Beatriz to the Holy Office after hearing about her previous marriage. This was not an easy act for him. Diego confessed that "separating from her would be like having one of his eyes taken out."[42] She was found guilty and sentenced to a five-year exile from the archdiocese of Mexico.

Although Beatriz did not have any children, her family history demonstrates at least two generations of African-indigenous unions. She represented the outcome of the first generation formed by her *negro* father and her *india* mother. Her marriages represent the second generation. In her first, she found an *indio* spouse, and in her second, a *negro*. Had she borne children by Diego López, *indio*, or Diego López, *negro*, they would have been Afro-indigenous and likely labeled *mulato*. Moreover, her story illustrates the ease with which Beatriz was able to move between the various social and cultural spaces of early New Spain and interact with a diversity of people, including *indios, mestizos, negros, mulatos, morenos,* and *españoles*.

A final example of African-indigenous families can be seen in the life and marriages of Gonzalo Hernández.[43] Gonzalo was born around 1526, in the town of Amatitlan, to Juan, *negro*, a slave of Alonso Avalos, and María, *india*, a native of Mexico City. Around 1550, he married a *mulata* named Francisca Rangel in Amatitlan. Gonzalo and Francisca lived as husband and wife for two years. After those two years and the birth of a child, Francisca left abruptly and disappeared. For almost three decades, Gonzalo sought to find her, but to no avail. In 1579, he received word that she had died and presented that evidence to the ecclesiastical authorities in order to receive permission to remarry. Once declared free of matrimony, he sought a marriage to Catalina

García, an *india* from the pueblo of Maquilí. Prior to this second marriage, Gonzalo asked permission of Catalina's family and town elders. They agreed and the couple was wed.

Four years after Gonzalo's second wedding, he received word that Francisca was alive and living on an *estancia* in Michoacan, *amancebada* with a *negro*. In order to verify the news, Gonzalo traveled to Michoacan and confronted her. Although he had hoped to bring her back to the authorities so that they might adjudicate his matrimonial situation, her *negro* lover and several *mulatos* prevented him from doing so. To discharge his conscience, Gonzalo denounced himself to the Inquisition, stating that he sincerely wished to return to married life with Francisca, since theirs was the only valid marriage. Unlike in many cases of bigamy, after a thorough trial Gonzalo was acquitted by the tribunal. According to their verdict, by presenting evidence of Francisca's death—even if that evidence had been in error—Gonzalo had taken the appropriate steps required of Christians seeking to remarry, and in so doing he had treated the sacrament of marriage with respect.[44]

In this case, both Gonzalo and Francisca were Afro-indigenous *mulatos* born in the town of Amatitlan. According to her testimony, Francisca's mother was an *india* originally from the pueblo of Içatlan, but she did not mention her father. Presumably her father was a *negro* or a *mulato* like Gonzalo's father. Given that she would have been born around 1536, it is very likely that her father was a slave or servant sent to the region during the formative years of its economic development. He may have worked in the newly discovered mines or on a rural estate supporting that industry.[45] As children of African-indigenous unions, their marriage, contracted in an indigenous community, represented a second-generation union between two Afro-indigenous *mulatos*.

Additionally, both Gonzalo and Francisca manifested strong ties to indigenous culture. For example when Francisca left Gonzalo, she chose to live with her indigenous mother in a *pueblo de indios*. Similarly, when declared free from his first marriage, Gonzalo found a new spouse in Maquilí, another *pueblo de indios*. His choice to ask for Catalina's hand in marriage from her family and from the local *indios principales* demonstrates his familiarity with native culture, his comfort in a native community, and his fluency in a native language. The witnesses to the second marriage did not speak Spanish, instead providing their testimony to the tribunal in Nahuatl through a translator. This suggests that Gonzalo likely communicated with his second wife—and probably his first wife's mother—in Nahuatl, not Spanish.

As in the previous cases, Gonzalo's marriages and family history illustrate that ties between natives, Africans, and individuals of African descent frequently spanned multiple generations. Individuals born of African-indigenous unions tended to become acculturated to native cultural norms and fluent in native languages. Later in life, this fluency could lead to the creation of marital ties and social bonds between Afro-Mexicans and indigenous persons. Ultimately these cases highlight the important cultural and familial connections that likely bound many of Mexico's *mulatos* to their *indio* kin.

VARIABILITY IN *MULATO* ASCRIPTION

The cases from this chapter demonstrate that in sixteenth-century New Spain, the label *mulato* could be applied to a broad range of individuals whose ancestry could include Africans, Native Americans, and Europeans. As a result of these ascriptions, the label *mulato* homogenized a vast range of lived experience. Most significantly, this chapter has demonstrated that this homogenization has hidden an important subgroup of *mulatos* born of African-indigenous unions. Yet this tendency also suggests that the variables that influenced the ascription of the *mulato género* may have differed from those that influenced the ascription of the *mestizo género*.

The preceding chapter highlighted the reality that contemporaries did not automatically apply *mestizo* to all individuals of mixed Spanish-indigenous ancestry. Instead, the ascription of *mestizo* relied heavily on the perception of one's social networks and cultural affinities. Those individuals perceived to be close kin of *españoles*, raised as a family member, and integrated into the social and economic networks of *españoles* were likely to be tacitly accepted as *españoles* even if they were born of an *español-india* union. Conversely, if an individual born of such a union was raised by an *india* mother, living and working with other *indios*, the person was likely to be ascribed the label of *indio*.

Thus, at least in the sixteenth century, the *mestizo* label represented a liminal one, which applied to individuals of presumed mixed Spanish-indigenous ancestry who were not clearly incorporated into either parent *género*.

In contrast, this study has not found as great a degree of variability among individuals commonly ascribed *mulato*. Few cases demonstrate differential ascription by *mulatos'* contemporaries. In most cases, persons labeled *mulato* were labeled as such by all witnesses. Nevertheless, a few individuals did receive variable ascriptions by their contemporaries. Such cases can illustrate the range of variability possible for those individuals commonly regarded to be *mulatos*.

Variation tended to occur when an observer perceived an individual as being more indigenous (*mestizo, indio*) or more African (*negro, moreno*). No *mulato* showed variability in both directions. As with variability along the Spanish-indigenous spectrum, variability in *mulato* ascription mirrored social and cultural ties to a parent group. An example of this can be seen in the person of Luisa, a slave.[46] She was suspected of being the first wife of Juan Perales, a *mulato* accused of being twice married. Most witnesses, including *mulatos, españoles,* and *negro* or *moreno* slaves, referred to Luisa as a *mulata*. In her own testimony, she described herself as a *"mulata esclava."*[47] In contrast, her mother, a slave named Juana, described Luisa as *"de color morena"* (*morena* in color).[48] Juana used the same phrase to describe herself, although most witnesses called her a *negra*.

Juana's use of the phrasing *de color* and the category of *morena* highlight two important aspects of *género* ascription among individuals of African descent. First, Juana's use of *de color* represents a physical characterization of skin color over a specific *género* ascription.[49] Her statement could be read as signifying that she and her daughter "had the color of" or "looked liked" *morenas* without actually ascribing either woman to that *género* category. Prefixing a *género* label with *de color* served to ameliorate the negative association of that label by weakening the link between the *género* label and the individual being described. Although individuals could conceivably use this phrase to reference the physical color of any *género*, in the documents examined for this study individuals only used the *de color* construction with *géneros* denoting African descent: *negro, mulato, moreno,* or *loro*.[50] Additionally,

Juana's choice to use *"de color morena"* for both herself and Luisa may have served to underscore their familial relation in an attempt to bolster the weight of her testimony in the case against Juan Perales.

Second, Juana's statement illustrates the use of *moreno* as an alternative to *negro* in describing individuals of African descent. In the sixteenth century, the Castilian word *moreno* had various meanings depending on context. As a pure color referent it implied a brownish hue and could appear in descriptions of individuals of various *géneros*.[51] In such contexts *moreno* functioned as an adjective describing an individual's features, such as one's beard, face, or body.[52] Nevertheless, in various sixteenth-century documents, *moreno* could be ascribed to individuals in lieu of *negro*.[53] In the case against Juan Perales, several enslaved persons of African descent called themselves *morenos*. Despite those self-ascriptions, when several of these witnesses ratified their statements, the Inquisition's notary described them as *negros*. This suggests that among individuals who could be considered *negros, moreno* represented a preferable self-ascription. In other words, when used as a *género* category, *moreno* represented a kinder, more polite word for *negro*, a euphemism.

Most frequently, slippage occurred between *negro* and *moreno*, not between *moreno* and *mulato*, although this case provides evidence of that possibility. For example, Juana's statements, even qualified by the phrase *de color*, place Luisa on a *mulata–morena* spectrum. Additionally, Juan Perales described his presumed second wife, Juana Hernández, as a *morena* despite all other witnesses choosing to label her a *mulata*. In the case of both Luisa and Juana, the possible slippage between *mulata* and *morena* may reflect these two women's close association with slavery. Luisa was a slave, and, although Juana Hernández was free, she had close associations with her enslaved *mulato* father and other enslaved persons. In this instance, the slippage between *mulata* and *morena* likely resulted from the women's association with slavery and their social ties to other *negros* or *morenos*.

Another example of slippage between *mulato* and African *géneros* can be seen in the case against Mariana de la Cruz.[54] As in the previous example, most observers described Mariana as a *mulata*. The majority witnesses were of African descent, described as *mulatos* and *negros*, and some were enslaved. Mariana described herself as a *"mulata libre"* and gave her parents as Juan Capitan, an enslaved *negro,* and Marta, an *india mexicana.* Yet two references to Mariana suggest that she could be perceived differently. In her first interview, the Inquisition notary described her as *"una negra amulatada"* (a *mulata*-like *negra*) when recording her entrance into the courtroom.⁵⁵ The notary's description labeled Mariana a *negra* but implied that something about her appearance made her *mulata*-like. Similarly, Isabel, an enslaved *negra,* vacillated in ascribing a *género* to Mariana.⁵⁶ Isabel described her as "Mariana *mulata negra libre."*⁵⁷ Here the word *negra* likely functioned as an adjective modifying *mulata* rather than as a separate *género* label. This reading would imply that Mariana had darker-hued skin. Together these two ascriptions suggest that despite her Afro-indigenous parentage, some contemporaries perceived Mariana as being somewhere between a *mulata* and a *negra.* In this case, Mariana maintained strong social ties to other *mulatos* and *negros,* including many slaves, and such close connections may have led contemporaries to perceive her as more like a *negra* than other *mulatas.* The next chapter further examines the cases of Mariana de la Cruz and Juan de Perales to illustrate the importance of elaborate Afro-Mexican social networks in facilitating *mulato* marriage patterns.

Although these cases lack direct physical descriptions, these ascriptions hint at the issue of phenotype. The phrase *de color* and the adjectival use of *amulatada* or *negra* suggest that physical appearance contributed to the process of ascription. Unfortunately the lack of phenotypical descriptions inhibits the historian's ability to gauge the degree to which perceived physical attributes correlated to ascriptions of *negro* or *mulato.* In all likelihood, the individuals who made such ascriptions did so because the subjects in question manifested both socio-cultural *and* phenotypical affinities to *negros.*

At the same time, connections to indigenous society and culture could blur the line between *mulato* and *indio.* An excellent example of this can be seen in Madalena Osorio. In 1588, she married Pedro Gonzáles, a *mulato,* on an *estancia* near Antequera.⁵⁸ In seeking permission to marry, Pedro had falsified claims that his first wife had died. The investigation into his double marriage recorded numerous ascriptions of Madalena's *género.* Universally individuals referred to her as an *india.* Witnesses included several *mulatos* and the priest who had celebrated her marriage to Pedro. Even the Inquisition notary labeled her an *india* when she was called before the court. When stating her name and personal details, Madalena did not self-ascribe any *género*. "She said that she is called Madalena Osorio and is the daughter of Francisco Polito *mulato* and of Ana Díaz *india*, wife of Francisco Polito, who are now deceased and were *vecinos* and *naturales* of Mexico [City] in the barrio of San Juan and that there she has relatives of both but since she left that land while very young she does not know their names."[59] Even after providing her parentage, when the notary recorded her verification of the transcription he called her an *india* and stated that she was a *ladina* (capable of speaking and understanding Castilian). Such notations generally appeared only after testimony presented by *indios*.

Madalena's biography provides some clues as to why contemporaries perceived her as an *india*. Her upbringing in Mexico City's largest indigenous neighborhood, San Juan de los Naturales, likely led to her acculturation to Nahua society and culture. That cultural preparation could have facilitated her interactions with Nahuatl speakers and communities scattered throughout colonial New Spain. After leaving Mexico City as a child, she spent at least ten years in the rural region around Oaxaca, most that time living on multiethnic *estancias*. On those rural estates she interacted with *españoles*, *mulatos*, and *indios*. Her contemporaries may have perceived her as an *india* because of associations and relationships she forged through shared residence with other *indios*. Ultimately, despite being of African descent, Madalena's lifestyle and social perception led her contemporaries to consider her an *india*.

Another instance of *género* slippage influenced by Afro-indigenous ancestry and lifestyle can be found in the case against Juana Augustina, mentioned at the start of this chapter. Throughout most of the case, witnesses referred to her as a *mulata*, and, although she did not self-ascribe any *género*, she did note that her parents were a *mulato* and an *india*. In her first audience with the Inquisition, the notary stated that the court did not ask for her to provide an account of her life (*discurso de su vida*) because she was "a *mestiza mulata* raised in this land."[60] The ascription of *mestiza mulata* does not appear in any other source. As with the previous example of a *mulata negra*, the phrase conveys a sense that Juana is a *mestiza* who appears *mulata*-like. Although we do not know what Juana looked like, her biography certainly suggests that she was acculturated to indigenous language and society. The notary's ascription likely resulted from his holistic perception that her appearance, parentage, and lifestyle fell somewhere between what would be expected for a *mestiza* and a *mulata*.

The most unique case of variable ascription examined in this study can be found in a criminal case from 1581. In the spring of that year, Antonio de Espejo, a Spanish *estancia* owner, killed two of his cowboys in a rage-fueled dispute near Celaya.[61] One of the victims, Andrés Vásquez, represents an interesting example of differential *género* ascription along the African-indigenous spectrum. Various witnesses described Andrés as an *indio, indio mexicano, indio ladino, indio amulatado, indio como mulato, indio que parecia mulato, mulato medio indio, mulato,* and *mulato, hijo de mulato e india.* Initial testimony in the case was collected at an *estancia* known as Aguas Calientes. Residents there tended to call Andrés an *indio*. The claim that he was an *indio mexicano* corroborates other testimony that he was born in Toluca, a Nahuatl-speaking community. Accounts by several Nahuatl-speaking *indios* further indicate that he was able to communicate with them in Nahuatl as he lay mortally wounded. On the other hand, the ascription of *indio ladino* emphasized his fluency in Castilian.

Additional testimony solicited by the prosecutor recorded ascriptions of Andrés as an *indio amulatado, indio como mulato, indio que parecia mulato,* and *mulato medio indio.* The *fiscal* (prosecutor) chose to describe Andrés as a *mulato* in the questions put before the witnesses. When witnesses responded to those questions, their ascriptions of Andrés varied according to their own *género* and their relationship to him. Many of his fellow cowboys—men predominantly labeled *mulato*— called Andrés a *mulato*. In contrast, the *indios* interviewed chose to modify the fiscal's ascription of *mulato* by including some reference to *indio*. All the indigenous witnesses spoke Nahuatl or Otomí. Four *indio* witnesses described Andrés as an *indio como mulato*. Two chose to describe him as a *mulato medio indio,* and one used the phrase *indio que parecia mulato*. These constructions suggest that, to varying degrees, *indios* perceived Andrés as being somewhat like them but also different, more like a *mulato* than an *indio*.

The diversity of ascriptions for Andrés provides a window into the complexity of *género* ascription in early New Spain. While most Inquisition cases show little variation in the ascription of *géneros,* such uniformity may not have been universal in all contexts. In the Inquisition cases examined here, witnesses tended to be acquaintances, friends, or relatives of each other. The familiarity between the individuals investigated and interviewed by the Inquisition may have led to more consistent ascriptions in those cases. In contrast, the criminal case into the death of Andrés Vásquez interviewed a wide range of people, some of whom had known Andrés for a long time, others who hardly knew him. Increased variability in *género* ascription would not be surprising in contexts where witnesses had little contact or shared experience with the individual being described. Observers might construct their ascription in idiosyncratic ways, each basing evaluation on slightly different attributes of the person being observed. This variability might be more representative of the ascriptions made between strangers or people who did not know each other well. Certainly, the various ascriptions provided for Andrés show definite differences that can be traced to the length and frequency of relationships and the relative differences between observer and observed.

Despite the variability described above, the extant documentation suggests that in most cases observers agreed in ascribing an individual to the *mulato género.* The basis for this conformity cannot be easily accessed. The brief and limited physical descriptions that have been preserved make it impossible to identify if there was a consensus on what *mulatos* looked like. Phrases like *de color* suggest that appearances and physical traits certainly factored into the process of ascription but do not provide sufficient evidence for a strong physical or phenotypical influence in the ascription of *mulato.* Similarly, the variability in lived experience, parentage, and cultural affinities suggests that the ascription of *mulato* could not easily rest in a shared lifestyle or specific cultural modes. Yet colonial subjects seemed to largely agree on who should be labeled a *mulato* even while the individuals labeled *mulato* varied so widely. The term *mulato* clearly meant something to colonial subjects.

Within all the diversity found in the lives and experiences of early colonial *mulatos,* the commonality that led to their ascription as *mulatos* appears to be known, or presumed, *partial* African descent. In other words, for early colonial subjects a *mulato* was someone who was or could have been descended from a *negro*. Alternatively, individuals of known or presumed wholly African ancestry—African-born individuals and those born of endogamous African unions—were ascribed as *negros,* or *morenos*. While there could be some slippage between *negro* and *mulato* in particular cases, most early colonial subjects concurred in their ascriptions of *negro* or *moreno,* with such categorizations rarely overlapping with *mulato*. Although *mulato* appears to have referenced partial African descent, the specific observations that led colonial subjects to categorize individuals as *mulatos* likely varied depending on the actual relationships between observer and subject. When making ascriptions, it cannot be forgotten that colonial subjects read lineage into cultural and social markers. Consequently, in some cases known ancestry or parentage likely played a role, in others physical appearance was a factor, and in others social networks or cultural traits factored into ascription. Regardless of what observations contributed to the process of ascription, colonial subjects largely agreed that the category of *mulato* applied to individuals who manifested some degree of Africanness, real or imagined, but who were not perceived to be wholly African.[62]

The logic behind this pattern of ascriptions suggests that the labeling of *mulatos* and *mestizos* operated differently, at least in the sixteenth century. *Mestizo* functioned as a category of liminality. Individuals became *mestizos* when they could not manifest sufficient social connections, cultural traits, or physical attributes necessary to be considered *españoles* or *indios*. In effect, the label *mestizo* applied to individuals who failed to meet the social and cultural threshold for inclusion in one of their parent categories. In contrast, *mulato* appears to have marked individuals who manifested a degree of partial Africanness, as defined through some combination of social, cultural, and physical attributes. In another way, *mestizo* ascription relied on a lack of social, cultural, or physical traits sufficient for ascription as *español* or *indio*. *Mulato* ascription followed the perceived presence of traits associated with partial African ancestry.

While both *mestizo* and *mulato* served to exclude individuals from parent categories, the permutations of what might be considered partial

Africanness led to more consistent ascriptions of *mulato*. Even if two observers relied on different markers they might both agree on some measure of partial Africanness. In contrast, the ascription of *mestizo* required observers to agree that an individual did not manifest sufficient traits to be considered either an *español* or an *indio*. In other words, the threshold of observed traits required to consider someone a *mulato* was likely lower than the threshold for considering someone a *mestizo* and made it more likely that observers would agree on the ascription of *mulato* even if they did not consider the same constellation of traits. Consequently, in the sixteenth century, *mulato* served as a catchall for persons known or presumed to be of mixed African ancestry, even if they may have manifested social and cultural traits common to other *géneros*.

CONCLUSION

The overall range of diversity found within New Spain's *mulato* population cannot be understated. This chapter has examined several important aspects of that diversity. Most significantly, qualitative and quantitative analysis suggests that during the sixteenth century a large percentage, possibly a majority, of *mulatos* in New Spain were Afro-indigenous. The lives of these individuals reveal the important connections that existed between Africans and indigenous people in the early colonial period. Moreover, the cultural formation of Afro-indigenous *mulatos* made them proficient in moving within and between the various cultural spheres of early colonial society. Their ties to indigenous communities fostered continued Afro-indigenous unions over time and established strong cultural and familial ties between both groups, the significance of which has only begun to be examined.

In addition, the diversity of lived realities among early colonial *mulatos* provides clues as to the considerations that factored into the ascription of the *mulato* label. This examination suggests that colonial subjects ascribed *mulato* to those individuals they presumed to be of partial African descent. In making such an ascription, colonial subjects gauged multiple observed qualities and behaviors and could conflate social and cultural attributes with lineage. This standard differed from that of *mestizo*, which applied to individuals unable to manifest the characteristics of either *español* or *indio*. The underlying logic of *mulato* ascription has tended to homogenize our understanding of *mulatos* by masking the diversity that could exist among such individuals. Yet the homogenization of the *mulato* label should not blind historians to the diversity of experiences, choices, and opportunities that existed for individuals who were ascribed this label in the early colonial period. This chapter's exploration of Afro-indigenous *mulatos* represents an attempt to recover the uniqueness manifested by those ascribed *mulato*. The chapters that follow continue in this vein by exploring the diverse ways that *mestizos* and *mulatos* experienced marriage and work in the early colonial period.

CHAPTER 5

MARRIAGE

> It is necessary to charge persons to come to the defense and aid of the *indios* of [Mexico] city and its surroundings and in doing so free them and relieve them from the *negros, mulatos,* and *mestizos* so that they are not killed or robbed. Only one hundred leagues from here in a pueblo without a corregidor, a single *mulato* would be capable of causing unrest or even plundering it. Worse still, this kingdom is so vast that all the delinquents and those of ill repute, *mestizos* and *mulatos,* would put themselves up in *pueblos de indios,* which would result in great harm, completely destroying the [pueblos], taking refuge there, and hiding where the justices cannot arrest them for their crimes. The number [of these] could grow so much that there would be no secure roads.
>
> *Audiencia of Mexico, 1606*

On April 9, 1575, Don Francisco de Zarate, *chantre* and *provisor* (cantor and ecclesiastical judge) of the cathedral of Antequera (Oaxaca), received information that Marcos Ruiz, a *mestizo,* had committed a heretical crime against the sacrament of marriage by marrying Leonor de Castañeda, a *castiza,* while his first wife, Catalina Selada, a *mulata,* still lived.[1] When interviewed, Marcos stated that he was twenty-seven years old and the son of Pedro Ruiz, a conquistador of Oaxaca, and an unnamed *india.* At the time of his trial, he worked as a muleteer operating out of Antequera. The trial's records help highlight key contextual factors facilitating early colonial marriage trends. Most significantly, each of his marriages occurred in a slightly different social and cultural space.

According to witnesses, his first marriage was contracted in Santiago de Guatemala, around 1570. Marcos's work as a muleteer likely brought him to Santiago, where he entered into close relationships with a number of Afro-Guatemaltecos. He found lodging in the home of Catalina Marroquín, a free *negra* and former slave of the bishop of Guatemala. In her home Marcos met Catalina de Selada, a *mulata*. She was the daughter of Juan de Selada, a *moreno,* and Isabel, an *india.* Most witnesses recalled that Juan de Selada threw the couple a large wedding feast after their nuptials. Although the case does not document their full courtship, in all likelihood Marcos's associations to the Seladas and other Afro-Guatemaltecos were likely the result of social and residential proximity. As a foreigner in town, seemingly without an entrée into Spanish circles, Marcos found a residence in the home of a freed slave and became part of a largely Afro-Guatemalan network of friends and family.

Although his occupation cannot solely account for this social network, his social affinities mirrored those of other muleteers.[2] In his study of sixteenth-century Santiago de Guatemala, Robinson Herrera noted that muleteers worked frequently with African slaves and others of African ancestry.[3] Consequently, it is not surprising that Marcos found friendship and accommodation among a local group closely connected to his occupation. Moreover, the issue of residence—his physical space—cannot be overlooked. By living in the home of a freed slave he further associated himself with individuals of African descent in the eyes of the Spanish elite and likely deepened his social ties with Afro-Guatemaltecos.

Marcos's second wedding took place several years later, around 1573, in his hometown of Antequera. There he entered into a relationship with Leonor de Castañeda, a *castiza.* According to Marcos, the ceremony was a major event attended by local notables, including the *alcalde ordinario* (local magistrate) Diego Pacheco. In Antequera, Marcos appears to have lived and moved in a very different social network. Antequera was his home. He had been raised there and was publicly known to be the son of one of its original conquistadors. This likely made a great deal of difference. While *españoles* in Guatemala would have simply seen him as a *mestizo* muleteer with *mulato* and *negro* friends, in Antequera he was a known descendent of the conquest-era elite. Although the case documentation does not describe how Marcos met his second wife, Leonor, their well-attended wedding suggests largely Spanish social connections.[4]

This differential positioning of an individual universally described as a *mestizo* highlights the reality that *género* ascriptions only provided a rough guide to an individual's place in the social order. Individuals ascribed to the same *género* constructed diverse social networks that grew out of shared occupations, residences, and cultural affinities. Cases like that of Marcos can help illustrate how the social relationships of *mestizos* and *mulatos* helped to shape the patterns of marriage in early colonial New Spain. Although *mestizos* and *mulatos* manifested different marriage trends, in each case their patterns of marriage reflect the ways that members of those *géneros* sought and created community.

This chapter argues that in the sixteenth and early seventeenth century, the unique social position of *mestizos* and *mulatos* led them to enter exogamous marriages more frequently than their contemporaries from other *géneros*. While *mestizos* and *mulatos* resembled each other in their degree of exogamy, their specific patterns of exogamy differed. *Mestizos* tended to marry *españoles* or *indios*, and *mulatos* tended to marry *negros* and *indios*. In each case, the patterns of endogamy and exogamy manifested by *mestizos* and *mulatos* speak to the importance of shared social, cultural, physical, and economic spaces in fostering marital unions. In this sense, the marriage patterns of *mestizos* and *mulatos* provide a way to examine the lived reality of colonial subjects and the myriad ways they related to other members of their society. The observed diversity of social networks and marital partners suggests that *mestizos* and *mulatos* occupied a unique space within colonial society, one that allowed them to form ties with a wide array of their contemporaries.

SOURCES

The findings of this chapter are based on two separate but related source bases: parish marriage records and Inquisition cases, primarily those investigating multiple marriages. Both documentary genres have benefits and drawbacks that shape and limit the findings that can be drawn. Parish records provide the best means to examine large-scale marriage patterns in a systematic and quantitative way. Unfortunately for the historian, few parish records from sixteenth-century Mexico exist, and most extant records from that century date only from the 1590s.[5] Moreover, some sixteenth-century parish records contain no *género* labels, others provided *género* ascriptions, and others avoided *género* labels but still recorded legal status.[6] Even when labels were recorded, historians of race have voiced uncertainty over who determined the ascribed race of individuals recorded in parish records.[7] Consequently, this analysis relies on parishes whose records consistently applied *género* labels during the period under study even though the records do not indicate who provided the ascriptions. Yet, even where available, parish records alone cannot provide the social and cultural details necessary for interpreting the marriage trends they contain.

To contextualize marriage data, scholars of later periods have frequently turned to parallel sources, including baptismal records and censuses that provide residential and occupational data.[8] Unfortunately, the similarly poor preservation of baptismal records and even less consistent *género* ascription in those sources make synchronic analysis of several local data sets very difficult and completely preclude the application of "nominal record linkage" as employed by Patricia Seed and Douglas Cope.[9] In the absence of other local data suitable for interpretation, the necessary qualitative information must be garnered from other documentary sources.

Inquisitorial records, particularly cases investigating double marriage, can provide such qualitative data. In his study of colonial bigamists and their lives, Richard Boyer noted that, with the exception of their crime, most bigamists were otherwise normal members of society. Even though their crime made them stand out, most individuals contracting plural marriages did so to "fit in and settle in" their communities.[10] The very mundane nature of marriages, including heretical ones, ensures that Inquisition cases provide unique vantages into the process of spouse selection by *mestizos* and *mulatos*. On the other hand, the context of production insures that the cases they document are by no means random. The individuals investigated frequently violated both ecclesiastical law and social norms. The fact that these cases involved lower-ranked individuals of mixed ancestry adds further complexity to the problem. Was *género* a factor in the denunciation of such individuals or in the decision to pursue the case? In general, early modern judicial systems placed greater emphasis on the regulation and punishment of social inferiors than elites.[11] Additionally, how might the *género* of the defendant and those of their spouses shape the initial complaint? One can imagine that if a *mestizo* married to an *española* attempted to remarry an *india* or a *mulata* the scandal caused by the abandonment of the *española* might lead to a greater chance for denunciation than if a *mestizo* married to an *india* tried to remarry another *india*. Vagaries such as these make systematically accounting for possible biases in the extant corpus of such cases almost impossible. Despite these downsides, the analysis of qualitative inquisitorial cases alongside quantitative parish data can help overcome the weaknesses of relying on either source base separately.

Several important trends can be discerned from the available data. *Mestizo* social networks facilitated marriages to *españoles, indios,* or other *mestizos*. Within that pattern, *mestizas* tended to marry *españoles* more frequently than their male counterparts, especially when well integrated into Spanish households. A comparable pattern existed among *mulatos*. Most *mulatos* found spouses among *mulatos, indios,* or *negros*. Over time *mulatos* became more endogamous. The increased endogamy of *mulatos* occurred concurrently with the construction of Afro-Mexican social networks that facilitated relationships between *mulatos* and other individuals of African descent. Finally, even as *mulatos* became more endogamous, between one-fifth and one-third of *mulatos* married individuals of indigenous ancestry.

PARISH MARRIAGES, 1576–1641

The parish records analyzed for this study were drawn from two parishes: the Parroquía de la Santa Veracruz (Mexico City) and the Real y Minas de Santa Fe de Guanajuato.[12] These parishes represent ideal locations for examining marriage patterns within a demographically varied population. The Mexico City parish provides a useful window into urban patterns in a residentially mixed neighborhood. Despite the lack of detailed censuses in the early colonial period, an ecclesiastical census from 1571 provides a basic demographic picture of Mexico City.[13] The census lists Santa Veracruz as having 950 *españoles* and 2,700 *indios*. By comparison, the parish served by the cathedral, Asunción Sagrario, hosted almost 8,000 *españoles* and just over 3,000 *negros*. The census does not list any *indios* resident in Asunción Sagrario nor does it mention *mestizos* or *mulatos* in any parish.[14] My selection of Santa Veracruz was partly due to its greater degree of mixed residents. While *indios* certainly worked and lived within the boundaries of Asunción Sagrario, *españoles* and *negros* greatly outnumbered indigenous residents. On the other hand, Santa Veracruz had demographics slightly more consistent with the colony as a whole, given its closer proximity to largely indigenous neighborhoods. In this sense, Santa Veracruz occupied a middle ground in early Mexico City. The parish was located to the west of the main plaza, which housed the cathedral and viceroyal palace. This location placed it at the edge of the sixteenth-century city and on the main roadway and causeway linking the city to the large indigenous community of Tacuba. To the north, the largely indigenous parish of Santa Catarina Virgen y Mártir and the indigenous community of Tlatelolco bordered Santa Veracruz. To the south, Santa Veracruz bordered the area served by the friars of the Convent of San Francisco and the largest indigenous parish of the greater urban area, San Juan de los Naturales. The varied demographics of Santa Veracruz can be explained by its location on a major trade artery (Mexico–Tacuba) and its proximity to both the largest concentration of Spanish residents (Asunción Sagrario) and the large centers of indigenous subjects (Tlatelolco, San Juan de los Naturales, and Tacuba).

In contrast to Santa Veracruz, the records from Guanajuato provide insights into the patterns formed in a rural region shaped by the mixed labor force of mining. The mines of Guanajuato were discovered between 1548 and 1552, not far from the main route connecting Mexico City to Zacatecas.[15] At the time of the discovery of silver, the Guamare indigenous people sparsely populated the region surrounding Guanajuato. The discovery spurred an influx of miners along with ranchers interested in raising livestock to support the mines. Unlike

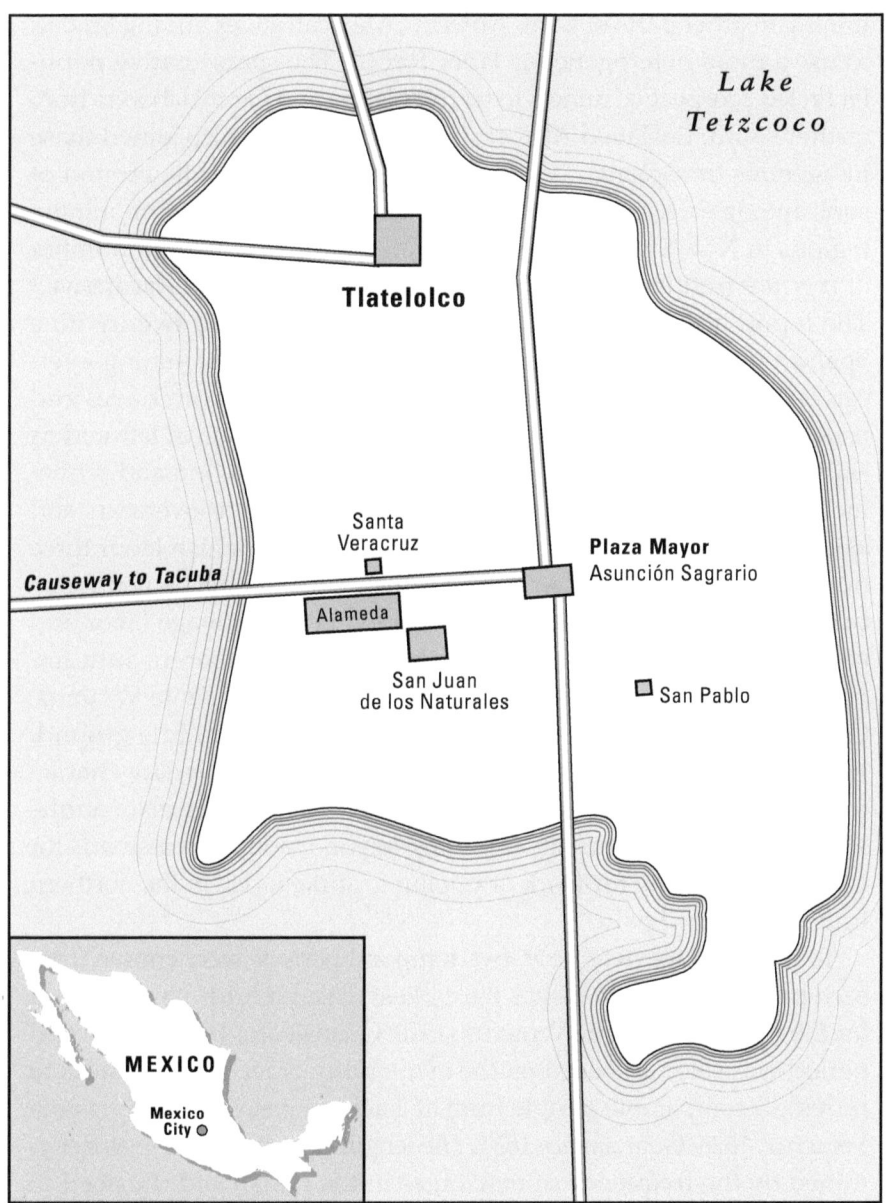

Map 1. Sixteenth-century Mexico City and Tlatelolco, including the parishes of Asunción Sagrario, San Juan de los Naturales, Santa Veracruz, and San Pablo. Copyright © 2016 by the University of Oklahoma Press. All rights reserved.

mining in other parts of Latin America, Mexican silver mining tended to use a more heterogeneous labor force.[16] The sparse native population led prospective miners to recruit Nahua and Otomí laborers from farther south. Enslaved Africans and some *mulatos* also joined these indigenous transplants.[17] Guanajuato represents a middle ground of sorts among early colonial mining centers. In a 1597 report on mining regions in New Spain, Guanajuato ranked fourth in overall number of *ingenios* (refining mills), behind Pachuca, Taxco, and Zacatecas.[18] The report also noted that the community supported twenty-nine Spanish mine operators, placing it fourth in number of mining interests. While *indios* predominated, a small number African slaves and *mulatos* worked in mining gangs (*quadrillas*), while most labored as skilled workers in various jobs relating to ore extraction and refinement.[19] Although a clear minority, *españoles* worked as overseers and skilled tradesmen. In the 1590s, the overall non-Spanish labor force numbered over six hundred.[20] The settlement's miners owned forty-two slaves. Indigenous labor was divided between wage labor and corvée labor supplied by the *repartimiento*. Wage laborers outnumbered *repartimiento* labor, 415 to 166. Like the parish of Santa Veracruz, Guanajuato represents a demographically diverse middle ground. While it was not the largest mining center, ethnic diversity characterized its labor force. Finally, Guanajuato's location off the main north–south trade artery of the silver mining region made it a crossroads for individuals looking for work or hoping to strike it rich in the northern frontier of New Spain.

To track change over time, two temporal periods were chosen from each parish. For both parishes the earliest extant records were selected for the first period: Santa Veracruz, 1576; Guanajuato, 1605. The second period was selected based on the availability of records and so as to provide a comparable sample from at least one generation later: Santa Veracruz, 1626; Guanajuato, 1631. The length of each sample was determined by the frequency of marriages in the parish and the need to collect a sufficient sample size for comparison. The greater frequency of marriages in Santa Veracruz allowed for five-year samples, while the lower frequency in Guanajuato necessitated ten-year samples. Although the early periods examined for each parish are separated by almost thirty years, the later conquest and slower development of

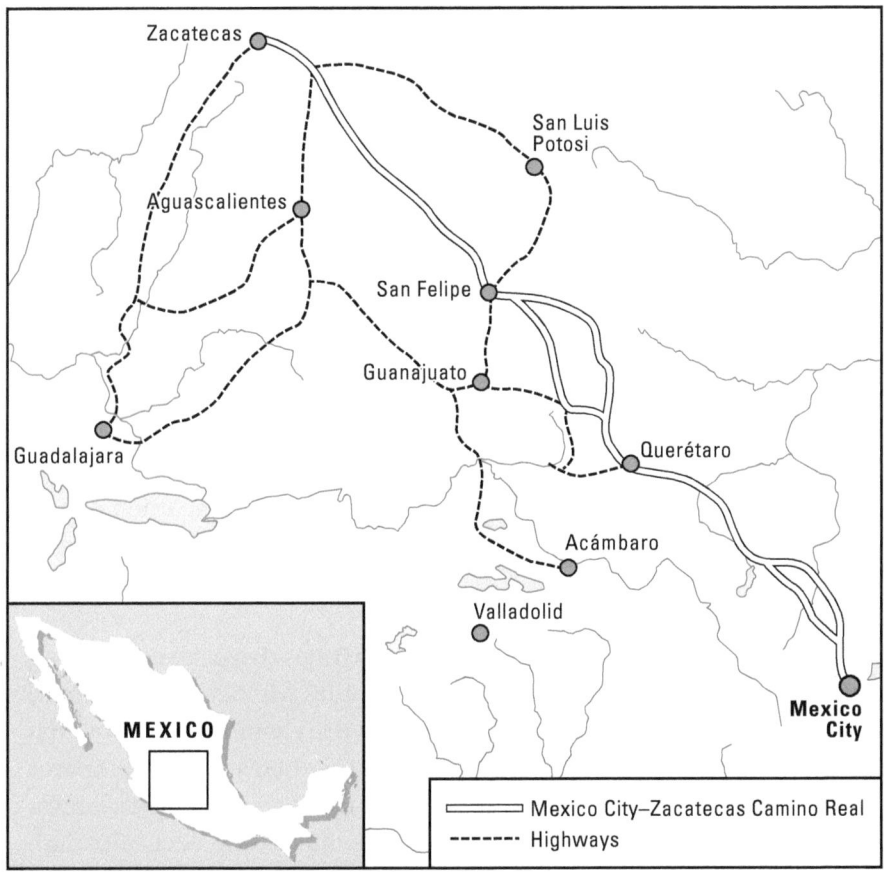

Map 2. Northern New Spain, including trade routes between Mexico City and various mining and ranching communities. Copyright © 2016 by the University of Oklahoma Press. All rights reserved.

the north means that the early data for both parishes preserves the marriage patterns from approximately fifty years after the foundation of each community.[21]

The most significant divergence between the two data sets lies in the preservation of *indio* marriages. For Guanajuato, marriage registers exist for *españoles* (including *mestizos, mulatos,* and *negros*) and *indios* for both periods. While Santa Veracruz has *español* and *indio* registers for the early period, there is no evidence of an extant *indio* marriage register for the later period. In the extant Santa Veracruz registers,

Table 5.1
COHEN'S KAPPA FOR SANTA VERACRUZ AND GUANAJUATO

	Early Period	Later Period
Santa Veracruz	.639	.777
	(1576–1581)	(1626–1631)
Guanajuato	.676	.727
	(1605–1615)	(1631–1641)

women of all *géneros* appear in both *español* and *indio* registers, yet only *indio* grooms appear in the extant *indio* register from the sixteenth century. Lacking an *indio* register for the seventeenth century, the data set does not record any marriages by *indio* grooms to women of any *género* for the later period.[22] Even lacking these marriages, the records from Santa Veracruz provide compelling evidence of marriage patterns among its residents.

During the periods under study, both parishes demonstrated strong endogamy. Scholars of marriage in colonial Mexico have gauged relative endogamy through the use of two statistical measures that account for group size and sex ratios. First, Cohen's kappa compares the number of actual endogamous marriages in a sample to the number of "expected" endogamous marriages that would occur through random paring.[23] Second, "conditional kappas" can be calculated for men and women of each *género* within the larger population to determine the degree to which they tend toward endogamy or exogamy. In each case, the calculation results in a value between -1 and 1. Values closer to 1 indicate increasing endogamy, values closer to 0 reflect more random pairings, and values approaching -1 suggest increasing preference for exogamy. The Cohen's kappa values for the four samples for this study range between .639 and .777, with the kappa increasing for each parish between early and later periods (see table 5.1). These values indicate a high degree of endogamy that increased over time.

Despite the strong overall trend toward endogamy, conditional kappa values demonstrate differences in the relative endogamy of different *géneros*. The parent groups of the colonial order (*españoles, negros, indios*) demonstrated greater endogamy than those of mixed

Table 5.2
MARRIAGES, SANTA VERACRUZ, 1576–1581

Spouses	española	mestiza	india	negra	mulata	Men
español	109	5	9	0	2	125
mestizo	4	10	6	0	1	21
indio	1	2	37	0	0	40
negro	0	0	5	8	1	14
mulato	1	1	3	5	0	10
Women	115	18	60	13	4	210

NOTE: Table combines slaves and free persons of the same *género*.

Table 5.3
CONDITIONAL KAPPAS, SANTA VERACRUZ, 1576–1581

Género	Male	Female	Combined
español	0.717	0.871	0.787
indio	0.895	0.526	0.663
negro	0.543	0.588	0.565
mestizo	0.427	0.506	0.463
mulato	–0.019	-0.050	–0.028

ancestry (*mestizos* and *mulatos*). In the early period these differences were quite large. Tables 5.2–5.5 present the marriage patterns and conditional kappas for each parish's early period.

In each early sample, *españoles* manifested the greatest endogamy of parent *géneros*, followed by *indios* and *negros*. In his study of late-seventeenth-century Mexico City, Douglas Cope found that rates of endogamy correlated with *género* size: the larger the group, the greater tendency toward endogamy.[24] The samples examined for Santa Veracruz and Guanajuato did not show that trend. *Españoles* and *negros* tended to be more endogamous regardless of their relative size in the population. For example, in early Guanajuato, the thirty-one *españoles* tended more toward endogamy than the almost three hundred *indios*. In early Santa Veracruz, the smaller *negro* population similarly manifested a greater tendency to intermarriage than did *mestizos*. Such

Table 5.4
Marriages, Guanajuato, 1605–1615

Spouses	española	mestiza	india	negra	mulata	Men
español	15	0	0	1	0	16
mestizo	0	0	1	0	1	2
indio	0	1	143	0	5	149
negro	0	0	1	4	2	7
mulato	0	1	5	0	1	7
Women	15	2	150	5	9	181

NOTE: Table combines slaves and free persons of the same *género* and excludes *chinos* ($n = 1$).

Table 5.5
Conditional Kappas, Guanajuato, 1605–1615

Género	Male	Female	Combined
español	0.932	1.000	0.965
indio	0.765	0.736	0.750
negro	0.559	0.792	0.656
mulato	0.098	0.075	0.085
mestizo	–0.011	–0.011	–0.011

variance reflects the strong social pressures operating among *negros* and *españoles* regardless of their relative size.

For *españoles*, especially women, marrying outside of the *género* could diminish one's social standing in the eyes of contemporaries. In contrast, the low relative status ascribed to *negros* increased the difficulty of finding spouses outside their *género*. This pattern manifested itself most strongly among enslaved *negras* who tended to find fewer grooms from other *géneros* than their male counterparts, a trend that other studies on colonial marriage patterns have noted.[25] In contrast to Cope's findings, these parishes show that in an early period parent *géneros*, regardless of relative size, tended toward more endogamy than *géneros* of mixed ancestry.

In the early period of each parish, the conditional kappa for *indios* fell between *españoles* and *negros*; however, the patterns of men and women of this *género* varied between each parish. In Guanajuato, *indio* brides and grooms tended to marry similarly. Regardless of gender, *indios* married other *indios* or they married *mulatos*. In 1605, *indios* and *mulatos* represented the two largest groups in the mining community. *Indios* accounted for 86 percent of the mining town's residents, while *mulatos* comprised 9 percent.[26] The data suggest that within this community *indio* men and women were equally likely to choose spouses from among the *mulatos* with whom they lived and worked. In Santa Veracruz, *indias* married grooms from other *géneros* far more frequently than their male counterparts. In choosing exogamous spouses, *indias* favored *españoles* and *mestizos* over *negros* and *mulatos*. The frequency of *español-india* unions may reflect a dearth of marriageable *españolas*. The low rate of female immigration led to a gender disparity among *españoles*. Especially in the late sixteenth century, this benefited some *mestizas*, as will be discussed below. The marriage patterns suggest that *españoles* may have turned to *indias* when unable to find *españolas* or *mestizas*. Additionally, as members of the kingdom's largest *género* group, *indias* were ubiquitous in the urban environment. They worked in Spanish households, on the streets, and in the markets. Men of most *géneros* would have had frequent interactions with *indias* in a variety of settings, interactions that may have fostered affective ties. Whatever the cause, the disparity between *indio* and *india* conditional kappas in Santa Veracruz indicates that *indias* were more likely to marry outside their *género* than their male counterparts.

In the sample from early Guanajuato, *mestizo* and *mulato* marriages resembled statistically random pairing. Nevertheless, men and women of these groups certainly did not marry by random chance. The frequency of *mulato-indio* unions likely reflects the interplay between demographics and occupation. *Indios* outnumbered *mulatos* by ten to one, and few other partners were present in any sizable number. *Españoles, mestizos,* and *negros* only represented 5 percent of the community's population. As was mentioned above, shared work, residence, and possibly kinship likely fostered ties between *mulato* and *indio* residents.

In the sample from early Santa Veracruz, *mestizo* marriages produced a kappa just below that of *negros*. In the last quarter of the sixteenth century, Mexico City's *mestizos* had already begun to favor *español*,

Table 5.6
MARRIAGES, SANTA VERACRUZ, 1626–1631

Spouses	española	mestiza	india	negra	mulata	Men
español	261	10	3	2	5	281
mestizo	8	18	3	1	3	33
indio	0	0	0	0	0	0
negro	0	2	8	138	5	153
mulato	0	10	2	5	17	34
Women	269	40	16	146	30	501

NOTE: Table combines slaves and free persons of the same *género* and excludes *castizos* (n = 6) and *chinos* (n = 4).

Table 5.7
CONDITIONAL KAPPAS, SANTA VERACRUZ, 1626–1631

Género	Male	Female	Combined
negro	0.862	0.921	0.890
español	0.846	0.932	0.887
mulato	0.468	0.535	0.499
mestizo	0.506	0.411	0.454
indio	NA	NA	NA

mestizo, or *indio* partners. Even though *mestizas* were more endogamous than *mestizos*, they married *españoles* slightly more frequently. In contrast, *mulatos* resembled the random pattern. There were no endogamous *mulato* marriages in Santa Veracruz. *Mulatos* favored *negras* or *indias*, while three of four *mulata* brides married two *españoles* and one *mestizo*. The small size of the *mulato* population likely facilitated marriages to partners from larger groups. Additionally, the absence of *españolas* seems to have benefited some *mulatas*. Taken together, both early samples indicate that *mestizos* and *mulatos* tended to marry outside their *género* more frequently than *españoles*, *negros*, and *indios*, and that when doing so *mestizos* and *mulatos* selected spouses in different ways.

In the later samples, parent groups remained more endogamous than *mestizos* and *mulatos*. The greatest change between early and later

Table 5.8
MARRIAGES, GUANAJUATO, 1631–1641

Spouses	española	mestiza	india	negra	mulata	Men
español	20	5	0	0	1	26
mestizo	1	13	8	0	1	23
indio	0	1	124	0	2	127
negro	0	0	3	34	2	39
mulato	0	1	15	2	12	30
Women	21	20	150	36	18	245

NOTE: Table combines slaves and free persons of the same *género* and excludes *chinos* ($n = 1$) and castizos ($n = 1$).

Table 5.9
CONDITIONAL KAPPAS, GUANAJUATO, 1631–1641

Género	Male	Female	Combined
negro	0.850	0.934	0.890
español	0.747	0.898	0.816
indio	0.940	0.643	0.764
mestizo	0.519	0.629	0.569
mulato	0.353	0.621	0.450

samples can be found in the rates of endogamy and conditional kappas for those of mixed ancestry (see tables 5.6–5.9). In both parishes *mestizo* and *mulato* marriages became more endogamous over time, although they still trailed behind *negros, españoles,* and *indios.*

The conditional kappas of the later samples from both communities fall into two clear clusters: one containing parent *géneros* and one for *mestizos* and *mulatos.* Almost every parent *género* became more endogamous. Only *españoles* in Guanajuato showed slight decrease in their conditional kappas. Among parent groups, *negros* went from being the least endogamous *género* to becoming the most endogamous. Such a shift may reflect the increased size of the marrying population and a growing number of slaves. In the period between the early sample and late sample, both parishes saw a large increase in the number of enslaved *negros* brought during the height of the slave trade between

1580 and 1640.²⁷ During this period, African-born slaves married more frequently than creole slaves and more endogamously.²⁸ Both parishes show evidence for this trend during their later sample. In each parish, *mestizo* and *mulato* conditional kappas increased from the earlier period but remained clustered together below the range of the parent *géneros*.

In Guanajuato, *indio* men represented the most endogamous group, slightly more endogamous than even *españolas*. In contrast, *india* brides participated in half of all *mulato* marriages and over one-third of all *mestizo* marriages. The conditional kappa for *indias* clustered more closely with *mestizas* and *mulatas* than it did *negras* or *españolas*. These patterns appear to be rooted in the gender disparities in the marriage pool. *Mestizo* and *mulato* men outnumbered their female counterparts in the marriage pool. *India* brides likely represented the most numerous group of free women in the settlement and therefore a reasonable choice for *mestizos* and *mulatos*.

Mestizos continued to find most spouses among other *mestizos* or among *españoles* and *indias*. In Santa Veracruz, *mestizas* married *españoles* more frequently than their male counterparts, but only slightly. In Guanajuato, the gender difference manifested itself more strongly: just under a quarter of *mestizas* married *españoles*. In contrast, only two of twenty-five *mestizos* married *españolas*. Over time, *mulatos* began to more clearly manifest a pattern of marriages to each other or to *negros* and *indios*. This tendency emerged strongest in Guanajuato with twenty-nine of thirty grooms finding spouses among *indias, mulatas,* and *negras*. Similarly, sixteen of eighteen *mulatas* married *mulatos, negros,* or *indios*. The *mulato-india* pairing appeared most frequently, suggesting sustained affinities between *mulatos* and *indias* in the mining camp. In Santa Veracruz, the lack of any *indio* grooms in the sample hinders the analysis of this trend. Even so, Mexico City *mulatos* manifested a slightly different pattern. Marriages to other *mulatos* and *negros* remained important and accounted for over half of *mulato* marriages. However, *mulato* men married *mestizas* more frequently than *negras* or *indias*, and, among *mulatas*, marriages to *españoles* were as frequent as those to *negros*.

The variation between the urban setting of Santa Veracruz and the rural mining camp of Guanajuato may explain some of these differences. Residents of Santa Veracruz may have manifested greater socioeconomic diversity within any specific *género* category than their counterparts in the north. For example, most *españoles* in Guanajuato formed part of a small clique of elite civil officials, mine owners, and overseers.[29] The early-seventeenth-century *español* residents of Santa Veracruz likely held a greater range of economic positions and social ranks. While a marriage between an *español* and a *mulata* in Guanajuato could prove socially disastrous to an *español* within that community, the same pairing might not have had the same impact in Mexico City, especially if the *español* and *mulata* were both members of the evolving plebian milieu.[30] Similarly, the increased frequency of *mulato-mestiza* marriages in Mexico City likely grew out of the greater incidence of quotidian interactions between men and women of these two groups within the ranks of non-elite urban residents. As late as the 1690s, *mulato-mestiza* marriages ranked as the second-most-frequent pairing for *mulato* men and *mestiza* women in Mexico City.[31]

Overall, the parish marriage registers reveal several important trends. First, *mestizos* tended to marry endogamously or with members of their parent groups, *españoles* or *indios*. Second, *mestizas* tended to marry *españoles* slightly more frequently than their male counterparts. Third, although initially highly exogamous, over time *mulatos* tended toward endogamy or marriages to *negros* and *indios*. Within this trend, marriages to persons of indigenous descent (*indias* or *mestizas*) remained important, accounting for one-fifth to one-third of all *mulato* marriages.

The rich narratives preserved in Inquisition cases can help elucidate the dynamics that produced the patterns observed in parish records. A close reading of such cases reveals that most marriage trends grew out of familial ties, occupation, and social networks. The following personal stories found within Inquisition cases provide glimpses into the lived experience of early colonial *mestizos* and *mulatos*. Their experiences attest to common patterns of life embodied in marriage trends as well as shed light on the diversity found within and between these *géneros*.

MESTIZO MARRIAGES

A good example of how occupation and cultural fluency could foster *mestizo* marriage patterns can be found in the case against Bartolomé Hernández.[32] Born in Puebla around 1540, Bartolomé was the child of Bartolomé Hernández, a *cantero* (stonecutter) from Puebla, and María Hernández, a *mestiza*. Although he did not know any of his grandparents, he was aware of a half-brother, Alvaro, on his father's side. Bartolomé had been trained as an *arriero* (muleteer) and spent much of his life traveling between Mexico City and Puebla. At the time of his trial in 1578 he worked primarily as a trader transporting honey from Actopan to Mexico City and Puebla.[33]

The Inquisition case revealed that Bartolomé had contracted marriages in two different social and cultural settings. In the 1560s, Bartomolé found himself living in the indigenous pueblo of Totomihuacan.[34] Work as a muleteer or trader likely drew Bartolomé to the community. Once there he entered into a relationship with an *india* named Veronica Ana. His time in Totomihuacan required fluency in Nahuatl and familiarity with Nahua culture. The witnesses to his life with Veronica Ana were *indios*, and these included Juan Matias, the father of Veronica Ana, Don Pedro de Morales, *gobernador*, and Luis de Castañeda, an *indio principal* and alcalde. All residents of Totomihuacan made their statements in Nahuatl. In 1563, the local friar, Bernaldo de Vargas, married Bartolomé and Veronica in a public ceremony attended by most of the community. The couple lived together in her father's home for many years and had three children. Sometime before 1570, Bartolomé left Totomihuacan and made his way to Tlaxcala.

Bartolomé appears to have established ties within this different social and geographic setting. Although his narrative did not elaborate on what brought him to Tlaxcala, his occupation likely played a role in his relocation. Once in the city, he began a relationship with Agustina de Collacos, a *mestiza*. This relationship began as a secret tryst between the two but was eventually discovered by Agustina's father, Pedro de Collacos. Neither partner described how the relationship began, although Agustina's sister suggested that Bartolomé may have been living in the Collacos home.

The Collacos family had strong ties to both Hispanic and indigenous culture. Pedro de Collacos had worked as the *nahuatlato* (translator of Nahuatl) for the bishop of Tlaxcala. Pedro de Collacos was married to an *india* named Mariá and had three daughters, all considered *mestizas*. In his testimony Bartolomé called Pedro a *mestizo*, although no other witnesses did so. Pedro's occupation made him an intermediary between *españoles* and *indios* and might have contributed to his ascription as a *mestizo*. Despite his ties to indigenous culture, Pedro manifested Spanish cultural values when he responded to the illicit affair between Bartolomé and Agustina. After discovering the liaison, Pedro demanded that Bartolomé marry his daughter. Iberian standards of honor considered the illicit sexual relationship of Pedro's unmarried daughter to be a stain on his honor and that of his daughter. If widely known, Agustina's premarital relationship with Barolomé would have cast doubt on her virtue and sullied her female honor.[35] In his inability to properly seclude his daughter from unwanted advances and protect her virginity, Pedro lost honor as father and head of house. By demanding that the lovers marry, Pedro sought to rectify the loss of honor through a public and legitimate marriage. Although Pedro succeeded in marrying his daughter to her lover, the marriage made Bartolomé a bigamist.

Bartolomé's marriages demonstrate the importance of shared spaces and culture. Bartolomé likely entered Totomihuacan as a trader or muleteer. There his fluency in Nahuatl, possibly acquired from his *mestiza* mother or while traveling, allowed him to find an indigenous bride and live among her fellow *indios*. Bartolomé's extensive stay in Totomihuacan suggests his comfort in that environment and the construction of extensive social ties to members of that community. Once in Tlaxcala, Bartolomé demonstrated the ability to live and interact within a Hispanicized social circle. Although the Collacos family had connections to indigenous residents of Tlaxcala, Pedro Collacos was an *español* or *mestizo* with strong relationships with Spanish ecclesiastical elites. Pedro's response to Bartolomé and Agustina's affair speaks to the predominately Hispanic cultural orientation of that household. Ultimately Bartolomé's occupation and familiarity with indigenous cultures had helped him find his first spouse, while physical mobility and ties to Hispanic society likely brought him into contact with his second.

Another example of *mestizos* finding spouses through occupation and shared residence can be seen in the case of Pedro de Carranza.[36] Born in 1544, Pedro grew up the illegitimate child of a conquistador, Pedro Carranza, and an *india* named Catalina. Although born out of wedlock, Pedro grew up among his relatives. At the time of his trial in 1572, he had maintained connections to a half-sister, Ana Carranza, an *española*. Through his half-sister, he was brother-in-law to Antonio de Espinosa, a Mexico City printer. Pedro had another *español* brother-in-law, Bernardo de Oñate, who worked as a *platero* (silversmith) and *ensayador* (assayer). These connections to extended *español* relatives helped him find a place as a *criado* (servant or dependent) in the home of Gonzalo Cerrezo, *alguacil mayor* of Mexico City. Cerrezo was married to María de Espinosa, who may have been the sister of his brother-in-law Antonio de Espinosa.

While in the Cerrezo home, Pedro met Inés de la Gama, an *española*, who also served the household as a *criada*. In the sixteenth century, term *criada*, or its male version *criado*, could have various connotations. Generally it described domestic servants and employees within a household. In some cases it could also refer to wards or dependents that lived more like kin than hired laborers.[37] According to Inés, Pedro served as *camarero* (steward or valet) to Gonzalo Cerrezo. In large Spanish homes, the *camarero* held a privileged position because of the intimate relationship his work fostered with the head of house.[38] Pedro likely acquired his post through the efforts of his Spanish relatives. The exact relationship between Inés and the Cerrezos cannot be determined. Bernardo de Oñate implied that she served Cerrezo's wife, possibly in a position analogous to that of Pedro. As an *española* born in Mexico City, her family probably facilitated her placement in the Cerrezo home.

While living with the Cerrezos, Inés and Pedro struck up a friendly relationship. He recalled that at times he would joke with the other *criadas*, sometimes pretending to marry each other. One day when María de Espinosa threatened to beat her *criadas*, Pedro interceded to stop the punishment by claiming that he and Inés had been married. The ploy failed and only angered María de Espinosa further. The encounter led to Pedro's dismissal from the Cerrezo home. Nevertheless, the relationship between Inés and Pedro continued. The couple's accounts of their actual marriage differed. Inés claimed that Pedro had proposed a real marriage about a month after he had left the Cerezo home. She had accepted, and they were wed in the home of Juan Bravo by Dr. Bravo, *provisor* of the archdiocese. Pedro recalled a different chain of events. He claimed to have traveled to Peru for several years. Once back, Pedro claimed, Dr. Bravo had contacted him and asked that he marry Inés in order to remove her from the Cerrezo home. Bravo feared that Inés's poor attitude would eventually lead María de Espinosa to punish her severely. Pedro confessed to the tribunal that he had only married Inés after Dr. Bravo promised to annul the marriage once Inés had left the Cerrezo home. Given their ages, Inés and Pedro were likely only in their late teens when they married, sometime around 1557. The marriage was not a happy one and only lasted a year or so. Inés claimed that Pedro did not treat her well and failed to provide for her support and welfare. She even claimed that he once threatened to kill her. Eventually the unhappy couple separated when Pedro told her to go off on her own. Inés made sure to note that even though she lived independently after their separation, she remained an honorable woman.

After leaving Inés, Pedro sought his fortune, eventually meeting Isabel de la Fuente, a *mulata*, while staying in the home of Hernán Núñez, a tailor. Isabel was the sister-in-law of Núñez. The couple married in 1567, after which Pedro and Isabel moved from Mexico City to an *estancia* owned by Francisco Rodríguez, a goldsmith, located near Coyoacan. There Pedro supported his family selling chickens and other goods. By the time of his trial in 1572, Pedro and Isabel had four children, Ana, Catalina, María, and Matías. When arrested by the Inquisition, Pedro insisted that his marriage to Inés had been annulled by the *provisor*. Unable to provide concrete proof of the annulment or witnesses to his conversations with Dr. Bravo, the Inquisition convicted him of bigamy.

Pedro's case illustrates the importance of shared residence in spouse selection. He met both his wives while living under the same roof. Shared occupation further contributed to his marriage to Inés. This marriage illustrates the ways in which some *mestizos* forged ties with *españoles*. As the son of a conquistador, Pedro found himself working as a dependent for a local official. Working in a Spanish household he interacted with other *criados* and *criadas* of various *géneros*. Within this shared setting of work and residence, the *mestizo* son of a conquistador married an *española* serving as a *criada*. His second marriage also occurred through shared residence. Although the case does not describe the inner workings of the Nuñez home, Pedro's stay there allowed him to meet Isabel de la Fuente, the sister-in-law of his host. Following their marriage, Pedro and Isabel set up a life for themselves, renting a place on an *estancia*. Pedro may have met his future landlord, a goldsmith, through his brother-in-law the silversmith. Finally, although *mestizo-mulato* marriages were relatively rare, Pedro's experiences illustrate how multiethnic membership of many households fostered a diversity of unions, both common and uncommon.

MARRIAGEABLE *MESTIZAS*

In the first century of colonial rule, the growth of Spanish society suffered from a very real problem of reproduction. Conquest-era emigration was heavily male, and the continued opportunities offered by campaigns of conquest through the 1540s and 1550s ensured a large population of *españoles* with few *españolas*. The surviving records of emigrants preserved in the Casa de Contratación (House of Trade) shows that from 1520 to 1539 women represented less than 7 percent of transatlantic passengers.[39] Of that number, only 54 percent were young unmarried women. The documentation does not provide the marital status of most male emigrants, unless they traveled with their family. Nevertheless, the disparity in numbers insured that, once in the Americas, *españoles* found themselves in a society profoundly lacking in *españolas*.

By the late 1540s, the problem of such a large single male population became apparent to the crown. By mid-century, the crown had begun to enact provisions insuring a more balanced emigration to the colonies. In 1544, and throughout the century, the crown ordered that men married in Spain wishing reside in the Americas were required to travel with their wives and children or they would be forced to return.[40] These laws sought to protect the sanctity of marriage by insuring that spouses lived together but also served to help ensure the growth of a stable Spanish population. The crown hoped that the emigration of families would help bring order to the male-dominated conquest-era society and reduce the gender disparity between Spanish men and women. Lamentably for the crown, these policies did not correct the disparity, and throughout the sixteenth-century viceroys complained about the proliferation of single men and their penchant for vagabondage.[41]

Even as the political and social order stabilized during the second half of the sixteenth century, the gender balance among European arrivals did not achieve parity. From the 1540s onward, women emigrants increased their overall percentage of all emigrants steadily. During the 1540s and 1550s, female passengers accounted for just over 16 percent of all emigrants, roughly fifteen hundred of nine thousand persons.[42] Of those, single women remained the majority but only just, accounting for 54 percent of all female arrivals. In the twenty years following 1560, female emigrants dramatically increased to 28 percent of all travelers, or five thousand out of almost eighteen thousand persons.[43] The percentage of single women grew slightly from 54 to 60 percent of all female emigrants. In the final twenty years of the century, women decreased slightly to 26 percent of all emigrants, or twenty-five hundred out of ninety-five hundred arrivals.[44] Of these, roughly 60 percent were unmarried young women. In short, even as Spanish colonial society became more stable and Iberian women began emigrating in larger numbers, single women traveling to the colonies never exceeded one-fifth of all emigrants. The demographics of *español* emigration to the Americas and the increased importance of marriage for social and political advancement helped create an environment in which *mestizas* became valuable social and familial commodities.

In a society lacking *españolas*, socially respectable *mestizas* were seen as viable marriage partners for those unable to secure the hand of an *española*. The families of *mestizas* recognized their value and in many cases protected these women even if they were illegitimate in the hopes that they could secure a marriage to an *español*. In most cases, the dominant factor facilitating *mestiza-español* marriages was the ability of the woman to maintain the standards of female honor expected of an *española*, especially chastity and public modesty.[45] Consequently, Spanish families sought to preserve the honor of their *mestiza* kin by sheltering them within the home or in the homes of other *españoles*. The following examples illuminate the important position *mestizas* held in their families and their role as potential spouses for *españoles*.

An example of a family treating its *mestiza* kin as it would an *española* can be seen in the life of Ana Melgarejo.⁴⁶ The daughter of Licenciado Velázquez and Juana, an *india* from Chalco, Ana was born around 1540 and grew up in Michoacan in the home of her father. She grew up alongside her half-sister Francisca Velázquez and after her father's death lived in the home of her brother-in-law, Juan Pérez Calvillo. None of the *español* witnesses who knew Ana called her a *mestiza,* suggesting she may have straddled the amorphous boundary between tacit *española* and *mestiza.*

Ana was a dependent of Juan Pérez Calvillo, who served as her guardian and had an interest in maintaining her honor and securing for her a socially advantageous marriage. In 1559, Pérez Calvillo met a new arrival in town, an *español* named Francisco Gutiérrez. At the time, Francisco worked as an assistant to the *alcalde mayor.* Previously he had participated in the conquest of the Yucatán and had some training in medicine. As Ana's guardian, Pérez Calvillo brokered a marriage with Francisco. Don Diego Pérez Negron Gordillo, *chantre* of the cathedral church of Michoacán, betrothed the couple in Juan's home.⁴⁷ Many other prominent members of Michoacán society attended the ceremony. Following their union, Francisco and Ana lived in Pérez Calvillo's home for a time before leaving to live in the home of Miguel Díaz, another *vecino* of Michoacán.

On the feast of San Francisco, while the entire town was out watching the processions, a man from Campeche noticed Francisco and Ana holding hands. He told several of the *vecinos* that he recognized Francisco and knew that he was married in Yucatán to a woman named Catalina de Vargas. This news spread rapidly, and Juan Pérez Calvillo acted quickly in defense of his sister-in-law's honor. Pérez Calvillo denounced Francisco to the *alcalde mayor,* and Francisco was investigated by ecclesiastical authorities under orders from the bishop. He was found guilty, publicly penanced, and branded for his crime. For her part, Ana acted quickly to have the marriage annulled by the bishop. Her request was granted, and she subsequently married two more times, in each case to an *español.*

Ana Melgarejo's case provides a window into understanding the place of socially prominent *mestizas* within the social order of the mid sixteenth century. Ana's life within her natal home and that of her brother-in-law mirrored that of unwed *españolas*. Her guardian brokered a marriage to an *español* whom he believed to have good prospects. After her marriage, Ana's family helped support the newlyweds. Once Francisco's past came to light, the speedy reaction by Pérez Calvillo demonstrates a concerted effort to protect Ana's reputation and future marriage prospects. The pace of the investigation also suggests that the community as a whole recognized the severity of Francisco's transgression and the need to secure a future for Ana. Moreover, Ana took an active part in rehabilitating her honor. Her successful petition for an annulment protected her status and ensured that she could seek a respectable marriage despite the dishonor brought by Francisco. Her efforts succeeded; she was able to remarry a Spanish merchant and later a Spanish tradesman in Mexico City.

Another case illustrating the privileged position of *mestizas* can be seen in the life of Mari Sánchez. Born around 1554, she was the *mestiza* daughter of Martín Alonso, *español,* and Juana Sánchez.[48] As a young woman she lived in Mexico City in the home of Andrés Moreno where she worked as a *criada*. Unfortunately we do not know how Mari came to live with Moreno. She was neither an orphan nor a foundling; her parents lived in a mining town. It is possible that Moreno was a distant kinsman or family friend. The testimony did not describe their relationship fully. Whether she lived as a ward or served as a domestic, her case demonstrates how her patron worked to preserve her honor in the face of scandalous behavior.

In 1570, at the age of sixteen, she began a friendly relationship with a young *español* named Pedro de Padilla. They had direct communication and sent notes through intermediaries. During the course of their conversations, Mari complained that her employers treated her poorly. Ostensibly acting in her interests, Pedro took it upon himself to intercede and remove her from her situation. Indeed, Mari's complaints may have been a subterfuge intended to spur Pedro into helping her escape the seclusion of her guardian's home. One night in late April 1570, Pedro sneaked into Mari's home and abducted her. After taking her to several other residences he left her in the care of an *india* named Agustina, possibly a relative of Mari. The investigation into Mari's disappearance proceeded quickly and Pedro was arrested. Moreno, Mari's employer, brought a suit against Pedro for taking the young *doncella* from his home. As her patron and guardian, Andrés had an interest in protecting Mari's honor for both her sake and his own. Any dishonor brought on a *criada* reflected on the honor of the family.[49] Faced with criminal prosecution and the possibility of capital punishment, Pedro agreed to wed Mari. Moreno and the authorities acted quickly, and the couple was married by clerics from the cathedral church of Mexico City within days of the abduction. Afterward Mari and Pedro lived together as husband and wife, and she bore him a child. After two years he abandoned her.

At the time of her abduction it was not known that Pedro had been married in Spain before arriving in Mexico. In the heated aftermath of Pedro's abduction of Mari, he had failed to disclose his previous vows. Once arrested by the Inquisition, Pedro argued that his marriage to Mari was not valid, as Andrés had coerced him into marrying her. According this logic, the coercion used by Andrés to force Pedro to marry his *criada* undermined the sacramental validity of the marriage, which required free will by both parties. In acquiescing, Pedro felt he was being deceitful to Andrés' interests but not violating the sacrament of marriage, as the union did not meet the spiritual prerequisites. In his confession, Pedro also noted that after the marriage he had asked the *provisor* to annul the marriage, but his petition was not acted upon. In the end, the inquisitors did not agree with Pedro's claims. He was sentenced to public penance, one hundred lashes, and perpetual exile from the Indies.

The events surrounding Mari's abduction illustrate that her employers had an interest in guarding their *criada*'s honor and protecting her marriageability. The rapid response of Moreno to her abduction suggests that the dishonor caused by her abduction threatened his honor as the head of house as well as her own female honor. Even if Pedro did not seduce or force himself upon Mari, her absence from Moreno's home in the company of a young man tarnished her reputation as a *doncella*. The subjective public view of such events was more important than an objective factual accounting, especially when honor was at stake.[50] By emphasizing that she was a *doncella*, Moreno asserted that in his home her feminine virtue was being protected and publicly acknowledged. Moreno's quick action sought to minimize the damage caused by her unchaste behavior and secure the least dishonorable result, a marriage. While we cannot know if Moreno would have supported a marriage between the two under normal circumstances, his emphatic demand that they be married certainly reflects his protection of her public honor and that of his family.

These cases do not represent the ideal. The fact that both of these women were married to men who were already married makes these cases somewhat exceptional. Nevertheless, the experiences of Ana and Marí provide a unique window into the marriage options available to some *mestizas*. In each case, social, residential, and cultural proximity to *españoles* proved crucial. Both Marí and Ana were well integrated into Spanish households. In Ana's case her family recognized and raised her, while Marí was integrated into a Spanish home via her status as *criada*. Similarly, each woman lived within the Hispanic cultural sphere and was cognizant of the value society placed on her sexual purity, her honor. Spanish guardians acted typically in brokering the marriages of honorable young women.[51] That the marriages did not result as their Spanish brokers would have hoped does not detract from the fact that these two women experienced marriage similarly to *españolas*.

These cases help illustrate the social relationships that allowed some *mestizas*, particularly those who were protected by their families and employers, to marry *españoles*. The protection they received allowed them to maintain social standards of female honor—they could claim to be *doncellas*.[52] Many of these women could bring important financial resources and social connections into a marriage, thereby increasing their value as spouses. In this regard, they were very similar to tacit *españolas*; however, unlike their counterparts, they were commonly regarded as *mestizas*. This was an important qualitative difference. In the eyes of their contemporaries they were not *españolas*; nevertheless, their embodiment of Spanish cultural norms allowed them to secure marriages to *españoles*. In this way, these cases show that in the early colonial setting the public ascription of *mestiza* did not necessarily prejudice a woman's marriage prospects.

MULATO SOCIAL NETWORKS

The incidence of *mulato* endogamy represents a significant diachronic trend. Herman Bennett has argued that the incidence of marriage between Africans and their descendants resulted from the formation of a creole consciousness in colonial Latin America. Through their exposure to Catholicism and shared experiences of juridical subjugation, Africans and their descendants fashioned new identities that helped underpin a commonly held sense of community.[53] Importantly, Bennett argues that this consciousness did not reflect a shared racialized identity among Afro-Mexicans.[54] Similarly, Frank Proctor found that while Africans and their descendents forged communities that transcended the *género* labels of *mulato* and *negro*, they did not develop an overtly political "racial consciousness."[55] The frequency of *mulato* endogamy in the late sixteenth century provides further evidence for the creation of creole communities composed of individuals of African descent. The narratives found in sixteenth century Inquisition records provide evidence that *mulato* endogamy and creole Afro-Mexican communities evolved out of social networks formed between *negros* and *mulatos*. Most endogamous marriages between *mulatos* occurred because the two spouses were members of the same Afro-Mexican social networks. Importantly, these Afro-Mexican networks included *negros, morenos, mulatos,* slaves, and freemen. The following cases provide some of the earliest examples of *mulatos* actively forging their own extended communities from among those with whom they lived, worked, and socialized.

An excellent example of the relationship between Afro-Mexican social networks and *mulato* endogamy can be seen in the Inquisition case against Mariana de la Cruz and Antonio Hernández.[56] Most contemporaries considered Mariana and Antonio to be *mulatos*, although in two instances Mariana was described as a *negra amulatada* and a *mulata negra* (as discussed in chapter 4). Despite moving through various parts of New Spain, Mariana spent much of her life among other Afro-Mexicans and through those social networks met her future spouses.

Mariana began her life in the north of New Spain. She was born to Juan *criollo negro*, a slave of Don Francisco Tello, and Marta *india* around 1565.[57] The details of her youth are sparse. She was born in the town of Zinapecuaro and eventually made her way to San Miguel de Chichimecas. Around 1585, she married her first husband, Antón Ximénez *negro biafora*, a slave of Hernando Altamirano, in the presence of many *indios* and *negros* from San Miguel. Isabel *negra* and Agustin *moreno*, a married couple, and slaves from the Altamirano household attested to the couple's marriage. Pedro, an *indio*, and Catalina, a *negra* slave of Altamirano, served as *padrinos* (godparents) at the wedding. After the wedding, Mariana and Antón took up married life together in the home of Altamirano. The couple bore a daughter, Andrea. Eventually, the slaves of Hernando Altamirano, including Antón and Mariana, were sent to Mexico City where they took up residence in the home of Doña Agustina Altamirano.

In Mexico City, Mariana began to make new social connections. On the feast of Saint John the Baptist, June 24, 1592, she met Antonio Hernández in front of a store. Both Mariana and Antonio confessed that they quickly entered into a nonmarital sexual relationship (*amancebamiento*) and were inseparable after meeting. In his own confession, Antonio stated that he was born to Antón, *negro* slave, and Lucía, *india*, in the town of Cuauhtitlan. He made a living working as a muleteer. Although neither party described the cause of their intense attraction, events moved quickly. The same day they met, Antonio took her to the home of Hernando Salazar, his employer. Mariana's daughter, Andrea, remained in the charge of Doña Agustina Altamirano. According to Mariana, she stayed in Salazar's home almost three weeks before she and Antonio left Mexico City. As the couple left Mexico City, they appeared to rely on Afro-Mexican networks. Once outside the city walls, Antonio left Mariana with a *negra libre* for several days. Eventually he returned and told her that he had secured transportation to Acapulco with a muleteer named Rosales. As a muleteer, Antonio likely relied on his fellow transporters to secure their passage to Acapulco. Antonio and Mariana began to call themselves husband and wife as they traveled to avoid suspicion and accusations of *amancebamiento*.

Once in Acapulco, Mariana began working for, and living in the home of, Francisco Barbadillo, *alguacil mayor* of the port town. Although Mariana and Antonio had been claiming to be a married couple, Barbadillo doubted them and insisted that the couple marry legitimately. In their marriage petition, two of Barbadillo's slaves attested to having known Mariana since she was a child in Michoacan. These connections to old friends may have secured her employment in Acapulco. The couple celebrated their marriage in May 1593. Baltasar de los

Reyes and María de Mendoza, *moreno* slaves of Barbadillo, served as their *padrinos*. After less than six months, word reached Acapulco of Mariana's previous marriage.

The allegations spread through the Afro-Mexican social networks that Mariana and Antonio had fostered. Sometime in mid 1593, Francisco Barbadillo traveled from Acapulco to Mexico City with some of his slaves. In Mexico City, Baltasar de los Reyes, a slave of Barbadillo and a *padrino* at Mariana and Antonio's wedding, met Mariana's first husband, Antón, and her father, Juan. After telling Baltasar of Mariana's abduction, Antón and Juan shared their story with Barbadillo. Although the testimony did not elaborate on how the slaves of Altamirano and Barbadillo came into contact, once they shared information about Mariana and Antonio the couple could not continue their clandestine affair. While in Mexico City, Baltasar received additional confirmation from a *negro* muleteer, possibly a colleague of Antonio who knew of the couple's flight to Acapulco. When the Barbadillo entourage returned to Acapulco, Baltasar denounced Mariana and Antón for their crimes. The Inquisition convicted Mariana for double matrimony and Antonio for willingly facilitating her crime.

Throughout her life Mariana moved within and between various Afro-Mexican social circles. In her youth, she lived among the slaves of her father's owner, Francisco Tello. In San Miguel she entered into a network of slaves owned by Hernando Altamirano. During this time, her social connections included some *indios* and Afro-indigenous couples. When the Altamirano slaves moved to Mexico City, she traveled with her husband. In Mexico City, she lived in the Altamirano house with her daughter. Yet the city afforded new connections. There she met Antonio, and their relationship began. His personal connections and occupation provided a means to leave the city. He sequestered her in his employer's residence and used a friendship with a *negra* to smuggle Mariana out of Mexico City. Antonio's ties to muleteers, including at least one *negro*, allowed him to secure passage to Acapulco. Once in Acapulco, Mariana's social connections to slaves she had known in Michoacan secured employment in the home of Barbadillo. Her lifelong ties to *negros* and *mulatos* formed the basis for several different local networks, and the largely Afro-Mexican composition of her communities influenced her marriage to other *mulatos*.

The life and marriages of Juan de Perales further illustrate the importance of Afro-Mexican social networks in fostering *mulato* endogamy. Born around 1547, Juan de Perales grew up in Mexico City and spend most of his adult life working as a carter (*chirrionero*).[58] In 1571, the Inquisition began an investigation into Juan's previous marriages. According to witnesses, around 1562 he married Luisa *mulata*, a *criada* of Gaspar de Miranda. Most of the witnesses to Juan and Luisa's relationship were *negros* and *mulatos*. Some were slaves of Miranda, although his social network included a freed slave, Cristobal Hernández, who worked as a *tundidor* (cloth shearer), and a slave of Don Luis de Velasco, Nicolás *moreno*. According to Luisa and others, the couple had been *amancebados* and had even exchanged "*palabras de presente*" (promise of marriage). After exchanging those vows, Juan wished to solemnize their union. At this point, Miranda objected, and Luisa changed her mind. Juan took his case to the archbishop, who ordered that the couple be wed. Furious over the marriage, Miranda sent his slave, Luisa, and her new husband, to live on an *estancia*. The couple lived together for several months before Juan left.

Several years later, Juan had returned to Mexico City and entered into a relationship with Juana Hernández, a *criada* in the home of Manuel Tarrique. Around 1569, Juan and Juana married. The witnesses to this second marriage included Juana's parents, María Hernández, *morena*, and Francisco Juárez, a *negro* slave of Don Luis de Castilla. Other witnesses included Juan Pérez, a *mulato criado* of Juan de Sámano, the *alguacil mayor*, and Pascual Núñez, a *negro* slave of Juan de Cuenca. After marrying, Juana learned of Juan's previous marriage and eventually, in 1571, asked her employer to denounce him. In response to the allegation and investigation, Juan cast doubt on the earlier marriage by attacking the credibility of its witnesses. He claimed that Nicolás *moreno* and his second wife Juana had "lascivious, carnal relations."[59] Witness on his behalf added that Juana had become pregnant during that affair. Juan also cast doubt on the testimony of his first wife's mother, Juana *de color morena*, by claiming that she hated him for having refused to marry Luisa. Finally, he further attacked Nicolás *moreno*, claiming that he was a bad Christian, a perjurer, and a drunk. This strategy insinuated sufficient doubt into the case, and for a time the Inquisition suspended its investigation.

In 1575, the Inquisition reopened the investigation after several elite Spaniards reported evidence against Juan. By late 1574, Juan, now calling himself Juan de Ayala, had begun working for Licenciado Avalos at a rural estate north of Mexico City. Juan asked his employer for permission to marry an *india* from a nearby town. As Juan and Avalos discussed the marriage, Cristóbal de la Cerda, *relator* (clerk) of the Audiencia, entered and recognized Juan. Cerda told Avalos that Juan had been investigated for double marriage in Mexico City and that both his suspected wives were alive. Cerda knew of Juan's past through various acquaintances. Gaspar de Miranda had complained about the first marriage occurring against his will. Blas de Miranda, probably kin of Gaspar, knew of Juan's marriage to an *india,* and other acquaintances had informed him of Juan's marriage to the *mulata* daughter of a slave owned by Don Luis de Castilla. After hearing of Juan's past, Avalos wrote to the Inquisition and informed them that Juan had fled and was presumed to be wandering among the *obrajes* of Mexico City working as a carder (*cardador*). The new evidence prompted a review of the case, after which Juan was convicted and sentenced for his crimes.

The voluminous testimony against Juan records his mobility and frequent association with other Afro-Mexicans. As a freeborn *mulato*, Juan traveled widely and appears to have worked in various trades, as a carter and a carder. His first marriage attests to close relationships with a group of *negros* and *morenos* connected to the Miranda household. After he fled that marriage, he found himself among another circle of *negros* and *mulatos* serving Manuel Tarrique and Don Luis de Castilla. These two networks did not exist in isolation. Several members knew each other. Nicolás *moreno,* a slave of Don Luis de Velasco, appears to have straddled both. The overlap between both Afro-Mexican networks likely reflects relationships between their masters. Don Luis de Castilla and Don Luis de Velasco were kinsmen, and at the time of the case both Velasco and Castilla served on the *cabildo* of Mexico City.[60] The ties between Spanish patrons did not end there. Gaspar de Miranda was father-in-law to Cristóbal de la Cerda, and, as *relator,* Cerda likely interacted with Velasco and Castilla both socially and in matters of city governance. The close ties between Spanish masters helps explain the interconnections between Afro-Mexican social networks comprised of their slaves and servants, and how Juan came to move between them.

Although these networks of urban slaves and servants represented part of Juan's social circle, he also moved rural networks that may have been more indigenous. The accounts by Avalos and Cerda suggest that he was comfortable living in the outlying *pueblos* north of Mexico City. After only a short time in that region, he had found an *india* he wished to marry. Additionally, his flight to the *obrajes* suggests some ties to that industry and possible networks comprised of its Afro-Mexican and indigenous laborers.[61] Overall, the marriages and movements of Juan de Perales provide a window into the ways that *mulatos* could move within and between social networks forged by Afro-Mexicans.

One final example further illustrates how *mulatos* negotiated a wide array of social networks. In 1558, Francisco de Hojeda, a Spanish *sedero* (silk weaver), and Elvira, a free *mulata*, bore a son, Diego de Hojeda.[62] Although his son was illegitimate, Francisco raised Diego within the family home alongside his legitimate siblings. As a result, in his youth Diego learned his family's trade while working for his father in Puebla and his grandfather in Mexico City. His family ties likely secured him a place working for Diego del Castillo, another *español* resident of Puebla. While in Castillo's home, Diego met an *india* named Catalina and in 1576 married her. Castillo and his wife served as godparents at the wedding, which took place in the main church of Puebla. After about a year, Diego left Puebla and traveled to Mexico City.

In Mexico City, Diego appears to have established a new social network with other Afro-Mexicans. Although he had family ties in Mexico City, after arriving he became involved with Ana, a *negra* slave of Martín Alonso, a local baker. After a time they exchanged vows in the home of Dr. Sedeño. The two witnesses to their betrothal were Catalina, a *negra* slave of Sedeño, and Angelina, a free *negra* fishmonger. Ana recalled that many other *mulatos* had gathered when they changed vows. After her owner died, Cristóbal de Pastrana, a local merchant, purchased Ana. Four or five months later, Diego left town, having taken up work as a *carretero* (cart driver).

Although seemingly distinct, the various social circles Diego moved through did not exist in isolation. Word of his marriages spread back and forth through various personal encounters between acquaintances. One avenue focused on Spaniards. Cristóbal de Pastrana, Ana's new owner, worked as a merchant in the arcades of the Mexico City plaza alongside Diego's grandfather, Juan de Hojeda. After Cristóbal acquired Ana and learned of her free *mulato* husband, Diego became the subject of conversation between the two men. After speaking with Juan de Hojeda, Cristóbal denounced Diego for his crimes. A second chain of communication emanated from within Diego's Afro-Mexican associations. In Puebla, Catalina *india*, Diego's first wife, learned of his second marriage through Manuel, a *negro* slave of María de Escobar.

Diego de Hojeda's experiences illustrate different ways that early colonial *mulatos* could forge social connections. His parentage and upbringing demonstrate a strong degree of familial support for his economic well-being and his preparation for work. Through his family Diego received training and employment. His marriage to an *india criada* suggests that his family may not have chosen to use their social connections to help find him a spouse. Instead, this Afro-indigenous marriage appears to have grown out of a shared residence in the home of his employer. In Mexico City, Diego moved within a different social circle. Despite having Spanish relatives in the community, Diego appears to have become part of an extended Afro-Mexican network of slaves and free people. Most importantly, this case demonstrates the way in which these networks could overlap, especially as gossip moved through them. The owner of Diego's second wife worked alongside Diego's grandfather. Although indigenous, Diego's first wife conversed with the household slaves of Spaniards in Puebla. This permeability reflects the overlapping nature of colonial social networks. Even though networks tended to map onto major *género* divisions (Spanish, Afro-Mexican, indigenous), specific individuals could move within and between several, just as information could flow through them, passing between masters and slaves, employers and employees, or friends and acquaintances.

Overall, the life stories preserved in Inquisition cases reveal that most *mulatos* participated in Afro-Mexican social networks. These networks did not exist to the exclusion of other circles of friends or acquaintances. While Afro-Mexican social networks helped facilitate *mulato* endogamy, the complexity of such other relationships can explain the factors that contributed to exogamous marriages. *Mulatos* frequently forged networks of friends, family, and acquaintances with individuals of other *géneros*. As chapter 4 has shown, a significant minority of *mulatos* were born from, or helped perpetuate, African-indigenous unions. Even in the cases discussed here, *mulatos* who participated in Afro-Mexican communities frequently had ties to indigenous persons. Mariana and Antonio were both born from *negro-india* unions. Juan de Perales traveled through indigenous *pueblos* and sought to marry an *india*. Diego de Hojeda married an *india* he came to know while living under the same roof. These cases highlight the complexity of relationships forged by early colonial *mulatos*. Many *mulatos* may have helped construct and perpetuate shared Afro-Mexican communities, but those networks did not exist in isolation from other personal and affective ties. Rather, they existed in addition to a host of other relationships formed through work, travel, residence, and family.

BEYOND EXOGAMY AND ENDOGAMY

In his recent study of Africans in seventeenth-century Mexico, Frank Proctor found that *mulato* and *negro* marriage patterns grew out of strong social networks that existed between these two *géneros*. In order to better contextualize the importance of Afro-Mexican community, Proctor suggested that *mulato-negro* marriages be construed as "intraracial" rather than interracial. In other words, the marriage patterns suggest that despite different *género* ascriptions, many marriages between *mulatos* and *negros* grew out of shared experiences and social ties and therefore should be considered endogamous pairings.

While sixteenth-century Inquisition cases provide strong evidence for the construction of shared Afro-Mexican social networks, the quantitative marriage data suggest that individuals labeled *mulato* married differently than those labeled *negros*. Across both parishes examined by this study, *negros* married other *negros* much more frequently than they married *mulatos*. *Negros'* tendency toward endogamy always exceeded that of *mulatos*, often by a considerable margin. The distribution of exogamous marriages also indicates divergence between *mulatos* and *negros*. In the early Santa Veracruz sample, as many *mulatos* married *españolas, mestizas,* and *indias* as married *negras*. In the seventeenth-century sample, almost one-third of *mulatos* married *mestizas,* while only half as many married *negras*. At the same time, as many *mulatas* married *españoles* as married negros. In the early Guanajuato sample, ten of sixteen *mulato* marriages involved *indio* spouses. Only one quarter of *mulatos* married other Afro-Mexicans. In the later sample from Guanajuato, *mulato*s married more *indias* than *negras* or *mulatas* combined. Fewer *mulatas* married men of other *géneros,* but as many married *indios* as married *negros*. Taken as a whole, the quantitative and qualitative data suggest that while Afro-Mexican communities of the late sixteenth and early seventeenth century brought together *negros* and *mulatos,* their marriage patterns suggest that individuals of these *géneros* found spouses in different ways. In the period covered by the later sample, most *mulatos* were free while most *negros* were enslaved. The free status of *mulatos* allowed them greater physical and social mobility. Although *mulatos* and *negros* formed social networks based on shared kinship, friendships, residence, and occupation, *mulatos* could move between many social networks and in doing so experienced marriage differently than *negros*.

Nevertheless, Proctor's claim—that traditional measures of exogamy versus endogamy tend to mask social ties that existed across *género* categories—represents an important corrective for scholars of colonial Mexico. Many of the cases examined in this chapter and the next chapter suggest that ascribed *género* labels did not inhibit individuals' ability to create and maintain diverse social networks and find spouses from within those communities. In fact, these cases speak to ways in which particular contexts might have forged "intraracial" unions between individuals from different *géneros*. For example, a union between an Afro-indigenous *mulato* and an *india* born and raised in the same *pueblo* represents as much of an intraracial union as that between a *mulato* slave and a *negra* slave living in their master's home. Similarly, the brokering of a marriage between a *mestiza* raised by her Spanish family and a young *español* acquaintance suggests the operation of intraracial dynamics more than interracial ones. The importance of particular relationships in fostering marriages reminds us that overall patterns of marriage derived from the experiences of specific individuals situated within their own complex webs of social connections and affinities. Only by understanding how colonial subjects formed communities and navigated social ties can we fully understand the dynamics of marriage in the colonial period.

Although social position and social networks shaped how *mestizos* and *mulatos* experienced marriage, they did so in slightly different ways. Many *mestizos* had ties to Spanish kin and relatives, connections that could facilitate marriages to *españoles*. Not all *mestizos* benefited in this way. In other cases, kinship ties to *indios* and other *mestizos* formed the basis for social networks. *Mulatos* shared familial ties to *negros, mulatos,* and *indios*. Sustained Afro-Mexican social networks represented an important mainstay of *mulato* communities. For both *mestizos* and *mulatos*, residence and occupation could help establish social relationships with patrons or with other members of multiethnic households. The diversity of colonial homes fostered interethnic relationships and served to make them a nexus where different social networks intersected. Many exogamous relationships grew out of relationships nurtured by shared residence. Finally, these cases attest to the mobility of *mestizos* and *mulatos* and their ability to construct new networks as they moved into different communities.

Overall, examining how *mestizos* and *mulatos* experienced marriage reveals the fluidity of early colonial society. Individuals of all *géneros* lived and worked alongside one another, often sharing very intimate spaces. In many cases, *mestizos* and *mulatos* relied on diverse kinship networks, cultural proficiencies, occupation, and shared physical spaces to create communities of friends and acquaintances. Even though most *mestizos* and *mulatos* married spouses from their *género*, the exogamous marriages that did occur speak to the ability of *mestizos* and *mulatos* to form multiple social networks and form affective ties to individuals from various other *géneros de gente*.

The social and spatial mobility demonstrated by *mestizos* and *mulatos* helps contextualize the difficulty that colonial administrators faced when seeking to solve the perceived problems caused by members of these groups, the subject of chapter 2. *Mulatos'* and *mestizos'* wide-ranging social and cultural ties transected the juridical ideal of a society divided between a Spanish republic (including *mestizos, mulatos,* and *negros*) and an indigenous republic. Yet the factors that contributed to these diverse social networks resulted from patterns of Spanish colonialism. The lack of *españolas* in early colonial society led to relationships between *españoles* and *indias,* and in some cases *negras.* These relationships helped produce individuals who would be ascribed as *mestizos* and *mulatos.* The sustained imbalance of transatlantic migration over the sixteenth century perpetuated this trend. Colonial patterns of economic development frequently relied on *negro* and *indio* laborers, similarly facilitating the growth of Afro-indigenous *mulatos.* In addition, Spanish homes, businesses, and estates became crucibles of interaction where employees, dependents, and slaves of various *géneros* intermingled, forming multiethnic families and communities. From these diverse origins, individuals of mixed ancestry became exposed to different cultural traditions. Often acculturated to both Hispanic and indigenous ways of life, *mestizos* and *mulatos* formed social and affective ties that crisscrossed those cultural boundaries. In doing so, they utilized the full range of cultural and social connections available to them while simultaneously exposing the disjuncture between the Spanish juridical construction of difference and the complex web of social, cultural, and economic relations forged by colonial subjects. The following chapter continues the examination of the place of *mestizos* and *mulatos* in early colonial society by exploring their experience of work and occupation. As with marriage, the varied origins and social networks of *mestizos* and *mulatos* led to a diverse set of occupational experiences.

CHAPTER 6

Occupation

> Juan de la Peña, on behalf of the *mulatos* of [New Spain], has informed me that as a result of spending the majority of their time occupied working in mines, and tending livestock on *estancias,* and [doing] other things outside of settled areas they are not indoctrinated or educated in Our Holy Catholic Faith, as would be just, and they suffer detriment to their souls and consciences and to their salvation; in this, God, Our Lord, has been and is very disserved.
>
> Royal cédula *addressed to the archbishop of Mexico, 1569*

In 1564, Juan Méndez, a *mestizo,* appeared to be leading a comfortable life.[1] He owned his own business working as a shoemaker in Antequera (Oaxaca). He was married to Catalina Sánchez, a *mestiza,* who had been given a five-hundred-peso dowry by her employer, Francisco de Heredia. In June of that year, word began to spread that Juan had been married previously to an *india* named Juana. In response, Juan hastily fled town. After leaving his store in the hands of one of his workers, a *mestizo* named Hipólito García, he scribbled a quick letter to Catalina lamenting the trouble he had caused, and he fled, taking her dowry with him. While the case against Juan is not complete, it provides evidence for the socioeconomic position held by Juan and his second wife, Catalina.

Juan Méndez's quick disappearance from Antequera allowed him to avoid an interrogation by the ecclesiastical court. However, even without direct testimony from Juan, the case provides numerous details about his life. We know that he worked as a shoemaker, owned his own store, and employed others. The last person to see him in town was Hipólito García, who believed that Juan had left to visit a rural *estancia*. Juan's ownership of a shoe store suggests that he had both professional training and access to capital. While many *mestizos, mulatos,* and *indios* worked in skilled trades, in the sixteenth century few non-Spanish individuals had the capital to set up independent operations. Consequently, Juan's store represented a considerable economic asset, one that placed him solidly within the ranks of entrepreneurial tradesmen.

Juan's flight infuriated Francisco de Heredia because Juan stole the dowry that Francisco had provided for his *criada*.[2] Francisco's five-hundred-peso gift to Catalina represented a substantial financial resource. The crown paid many conquistadors less than five hundred pesos in annual pensions. A common laborer would need to work sixteen years to earn as much. It was three times the annual salary of a parish priest and roughly the annual salary of an *alcalde mayor*.[3] Although some of the most prominent families of New Spain gave their daughters dowries valued in tens of thousands of pesos, five hundred pesos represented a substantial sum for most *novohispanos*.[4] The fact that Heredia had offered to support Catalina's marriage to Juan indicates his support of the couple's marriage and his desire to provide for the couple's future. A marriage to a social inferior or wastrel would not have warranted such support. Moreover, the dowry provides strong evidence that Francisco Heredia had a significant connection to Catalina. Although a patron-client relationship would have warranted some form of support in a marriage, his donation of five hundred pesos to a *mestiza criada* suggests that their relationship was deeper than that between employer and employee. In this case, the amount of support may hint that she was an illegitimate daughter of his—or that of a close relative. Francisco's willingness to provide for her certainly placed her within the ranks of the marriageable *mestizas*.

The testimony presented in the case did not identify Juan Méndez's parents directly. Witnesses described him as the son of an *español*, presumably with an *india*. An *española* named Catalina Alonso admitted that Juan was the son of her first husband. This admission suggests that Juan had been raised as an illegitimate child in his father's house.

Catalina Alonso's own family ties reveal that Juan's extended kin included several prominent figures. She was the widow of a man named Hernán Gómez de Valverde, a *vecino* of Antequera and possibly Juan's father. One of Catalina's sons served as a canon in Antequera's cathedral. This son told her that Juan had fled to Havana, where he was living with a *mulata*. The family's awareness of Juan's whereabouts further supports sustained ties to his father's family. The support and recognition of his father likely explains Juan's ability to learn a trade and run his own business.

Juan Méndez and Catalina Sánchez represent very tantalizing examples of sixteenth-century *mestizos*. On the one hand they fit the archetypical stereotype used to denigrate those of their *género*—both were likely illegitimate.[5] On the other hand, their economic position compared favorably to *españoles*. Juan worked as a tradesman and owned his own store, a unique position given that most *español* tradesmen did not own their own stores. Similarly, Catalina's substantial dowry represented a significant financial asset.[6] While their wealth paled in comparison to the wealthiest *español* families, their socioeconomic status exceeded the majority of colonial subjects and placed them within the middling ranks of Hispanic society.

The relationship between socio-racial categories and occupation has been widely examined for the late seventeenth and eighteenth century.[7] Scholarship has found that although race and occupation could be closely linked, ascribed *género* did not determine occupation, nor did occupation imply membership in a particular *género*—with the possible exception of elite bureaucratic positions that excluded non-Spaniards. Moreover, several scholars have noted that *mestizos*— and to a lesser degree *mulatos*—occupied an "ambiguous middle layer" in the occupational hierarchy.[8] In contrast to the detailed work on the seventeenth and eighteenth centuries, the occupational and socioeconomic positions of sixteenth-century *mestizos* and *mulatos* remains largely unexamined. Part of this lacuna can be attributed to a lack documents that provide comprehensive occupational data for early colonial communities.

In order to assess the range of occupations held by *mestizos* and *mulatos*, my analysis relies on two sources. The largest collection of cases comes from the records of the Inquisition. Although occupation was not recorded for every witness or defendant, many men chose to name their occupation. Only a handful of women declared an occupation. Occasionally men and women referenced their occupation or that of others in their testimony. The second set of sources examined here are licenses granted by the viceroy allowing non-Spaniards to carry swords and daggers. Arms licenses provide a unique window into the ways in which non-Spaniards sought to demonstrate their personal honor and social status through access to restricted sumptuary items.[9] The text of most arms licenses contains concise descriptions of the lives of their recipients, including references to occupation. While both source bases have preserved a range of individual experiences, neither represents a random cross-section of colonial subjects. Consequently, neither provides clear evidence for the overall distribution of occupations among *mestizos* and *mulatos*.

Nevertheless, the occupations preserved in Inquisition cases and arms licenses offer a means to gauge the range of jobs held by *mestizos* and *mulatos* and the multiple contexts that influenced employment. The rich details preserved in Inquisition cases help elucidate the social and cultural place of individuals and the factors that influenced their employment. Arms licenses grant access into the lives of upwardly mobile individuals. The details of their petitions help to illustrate the ways in which aspiring *mestizos* and *mulatos* attempted to gain social status. Additionally, the cases examined came from a variety of communities, urban and rural, large and small. This geographic and residential diversity further illustrates the multiple experiences of early colonial *mestizos* and *mulatos*. Overall, the analysis presented here focuses more on the occupational and economic possibilities available to *mestizos* and *mulatos* during the early colonial period and less on their overall distribution in the workforce.

A close reading of Inquisition cases and arms licenses reveals some of the ways that early colonial *mestizos* and *mulatos* acquired occupations and participated in the workforce. These sources reveal that *mestizos* and *mulatos* worked in a wide range of trades and occupations. Tables 6.1 and 6.2 list the occupations held by men and women. *Mestizos* and *mulatos* reported a comparable range of urban and rural occupations and shared six of the top seven most common occupations. Even within this limited sample, men of both *géneros* held a wide array of skilled trades. For some, family connections facilitated the acquisition of specialized skills and allowed individuals of mixed ancestry to enter the ranks of tradesmen and artisans. In other cases, the need for labor drew *mestizos* and *mulatos* into occupations reliant on wage labor. In those cases, many individuals of mixed ancestry entered occupations tied to commerce, animal husbandry, and agriculture. *Mestizos* appeared to have greater access to more prestigious employment opportunities, with several men working as tradesmen and artisans in relatively exclusive professions, such as gilder, silversmith, and gold leaf maker. At the same time, some *mulatos* lived and worked as slaves. Most women served as *criadas* in the homes of *españoles*, although some carved out other careers for themselves. Overall, the occupations in the sample tend to indicate that by the end of the sixteenth century, *mestizos* and *mulatos* already inhabited a middle layer of the labor force, working as wage laborers in a variety of trades and occupations. The rich details of these cases illustrate how the diversity of social and cultural backgrounds among *mestizos* and *mulatos* contributed to their varied participation in the labor force.

ARTISANS AND TRADESMEN

Many tradesmen maintained close relationships with *españoles* as patrons or fellow tradesmen. Alonso Ruiz, the lone silversmith (*platero*) of the sample, represents a good example of a *mestizo* tradesman with ties to *español* associates. Alonso was born in Santiago de Guatemala to Bartolomé Ruiz and an *india* sometime around 1540.[10] He did not name his mother in his statements, suggesting he may not have known her or that he was trying to more closely associate himself with his father. By 1564, Alonso had moved to Mexico City where he had married María de Morales, the daughter of Gonzalo de Morales and niece of Bachiller Ribas. In that year, Alonso found himself before the ecclesiastical court of Mexico City when former acquaintances from Guatemala came to Mexico and denounced him for having been previously married to Catalina Ruiz, an *india*. Most witnesses knew that Alonso worked as a silversmith in Guatemala and Mexico. Alonso likely received training as a silversmith when he was young in Guatemala.

Table 6.1
MESTIZO AND *MULATO* OCCUPATIONS, 1555–1657

	Mulatos	Mestizos
Muleteer	16	10
Cowboy or ranch hand	5	4
Tailor	5	3
Shoemaker	5	3
Slave	5	
Auxiliary*	3	1
Farmer or rural landowner	2	5
Carter	2	1
Sailor	2	
Shearer	2	
Silk weaver	1	1
Cacao merchant	1	
Cattle rancher	1	
Estate manager	1	
Fruit vendor	1	
Master carpenter	1	
Meat merchant	1	
Merchant	1	
Servant	1	
Slave trader	1	
Sugar master	1	
Assistant constable		2
Ferrier		3
Baker		1
Fish merchant		1
Gold leaf maker		1
Gilder		1
Locksmith		1
Rubber merchant		1
Silversmith		1
Stocking maker		1
Totals	55	41

*Auxiliaries were individuals who worked as dependents to Spaniards but were not otherwise given a job title; in some contexts they could have been called *criados*.

SOURCES: AGN, Inq., vols. 5, 10, 18, 26, 27, 29, 38, 47, 70, 94, 95, 98, 100, 101, 103, 104, 107, 108, 134, 137, 145, 147, 148, 184, 185, 186, 262; AGN, General de Parte, vols. 1, 2, 4, 5, 6, 7, 8; AGN, Reales Cédulas Duplicadas, vols. 5, 16, 18, 20, 23.

Table 6.2
MESTIZA AND *MULATA* OCCUPATIONS, **1564–1598**

	Mulatas	Mestizas
Servant	8	8
Slave	2	
Midwife	1	
Tavern owner	1	
Totals	12	8

SOURCES: AGN, Inq., vols. 25, 26, 27, 38, 48, 84, 94, 95, 101, 103, 107, 116, 137, 185, 186.

When he moved from Guatemala to Mexico he traveled in the company of a Spanish silversmith. The testimony provided in the case indicates that he maintained extensive professional and social connections to the silversmiths of Mexico City once he arrived. After being arrested and questioned by the Inquisition he was released pending the final decision of the tribunal. During this time, his bail was posted and his person guaranteed by a Spanish silversmith named Manuel Tarrique. While a fellow tradesman was supportive enough to provide his bail, Tarrique's support had limits. After Alonso tried to escape, Tarrique wrote to the court in order to try to retract his bond because he was fearful that Alonso might flee again. Nevertheless, Tarrique's initial offer of assistance may have reflected social ties forged through shared occupation.

The life of the locksmith Graviel Carrasco provides a useful illustration of early colonial mobility and a *mestizo* who became drawn into the extended conquests of the mid sixteenth century.[11] Graviel was born in the early 1540s to Pedro Carrasco, a *vecino* of Michoacan. As a teenager, Graviel sought his fortune by joining the expedition to Florida led by Don Tristán de Luna y Arellano. As the expedition was preparing to leave, Graviel found himself in Xalapa near the port of Veracruz. During that time many men entered into sexual relationships with native women. In order to continue those relationships, it became common for the men to say that they had married the *indias* in the hopes of avoiding accusations of *amancebamiento* and so that they might bring those women on the expedition. Like so many would-be conquistadors, Graviel began a relationship with an indigenous woman, one named María. She would accompany him on the expedition to Florida; later he would describe her as his *criada*. When the expedition failed and its members returned to Mexico, Graviel and María traveled to Guatemala where they settled in the town of San Cristóbal de los Llanos. During the time that they were together, Graviel and María had two sons and a daughter. While living in San Cristóbal, Graviel worked as a blacksmith serving the local indigenous residents. Eventually Graviel made his way from San Cristóbal through Oaxaca and on to Mexico City. During this time he married two more times, to *mestizas*. By the time of his trial in 1565, Graviel had taken up work as a locksmith in Mexico City.

Unfortunately the case does not specify when Graviel received his professional training in blacksmithing and as a locksmith. It is unclear what occupation Graviel had at the time he joined the expedition to Florida. At that time, he would have been around sixteen years old and may have already received instruction in blacksmithing. After returning and finding himself in a rural, largely indigenous area, he took up his trade there. He may have taken up the related profession of locksmith after moving back to Hispanic settlements. Regardless of how he acquired training, Graviel's training in metalworking allowed him to earn a living in a variety of locations.

Like the other *mestizo* tradesmen, Graviel demonstrated strong integration into Hispanic society. Almost all of the individuals interviewed in his trial were Spaniards, and all of the men who provided details of his participation on the expedition were Spanish. His ability to navigate Hispanic society as well as his desire to further his prospects through military service suggest that he had been raised within Hispanic culture. His sojourn among *indios mexicanos* in Guatemala hints that he was likely also comfortable in indigenous contexts. For a time he lived in a largely indigenous community, plying his trade among its residents. His willingness to settle and work in such a community implies a degree of familiarity with Nahua culture and language. Nevertheless, he was eventually drawn back into Hispanic society.

An example of family ties possibly facilitating entrance into trades can be seen in the case of Pedro Sánchez de Reyna.[12] In 1569, Pedro faced charges of blaspheming in Nahuatl while with a group of *indios*. Born sometime around 1544 in San Ildefonso Villa Alta, Pedro was initially raised by his father, Bartolomé Sánchez de Reyna. Pedro fit the stereotype of *mestizo* illegitimacy, although he was unusual in that his father was a cleric. During the trial, Pedro stated that he worked as a tailor. Unfortunately his occupation did not have much bearing on the proceedings and was not discussed in detail. Nevertheless, the testimony provides ample indication that Pedro was very close to his family and well integrated into Antequera's Hispanic elite. Despite the sacrilegious nature of his own birth, many of the witnesses presented on his behalf spoke to his family history and his good repute. For example, Cristóbal Robles noted that Bartolomé Sánchez de Reyna worked to instill "good Christianity" in Pedro. After his father's death, Pedro had moved to Antequera where he lived with "honorable people and Christians" in the home of his uncle Francisco Gutierrez. Several other witnesses noted that he was married and lived an honorable life. Sebastián de Salas, an *indio*, noted that Pedro and his wife, Magdalena *india*, lived "with all tranquility and honesty." As an adult, he was well respected by those he knew, including other Spaniards and members of the clergy. Although the details of his profession are sparse, his integration into the social networks of his extended *español* family likely facilitated his training as a tailor.

Close ties to Spanish parents and relatives were not exclusive to *mestizos*. Some *mulatos* benefited from these connections as well. Diego de Hojeda, discussed in the last chapter, represents an excellent example of a *mulato* with strong multigenerational ties to his Spanish relatives.[13] Diego was born around 1558 to Francisco de Hojeda, an *español*, and Elvira, a free *mulata*. Diego grew up in his father's home alongside his legitimate half-siblings. There he learned to be a *sedero*, the family trade.[14] He practiced the trade in Puebla and Mexico City and finished his training under the direction of his grandfather, Juan de Hojeda. Diego would eventually leave that trade and begin working as a carter (*carretero*) traveling between Mexico and Veracruz. The testimony of his case does not provide any clues as to why Diego abandoned the family trade for that of a seemingly less prestigious occupation. By the time of his trial he had relocated to Zacatecas, where he continued to work as a transporter.

After contracting two marriages, Diego may have hoped that staying on the road would decrease the likelihood of his being discovered. This was not the case. His second wife's owner and his grandfather both worked in the arcades of Mexico City's market. The two men shared knowledge of Diego's marriages that eventually led to his denunciation and arrest. During his interrogation, Diego attempted to use his training as a *sedero* to ameliorate his punishment. After confessing to the marriages, Diego dropped to his knees and clasped his hands, and cried out, "I plead penitence and mercy because I did not do it [double marriage] out of malice or to make a mockery of Holy Matrimony, and in payment of my crime I will work in [a] monastery serving in my occupation as a *sedero*, which I know how to do quite well."[15] Unfortunately, this last-minute appeal did not sway the court, and it did not sentence him to practice as a *sedero*. While family connections could help establish *mestizos* and *mulatos* in skilled trades, receiving training did not guarantee a lifelong career, as can be seen in Diego's shift from *sedero* to *carretero*. He was not alone in abandoning a skilled trade for another occupation.

Another example of this can be seen in the case against Jusepe de Molina.[16] In 1599, Jusepe was denounced by his half-brother for being married twice, first to Doña Mariana D'Espinosa, an *india principal*, and then to Mari López, a *mestiza*. Born around 1560, Jusepe was raised by his father, Juan de Molina, and retained close connections to his *español* half-siblings. As a child he was given a basic education in the *colegio de niños*, the school established for educating *mestizos*. Later his father apprenticed him to a farrier, Francisco Rodríguez. Yet, despite the benefits of his education, Jusepe did not enter that trade. Although his case does not clearly indicate how he supported himself, there are clues to suggest that he found employment in low-skill, rural occupations.

After he and his first wife separated, Jusepe travelled to the northern frontier. For two years he traveled around the *estancias* of the Chichimecas and between the northern settlements of Guadalajara, Pátzcuaro, and Zacatecas. After a brief return to Mexico City, Jusepe spent ten more years in the northwest around Compostela (today's Morelia) and in Michoacan. His time on *estancias* may suggest that he sought seasonal employment working with livestock. At some point during his travels he fought in the ongoing war waged against Chichimeca groups along the frontier. Several acquaintances described scars on his head that were the result of arrow wounds he had received. After his second marriage, Jusepe managed a number of mares as part of her dowry. The case is silent about how Jusepe used the animals. Nevertheless, it is plausible that Jusepe hoped to use the animals as breeding stock. At the time of his arrest, he and Mari had been married for four years, and the couple owned thirty mares. Jusepe also owned a *jineta* saddle and stirrups. The size of the couple's herd and his ownership of tack support the notion that he had taken up animal husbandry. Although Jusepe found his way into a stable profession, it was certainly not the occupation to which his father had him apprenticed.

The cases of Diego de Hojeda and Jusepe de Molina are excellent examples of how families could provide occupational training to their *mulato* and *mestizo* sons. Unfortunately they do not provide clear indications of why these two men did not continue on in those trades. It might be tempting to attribute their lack of advancement as being a by-product of discrimination against their *género*, but such a view does not corroborate with the details of their lives and those of other tradesmen. In the cases examined here, *género* did not seem to be an impediment to training or the formation of social ties with other tradesmen.[17] For most men in this sample, familial connections and support appeared to trump the prejudices mapped onto non-Spanish *géneros*. Moreover, once established in trades, *mestizos* and *mulatos* often maintained close ties to other tradesmen, frequently living, working, and associating with other men in those professions. That some of these men chose to leave their profession should not be construed as evidence that they were not welcome in those trades. Rather, the mobility seen in the cases of Diego Hojeda and Jusepe Molina suggest that these men were well aware of the occupational possibilities available to them and chose to work in a job that best suited their needs and desires. In fact, on the whole, the life stories of *mestizos* and *mulatos* illustrate that most of these individuals were cognizant of the variety of employment opportunities available and moved between jobs as they sought fit.

In fact, even some *mulatos* lacking Spanish familial connections were able to receive training and enter the ranks of skilled labor. A very early example of this can be seen in the case of Luis Hernández, discussed in chapter 4 for its portrayal of Afro-indigenous families.[18] Born sometime around 1530, Luis worked as a tailor in Mexico City. Although Luis only mentioned his profession in passing, his case provides some tantalizing clues. Luis was an Afro-indigenous *mulato*. His mother was an *india* who did not speak Castilian and instead provided her testimony in Nahuatl. The testimony in the case suggests that he and his first wife, Agustina, were well integrated into the indigenous social circles of their mothers. In contrast, no one mentioned the name or *género* of Luis's father. Yet the fact that Luis was called a *mulato* and raised by his indigenous mother suggests that his father was likely a *mulato* or a *negro*, possibly a slave. There are several possibilities for how Luis learned his trade. If his father was a slave or servant of a Spanish tailor, Luis may have entered his profession via his father's training or influence. On the other hand, textile production was not an exclusively Spanish profession. Trades like weaving or tailoring were common prior to the arrival of the Spanish. As a result, Luis may have received training via his connections to indigenous tradesmen thanks to his close association with his *india* mother. Although the specifics of Luis's occupational history can only be inferred, he demonstrates that at least some first-generation Afro-indigenous *mulatos* practiced skilled trades in mid-sixteenth-century New Spain.

Luis Hernández was not unique in his ability to enter a skilled trade without Spanish familial connections. The case against Diego Ximénez similarly provides a window into how Afro-indigenous *mulatos* entered skilled trades.[19] Diego was born in San Pedro, Honduras, sometime around 1536 to a *moreno* named Diego and an *india* named María Inés. As a young boy he worked as a servant for a Spaniard named Juan Ximénez. At the age of thirteen, Diego married Inés, an *india criada* of Juan Ximénez. During this time, Diego received training as a shoemaker. The couple lived in San Pablo for ten to twelve years, after which Diego traveled to San Salvador and Guatemala. During this time he did not practice his trade as a shoemaker, instead working as a muleteer transporting goods.

Before Diego could return to Inés, he received word that she had died. Eventually he made his way to Antequera, where he met and married an enslaved *negra* named María Sape while staying in the home of Antonio Gómez. Diego continued to work as a muleteer transporting goods to the port of Guatulco. During this time he was investigated for bigamy, but he was eventually acquitted after the court determined that Inés had died prior to his marriage to María.

Although the son of a *moreno* and an *india*, Diego was able to use his connection to a Spanish patron to receive specialized training as a shoemaker. It may be possible that one or both of Diego's parents served Juan Ximénez. Although the social ties that connected Diego to his Spanish patron remain obscure, his case illustrates how Spanish patrons could provide occupational training to their dependents of mixed ancestry. Despite his training in a skilled trade, Diego struck out on his own, choosing to work as a muleteer rather than a shoemaker. Although this would seem to suggest his abandonment of that skilled trade, it is possible that Diego's choice to work in transportation was part of a longer-term strategy for accumulating wealth and working as a shoemaker. Prior to his first wife's death, Juan Gómez, an *español* acquaintance, asked why he continued to work as a muleteer away from Inés. Diego replied that he would only go on one or two more trips in order to save up money before returning to his wife.[20] This statement suggests that Diego had a plan for the future that required capital. He might have been saving money to help establish himself as a shoemaker in Antequera.

Mestizo and *mulato* tradesmen manifested a range of experience. Most entered their profession via some connection to Spanish family or patrons. Once in professions, these men could form strong ties to their associates. Yet even those who had strong ties to their occupation and fellow tradesmen could choose to change careers. In such cases, social and physical mobility afforded *mestizos* and *mulatos* access to a variety of alternatives. Some men looked to military service in the hopes of social advancement. Others looked to rural areas and the opportunities offered in transport and commerce. The tantalizing stories preserved in these cases hint that a variety of social experiences and cultural affinities could lead *mestizos* and *mulatos* into and out of skilled trades.

COWBOYS AND MULETEERS

While roughly half of the *mestizos* and *mulatos* examined here worked as tradesmen or artisans, the other half worked in lower-skilled, often rural occupations. There existed much less variety in these occupations, with most men working as either muleteers or ranch hands (cowboys).[21] In fact, these two occupations represent the two most commonly held jobs by *mestizos* and *mulatos.* There are a number of factors that likely drew men of mixed ancestry into these occupations. First, Spaniards tended to settle in larger cities or towns, with all but the most entrepreneurial eschewing rural areas. As Hispanicized individuals, *mestizos* and *mulatos* made ideal employees for such Spanish entrepreneurs in need of laborers. Second, with the Spanish population concentrated in larger urban areas, the need to provide foodstuffs, raw materials, and trade goods to those residents created a demand for rural labor in transportation, agriculture, and livestock ranching. Additionally, the lower prevalence of *españoles* in the countryside likely reduced the degree of prejudice or discrimination felt by non-Spaniards. Third, based on the experiences of the men in this sample, these professions required little prior training and could be learned on the job.[22]

Although mining represented a large sector of the rural economy, few of the *mestizos* and *mulatos* examined here worked directly in ore extraction or refining. As the marriage data from Guanajuato shows, many *mulatos* lived and worked in mining communities. Unfortunately, none of the stories of the men or women who worked in the mining industry were preserved in the cases examined here. Nevertheless, the muleteers and cowboys in the sample provided raw materials and trade goods to mining camps, and their experiences illustrate the ways in which rural labor helped connect the major sectors of the colonial economy.

The single most common profession was that of muleteer. As was seen above, this occupation could even lure skilled tradesmen from urban areas. Although many men worked as muleteers, there is no evidence that any of the men examined here owned their own animals. Such a situation is not surprising. Animals represented a large capital investment. Most pack trains in the sixteenth century consisted of several dozen animals.[23] The cost to purchase, outfit, and maintain so many animals made the ownership of pack trains difficult for anyone of modest means. Consequently, merchants became the primary owners and operators of mule trains.[24] Over the course of the sixteenth century, the number of mule trains greatly increased as the government moved to restrict native transporters (*tamemes*) over concerns of abuse and overwork.[25] The sustained growth of this industry over the sixteenth century created new occupational opportunities for those men willing to spend days on the road traveling through difficult and often dangerous terrain. The average mule train required one handler for every four to five animals, between three to ten muleteers in all.

Given the labor required to manage pack trains, muleteering became a reasonably well-remunerated occupation. Although wage data is sporadic, annual salaries for muleteers ranged between thirty and two hundred pesos, with a middle range around fifty pesos.[26] Much of the diversity in wages can be attributed to differences in *género*, with Spaniards receiving the highest pay and *indios* the lowest. Additional variation can be explained by various factors, including work experience, trade route, and the likelihood of hazard or danger. If most *mestizos* and *mulatos* made fifty pesos per year they would have earned roughly 70 percent more than unskilled manual laborers, whose wages averaged thirty pesos a year.[27] By the mid to late sixteenth century, the average unskilled wage laborer lived at a subsistence level—thirty pesos a year provided enough for food and housing but not much else.[28] The increased wages earned by muleteers at least allowed for the possibility of some long-term savings and upward mobility. In this context, Diego Ximénez's choice to put aside shoemaking in order to generate some capital as a muleteer might be seen as a financially astute decision, even if it represented a step down in perceived status.

While some men became muleteers for a short period, others worked in it for much longer. An example of this can be seen in the case of Antón Hernández, an Afro-indigenous *mulato* born in Mexico City to Antón *negro*, a slave of Juan de la Serna, and Lucía, an *india* from Coatitlan.[29] After being raised in the home of Juan de la Serna, Antón left at age fifteen and took up muleteering sometime around 1583. For eleven years, Antón worked transporting goods between Mexico City, Veracruz, and Acapulco. In 1593, he was arrested for being complicit in bigamy by marrying Mariana de la Cruz, a *mulata*, while knowing that she was already married. His occupation likely facilitated their crime because it allowed him to help Mariana move from Mexico City to Acapulco in the hopes that they might avoid suspicion. Another example of a lifelong transporter can be seen in Juan de Perales.[30] Like Antón, he was born and raised in Mexico City. Known as a *mulato,* he did not declare his parentage. Ever since he started working, Juan had been employed as a carter (*chirrionero*) traveling between Mexico City, Veracruz, and Zacatecas. At that time of his trial in 1575, Juan worked as a carter for a Spaniard named Hontiveros. Despite the fact that muleteers and carters likely made more than a subsistence wage, neither Antón nor Juan confessed to owning any property at the time of their trials.

This was common. During trials, the tribunal required that defendants declare their property to pay for costs of imprisonment and trial. Few *mestizos* and *mulatos,* regardless of occupation, declared any property, as will be discussed further below. Although it is possible that most *mestizo* and *mulato* defendants owned nothing beyond the clothes on their backs, some may have chosen to keep silent about property they owned or debts owed to them by others. One can imagine that defendants willfully failed to declare small amounts of cash, extra clothing items, simple tools, or money owed by others in the hopes of retaining some savings after their trial. Stereotypes of their *género* may have predisposed the tribunal to presume that their material wealth was minimal and accept declarations of poverty. The court may have weighed the possible value of undeclared property against the cost of investigation and collection of those goods.

The property declared by Manuel Díaz, a Portuguese-born *mulato* and muleteer, provides a glimpse at life on the road.[31] Like others Manuel chose muleteering after practicing several other occupations. Prior to arriving in the New World, Manuel had lived in Portugal and travelled to Naples and "the East."[32] When he arrived in New Spain, he settled near Veracruz in the region around Jalapa. He did some work as a fisherman, possibly drawing on skills he had learned back in Portugal.[33] Most witnesses referred to him as a muleteer but not one who owned his own animals or carts. Domingo Pérez, also from Portugal, noted that in the past Manuel had been in charge of a mule train owned by Pedro Gómez. Manuel's own declarations reinforce the fact that he worked as a muleteer but did not have his own pack animals or wagons. When arrested, he declared his property as follows:

> Firstly, a grey horse
> a *jineta* saddle and *estradiote* stirrups
> an old *jinete* bridle and spurs
> an old blanket
> a tent made of local [Mexican-made] fabric
> a crossbow with its quiver
> a tool bag with pliers, hammer, and butteris
> an old black cloak
> old blue breeches
> a local blanket
> a black raincoat that he is carrying
> breeches made of local cloth
> a machete
> eleven *reales* in cash.[34]

This list of property represents the essentials of someone who lived on the road. Manuel had his own horse and tack. He owned a tent. He had several blankets to sleep on and all the clothing and apparel necessary for long trips. Moreover, he had a small tool kit to help him maintain his animals and property. Finally, he owned weapons to protect himself and his property from bandits and vagabonds. While Manuel's property does not illustrate vast wealth, his list of goods illustrates that he earned a wage above subsistence and chose to invest those earnings into tools and goods beneficial to his profession.

After muleteers, the next most common profession was that of cowboy or ranch hand. Like muleteering, the raising of livestock was a major part of the colonial economy and a major area of growth throughout most of the sixteenth century. In Mexico, sheep and pigs were the first two domesticates to be introduced in large numbers. Over the course of the sixteenth century, livestock production increased dramatically.[35] Livestock provided meat for consumption in New Spain, hides for local production and export, and tallow for soap and candles.[36] Sheep provided mutton for local consumption and wool for use in the growing textile industry.[37] The discovery of silver created an additional outlet for goods produced by ranchers. Miners had a great demand for meat, tallow, and hides, all of which were essential to the operation of mines and the subsistence of mining communities.[38]

The rapid growth of pastoralism and the economic demand for animal products necessitated laborers to raise, tend, and manage livestock. Livestock production did not favor small-scale ownership. Especially during the mid sixteenth century, the rapid increase in herd sizes and the corresponding drop in market prices made ranching viable only in large numbers. Consequently, cowboys, herders, and ranch hands worked for Spaniards who owned large herds. Like muleteering, the specialized knowledge necessary for these rural jobs was significantly lower than the trades and likely made it easier for men to learn on the job. Finally, the fact that many *mestizos* and *mulatos* had ties to indigenous communities placed them in close proximity to rural pastoral estates.

A good example of early colonial cowboys can be found in a 1581 criminal case brought against Antonio de Espejo.[39] In April of that year, Espejo murdered two cowboys and injured a third over the course of one week. The conflict between Espejo and his men erupted over whether or not the time had come for the cowboys to brand young animals out on the range. While Espejo insisted that his men travel from their main *estancia* near Celaya into the grazing lands to the north, the men feared that it was too early in the season and that they might run into Chichimec raiders on the journey. As the investigation unfolded, the testimony of cowboys and other estancia residents provide a window into life on a pastoral estate. Most importantly, the estate had a multiethnic assortment of residents drawn from a variety of colonial *géneros*. *Mulatos* comprised the majority of residents. In some cases their *negro* and *indio* parents lived on other estancias or in *pueblos de indios*. Similarly, some *mestizo* residents had *indio* kin nearby. Moreover, marriages crossed all *género* categories with *mestizo-mulato, mulato-indio,* and *mestizo-indio* marriages occurring among the estancia residents.[40] Ties between the cowboys and *indios* were strong enough that several of the men fled Espejo's wrath by taking refuge in the nearby *pueblo* where their wives lived.

On the whole, the investigation unwittingly uncovered a community in which *mestizos, mulatos, indios,* and *negros* lived side-by-side on various pastoral and agricultural estancias as coworkers, friends, and relatives. To be sure, *españoles* were not absent; at least in this case the only Spaniards regularly resident on the estancias were the *mayordomos* who oversaw the day-to-day business needs of the operations. Below them were *caporals* (foremen) that managed the ranch hands directly and oversaw the herds. While *mayordomos* tended to be *españoles*, the caporals were mainly *mulatos*. Although the testimony of the case suggests that most laborers on Espejo's estancias were born in the region, the men clearly made a choice to work as cowboys and ranch hands and were reasonably well remunerated for their labors. In testifying against Antonio de Espejo, Gerónimo López, a *castizo* cowboy, noted that each of the cowboys working for Espejo had been paid fifty *pesos* of advance salary for their work.[41] The loss of this advance pay may have prompted some of Espejo's rage as some of the men had chosen to flee with their pay rather than risk travel in areas of Chichimec activity. The wages paid to Espejo's cowboys nearly matched the average income of men working as muleteers. Like muleteers, cowboy salaries likely varied according to *género,* experience, and skills. In contrast to the average wage of fifty pesos for a cowboy, Francisco Muñoz, a *mayordomo* of Espejo, was owed over eight hundred pesos for three and a half years of service, suggesting an annual salary of over two hundred pesos—four times that of the non-Spanish cowboys working for him. Nevertheless, the fifty pesos a year that the cowboys earned represented a good wage, one that could allow for modest savings over time.

Despite the fact that cowboys received reasonable salaries, they also faced serious dangers. After all, the conflict between the men and Espejo revolved around fears that their job would put them at risk of a Chichimec attack. Such fears were not unfounded. In the same year that Espejo and his men came into conflict, Don Lope de Sosa, another livestock magnate, wrote to the viceroy to inform him of a Chichimec raid that had befallen several of his employees:

> On the fourteenth of this month of June . . . [the cowboys] saw a herd of mares coming down the mountainside. . . . They went after them, six young *españoles*, three *mulatos,* and a *negro* with the intent to collect them. . . . They noticed that they were being driven by six *indios chichimecos* outfitted for war riding large horses with bows

and arrows.... The [cowboys] were unprepared to fight because they carried no weapons other than one harquebus and one sword, two leather doublets, three *garrochas* and three butcher knives.... The cowboys took up arms and defended themselves with such tenacity that five of the six [*indios*] were wounded.... Luckily they dismounted [the *indios*]; men and horses wounded, they fought hand to hand not caring if the *indios* surrendered.... Once they had subdued the indios they used their butcher knives and stabbed them, killing them.[42]

Sosa's account provides a chilling view of the violence that could break out between Chichimec raiders and those who worked the northern frontier. Although anecdotal, the violence described by Sosa provides a vivid glimpse of the dangers faced by many *mestizo* and *mulato* cowboys who braved uncontrolled territory for the modest pay of fifty pesos a year.

In contrast to tradesmen, *mestizo* and *mulato* muleteers and cowboys did not appear to enter these professions through connections to *españoles*. Although their employers were most often *españoles*, the demand for labor primarily drew men of mixed ancestry into these occupations. Life on the road or in the countryside was often dangerous and difficult. Men in both professions could face the dangers of highwaymen and Chichimec raids. For muleteers the work of transporting goods was incessant. When asked about the whereabouts of a fellow muleteer, Diego de Hojeda lamented, "I don't know where he is, because those that are muleteers never stop."[43] Yet, for all the hardships of such work, the wages exceeded substance and likely provided some possibilities for savings.

TRANSATLANTIC CROSSINGS AND THE SLAVE TRADE

Although many *mestizos* and *mulatos* worked in jobs intimately tied to commerce and the Atlantic world, few actively participated in transatlantic trade. Nevertheless, at least two Iberian-born *mulatos* arrived in New Spain thanks to their training as sailors. One of these men, Manuel Díaz, was mentioned above for the assortment of property he acquired as a muleteer. Yet that was a second career for him. Before arriving in New Spain, Manuel had traveled throughout the Mediterranean. He was born in Alvor, Portugal, around 1523. At a young age, Manuel became a "man of the sea."[44] At the age of twenty-four, he left for a longer maritime voyage that took him to the east. On that trip he spent time in Naples and the eastern Mediterranean. Once he returned from the Levant, Manuel left Portugal and headed to New Spain. Only after arriving in Mexico did Manuel leave the sea behind to take up muleteering. Although it is unclear what caused him to leave maritime life behind, the transition might have been gradual. At least one witness in his case described Manuel as a fisherman, suggesting that he had moved from trade ships to fishing boats before taking to the roads as a transporter.

Another example of an Iberian-born *mulato* using maritime trade to reach the Americas can be seen in the case against Antonio de Arenas.[45] Antonio was born in Estremoz, in the Alentejo region of Portugal, sometime around 1550. His father, Gaspar de Arena, was an *escribano* and was married to Antonio's mother, Isabel de Correa, a *negra*. Although hailing from an inland settlement, Antonio quickly found his way to the sea and worked in a variety of maritime positions. According to his statements, at age eight he had signed on as a *paje* (page or cabin boy), later working his way up to serve as a *grumete* (sailor apprentice) and then a sailor.[46] Eventually he found his way to New Spain after working as crew on a slave ship that collected its human cargo at Cabo Verde. Once in New Spain he abandoned the maritime life and traveled to Mexico City and Zacatecas and eventually settled in Istlahuaca. In 1578, the Inquisition convicted him of bigamy and sent him back to the sea for a four-year term as an unpaid oarsman of His Majesty's galleys.

The examples of Manuel and Antonio demonstrate an important means by which some Iberian-born *mulatos* entered the colony. Most of the Iberian-born *mulatos* in this sample were born in the Algarve of Portugal or in Andalusia. Both regions were heavily oriented toward maritime commerce, and many men there had some experience with naval trades. In fact, most of the witnesses in the cases against Antonio de Arenas and Manuel Díaz were Portuguese or Castilian men who declared their professions as mariners or fishermen. Certainly not all of these men continued those professions in New Spain. Both Manuel and Antonio abandoned the sea, eventually finding work inland. Nevertheless, these cases demonstrate that for many men born in the coastal regions of Iberia, the maritime life and heavy commercial traffic between Iberia, Africa, and the Indies provided an ideal means of immigration. The draw of the American colonies affected *mulatos, portugueses,* and *españoles* alike. It is not surprising that some Iberian-born *mulatos* used work in maritime commerce as a means to enter the Americas.

Antonio's participation in the growing transatlantic slave trade is also important. During his life, the Spanish crown authorized a trade in slaves via the *asiento* system that sold licenses in bulk primarily to Portuguese traders who had access to the Portuguese entrepôts of West Africa. Ships involved in the trade were required to present their licenses and register their voyages with the Casa de Contratación in Seville before departing for Africa and then the Americas.[47] Sailors who signed on to ships in Cadiz or Seville could find themselves on such voyages. Antonio was not unique in being an individual of African descent who became involved in the maritime trade in human beings. In 1601, several decades after Antonio's travels, Juan Sardina, a *mulato,* petitioned the viceroy of New Spain for the right to carry a sword and dagger.[48] In his petition, he noted that he was the illegitimate son of Captain Juan Alvares Sardina. He had worked on his father's slave ship based out of the Portuguese kingdom of Angola. Juan Sardina arrived in New Spain with a cargo of thirty slaves and had been entrusted to sell those slaves in Mexico. Having become accustomed to adorning himself with a sword for his personal protection and honor, Juan was upset when the *justicias* in Mexico prevented him from carrying the weapons. In response, he petitioned the viceroy for a license, claiming that he had worn the weapon in the Canaries, Angola, and Cartagena. The viceroy agreed, and Juan received his license. Like Antonio, Juan was of African descent and had become involved in the transatlantic slave trade. Their cases demonstrate how some free individuals of African descent could become active agents in the lucrative overseas trade in human captives.

Just as some *mulatos* participated in the transatlantic slave trade, so too were some born into bondage. In Inquisition cases examined here, seven *mulatos* were known to be slaves. Since legal status followed the "law of the womb," all of these individuals, five men and two women, were born to enslaved women. Of the seven, three were born in Spain and two in Mexico. Most of these *mulatos* worked as domestic slaves in their owners' homes. For example, Joaquín de Santa Ana was the slave of Don Carlos de Sámano, a tailor.[49] Similarly, Isabel, *mulata*, was owned by Juan Ruiz and had attended him and his family on their transatlantic journey to New Spain.[50] All but two of these enslaved *mulatos* were investigated by the tribunal for blasphemy. In particular, they were said to have renounced God immediately before or during physical punishment by their masters. This phenomenon has been studied by several scholars, including Frank Proctor and Javier Villa-Flores.[51] In blaspheming, these slaves engaged in a process of contestation and negotiation over the master-slave relationship and the legitimacy (or not) of physical punishments. Unfortunately these cases, unlike bigamy investigations, generally did not produce much testimony outside of the particulars of the heretical statements of the slaves. Consequently we know less about the lives of these slaves, other than their poor treatment, than we do of free *mulatos* investigated for other crimes.

WORKING WOMEN

While men held a wide array of occupations, the women in this sample did not. The vast majority of women who declared occupations served as *criadas* (servants or maids). Such a finding is not surprising. Throughout the colonial period domestic service represented the most common occupation for women.[52] While a majority of female laborers fell into the category of *criada*, not all *criadas* were equal. As has been discussed above, the term *criada* (or *criado*) could refer to a dependent of the household, including kin or wards, and to domestic servants. Among the small number of women in this sample, the difference between a *criada* servant and a *criada* dependent appeared to map onto *género* lines. Although the same number of *mestizas* and *mulatas* fell into this category, *mestizas* more frequently shared familial or social ties to their employer. In contrast, the *mulata criadas* found in this sample worked as hired domestic servants. Given the small sample of women, the observed differences between *mestizas* and *mulatas* provide suggestive clues into the ways in which women of mixed ancestry experienced life as *criadas*.

An excellent example of a *mestiza criada* can be seen in the opening case of this chapter. Catalina Sánchez served as a *criada* but clearly had a deeper relationship with her employer than can be explained by labor alone. The five-hundred-peso dowry given by Francisco de Heredia suggests that the two shared a social bond that transcended a normal patron-client relationship between a head of house and his domestic workers. Unfortunately for the historian, the case does not provide clear evidence for the nature of the bond that underpinned such a generous gift.

To a lesser degree, the case of Mari Sánchez, discussed in the last chapter, illustrates a similar situation.[53] Mari lived as a *criada* in the home of Andrés Moreno. After she was abducted by Pedro de Padilla, Moreno acted quickly to organize a search for her. Once she was found, Moreno initiated legal proceedings to force Padilla into a marriage. Moreno's swift action to protect Mari's honor and secure a marriage indicate that his concerns transcended those of an employer worried about lost labor. Moreno did not appear to be related to Mari; nevertheless, his actions hint that she may have lived as a ward in his home.

A clearer example of the special position occupied by some *mestiza criadas* can be seen in the life of Madalena Pérez.[54] In 1575, a young *español* named Martín de Salvatierra arrived in the Valle de Atlisco. He found a place in the home of Manuel Pérez. After a time, Martín became enamored of Manuel's *criada* and illegitimate daughter, Madalena. Various witnesses described Madalena as a *mestiza* or a *castiza*. Moreover, most *español* witnesses agreed that she was an honorable *doncella*, indicating that while in her father's home she lived according to Spanish standards of female honor and sexual propriety. Once the relationship between Martín and Madalena came to light, her father objected to their union. This conflict led to a legal battle between Manuel and Martín over the couple's right to marry. After a protracted suit, the couple's desire overcame the parental objections, and the ecclesiastical authorities allowed them to marry.[55] The marriage would eventually by annulled once it became known that Martín had taken vows as an Augustinian friar.

Although most of the Inquisition's investigation focused on Martín's actions, the case does elucidate the life of Madalena Pérez. She was publicly known to be the illegitimate daughter of Manuel Pérez and lived in his home under his protection. In testimony presented by Manuel, he did not openly acknowledge his paternity, instead calling Madalena simply his *criada*. Yet other witnesses, including his nephew, did not hide the paternal connection between Manuel and Madalena. Although he did not openly claim her as his daughter, we know that Manuel was keenly interested in her prospects. The fact that witnesses emphasized her sexual purity by calling her a *doncella* demonstrates that Manuel had protected Madalena's honor and that she had presented herself as a virtuous young woman. Although Martín may have hoped that a marriage to Madalena would forge a social connection to her father and to the community, the cause of Manuel's opposition cannot be determined. Maybe Martín did not have sufficient social standing or economic prospects to warrant a marriage to his daughter. Maybe Manuel had reservations about Martín's truthfulness; certainly we know he was lying about his past. Or maybe Manuel simply did not want to lose a productive member of his household. Whatever the reasoning, Manuel's actions demonstrate that Madalena was more than a *criada*; she was his illegitimate daughter and a woman whose prospects he fought to protect.

Some *mestiza criadas*, like most *mulatas* in this sample, were hired domestic workers who appear to have lacked social or kinship ties to their patron. A number of women's biographies highlight that such employment could be of varying terms, with some women working for several families over the years. For example, Ana Martín, a *mestiza criada*, lived an itinerant life.[56] She was born in Puebla around 1542 to a Portuguese settler and an *india*. During the 1560s and 1570s she traveled between Puebla and Mexico City, and later to Ixmiquilpan. This mobility led her to seek employment in several households. In Mexico City she worked for Madalena Guillén, and after arriving in Ixmiquilpan she entered the service of Ana Sarpara. It was likely in the service of Ana Sarpara that she met Pedro Márques, an *español* carter, whom she married despite her first husband, Juan Flores, a *mestizo* muleteer, still being alive.

Although *criadas* did not necessarily forge deep bonds with their employers, they could benefit from their patron's status. For example, when Juana Hernández, a *mulata criada*, discovered that her husband, Juan de Perales, had taken another wife, she asked her employer Manuel Tarrique to see that Perales was investigated and punished for his actions.[57] At other times the patron-client relationship could be less generous. For example, in her trial for double matrimony, Francisca Ramírez, a *mulata criada*, insisted that her mistress, Juana de Espina, had forced her to marry one of the household's *negro* slaves, Juan Biafara, while she was still a girl.[58] Furthermore, when questioned about her sexual life, Francisca admitted that she had engaged in sexual intercourse before she married when Pedro de Peña, a relative of her employers, forced himself on her.[59] Sadly, such abuse was not uncommon for women working as domestic laborers, regardless of *género*.[60]

A vivid example of the vicissitudes and dangers that *criadas* could encounter can be seen in the life of Juana Agustina, the *mestiza mulata* discussed in chapter 4.[61] After having been orphaned by her parents, Juan Martín, *indio*, and Catalina, *mulata*, she was raised by another *indio-mulata* couple.[62] Her patrons saw her married to an *indio* named Juanillo. She lived with Juanillo for a time. Eventually Juana's *mulato* uncle, Juan Cantero, took her from her husband's home. The two traveled to Guadalajara, where he placed her in the home of Diego de Ribera, an official serving in the cathedral. Juana continued working in Ribera's home until he died. With the death of her employer, the *licenciado* Altamirano had her placed in the home of Hernando de Cisneros.

While Juana Agustina served as a *criada* in the Cisneros home, a *mestizo* named Agustín de Vega abducted her and took her from Guadalajara to an *estancia* near Ocotlan. Soon after her arrival, the prior of Ocotlan removed her from Agustín de Vega and had her placed in the home of Pedro Brizeño Gaytán. Unfortunately Juana's unwilling journeys did not end there. While she was working in the home of Brizeño Gaytán, a group of men, including two *españoles* and a *mulato*, abducted her a second time. The men took her to an *estancia* owned by García de Contreras, the father of one of the abductors. Once there, they used threats and intimidation to convince her to marry a *mulato* resident named Pedro. Later she admitted to being too terrified to declare her previous marriage.

Eventually word of this second marriage returned to Pedro Brizeño Gaytán, who denounced Juana to the Inquisition. Although he made the denunciation, Brizeño Gaytán emphasized that Juana had been abducted from his home and appeared to use the investigation as a means of removing her from the men who had kidnapped her. Although the investigation did lead to her removal from the *estancia*, it also resulted in a conviction. The tribunal was somewhat lenient with its sentencing, and at least one member voted that her punishment not include whipping. Part of her sentence included one year of service in the convent of Santa Mónica so that she did not "wander about aimlessly."[63]

Although tragic, this case illustrates how powerless some *criadas* could find themselves. Juana Agustina experienced a perfect storm. As an orphaned Afro-indigenous woman, she was completely dependent on her Aro-indigenous caregivers. When they sought to marry her at a young age she had no recourse. Eventually, her nonresident uncle secured her employment as a *criada* in a prominent Spanish household. For a time this strategy worked and Juana made a life for herself as a *criada*. Yet even in a Spanish home her she found herself vulnerable and without strong protectors. After two abductions she found herself alone and on a rural *estancia* being forced to marry a man she did not know. Although her patron at the time appeared to be sympathetic to the plight faced by his *mulata criada*, he did not intercede on her behalf as quickly or as decisively as the patrons of *mestiza criadas* caught in similar situations. Although an extreme case, Juana Agustina's life illustrates how vulnerable women could be as *criadas*.

Although most women in this study worked as domestics, employment opportunities for women had grown by the late sixteenth century, and women of all *géneros* found themselves in a variety of economic niches, from petty merchants to tradeswomen.[64] Evidence for this process can be seen in the two *mulatas* who found employment in other occupations, one as a midwife (*partera*) and the other a tavern owner (*tabernera*).[65] Barbola de Zamora, a *mulata* born in Spain, was twice investigated for questionable practices bordering on witchcraft, *hechicería*. In 1565, she was accused of saying heretical and superstitious prayers and using questionable techniques to cure the "evil eye." She was married to a Spaniard, Urbán de Balderas, and lived in the mines of Zacatecas. After a thorough investigation of how she treated newborn children, it was determined that she was not guilty of heretical crimes or witchcraft but was simply ill versed in the proper technique for baptism in extremis.[66] She was ordered to refrain from using any unsanctioned cures for illnesses and to learn the proper form for baptism from the local priest.

Five years later, she was again investigated for practicing *hechicería*. This time she was accused of soliciting *indios chichimecos* to use peyote in order to divine the location of lost objects. Witnesses also claimed that she said that one could pray to a spirit she called the *"anima sola"* in order to find missing persons or to win the heart of one they desired. This time the inquisitors found her guilty, ordered her to public penance, and mandated a four-year exile from the mines. Her case is interesting in that it is clear that she found gainful occupation as a midwife but also practiced a variety of popular folk remedies. Even though she was Iberian-born, once in New Spain her practices reflect some syncretism with native belief, as she accepted indigenous practices as efficacious.[67] While a full examination of *hechicería* and cultural syncretism among Africans and their descendants is beyond the scope of this work, Barbola represents an important example of how some marginal individuals found economic benefits through superstitious practices that may have blended African, European, and indigenous beliefs.

The other *mulata* to declare a profession other than *criada* was Ana Cavallero. Like Barbola, Ana was born in Iberia. In 1574, she was accused of heretical statements by several of her neighbors. She lived in the central part of Mexico City's *traza* near the Dominican monastery. She ran her own business by selling wine and bread out of her home. The fact that she managed a tavern suggests that she was more successful than other female vendors of alcoholic beverages who operated on the street or in market stalls.[68] Unfortunately, selling alcoholic beverages and dealing with ribald customers came with its own disadvantages. According to Juan Bautista Gallegos and his wife, Doña Luisa de Villalobos, one day while they were walking by they overheard Ana saying, "It's better to be happy with your lover than unhappy in marriage."[69] One can imagine that a conversation had sprung up concerning a marriage gone sour or the first bloom of a love affair. Although she denied the statement, her neighbors' testimony led to her being convicted of blasphemy and sentenced to penance and a fifty-peso fine. This case is interesting in that two Spaniards, including a *doña*, chose to denounce their relatively successful *mulata* neighbor over an offhand statement. The phrase she uttered was quite common, and many individuals were investigated for having made similar claims. Although certainly heretical in its rejection of sacramental marriage, it would seem to have been a minor matter.[70] Nevertheless, Juan Bautista and Doña Luisa chose to pursue a denunciation. While hearing such a comment may have scandalized them, it is certainly possible that they chose to use Ana's moral slip to their advantage. Given that Ana ran her own store that sold wine, it is likely that they were upset over a *mulata* running an establishment that promoted drunkenness and public disorder in their block or were simply jealous of her economic success. As early as 1545, complaints from *vecinos* and prelates in Mexico City had resulted in royal *cédulas* seeking to restrict the sale of wine and prevent public drunkenness among *indios* and *negros*.[71] The spiritual complaint leveled against Ana Cavallero very well might have reflected her Spanish neighbors' temporal concerns over drunks on their street. In this respect, her denunciation may have been prompted more by her financial acumen and success than by her irreverence.

The fact that the two most successful *mulata* businesswomen came from Iberia is telling, although not conclusive. Barbola and Ana may have had more experience with Spanish business practices and the acquisition of marketable skills in Iberia than their often American-born counterparts—many of whom were Afro-indigenous. Both were born free and knew their Spanish fathers, suggesting a greater degree of familial connection and support than some *mulatos* who only knew their mothers. In the case of Barbola, we know she was married to a Spaniard, likewise suggesting better than average connections to

Spanish society. While their cases are probably idiosyncratic, they do suggest that in the early sixteenth century some *mulatas* could find employment on their own as businesswomen or skilled practitioners.

PERSONAL PROPERTY

One final way of gauging the economic success of individuals is through an analysis of the property they owned. As was mentioned above, the Inquisition asked defendants to declare any property or assets they owned. Few *mestizos* and *mulatos* did so. Overall, eleven defendants—five *mulatos* and six *mestizos*—declared property (see tables 6.3 and 6.4). Other defendants may have owned small amounts of property that they successfully hid from the court. Despite being a limited sample, there were some suggestive trends in property ownership that may highlight differences in the types of objects owned by men and women. In general, women owned more clothing and domestic items, and men owned weapons, tools, and animals. These differences may reflect ways that men and women chose to spend their income. Men appear to have invested in the items important for their employment and social status. Women's investment in clothing may represent a form of savings that could be used as collateral or liquidated when necessary.

The most common difference between men and women was in their ownership of clothing. Only two of six male defendants owned clothes, while four of five women declared clothing as property. The amount of clothing owned could be quite variable. The few items of clothing owned by the two men, Manuel Díaz (the *mulato* muleteer discussed above) and Diego Rodríguez del Pozo (a *mestizo* cowboy), likely represented changes of clothing. On the other hand, some of the women owned significantly more clothing, including men's apparel. For example, Mariana de los Reyes, a *mulata,* owned multiple petticoats, shirts, and skirts as well as trousers and a men's shirt and doublet. While today we are accustomed to owning many outfits and pieces of clothing, in the sixteenth century clothing was relatively much more expensive. These women may have seen the clothing they owned as an investment or a valuable means of obtaining credit if necessary.[72] Clothing

Table 6.3
PROPERTY HELD BY *MULATO* DEFENDANTS

	Date and Place	Goods	Occupation
Isabel Díaz	1574, Mexico City and Puebla	A chest Petticoats *Huipiles* (blouses)	*criada*
Manuel Díaz	1572, Xalapa	A grey horse A *jineta* saddle with *estradiote* stirrups An old *jinete* bridle Spurs An old blanket A tent made of local fabric A crossbow with its quiver A tool bag with pliers, hammer, and butteris An old black cloak Old blue breeches A local blanket A black raincoat Breeches made of local cloth A machete Eleven *reales* in cash	muleteer, fisherman
Juana Ramirez	1574, Mexico City and Taxco	Fifteen *pesos* held by Juan (*indio*) A trunk A doublet Two shirts Twenty pesos	*criada*
Mariana de los Reyes	1585, Tuxtla	Trousers (*zaraguelles*) of green cloth An old blue petticoat A shirt of Rouen [cloth] made of cotton, with wide, threadbare sleeves A green *faldellín* (skirt) A men's doublet with silk buttons A blanket of three and a half varas Some skirts made from Campeche fabric Blue wool stockings A green skirt with a purple velvet fringe	
Francisco Rodríguez	1579, Coatzacoalcos	Two female burros on the *estancia* of Francisco Ortiz A burro on the *estancia* of Juan Beltrán Cota One hundred cows on the *estancia* of Francisco Ortiz 150 pesos in *reales* lent to Francisco Ortiz with a receipt Fifty and some odd pesos owed by Alonso de Tapia Eighty pesos that Juan Beltrán Cota collected on his on his behalf A business contract with Francisco Ortiz	cowboy

SOURCES: AGN, Inq., vols. 94, 101, 108, 137.

Table 6.4
PROPERTY HELD BY MESTIZO DEFENDANTS

Name	Date and Place	Goods	
Diego Díaz (alias Rodríguez)	1575, Cuernavaca	A small house or shack (*casilla*) worth ten or twelve pesos	
Bartolome Hernández	1578, Puebla	A horse A *jinete* saddle A harquebus A sword	

Beatriz Hernández	1572, Taxco	A small chest with key, containing:
		    A small sack of cacao which according to Pedro Coyote (husband) contains 8018 cacaos
		    Some local blankets (*mantas*)
		    A shirt of local cloth
		    A *marco* of silver polish
		    A lump of unrefined silver ore weighing up to one ounce
		    A wooden bed without sheets
		    A small scale for weighing silver	

Ana Martín (alias Beatriz	1572, Puebla	On her person
		    Tawny-colored skirts
		    A white *huipil*
		In the custody of Bartolomé García
		    Two mattresses
		    A bed made of cotton with its wooden frame
		    A chest with linens, including two pesos worth of new locally made tablecloths
		    Two handkerchiefs, one black, one white
		    A bolt of homemade cotton fabric five varas long
		    Two brass candlesticks
		    Seven bundles of meat and flour
		    Three carafes for wine
		    [Illegible]
		    An *artesa* [trough]
		    Four good horses, three equipped with packsaddles, the other a tamed colt. [Ana] heard that Bartolomé García, carpenter, sold the colt to another carpenter named Arcintega for one hundred *pesos de tepuzque*. [Arcintega was not a carpenter but a painter who lived in Mexico City]
			criada

continued

Table 6.4 (*continued*)
PROPERTY HELD BY MESTIZO DEFENDANTS

Name	Date and Place	Goods	

		An iron skillet
		An iron grill
		Three small images made locally
		Four white skirts
		A trunk like those of Mechuacan,
		    full of *chuchumite prieto*
		    [a native dye]
		Two tables, a large one and a small one
		Three sitting chairs
		Two large benches	

Jusepe de Molina	1600, Compostela and Mexico	Thirty mares large and
		    small and a horse
		    for collecting them
		An old sword carried on his belt
		An old cape of London,
		    breeches of the same,
		    and an old doublet
		Six bushels of corn
		Two old chests
		A medium-sized sidesaddle
		A *jinete* saddle with *jinete* stirrups
			farrier

Diego Rodríguez del Pozo	1572, Xiquilpa	Two very old horses
		An *estradiote* saddle
		Two pairs of stockings, one of yellow
		    taffeta and the other of white
		    kersey cloth
		A black cape, on his person
		Two velvet caps, on his person
		An ill-treated sword
		Jinete spurs
			cowboy

SOURCES: AGN, Inq., vols. 94, 95, 100, 104, 262.

could easily be pawned or used as collateral. While the clothing owned by Manuel Díaz was clearly worn from daily use, the clothing owned by many women in the sample was not described as worn or old, suggesting that they might have been keeping the clothing for its material value rather than day-to-day use.

While women tended to own more clothing, men were more likely to own weapons, animals, and tools or tack. Four of the six men owned weapons of some kind. Three of the men owned swords. That the sword-owning men were all *mestizos* is not surprising. During the late sixteenth century, the legal norms for sword ownership underwent a slight change. Early royal *cédulas* had prohibited any sword ownership by *mulatos,* while allowing *mestizos* to petition for licenses to carry swords. By the late sixteenth century, many *mestizos* had begun to carry swords even without the requisite license. Despite the fact that no changes had been made to the legal code, by the 1590s viceroys began to uphold *mestizo* ownership of swords as a right, even without prior authorization.[73] On the other hand, *mulatos, negros,* and *pardos* were still prohibited unless given a license by the king or viceroy. The fact that three of the four *mestizos* in this sample had taken to carrying swords suggests that like many of their contemporaries, they hoped to use these weapons as a symbol of honor and status as well as an important tool for self-defense.

Five of the six men owned animals, although for different purposes. Three of the men owned animals for their personal use. For example, the muleteer Manuel Díaz owned his own horse and tack. Similarly, Bartolomé Hernández, a *mestizo,* owned a horse and saddle, while Diego Rodríguez del Pozo, a *mestizo* cowboy, owned two old horses and a saddle. In contrast, Jusepe de Molina (discussed above) and Francisco Rodríguez, a *mulato* cowboy, owned substantially more animals and were likely engaged in animal husbandry. While Jusepe managed thirty mares that had been given to him in a dowry, Francisco owed several burros as well as a hundred head of cattle. Although the case against Francisco does not specify how he came to own so many animals, his declaration of property suggests that he was an astute economic actor who had use partnerships with Spaniards to profit from ranching.[74] In addition to the animals he listed, Francisco noted that several Spaniards owed him over two hundred pesos. He also was in possession of a written business contract with Francisco Ortiz, a Spanish rancher and one of his debtors. Francisco's ability to extend substantial credit to neighboring Spaniards and enter into business agreements suggests that he had been relatively successful as a cowboy and had begun to transition from a ranch hand to a ranch owner.

Although most men who declared property owned animals, so too did one woman, Ana Martín.[75] Of all those declaring property, Ana declared the largest number of items. While most of the items she declared were household goods, she also claimed to own four horses. Three of these animals were equipped with packsaddles, while the other was a colt. At the time of her arrest the colt had just been sold for one hundred *pesos de tepuzque*.[76] The tack that the animals were equipped with suggests that Ana might have had economic interests beyond her work as a *criada*. The packsaddles might suggest that she rented the animals to transporters or managed a small transportation business on the side. Furthermore, her remaining assets suggest that she had most of the material goods necessary to set up her own home. The inventory of property included a mattress and bed frame, benches, tables, linens, cookware, foodstuffs, and religious images. Unlike other defendants with property, Ana's list of goods looks the most like what one would expect to find in a fully furnished household.

One of the least common goods declared by defendants was currency. Of the eleven persons in the sample, only three declared any cash on their persons. The muleteer Manuel Díaz carried eleven reales or just under a peso and a half. This likely represented enough cash to purchase food while traveling on the road. Juana Ramírez, an Afro-indigenous *criada*, reported a much greater sum. She not only had twenty pesos in specie but had also given fifteen pesos to an *indio* named Juan. This was a sizable amount of savings that might have represented a conscious decision to save wages earned as a housekeeper. Additionally tantalizing is the fact that she was married to an African slave, named Antón (technically she was married to two African slaves, both named Antón). Her unusually large stash of cash may have been intended to help buy the freedom of her enslaved husband. Finally, and most uniquely, Beatriz Hernández, a *mestiza* living in Taxco, declared currency in the form of cacao beans.

In the pre-Columbian period cacao beans represented one of the most versatile mediums of exchange in everyday transactions. During the early colonial period, the difficulty in supplying enough specie—particularly small denominations—insured that the traditional use of cacao beans as currency remained viable.[77] In the case of Beatriz Hernández, the eight thousand plus cacao beans she owned represented a sizable savings. In 1555, Viceroy Velasco ordered that cacao beans be valued at one hundred and forty to a real; however, the actual exchange rate may have varied between forty and two hundred cacao beans to the real.[78] Using an average of one hundred cacao beans to the real, Beatriz had approximately ten pesos worth of cacao, or roughly three months of wages for an unskilled day laborer. In addition to cacao she also owned several mantas (bolts of cotton cloth). These may have also represented a currency-like item, as in the pre-Columbian period mantas were used as a larger medium of exchange than cacao beans. But her economic activities did not end there. Beatriz also owned a lump of silver ore weighing one *onza* (approximately one ounce), a scale used to weigh silver, and silver polish. As a resident of a prominent silver mining zone, Beatriz and her husband Pedro Hernández Coyote, an *indio*, likely hoped to profit from the mining and refining process. In her testimony she described Pedro as a *rescatador* (refiner), suggesting that these goods were likely used to support Pedro's work and their household income.

Overall, the property listed by these defendants is modest. Most individuals only owned a few items. Women tended to own clothing or domestic goods while men owned weapons or animals. In each case the property owned roughly paralleled the occupations held by their owners. Despite the limited sample and the modest amount of property, several of these individuals should be recognized for being relatively successful economic actors. The cowboy Francisco Rodríguez had managed to become a small-scale rancher and creditor. Beatriz Hernández sought economic advancement by participation in the local industry of silver mining and refining. Ana Martín far surpassed the modest place held by most *criadas* and was able to outfit her own household as well as manage several pack animals. While many of their contemporaries were likely less successful, these individuals demonstrate that economic success, as measured through accumulated material wealth, was not outside the reach of *mestizos* or *mulatos*.

CONCLUSION

This chapter shows that as early as the 1560s and 1570s—only two generations removed from the conquest—some *mestizos* and *mulatos* had moved into the ranks of tradesmen and artisans or had acquired reasonably well remunerated jobs in key sectors of the colonial economy. Although limited in number, these cases illustrate the variety of occupations held by men and women of mixed ancestry during the late sixteenth century. The diversity of employment among *mestizos* and *mulatos* reflects a variety of factors. Most broadly, the cases examined here suggest that in the early colonial period there were jobs to be had and that one's *género* need not necessarily define one's occupational choices. At the same time, individuals' social position and cultural affinities did shape their participation in the labor force.

Ties to Spanish family or patrons could provide men with training and employment. The extent and duration of support could vary depending on circumstance, and some men of mixed ancestry chose to leave skilled trades to take up other occupations. The demand for labor in rural areas drew *mestizos* and *mulatos* from various backgrounds. Although life as muleteers and cowboys could be difficult and dangerous, the work paid reasonably well, and men in these jobs manifested a reasonably large degree of spatial mobility. In some cases, *mestizos* and *mulatos* living in rural areas formed and maintained social and familial connections to *indios*. These affinities may have facilitated their entry into rural occupations or helped them form community in regions dominated by *pueblos de indios*. Most women who worked served as *criadas*, yet the experiences of *criadas* could vary. Some women, possibly more *mestizas* than *mulatas*, lived as wards and served patrons who protected them in various ways. Other *criadas* appeared to work as hired help and did not benefit from the same degree of patron support.

Although financial and economic success can be hard to determine from the available evidence, some men and women of mixed ancestry did appear to be successful entrepreneurs. Juan Méndez and Ana Cavallero ran their own businesses that included storefronts. The cowboy-turned-rancher Francisco Rodríguez had become a small-time creditor to his *español* neighbors. Even *criadas* like Ana Martín and Beatriz Hernández managed to accumulate a sizable assortment of personal property that likely supported small-time business dealings. Overall these cases attest to the real possibility of social and economic success among early colonial *mestizos* and *mulatos*.

While the cases in this chapter do not represent an overall cross section of *mestizo* and *mulato* occupations, they do provide powerful examples of how men and women entered occupations, moved between jobs, and were able to find some economic success. Certainly discrimination limited the available opportunities, but social networks and family ties proved useful to overcoming abstract prejudice. As in previous chapters, the cases examined here reveal the diversity of lived experience among *mestizos* and *mulatos*. Men and women of these *géneros* came from a variety of backgrounds, operated within various social networks, and moved through different cultural spaces. The variability in origins and social position contributed to their diverse experience in the labor force. Individuals' family ties, patrons, birthplace, and cultural formation could all contribute to their choice of occupation or occupations. Moreover, these cases demonstrate that *mestizos* and *mulatos* were not hapless victims of chance in an unfavorable labor market. Rather, their own choices, resourcefulness, and support networks significantly contributed to their socioeconomic position. While certain limits existed, and entrance into skilled trades required patronage and support, by the end of the sixteenth century the diverse backgrounds of early *mestizos* and *mulatos* contributed to the various ways they participated in the colonial economy.

Conclusion

This book shows that during the late fifteenth and early sixteenth century, Spanish exploration and colonization of the Americas led to the creation of new categories of difference—*géneros de gente*—to describe the varied population of Spanish America. The creation of those categories represented a recursive process. Initially, explorers, conquistadors, and settlers created categories to define the various people who came to inhabit the new Spanish American landscape. Over time, stereotypes based on older conceptions of difference and new colonial realities were mapped onto these colonial *géneros.* In response to petitions and reports from the Americas, the colonial legal system integrated those stereotypes into juridical codes that privileged certain *géneros*, such as *español,* while imposing burdens and restrictions on others. The legal codification of *géneros de gente* helped perpetuate and promote the stereotypes associated with each *género.* However, these juridical norms did not rigidly circumscribe the lives of colonial subjects. In fact, many individuals of mixed ancestry, *mestizos* and *mulatos,* lived in ways that belied legal restrictions and popular stereotypes. As a result of their diverse origins, social networks, and cultural formation *mestizos* and *mulatos* did not conform to any monolithic standard. Men and women of these *géneros* married a diversity of spouses, and members of *géneros* that by law should never have associated with one another came to forge close social and affective ties. In the early colonial period, economic opportunities abounded, and many individuals of mixed ancestry were able to forge social bonds that allowed them to hold well-paying jobs affording the possibility of economic advancement. The diverse lived experiences of *mestizos* and *mulatos* provide a counterpoint to the social stereotypes embodied in colonial laws.

The disjuncture between abstract prejudices entrenched in law and the diverse experiences of individuals of mixed ancestry provides a means to better understand the interrelationships within early colonial society and the nature of Spanish colonialism. In particular, this book highlights an important contradiction present within Spanish colonialism. From the outset, Spanish colonial expansion into the Americas relied on private individuals. Conquistadors and early settlers participated in the process of conquest and colonization in order to gain recognition from the crown and improve their positions. Even after the monarchy began to appoint royal officials to govern, government institutions relied on colonial subjects' complaints, reports, and petitions in order to understand problems on the ground, real and imagined. The juridical construction of *géneros de gente* grew out of this dynamic. Colonists mobilized this language of difference to describe the varied people present in colonial society and the problems that arose as a result of the interactions between different groups. By appropriating this language and imbedding it within the legal code, the monarchy sought to address the concerns of its subjects. However, to be effective, laws require implementation and compliance. Colonial subjects needed to accept and abide by the specific laws for those laws to have their intended effect. The examination of *géneros de gente* illustrates that, for a number of reasons, colonial subjects in early New Spain did not abide by the spirit or letter of the laws that their own petitions and complaints had helped produce.

This discrepancy reveals a tension inherent to the Spanish colonial experience. Colonial subjects of all *géneros* wanted *buen gobierno* and a responsive government. Yet, at the same time, subjects did not want policies of *buen gobierno* to impinge upon their ability to pursue their interests. From the earliest decades, complaints over the violence, real or imagined, perpetrated by *negros* against *indios* and *españoles* led to laws restricting the mobility of slaves and placed greater responsibilities on slave owners to prevent such violence. Yet Spaniards routinely violated such laws when they did not align with their particular interests. Officials and prominent citizens armed slaves as bodyguards even when others complained that those *negros* harmed *indios* and caused civil unrest. *Encomenderos* and entrepreneurs used *negro* slaves or hired *mulatos* and *mestizos* to oversee *indio* laborers on rural estates even though the presence of such persons violated the basic principles that underpinned the two-republic system. Complaints over *mestizo* scriveners, *encomenderos*, and priests led to restrictions on men of that *género*. At the same time, Spaniards carefully guarded their *mestiza* daughters for marriage and helped provide for the economic futures of their *mestizo* sons. On the whole, colonial subjects desired royal action when general circumstances hurt their interests but flouted such prohibitions when the legal norm or social convention encroached on their particular actions or desires.

This fundamental contradiction within Spanish colonialism reflects the complex interrelationships that existed between individuals of all *géneros* from the outset of Spanish colonialism. *Indios, mestizos, mulatos, negros,* and *españoles* did not exist in isolation from one another. Ties of patronage, kinship, residence, occupation, and culture bound members of all *géneros* to their contemporaries. Although the law could define the juridical place of a *mestizo, mulato, indio,* or *negro,* in reality no one conformed to that abstraction. The various lives examined in this study have illustrated the myriad ways that colonial subjects lived together. Well-born *mestizos* grew up in the homes of Spaniards, where they worked alongside *indio* servants and *negro* slaves. In other cases, children born to Spanish fathers and indigenous mothers seemingly disappeared. Those accepted into Spanish society lived as *españoles,* becoming integrated into the developing creole society. In contrast, indigenous society incorporated other children of mixed *español-indio* unions who came to live and work as *indios.* Similarly, some *mulatos* grew up in *pueblos de indios* among indigenous kin and found work on rural estates owned by Spaniards. Other *mulatos* lived and worked in Spanish homes or businesses, forging social networks with other Afro-Mexican slaves and servants. Overall, kinship, residence, occupation, and patronage fostered relationships that allowed the lived experiences of particular individuals to deviate from the abstraction of juridical norms and racial stereotypes.

The diversity among early colonial *géneros de gente* raises questions about their underlying meaning. If any particular term could be applied to such a diverse array of people, what did it signify? In her study of *mestizos* in colonial New Granada, Joanne Rappaport has argued that *mestizos* did not represent a "sociological group." Instead, the labels of *mestizo* and *mulato* served as categories to which people were assigned.[1] The diversity visible among Mexican *mestizos* and *mulatos* supports this assertion. However, *mestizo* and *mulato* did mean something to colonial subjects. Even though the range of lived experience challenges the view that *géneros* represented shared sociological groups, colonial subjects, including *mestizos* and *mulatos*, shared a set of understandings of how to categorize one another.[2] In the early colonial period, *mestizo* functioned as a category of exclusion from either *español* or *indio*. Individuals labeled *mestizo* lacked sufficient social or cultural attributes to be considered either Spanish or indigenous. In contrast, the ascription of *mulato* seems to have been based in the presence of social, cultural, and likely physical attributes denoting partial African ancestry. In each case, a shared cultural logic facilitated the process of ascription, even though neither group manifested a strong corporate identity, at least in the sixteenth century. In later centuries, *mulatos* would come to form corporate identities linked to their shared ascription, especially when their racial categorization overlapped with institutional memberships.[3]

Although this study has focused on the sixteenth and early seventeenth centuries, the patterns of lived experience found among *mestizos* and *mulatos* help shed light on the *longue durée* of racial experience in colonial Mexico and suggest avenues for future research. Most significantly, the possibility that roughly half of late-sixteenth-century *mulatos* may have been Afro-indigenous greatly expands our knowledge of early African-indigenous interaction in Spanish America and complicates our understanding of the origins of early Afro-Mexicans. Such findings bolster a growing body of scholarship that has begun to uncover the multitude of ways that Spanish colonialism, purposefully or inadvertently, brought Africans into contact with Native Americans.[4] At the same time, the existence of sixteenth-century Afro-Mexican social networks, which could include *mulatos* of various ancestries, adds to a growing body of scholarship that has demonstrated the importance of shared community among colonial *negros* and *mulatos*.[5] Yet gaps in our knowledge persist. The primary temporal focus of this study ends just as the slave trade to New Spain began to grow in intensity. How did the patterns of early colonial African-indigenous interaction persist as many more *bozales* entered the kingdom? Did the changing scope of the slave trade alter the factors that had facilitated the rise of sixteenth-century Afro-indigenous *mulatos*? Did these *mulatos'* position between indigenous society and Afro-Mexican social networks perpetuate ties between these two groups even as Afro-Mexican demographics changed dramatically?

The marriage patterns of early colonial *mestizos* and *mulatos* show that these two *géneros* engaged in a greater degree of exogamy than the parent groups (*españoles, negros,* and *indios*). Scholars of the late seventeenth and eighteenth century have found similar patterns.[6] Across time and space, *mestizos* and *mulatos* appear to have contracted a more diverse array of marriages than other groups. The specific permutations of these unions cannot be divorced from the social, cultural, and historical context of the communities in which they lived.[7] Nevertheless, the findings of this study suggest that the diversity found within these two *géneros* afforded *mestizos* and *mulatos* a myriad of connections to other individuals within society. These connections facilitated affective ties and in turn resulted in exogamous unions. Further research into the social and cultural networks of *mestizos* and *mulatos* in particular communities at particular times can help better illuminate the forces that facilitated exogamy over time and space. Similarly, the varied social and cultural backgrounds of early colonial *mestizos* and *mulatos* facilitated entrance into a wide range of occupations and had already come to represent a middle layer of the colonial labor force. This finding parallels occupational data found for later periods.[8] Unfortunately the lack of systematic occupational data for the sixteenth century inhibits direct correlations through time. Nevertheless, this study posits that the diverse backgrounds of *mestizos* and *mulatos* facilitated their presence in a myriad of jobs and occupations. Future research into the importance of family connections, social networks, cultural affinities, and residence can help us better understand the forces that contributed to *mestizo* and *mulato* patterns of work through time.

Finally, this analysis of difference and lived experience of racial minorities in early colonial Mexico speaks to the broader history of race in the Atlantic world and beyond. While racial categories and racial stereotypes represent some of the most profound legacies of the Age of Exploration, particular articulations of race and racial categories were the product of their own historical development. In the case of Mexico and Spanish America, conceptions of difference evolved out of preexisting modes of thinking and seeing. From the outset, categories of difference were based in the language of privilege, power, place, and religion. As Europeans began to construct an understanding of the New World and its people, those existing modes of thinking changed and adapted to new realities. Older notions of difference morphed and were recombined to describe new groups of people. In doing so, these categories elided social, cultural, and physical characteristics. The terminology that resulted maintained its connection to relations of power but came to reflect the complexities of a colony populated by diverse subjects descended from a triad of founding groups. Yet the outcome of this process, the *géneros de gente* of sixteenth-century New Spain, were not yet races, even though such terms had begun to adopt certain racial attributes.[9] Most importantly, they encoded racial notions that linked moral and social stereotypes to particular categorizations associated with lineage, culture, and phenotype. Nevertheless, the process of ascription remained rooted in complex assessment that privileged social and cultural attributes over purely physical ones.

This framework of difference was neither monolithic nor could it be. Like other colonial empires, Spanish rule relied on the acceptance of those it governed. The disjuncture between abstract legal constructions of difference and lived experiences highlights the ways in which Spanish colonialism was bounded by the wills and whims of its own subjects—even those being denigrated by increasingly racial notions of difference.[10] The important contingencies that mediated and molded the perception of difference and racial categories in colonial Mexico speak to the complex social connections that bound all members of colonial society together. As we further explore how race was constructed over time and space, we must remain cognizant of the forces that fostered disjuncture between abstract prejudices and the lived experiences of race in particular places and times. In this regard, the example of early colonial Mexico provides a powerful model of how difference was defined in the early modern world, but also how it could be hidden, mitigated, confused, or transcended.

NOTES

ABBREVIATIONS

AGI   Archivo General de Indias
AGN   Archivo General de la Nación

INTRODUCTION

1. Restall, Sousa, and Terraciano, *Mesoamerican Voices,* 65. Original translation from Nahuatl by James Lockhard with modifications by Lisa Sousa and Kevin Terraciano.

2. "Carta de Fray Nicolas de Witte a S. M.," Archivo General de Indias (hereafter AGI), Mexico 280, N. 57.

3. Martínez, *Genealogical Fictions,* 161–67.

4. Boyer, "Negotiating Calidad"; Bristol, *Christians, Blasphemers, and Witches,* 26–27; Rappaport, *The Disappearing Mestizo,* 38–42.

5. Covarrubias Orozco, Arellano, and Zafra, *Tesoro de la lengua castellana,* s.v. "casta," 473.

6. The history of these concepts receives fuller treatment in chapter 1. For historical accuracy I have tried to limit my use of both terms in this book. Nevertheless, to maintain continuity with the existing literature, I refer to *castas* or the *sistema de castas* where appropriate.

7. Hering Torres, "Purity of Blood," 31–33.

8. Cañizares-Esguerra, "New World, New Stars."

9. Chance and Taylor, "Estate and Class in a Colonial City," 482–83; Chance and Taylor, "Estate and Class: A Reply"; Israel, *Race, Class, and Politics*; McAlister, "Social Structure and Social Change," 36; McCaa, Schwartz, and Grubessich, "Race and Class," 433; Mörner, *Race Mixture;* Mörner, "Economic Factors and Stratification."

10. Cope, *The Limits of Racial Domination;* Seed, "Social Dimensions"; Valdes, "Decline of the Sociedad de Castas."

11. Martínez, *Genealogical Fictions,* 12–13.

12. Palmer, *Slaves of the White God;* Bryant, *Rivers of Gold, Lives of Bondage;* Proctor, *Damned Notions of Liberty.*

13. Bennett, *Africans in Colonial Mexico;* Carroll, *Blacks in Colonial Veracruz;* Mondragón Barrios, *Esclavos africanos en la Ciudad de México;* Restall, *The Black Middle.*

14. Bristol, *Christians, Blasphemers, and Witches;* Vinson III, "Race and Badge"; Vinson, *Bearing Arms for His Majesty;* Vinson and Restall, "Black Soldiers, Native Soldiers"; Germeten, *Black Blood Brothers.*

15. Bristol, "From Curing to Witchcraft"; Lewis, *Hall of Mirrors;* Megged, "Magic, Popular Medicine and Gender."

16. Althouse, "Contested Mestizos, Alleged Mulattos"; Sierra Silva, "From Chains to Chiles"; O'Toole, *Bound Lives;* Brockington, *Blacks, Indians, and Spaniards;* Carroll, "Los Mexicanos negros"; Restall, *Beyond Black and Red;* Robert C. Schwaller, "*Mulata, Hija de Negro y India.*"

17. Owensby, *Empire of Law,* 8.

18. Cañizares-Esguerra, *How to Write the History of the New World,* 9–10; Silverblatt, *Modern Inquisitions,* 27; Sweet, "Iberian Roots."

19. Geertz, *The Interpretation of Cultures,* 6–10.

20. Restall, "History of the New Philology."

21. Contemporaries generally called the dominant language *castellano*. For clarity I have generally used the modern name, Spanish.

22. Vinson, "Introduction," 9.

Chapter 1

Epigraph: "Carta de los conquistadores y pobladores antigous a S.M.," 1564, AGI, Mexico 168, N. 101, fs. 303–6v. "[L]os españoles della crecen e multiplican mucho y syn los españoles que aqui nacen e vienen de esos reynos ay gran numero de mulatos y mestizos jente muy mal enclynada pero valientes y determinados para qual quier desverguenca y conviene a raygar e perpetuar v. mag jente noble en su servicio para defensa dellos y yncovinyentes que la jente ruyn podra causar."

1. In this chapter I have chosen to use the term "Iberia" rather than "Spain." In the fifteenth and sixteenth century, *España* had not become the common descriptor for the kingdoms under the control of the monarchs of Castile and Aragon. Consequently, my use of "Iberia" should be interpreted here to refer to the multitude of holdings joined dynastically through the marriage of Ferdinand of Aragon and Isabella of Castile that would later come to be known as the *reinos de España,* or more commonly *España*. While much of the material in this chapter would also pertain loosely to Portugal, an examination of pan-Iberian beliefs is beyond the scope of this work.

2. Kamen, *Spain, 1469–1714*, 8–12.

3. Ruiz, *Spanish Society*, 6.

4. Dominguez Ortiz, *Las clases privilegiadas*, 71.

5. Gerbet, *La nobleza en la corona de Castilla*, 46. Unfortunately, a discussion of the vagaries of entrance into the *hidalguia* is beyond the scope of this work.

6. Collantes de Teran, *Sevilla en la baja edad media*, 253.

7. For examples of this view, see the letters of the viceroys of New Spain, AGI, Mexico vols. 19–27 (1536–1609). Especially as Iberian immigration increased toward the end of the sixteenth century, the viceroys regularly applied these terms to the lower-status immigrants that were flooding into the colony. In 1594, Viceroy Don Luis de Velasco complained bitterly about the *gente perdida* that had recently arrived. "Carta de don Luis de Velasco a S.M.," 1594, AGI, Mexico 22, N. 128, fs. 8.

8. A good example of these terms being used can be seen in the *probanzas de merito* (proofs of merit) from the conquest era. Many conquistadors chose to use this moral language of status to advance their claims for compensation and royal privileges. See "Informaciones de Méritos y Servicios," AGI, Patronato, S. 3.

9. María Elena Martínez has argued that the popular and institutional emphasis on verifying religious genealogy in Spain grew in importance during the fifteenth century and became common in the sixteenth century. She also argues that the preoccupation with religious descent was central to the formation of Latin American terms for racial difference. My argument here builds upon that assumption and highlights that other categories of difference factored into new American terminology. Martínez, *Genealogical Fictions*, 40.

10. Covarrubias Orozco, Arellano, and Zafra, *Tesoro de la lengua castellana*, 473.

11. Corominas, *Diccionario critico etimologico*, vol. 1, 914. According to Corominas, the first Portuguese usage to describe the social structures of India was in 1516, with the English adoption in 1588.

12. Covarrubias Orozco, Arellano, and Zafra, *Tesoro de la lengua castellana*, 1396. "Raza: la casta de caballos castizos, a los cuales señalan con hierro para que sean conocidos. Raza, en el paño, la hilaza que diferencia de los demás hilos de la trama. Parece haberse dicho quasi reaza, porque aza, en lengua toscana, vale hilo, y la raza en el paño sobrepuesto desigual. Raza, en lo linajes se toma en mala parte, como tener alguna raza de moro o judio."

13. Kamen, *The Spanish Inquisition*, 239.

14. Ibid., 238–41; Martínez, *Genealogical Fictions*, 45. Kamen and Martínez differ in their view of the societal consequences of these statutes. Kamen noted that the number of institutions with such statutes was relatively small. For example only six sees required proofs and many Castilian city councils did not impose similar restrictions. Moreover, he found that many institutions had ambivalent attitudes toward the enactment of such statutes as well as the rigidity of their application. Martínez counters that although the number of institutions with such statutes was small, those that did maintain purity laws were some of the most

prestigious in the kingdoms. Consequently their prestige helped promote their particular construction of ethno-religious purity.

15. Martínez, *Genealogical Fictions*, 66–68.

16. Ibid., 74. The phrase *publica voz y fama* and its analog *publico y notorio* appear frequently in legal documents recording testimony and reflect the importance of communal consensus in determining the veracity of an individual's claims. Other genres of documents include *probanzas de merito* and *interrogatorios*, questionnaires used by the prosecution and defense in criminal or Inquisition cases.

17. Ibid., 142–71.

18. Herzog, *Defining Nations*, 2.

19. Ibid., 67.

20. Collantes de Teran, *Sevilla en la baja edad media*, 214–18.

21. For example, see AGN, Inq., vol. 2, exp. 1 (*alemán*); vol. 9, exp. 6 (*inglés*); vol. 14, exp. 36 (*flamenco*); vol. 31, exp. 4 (*francés*); vol. 75, exp. 16 (*vizcaíno*). By the late sixteenth century, religious conflict arising due to the Protestant reformation led to increased suspicion of persons from northern Europe, especially the German states and the Low Countries.

22. Forbes, *Africans and Native Americans*, 75–79. *Esclavos blancos* represented a diverse lot, the majority being of Muslim descent enslaved during the Reconquest or in North Africa. See Pike, "Sevillian Society."

23. Cortes, *La esclavitud en Valencia*, 56–59.

24. Franco Silva, *Esclavitud en Andalucia*, 49.

25. Ibid. See also Boyd-Bowman, "Negro Slaves."

26. Many examples of this can be found in matrimonial records for Mexico. For example: "Leonor de color morena de tierra de Biafara," AGN, Matrimonios 128, exp. 25, 1583.

27. Herzog, *Defining Nations*, 24–29.

28. Ibid., 29–31.

29. Ibid., 18.

30. For excellent theoretical work on the way culture shaped the dynamic interaction of Europeans and non-Europeans in the early modern period, see Sahlins, *Islands of History*, xiv. In examining the interaction between James Cook and the Hawaiian Islanders, Sahlins highlights the importance of the "structure of the conjuncture." This theoretical view focuses on understanding the cultural constructs and predispositions that influence both sides of any encounter. In this case Cook and Hawaiians structured their understanding of the other through their own historically based cultural filters. James Lockhart has proposed a similar argument for the encounter between Spaniards and the native peoples of the Americas. See Lockhart, *Of Things of the Indies*, 99. The phrase he uses to describe the same process is "double-mistaken identity." Similarly to Sahlins, Lockhart emphasizes that each side of the encounter could only view the other side through its own existing cultural framework.

31. Most scholars who use *casta* and *castas* to describe persons of mixed-ancestry have studied the seventeenth and eighteenth centuries during which these

terms came to be applied as such. For example, see Carrera, *Imagining Identity;* Chance and Taylor, "Estate and Class in a Colonial City"; Chance and Taylor, "Ecology of Race and Class"; Cope, *The Limits of Racial Domination;* Katzew, *Casta Painting;* Kuznesof, "Raza, clase y matrimonio"; Lewis, *Hall of Mirrors;* McAlister, "Social Structure and Social Change"; McCaa, Schwartz, and Grubessich, "Race and Class"; Mörner, *Race Mixture;* Seed, "Social Dimensions"; Valdes, "Decline of the Sociedad de Castas"; Vinson, "Studying Race from the Margins."

32. Sixteenth-century *reales cédulas* only use *casta* in either its ethno-religious sense or to reference breeding stock. For example, "Real Cédula dando licencia a Iñigo Ortiz de Retes para llevar un chino a Nueva España," 1548, AGI, Indiferente 1964, L. 11, fs. 106. This *cédula* notes that the *chino,* a native of China, could be taken to New Spain because he was not *"de casta de moros."* Another example: "Real Cédula al lugarteniente de gobernador . . . sobre que no le echen en sus dehesas caballos ruines que le dañen su casta," 1536, AGI, Santo Domingo 2280, L. 2, fs. 92. This *cédula* references the problem of bad breeding stock, *caballos ruines,* being introduced to pastures with better-bred horses, *caballos de casta.* Even as late as 1602, the Spanish crown used *casta* to refer to animal breeding: "Real Cédula al Virrey de la Nueva España que envie a las Philipinas algunas labradores yeguas y cavallos para casta como esta ordenado," 1602, AGI, Filipinas 329, L. 1, fs. 41v–42.

33. Boyer, "Negotiating *Calidad*"; Bristol, "From Curing to Witchcraft"; Jackson, "Race/Caste and the Creation and Meaning of Identity."

34. "Real cédula que manda que las peticiones se hagan con informaciones," 1528, AGI, Panama 234, L. 3, f. 127v-8v. Additionally, when the crown sought to prohibit *mestizos* from being ordained as priests, the *cédula* stated that *mestizos* were to be barred from the priesthood because they were not "reserved, virtuous, and competent and [do not have] the qualities [*calidades*] that are required for the state of the priesthood." "Cedula que manda que no se ordenen mestizos en ninguna manera," in Encinas, *Cedulario indiano,* vol. 4, 344. However, the *cédula* went on to warn that all care should be taken that vows should only be taken by "persons in whom occur the necessary abilities and qualities [*calidades*]." This second clarification highlights that other persons—not only *mestizos*—could lack the necessary *calidad* and should likewise be barred.

35. For example, a 1535 *cédula* ordering all *vecinos* and *moradores* (settlers) to provision themselves with weapons for the defense of the colony stated that the specific weapons to be held would vary according to the *"calidad de cada persona."* Presumably, wealthier persons with more status and responsibility would be required to carry and provide greater and more expensive armaments than those with fewer resources and status. "Cédula que manda que los vezinos de Mexico tengan en sus casas armas," in ibid., vol. 4, 36.

36. A similar justification for my use of *géneros de gente* appears in Robert C. Schwaller, "For Honor and Defense," 242–43.

37. Ayala, *Diccionario de gobierno,* vol. 10, 46. "Todo género de personas."

38. "Carta de Alonso Perez de Arza," AGI, Mexico 99. "Cada día creze este género de gente."

39. "Carta del Licenciado Ramírez de Cartagena," in Levillier, *Gobernantes del Perú*, vol. 7, 288.

40. AGI, Indiferente 1252. "Negros o con otro género de gente." This *legajo* contains an assortment of *cédulas* from the early seventeenth century seeking to rectify problems with the *repartimiento* system in both New Spain and Peru. This *cédula* was issued in Valladolid, November 24, 1601.

41. Ibid. "Negros, u otro género de servicio."

42. "Carta y memorial inserto de Diego Martinez," AGI, Mexico 123, N. 21. "Otros géneros de jente tributaria como son mulatos y mulatas negros chichimecos y chinos." *Chichimecos* referred to the indigenous groups that lived in the northern mining regions of New Spain. *Chinos* referred to people perceived to be of Asian descent in the colony.

43. "Seis Memoriales que António Rodríguez dio en el Consejo respectivos al buen gobierno de la Nueva España," 1606, AGI, Mexico 125, N. 18. "[Que] el dia de hoy habra en la Nueva España de cinquenta a sesenta mil negros y mulatos, y mestizos, que es el género de gente que conforme a rázon deben acudir al trabajo de la labor de las minas, y sacar el metal dellas, y en todos cinquenta mil hombres deste género, no se hallaran cinquenta hombres que se atrevan a subir del suelo de las minas una arroba de metal."

44. Ibid. "Conpre negros, o alquile Españoles, o otro género de gente o no tenga ingenio a costa de las vidas de los Indios."

45. Cervantes Saavedra, *Don Quijote*, vol. 2, 465, 812.

46. Covarrubias Orozco, Arellano, and Zafra, *Tesoro de la lengua castellana*, 967.

47. Phillips, *Slavery from Roman Times*, 69; Ruiz, *Spain's Centuries of Crisis*, 139–63.

48. Sweet, "Iberian Roots," 150.

49. Phillips, *Slavery from Roman Times*, 87.

50. Sweet, "Iberian Roots," 145–46.

51. Ibn Khaldun and Rosenthal, *The Muqaddimah*, 63, 117; Eannes de Azurara, *Cronica do descobrimento e conquista*, 137–38.

52. Braude, "The Sons of Noah"; Blackburn, "Old World Background," 90–97.

53. Braude, "The Sons of Noah," 134–38. According to Braude, early medieval texts rarely specified the geographic regions inhabited by the descendants of Noah's sons; however, over time, each descent group came to be more closely tied to particular regions. Before the fifteenth century, most scholars linked Ham to Asia, Japheth to Europe, and Shem to Africa.

54. Blackburn, "Old World Background," 94–95; Braude, "The Sons of Noah," 138; Sweet, "Iberian Roots," 148–49.

55. In other words, the historical development and cultural importance of slavery within sub-Saharan society notwithstanding, Muslims and Christians alike first came to know black Africans as slaves. For centuries, the volume of

the trans-Saharan slave trade and the servile condition of those slaves served to reinforce any pejorative ascriptions upon darker-skinned Africans brought north into the Maghreb and Iberia. For examples of scholarship on autochthonous traditions of slavery in sub-Saharan Africa, see Lovejoy, *Transformations in Slavery*; Miers and Kopytoff, *Slavery in Africa*; Phillips, *Slavery from Roman Times*, 114–27.

56. Blackburn, "Old World Background," 91–92; Sweet, "Iberian Roots," 148–49.
57. Ibn Khaldun and Rosenthal, *The Muqaddimah*.
58. Ibid., 59–60.
59. Ibid., 117.
60. Columbus, Anzoátegui, and Casas, *Los cuatro viajes*, 30–31. The extant account of Columbus's first voyage was heavily edited by Bartolomé de las Casas from Columbus's diaries. Nevertheless, in the text the entirety of the above quote was attributed to Columbus.
61. Ibid., 38.
62. Sweet, "Iberian Roots," 157; Russell-Wood, "Iberian Expansion," 27–28. The bulls in question were *Dum diversas* (1452), *Romanus pontifex* (1455), and *Inter caetera* (1456).
63. Cortés and Delgado Gómez, *Cartas de relación*, 140–41.
64. Ibid., 242.
65. Motolinía, *Historia de los indios*, 232–33.
66. Ibid., 238.
67. The Caribs were most frequently labeled cannibals. Whitehead, *Lords of the Tiger Spirit*, 1–3. As early as the account of Columbus's first voyage, Europeans noted the savagery and cannibalism of this group. During the course of the sixteenth century the Spanish crown regularly issued *cédulas* allowing settlers to enslave or kill Caribs who resisted Spanish domination. See AGI, Indiferente 418, L. 3, 194. As late as 1609, Spaniards continued to petition the crown for authorization to attack and subdue Carib groups outside Spanish dominion. "Las condiciones con que el Capitan Thome Cano vezino de Sevilla tomara a su cargo servir a su Magestad," 1609, AGI, Indiferente 1255.
68. "Carta del Arzobispo Pedro Moya de Contreras a S.M.," 1582, AGI, Mexico 336B, N. 160.
69. John F. Schwaller, *The History of the Catholic Church in Latin America*, 44–45.
70. Many of these protections were granted piecemeal over the first half-century of colonial rule but came to be permanently entrenched in the New Laws of 1542. "Ordenanzas a Observar en el Consejo y Audiencia de Indias," AGI, Patronato 170, R. 47. For a detailed examination of native access to the legal system and protections within it, see Kellogg, *Law and the Transformation of Aztec Culture*. The New Laws prohibited *"servicios personales."* This system had required native persons to provide unpaid labor and services to *encomenderos*. Following the New Laws, natives could still be required to provide labor to *encomenderos*

and other Spaniards through the *repartimiento de indios;* however, this system was more directly regulated by officials and required that any laborer be paid for his time.

71. Lewis, *Hall of Mirrors,* 18; McAlister, "Social Structure and Social Change," 358.

72. Don, *Bonfires of Culture,* 146–74.

73. John F. Schwaller, "Conversion, Engagement, and Extirpation." For other studies on these dynamics, see Don, *Bonfires of Culture;* Griffiths, *Cross and the Serpent;* Gruzinski, *Man-Gods;* MacCormack, *Religion in the Andes.*

74. López de Velasco, *Geografía y descripción universal,* 29–30.

75. See Deutsch, "Medieval Unity," 29; Baumer, "Conception of Christendom."

76. Jones, "Image of the Barbarian," 387–88.

77. Most notably, Christopher Columbus was Genoese. Many of the crews used in early transatlantic voyages would have been quite diverse, consisting of, among others, Portuguese, Castilian, Genoese, Venetian, and Catalan sailors.

78. "Instrucción a Fray Nicolás de Ovando," September 16, 1501, AGI, Indiferente 418, L. 1, fs. 39v. "Algunos xianos [cristianos] de las dichas islas . . . tiene[n] tomadas a los dhos yndios sus mugeres e fijas e otras cosas contra su voluntad."

79. "R. C. Sobre Casamientos de Españoles con Indios" in Konetzke, *Colección documentos para la historia formación social,* vol. 1, 77. AGI, Panama 233, L. 2, fs. 45v.

80. "R. Provisión para que se casen los Negros" in Konetzke, *Colección documentos para la historia formación social,* vol. 1, 99.

81. "Real provision sobre la capacidad y libertad de los yndios," in *Colección de documentos inéditos relativos al descubrimiento conquista y organización de las antiguas posesiones españolas de ultramar* (Madrid: Real Academia de Historia, 1885–1932), vol. 10, 144. AGI, Santo Domingo 1121, L. 1, fs. 120.

82. "Cedula que manda a la Audiencia de Mexico prouea y de orden como se recojan los hijos de Españoles auidos en Indias a pueblos de Christianos," in Ibid., vol. 10, 178; Encinas, *Cedulario indiano,* vol. 4, 342.

83. Even though the application of *indio* to Native Americans occurred as a result of poorly understood geography, by the sixteenth century, Spanish had fully incorporated the Americas as the Indies.

84. In 1523, Charles V issued a *cédula* ordering the Casa de Contratación (House of Trade) to prohibit foreigners from trading in the Indies or sending ships to do so. "A los oficiales que no dexen cargar nyngund estranjero pa las Indias," 1523, AGI, Indiferente 420, L. 9, f. 170v. Similarly, in 1538 foreigners were prohibited from serving on ships bound for the Indies. AGI, Indiferente 1962, L.6, fs. 150-v. In 1598, the crown went even further and ordered the expulsion of all foreigners resident in the Indies who were not recognized by their communities as *vecinos.* AGI, Indiferente 427, L. 30, fs. 473v-474. Foreigners could become naturalized as subjects of the crown, in which case they would have been exempt from any of these prohibitions.

85. Rodríguez-Salgado, "Christians, Civilised and Spanish," 234.
86. Ibid., 235–36.
87. Bennett, *Africans in Colonial Mexico*, 3; Lockhart, *Spanish Peru*, 175; Martínez, *Genealogical Fictions*, 135. Additionally, the term *ladino* could be used to describe slaves who although African-born had acculturated to Hispanic society.
88. López de Velasco, *Geografía y descripción universal*, 37–38. For another late-sixteenth-century example, see Acosta, *Historia natural y moral de las Indias*, 185. For a brief examination of the use of *criollo* in the intellectual history of Latin America, see Arrom, "Criollo."
89. De la Vega, *Comentarios reales*, folio 255.
90. Corominas, *Diccionario critico etimologico*, vol. 1, 943–44.
91. *Diccionario de Autoridades*, vol. 1, 306. The later terms used to describe European-born *españoles*, *gauchupín* and *peninsular*, do not appear in sixteenth-century documents consulted in this study. Neither of these terms appear in Boyd-Bowman, *Léxico hispanoamericano*.
92. Alonso, *Enciclopedia del idioma*, vol. 3 (N–Z), 2085.
93. Ibid., 3209.
94. López de Velasco, *Geografía y descripción universal*, 37–38.
95. Ibid.
96. Ibid. This statement is interesting as it suggests that *criollos* were less virtuous and more base than peninsular Spaniards as a result of the effects of both the physical environment on their mental development and due to the less-than-virtuous nature of the immigrants who parented and acculturated them.
97. Bartlett, "Concepts of Race and Ethnicity," 45–46. For an exploration of how these beliefs affected English beliefs and the rise of African slavery in British America, see Jordan, *White over Black*.
98. Cañizares-Esguerra, "New World, New Stars."
99. Ibid., 60–61; Martínez, *Genealogical Fictions*, 139.
100. Cañizares-Esguerra, "New World, New Stars," 63.
101. Ibid., 65.
102. Forbes, *Africans and Native Americans*, 106. The *Real Academia Española* also defines *loro* as "de color amulatado, o de un moreno que tira a negro." *Real Academia Española*, s.v. "loro," http://lema.rae.es/drae/?val=loro, accessed November 1, 2013.
103. Forbes, *Africans and Native Americans*, 109–10.
104. Ibid., 111.
105. *Indio* was used to describe the inhabitants of both the West Indies and the Indian subcontinent of the East Indies.
106. Covarrubias Orozco, Arellano, and Zafra, *Tesoro de la lengua castellana*, 1302. "El que es hijo de negra y de hombre blanco, o al revés, y por ser mezcla extraordinaria la compararon a la naturaleza del mulo."
107. Forbes, *Africans and Native Americans*, 132.
108. Ibid., 140–47.

109. Ibid., 147.

110. Mira Caballos, *Indios y mestizos*, 58; López de Velasco, *Geografía y descripción universal*, 43. This ascription can also be found in the 1552 letter by Nicolas de Witte, "Carta de Fray Nicolas de Witte a S. M.," AGI, Mexico 280, N. 57.

111. Covarrubias Orozco, Arellano, and Zafra, *Tesoro de la lengua castellana*, 1550.

112. Corominas, *Diccionario critico etimologico*, 816–18.

113. Numerous sixteenth-century examples can be found in documents originating in Panama and South America. For example, see "Lista de la gente que truxo la primera vez el general Pedro de Ortega," AGI, Panama 42, N. 21, fs. 633; "Francisco Cambahigo criollo sobre no deber pagar demoras," Archivo General de la Nación (AGNB), Bogotá, Colombia, Tributos 18, doc. 4, fs. 173–204.

114. Borah and Cook, "Sobre las posibilidades de hacer el estudio histórico del mestizaje."

115. "Cedula que manda a la Audiencia de Mexico prouea y de orden como se recojan los hijos de Españoles auidos en Indias a pueblos de Christianos," in *Colección de documentos inéditos relativos al descubrimiento conquista y organización de las antiguas posesiones españolas de ultramar* (Madrid: Real Academia de Historia, 1885–1932), vol. 10, 179; Encinas, *Cedulario indiano*, vol. 4, 342.

116. Altman, "Spanish Society," 439.

117. Covarrubias Orozco, Arellano, and Zafra, *Tesoro de la lengua castellana*, 1278.

118. McAlister, "Social Structure and Social Change," 355.

Chapter 2

Epigraph 1: "Carta de don Luis de Velasco, virrey de Nueva España, al Emperador Don Carlos," in *Cartas de Indias*, 263–64. "Esta la tierra tan llena de negros y mestizos, que exceden en gran cantidad a los españoles y todos desean comprar su libertad con la vidas de sus amos."

Epigraph 2: "Carta de don Luis de Velasco a S.M.," 1608, AGI, Mexico 27, N. 52. "Muchos son los negros mulatos y mestizos libres que hay en esta tierra por que la mala yerva siempre crece y no hay que fiar ni confiar dellos lo que es posible se haze para tenellos sugetos y es mejor sufrillos aqui do queden ser castigados que en los pueblos de indios donde tendran mas libertad y haren mayores excessos sin castigo."

1. Ots Capdequi, *Estado Español*, 9–10; Góngora, "Institutions and Founding Ideas," 79.

2. Excellent works tracing this process and its ideological debates can be found in: Góngora, *El estado en el derecho indiano*; Góngora, *Studies in the Colonial History of Spanish America*; Ots Capdequi, *Estado Español*; Zavala, *Las instituciones jurídicas*.

3. Góngora, *El estado en el derecho indiano*, 39.

4. Ibid., 29–35.
5. Góngora, "Institutions and Founding Ideas," 69.
6. Owensby, *Empire of Law*, 55.
7. Zavala, *Las instituciones jurídicas*, 30–43.
8. "Instrucción a Fray Nicolás de Ovando," Sept. 16, 1501, AGI, Indiferente 418, L. 1, fs. 39–42. "Instrucción a Don Antonio de Mendoza" in de la Torre Villar, *Instrucciones y memorias*, vol. 1, 92, 95.
9. Ots Capdequi, *Estado Español*, 17–18.
10. Ibid., 15–16; McAlister, *Spain and Portugal in the New World*, 184.
11. For example, the Laws of Burgos (1512) and the New Laws (1542) represent aberrations in that they represent broad-reaching, comprehensive legislation. Nonetheless, it should be noted that even these pieces of legislation were reactions against specific problems that had already arisen in the Indies. Their breadth can be correlated in large part with the need for expansive legislation in response to many interrelated problems.
12. Owensby, *Empire of Law*, 45–46.
13. Góngora, *El estado en el derecho indiano*, 238.
14. "El Fiscal de su Mag y Sevastian yndio con[tra] Carlos Pinelo y Ju° Ant° Lanz," 1581, AGI Indiferente 1231.
15. Although the principle of analogy existed from the outset of colonial rule, the process of codifying the laws of the Indies was begun by Juan de Ovando as president of the Council of the Indies. See Poole, *Juan de Ovando*, 144–46.
16. Encinas, *Cedulario indiano*.
17. *Recopilación de leyes de los Reynos de las Indias*.
18. For example, Mangus Mörner distinguished between two "scales of classification": one based in legal codes, the other on social status. Mörner, *Race Mixture*, 60.
19. Altamira, "El texto de las leyes de Burgos de 1512"; "Ordenanzas a observar en el Consejo y Audiencia de Indias" [New Laws], AGI, Patronato 170, R. 47.
20. "Cedula que manda ... que los encomenderos no vayan en ningún tiempo a residir con sus casas en los pueblos de sus encomiendas." Encinas, *Cedulario indiano*, vol. 2, 256–58.
21. "R. C. Que no haya negros en los pueblos de indios." Konetzke, *Documentos para la Formación Social*, vol. 1, 213.
22. AGI, Indiferente 427, L.30, fs. 295-v. "Cedula que manda que no se consienta que anden ni estén en compañía de indios ni en sus pueblos, mestizos ni mulatos ni negros." Encinas, *Cedulario indiano*, vol. 4, 341.
23. "Real Cedula para que los negros, mulatos y mestizos no vivan entre los yndios." *Colección de documentos inéditos relativos al descubrimiento, conquista y colonización de las posesiones españolas en America y Oceanía* (Madrid: Imprenta Española, 1864–1884), vol. 18, 164–65.
24. "Cap. De carta ... que manda de orden como los negros y mulatos no viven entre Indios." Encinas, *Cedulario indiano*, vol. 4, 342.

25. Pike, "Black Rebels"; Guitar, "Boiling It Down"; Beatty-Medina, "Caught between Rivals"; Tardieu, *Cimarrones de Panamá*; Deive, *Los guerrilleros negros*; Price, *Maroon Societies*; Guillot, *Negros rebeldes y negros cimarrones*; Rueda Novoa, *Zambaje y autonomía*.

26. Vega Boyrie, "El cimarronaje y la manumisión," 80.

27. "Virrey de Indias: ordenanzas sobre los negros y sus amos," AGI, Patronato 295, N. 104.

28. For early examples of free Africans traveling to the Indies, see "Francisco de color negro, horro," AGI, Contratación 5536, L.1, f.11; "Rodrigo de Ovando, negro horro," AGI, Contratación 5536, L.1, f. 125; "Juan Ramos de color negro, horro," AGI, Contratación 5536, L.1, f. 206.

29. Garofalo, "Shape of a Diaspora," 28–33.

30. "Cedula que manda que no passen a las Indias negros ladinos," in Encinas, *Cedulario indiano*, vol. 4, 384.

31. Bowser, *African Slave in Colonial Peru*, 3; Palmer, *Slaves of the White God*, 8–9; Peralta Rivera, *Mechanismos del comercio negrero*, 17–20.

32. "Que no se pasen Esclavos Blancos, Negros, Loros, Mulatos, ni Berberiscos," in *Recopilación de leyes de los Reynos de las Indias*, Lib. IX, Tit. XXVI, ley xvii.

33. Encinas, *Cedulario indiano*, vol. 4, 135, 381–83.

34. Peralta Rivera, *Mechanismos del comercio negrero*, 20–21. These monopolies were not exclusive. The crown continued to issue private licenses and smaller commercial licenses.

35. Palmer, *Slaves of the White God*, 10; Peralta Rivera, *Mechanismos del comercio negrero*, 22.

36. Palmer, *Slaves of the White God*, 10–11.

37. Peralta Rivera, *Mechanismos del comercio negrero*, 43–76.

38. Bowser, *African Slave in Colonial Peru*, 12; Palmer, *Slaves of the White God*, 3, 34–35.

39. Sweet, "Iberian Roots," 159–60.

40. "Carta de don Luis de Velasco, virrey de Nueva España, al Emperador Don Cárlos," in *Cartas de Indias*, 256.

41. "Tabla General en que van las Provincias del Arcobispado de Mexico con los Partidos," AGI, Mexico 112, R. 3, s/f.

42. Bowser, *African Slave in Colonial Peru*, 339.

43. Aguirre Beltrán, *La población negra de México*, 219; Bowser, *African Slave in Colonial Peru*, 341.

44. Gerhard, "A Black Conquistador"; Restall, "Black Conquistadors"; Restall, *Seven Myths*, 53–63.

45. For example, see the license to carry a sword granted to Sebastián de Toral, a *negro* conquistador in Yucatán, in AGN, General de Parte, vol. 2, exp. 489, 97–97v.

46. For a fuller discussion of the relationship between the right to bear arms and *género*, see Robert C. Schwaller, "For Honor and Defense."

47. For examples of Spaniards seeking arms licenses for slaves and servants, see AGN, General de Parte, vol. 3, exp. 332, fs. 155v-156; AGN, Reales Cedulas Duplicadas, vol. 5, exp. 562, fs. 139; vol. 18, exp. 217, fs. 256v. Although these examples come from the late sixteenth and seventeenth centuries, they demonstrate the common practice of arming African dependents engaged in dangerous rural work.

48. Royal officials often were allowed to have armed slaves within their retinues, and many wealthy private individuals followed suit. See "Licencia a Luis de Rivera, tesorero de la casa de moneda, para traer en su compañia esclavos negros con espadas," 1587, AGN, General de Parte, vol. 3, exp. 7 fs. 3v.

49. "Cedula que manda que los negros no puedan traer ni traygan armas, publica ni secretamente," in Encinas, *Cedulario indiano*, vol. 4, 388.

50. "Carta de D. Antonio de Mendoza, virey de Nueva España al Emperador," in *Colección de documentos inéditos relativos al descubrimiento, conquista y colonización de las posesiones españolas en America y Oceanía* (Madrid: Imprenta Española, 1864–1884), vol. 2, 198–200.

51. "Ordenanças de Veracruz" July 3, 1539, AGI, Mexico 350. This document contains a copy of Mendoza's 1537 orders.

52. Ibid., fs. 4v-5

53. "Cap de las ordinanças que se confirmaron para la ciudad de los Reyes," in Encinas, *Cedulario indiano*, vol. 4, 388–89.

54. "Cedula que manda ... que ningún negro trayga en las provincias del Peru, ningunas armas," in ibid., vol. 4, 389.

55. "Cedula que manda ... vean las licencias que se han dado ... para traer en su compañamiento, negros con armas," in ibid.

56. AGI, Indiferente 418, L. 1, fs. 39v. See also Konetzke, "Mestizaje y su importancia," no. 24, 215.

57. *Colección de documentos inéditos relativos al descubrimiento conquista y organización de las antiguas posesiones españolas de ultramar* (Madrid: Real Academia de Historia, 1885–1932), vol. 9, 22–23; "R.C. que las Indias se puedan casar con españoles" in Konetzke, *Documentos para la Formación Social*, vol. 1, 61.

58. "R.C. sobre casamientos de españoles con indios" in Konetzke, *Documentos para la formación social*, vol. 1, 77; AGI, Panama 233, L. 2, fs. 45v.

59. Seed, *To Love, Honor, and Obey*, 32–46; Rípodas Ardanaz, *Matrimonio en Indias*, 227–257.

60. "R. Provisión para que se casen los negros," in Konetzke, *Documentos para la Formación Social*, vol. 1, 99.

61. "R. C. que los negros se casen con negras," in ibid., vol. 1, 210.

62. Seed, *To Love, Honor, and Obey*, 32–46.

63. "Proceso del Santo Oficio de la Inquisición contra Juan de Villate," AGN, Inq., vol. 2, exp. 9, fs. 231, 232v.

64. "Cedula que manda a la audiencia de Mexico, provea y de orden como se recojan los hijos de Españoles ávidos en Indias, a pueblos de Christianos," in Encinas, *Cedulario indiano*, vol. 4, 342.

65. "Cap de la instrucion del virrey de la nueva España que manda se informe de la utilidad que se sigue de aver colegio de mestizos y mochacas perdidas," in ibid., vol. 1, 211.

66. Quoted in Castañeda Delgado, "El colegio de San Juan de Létran," 70.

67. De la Torre Villar, *Instrucciones y memorias*, vol. 1, 164. The founding date for this house is not as clear. It was probably founded concurrently with the *mestizo* school. The school continued to support *mestizas* in some form until the end of the century, by which time it had come to educate the daughters of the local Spanish elite. See AGI, Mexico 24, N. 21.

68. As will be explored more thoroughly later, references to the recognized children of elite Spaniards and indigenous women had a strong tendency to obscure their indigenous parents.

69. "Cap. de carta que su Magestad ... para que dexen volver a las Indias a mestizos que han venido de aquella tierra," in Encinas, *Cedulario indiano*, vol. 4, 287. "Cedula que manda que queriendo venir a estos Reynos alguna India con sus hijos que los hubo en Español la dexen venir a ellos con los dichos sus hijos," in ibid., vol. 4, 358.

70. "R. C. Para que ningún mestizo que no sea vecino pueda cargar indios," in Konetzke, *Documentos para la Formación Social*, vol. 1, 259.

71. "Sobre los casados que no llevan sus mugeres," AGI, Mexico 1088, L. 3, fs. 165v.

72. "Real Provisión para que se casen los encomenderos que estén solteros," AGI, Panama 235, L. 7, fs. 75. See also Marshall, "The Birth of the Mestizo in New Spain," 167.

73. Encinas, *Cedulario indiano*, vol. 4, 345–48. The prohibition against indigenous arms ownership was first established in the 1501 instructions to Governor Ovando, and it would be reiterated frequently, in 1534, 1536, 1551, 1563, 1567, and 1571.

74. "Cedula que manda al Licenceniado [sic] Castro que no consienta que mestizo ni Indio tenga ni trayga armas," in ibid., 344.

75. Flint, "Treason or Travesty," 28–31.

76. López Martínez, "Motín de mestizos," 376–77.

77. "Carta a S.M. del Licenciado Castro con larga relación del motín," in Levillier, *Gobernantes del Perú*, vol. 3, 235, 237.

78. "Cap. de carta ... sobre que los mestizos ni mulatos no tengan ni traygen armas," in Encinas, *Cedulario indiano*, vol. 4, 345. Toledo would not arrive in Peru until May 1569.

79. Levillier, *Gobernantes del Perú*, vol. 4, 48–251. Toledo included his comments on *mestizos* within a lengthy report made after a through visitation of the viceroyalty.

80. "Carta del Virrey Don Francisco de Toledo sobre su viaje y vista," in ibid., 131.

81. Ibid., 130.

82. "Puntos de la carta anterior y decretos puestos en ella," in ibid., 230–31.

83. "Cap. de carta . . . que manda no consienta que mulatos ni zambaigos traygan armas, ni mestizos sino fuere con su licencia," in Encinas, *Cedulario indiano*, vol. 4, 345. This order was the first to add *zambaigos* to the list of those groups prohibited from carrying weapons.

84. For example, see "Carta del Virrey Don Francisco de Toledo sobre su viaje y vista," in Levillier, *Gobernantes del Perú*, vol. 4, 127–29.

85. "Cedula que manda que se executen las leyes del Reyno en los casos de adulterio," in Encinas, *Cedulario indiano*, vol. 4, 344.

86. "Cedula que manda, que no se provean mestizos en oficios de escrivanos," in ibid., vol. 2, 362.

87. "Cedula que manda que no se den protectorias de Indios a mestizos," in ibid., vol. 4, 343–44.

88. "Cedula que manda que no se ordenen mestizos en ninguna manera," ibid., 344.

89. "Cap. de carta que su Magestad escrivio . . . que manda que la cedula que esta dada para que no se ordenen mestizos, se entienda solamente con los hijos de India o Indio y Español," in ibid., vol. 1, 173.

90. Martínez, *Genealogical Fictions*, 50.

91. "Cedula que manda al Licenceniado [sic] Castro que no consienta que mestizo ni Indio tenga ni trayga armas," in Encinas, *Cedulario indiano*, vol. 4, 344–45.

92. "Cap. de carta . . . que manda no consienta que mulatos ni zabaigos traygan armas, ni mestizos sino fuere con su licencia" in ibid., 345.

93. Robert C. Schwaller, "For Honor and Defense," 252–53.

94. "Cap. de carta que su Magestad escrivio a la audiencia de Guatimala . . . que manda que los hijos de los negros esclavos libres avidos en Indias, paguen tributo como los demas," in Encinas, *Cedulario indiano*, vol. 4, 391.

95. In 1574, Viceroy Martín Enriquez complained that male African slaves preferred unions with indigenous women because their offspring would be born free. A similar preference could have been created if native people saw unions with Africans as a means of removing the burden of tribute from their children. See "Carta del Virey de la Nueva España, Don Martín Enríquez al Rey Don Felipe II," in *Cartas de Indias*, 299.

96. "Cap. de carta que su Magestad escrivio a la audiencia de Guatimala . . . que manda que los hijos de los negros esclavos libres avidos en Indias, paguen tributo como los demas" and "Cap. de carta . . . que manda lo mismo que el capitulo arriba," in Encinas, *Cedulario indiano*, vol. 4, 391.

97. "Cedula que manda que todos los negros y negras, mulatos y mulatas libres que oviere en las Indias paguen tributo a su Magestad," in ibid., 390–91; "Imposición de un marco o más de plata a los esclavos libres," AGI, Patronato 275, R. 77.

98. Milton and Vinson III, "Counting Heads," para. 14.

99. "Información fecha a pedimiento de Juan Bautista de Cardona sobre cierto tributo que se le pide, 1583," AGI, Indiferente 1233.

100. A copy of the 1578 *cédula* is included in his *probanza*. Another copy can be found in AGI, Panama 237, L. 11, fs. 38v-39v.

101. "Carta del fiscal, Juan Quesada de Figueroa a S. M," AGI, Mexico 72, N. 40.

102. Vinson, *Bearing Arms for His Majesty*, 143–46.

103. "Que las negras, y mulatas horas, no traygan oro, seda, mantos, ni perlas," in *Recopilación de leyes de los Reynos de las Indias*, Lib VII, Tit. V, ley xxviii.

104. Martin, *Los vagabundos en la Nueva España*, 1–38.

105. "Carta del Virrey a S.M." Aug. 20, 1550, AGI, Mexico 19, N. 13, fs. 13.

106. Ibid.

107. "Cedula que manda al Virrey de la Nueva España provea como los españoles y mestizos y indios vagabundos que hubiere en aquella tierra se junten y hagan pueblos en que vivan," in Encinas, *Cedulario indiano*, vol. 4, 343.

108. By the 1580s, northward expansion brought Spanish settlers, miners, and ranchers into constant contact with hostile, highly mobile *chichimecos*. To attempt to pacify the region and bring greater order and security, colonial officials began to favor the founding and settlement of cities as a means to extend Spanish control over these new frontiers. An excellent articulation of this policy can be seen in an undated (1580s) letter by Esteban de Porres, *relator* of the Audiencia of Mexico. In this letter he suggests that various *"villas y lugares"* be settled by Spaniards, *"indios de paz,"* and *"negros y mulatos libres."* In his estimation, the founding of twenty *villas* of thirty *vecinos* would be far cheaper and more effective than continuous military expeditions. See AGI, Mexico 70, N. 144.

109. "Cedula que manda que ningún vagabundo español no casado, ni viva ni este en sus pueblos de indios, ni entre ellos," in Encinas, *Cedulario indiano*, vol. 4, 341.

110. "Cedula que manda a la audiencia del Nuevo Reino de Granada, se informen de los mestizos que ay en aquella tierra," in ibid., 342–43.

111. As late as 1590, Viceroy Velasco (the younger) and his predecessor, the Marques de Villamanrique, continued to complain that the collection of free-colored tribute was hindered by their mobility and lax recordkeeping by local officials. AGI, Mexico 22, N. 24.

112. "Cedula que manda al Virrey de la Nueva España, provea como los negros y mulatos libres vivan con amos conocidos, para que se puedan cobrar los tributos," in Encinas, *Cedulario indiano*, vol. 4, 390.

113. "Cap. XXVI Que se tenga cuidado con que los españoles mestizos y mulatos y vagamundos y zambaigos que ay entre los indios, no hagan insolencias, ni daños," in ibid., vol. 2, 314–15.

Chapter 3

Epigraph: "Carta del virey de Nueva España Don Martín Enríquez, al Rey Don Felipe II," in *Cartas de Indias*, 298. "De los mestizos no hago tanto caudal, aunque ay muçhos entre ellos de muy ruyn biuienda y de ruynes costumbres; mas, al fin, son hijos despañoles y todos se crian con sus padres que, como pasen de quarto o çinco años, salen de poder de las indias y siempre an de seguir el vando de los spañoles, como parte de que ellos más se honrran."

1. Most of these petitions and letters survive in the Archivo General de Indias in sections Patronato and Mexico. A shift can be determined within these documents over the course of the sixteenth century. While conquistadors, early settlers, and their immediate descendants wrote letters that suggested specific changes or policies for the new kingdom's social, political, and economic order, by the third generation (roughly 1580) letters directed to the crown tended to focus solely on gaining bureaucratic positions, grants of aid, or other markers of status within the increasingly mature colony.

2. Schwartz, "Spaniards, 'Pardos,' and the Missing Mestizos," 9–12.

3. Mangan, "Moving Mestizos," 275n4, 281; Rappaport, *The Disappearing Mestizo*, 96; Schwartz, "Spaniards, 'Pardos,' and the Missing Mestizos," 9–10.

4. Rappaport, *The Disappearing Mestizo*, 99; Mangan, "Moving Mestizos," 274–76.

5. Undoubtedly, many *mestizos*, including elite *mestizos*, were born of nonconsensual, possibly violent sexual encounters between Spanish men and native women. While this is a crucially important aspect of Spanish conquest and colonization, a discussion of sexual violence in the engendering of colonial *mestizos* is beyond the scope of this work.

6. Lockhart, "Social Organization and Social Change," 288–89; Kuznesof, "Ethnic and Gender Influences," 162.

7. Hesse, "Racialized Modernity," 645–46.

8. In his study of early Spanish Peru, Lockhart identified a very similar phenomenon occurring among that kingdom's conquest-era elite. Lockhart, *Spanish Peru*, 163–69. Similarly, Rappaport has shown that during the sixteenth century many Spanish families in the kingdom of New Granada incorporated children of mixed Spanish-indigenous ancestry into the ranks of *españoles*. Rappaport, *The Disappearing Mestizo*, 95–131; Mangan, "Moving Mestizos," 279–81.

9. Rappaport, *The Disappearing Mestizo*, 10–11. In examining the early Caribbean, Stewart Schwartz coined the term "missing *mestizos*" to describe those of mixed Spanish-indigenous ancestry not ascribed to the *género* of *mestizo*. Schwartz, "Spaniards, 'Pardos,' and the Missing Mestizos."

10. Rappaport, *The Disappearing Mestizo*, 73–74.

11. In this book, I have avoided an examination of Spanish-indigenous children born within the highest ranks of conquistador families—the likes of Martín Cortés or the various descendants of Montezuma. By focusing on lesser-known individuals I hope to demonstrate the relative predominance of this phenomenon during the formative years of the kingdom. See Chipman, *Moctezuma's Children*; Lanyon, *New World of Martin Cortes*; Kuznesof, "Ethnic and Gender Influences." Older works include Marshall, "The Birth of the Mestizo in New Spain," 168; Diggs, "Color," 415.

12. "María García Pareja vezina [sic] de México sobre que se le den 200 ps⁰ de renta que tenía Andrés García su padre conquistador," 1579–1584, AGI, Mexico 107.

13. The *probanza* was a typical document type of the sixteenth century. In general, supplicants to the crown framed requests for pensions and grants of income in the language of dire necessity regardless of actual situation. Consequently, we cannot judge based on the evidence presented how impoverished María Garcia may have been.

14. See AGI, Patronato 74, N. 1, R. 7. In 1520, the governor of Cuba sent Narváez to arrest Cortés for having violated the terms of his expedition. After a brief conflict, Cortés successfully recruited many of the new arrivals to his cause.

15. At the time of Cortés's arrival in Tlaxcala, Maxixcatzin was one of the most prominent of the local nobility. He was the *tlatoani* of Ocotelolco, one of Tlaxcala's main moieties, and possibly the titular leader of the community as a whole. See Lockhart, *The Nahuas after the Conquest*, 31; Hassig, "Xicotencatl," 35–40.

16. "María García Pareja," AGI, Mexico 107, fs. 8.

17. An extreme example of this can be found in similar petitions by Don Luis de Velasco (the younger). Prior to his appointment as viceroy, Velasco wrote many letters to the crown asking for financial aid to ameliorate his impoverished condition despite already being *encomendero* of several lucrative communities, the recipient of a massive royal pension, and kinsman to several of the wealthiest families in the colony. Schwaller, "The Private Correspondence of Don Luis de Velasco, the Younger."

18. AGI, Patronato 74, N. 1, R. 7. Their 1575 request was not granted by the Council of the Indies. The inability of Francisca and Gonzalo to receive remuneration for the services of Juan Gómez de Almaçan may have prompted María García to press her case in 1579.

19. This marriage was one of many made in Tlaxcala, before and after the conquest, that cemented alliances between the community's ranking elite and the members of Cortés's expedition. Hassig, "Xicotencatl," 39–40.

20. "Probanza de Xpoval Gentil," 1562, AGI, Mexico 97.

21. The title *"adelantado"* marked Francisco Montejo as the royally recognized leader of the expedition that conquered the Yucatán Peninsula. In her study of *mestizos* in the kingdom of New Granada, Joanne Rappaport similarly demonstrates how marriages to illegitimate daughters of the conquistador elite represented an integral part of the construction of early colonial Spanish social hierarchies. Rappaport, *The Disappearing Mestizo*, 104.

22. "Probanza de Xpoval Gentil," 1562, AGI, Mexico 97, fs. 2.

23. The *probanza* of Cristóbal Gentil does not give many details about Diego Montejo. However, it is very likely that he too was a tacit *español* born of the *adelantado* and an *india*. Like Isabel, Diego was also favored by Montejo and received an *encomienda*. See Chuchiak, "Sins of the Fathers."

24. Nazzari, "An Urgent Need to Conceal," 104.

25. For the use of socio-racial terms as epithets, see Lockhart, "Social Organization and Social Change," 288.

26. The Montejos were incredibly powerful in the sixteenth century. Beside wealthy *encomiendas* and financial grants in the Yucatán, the *encomienda* of Azcapotzalco had been given to the *adelantado* Francisco Montejo in return for his services in petitioning the crown during Cortés's 1519–21 conquest of Mexico-Tenochtitlan. The *encomienda* remained in the family at the time of this *probanza*, having been given to Doña Catalina as part of her dowry in her marriage to Alonso Maldonado.

27. In the sixteenth century the usage of the honorific *don* (and *doña*) was quite consistent for individuals. Rarely was a person referred to as *Don* by some and not by others. See Lockhart, *Spanish Peru*, 35–37. A 1571 document exists in which Diego Montejo refers to himself with the honorific. Unfortunately this document does not shed light on Diego's mother and only refers to him as "hijo del adelantado don Francisco de Montejo." See "Petición de don Diego Montejo, hijo natural de Francisco de Montejo, a don Carlos de Arellano para poder casar con Ana de Campos, viuda mujer que fue de Julián Doncel," November 22, 1571, private collection, Mérida. A transcription of this document was graciously made available to me by John F. Chuchiak.

28. "Alonso Rieros, hijo de conquistador. Memorial, informacion y recomendacion del obispo de Michoacan," 1542, AGI, Mexico 95, N. 50. The testimony in support of Alonso Rieros's claims was taken in Puebla de los Angeles.

29. Alonso Rieros signed a joint petition written by the members of Cortés's company requesting recompense for their services in the conquest of Mexico-Tenochtitlan. See Icazbalceta, *Colección de documentos,* vol. 1, 431–37.

30. AGI, Mexico 95, N. 50, fs. 1.

31. Ocelotepec is located south of Antequera (Oaxaca) and toward the Pacific coast, nestled in the slopes of the Sierra Madre del Sur. Gerhard, *A Guide to the Historical Geography of New Spain,* 187–88.

32. AGI, Mexico 95, N. 50, fs. 2.

33. AGI, Mexico 95, N. 50, fs. 4–5.

34. Lockhart, *Spanish Peru,* 166; Borah and Cook, "El estudio histórico del mestizaje," 185.

35. Although an early date, we know that some of his contemporaries also born of conquistadors and native women were then being labeled as *mestizos*. In the late 1540s, both the *cabildo* of Mexico City and the crown hoped to provide for these early *mestizos* through the creation of a school for *mestizo* children. "Cap de la instrucion del virrey de la nueva España que manda se informe de la utilidad que se sigue de aver colegio de mestizos y mochacas perdidas," in Encinas, *Cedulario indiano,* vol. 1, 211.

36. Gerhard, *A Guide to the Historical Geography of New Spain,* 188.

37. "Antonio de Leyba, hijo de Juan de Najera conquistador, pide un corregimiento (1552), Mexico," AGI, Mexico 280.

38. "Antonio de Leyba," AGI, Mexico 280, fs. 2.

39. "Cedula que manda que los vezinos de Mexico tengan en sus casas armas," in Encinas, *Cedulario indiano*, vol. 4, 36.

40. "Antonio de Leyba," AGI, Mexico 280, fs. 5v.

41. Tavárez, "Legally Indian," 96.

42. Haskett, *Indigenous Rulers*, 138–41.

43. Ibid., 48.

44. Ibid., 139; Rappaport, *The Disappearing Mestizo*, 72–73.

45. "Cedula que manda a la audiencia de las provincias del Peru, que no consientan que ningun Indio trayga armas," in Encinas, *Cedulario indiano*, vol. 4, 345.

46. AGN, General de Parte, vol. 5, exp. 336, fs. 73v-74.

47. AGI Santa Fe, vol. 528, L.1, f. 34r.

48. This tendency appears over time and space. In her study of New Granada, Joanne Rappaport traces how several caciques of the late sixteenth century negotiated their mixed ancestry by appealing to the most beneficial attributes of *españoles* and *indios*. Rappaport, *The Disappearing Mestizo*, 133–69. Peter Villella has demonstrated how native elites in late colonial Mexico, including some of mixed ancestry, employed similar rhetorical strategies to appeal to notions of Spanish honor and blood purity while simultaneously emphasizing their indigenous nobility. Villella, "Native Elites and the Discourse of Blood Purity."

49. Rappaport, *The Disappearing Mestizo*, 130.

50. "Meritos y servicios de Juan Gomez Almazán, Nueva España," AGI, Patronato 74, N. 1, R. 7, fs. 1.

51. Chance, *Race and Class*, 132–33, 175–76; Mörner, "Economic Factors and Stratification," 362; Diggs, "Color," 407; Seed, "Social Dimensions"; Chance and Taylor, "Estate and Class in a Colonial City," 482–84.

52. Rappaport, *The Disappearing Mestizo*, 97.

53. Kuznesof, "Ethnic and Gender Influences"; Chance, *Race and Class*, 98, 128, 132–33; Mörner, *Race Mixture*, 55; Diggs, "Color," 415; Chance and Taylor, "Estate and Class in a Colonial City," 462.

54. Cañizares-Esguerra, "New World, New Stars."

55. See "Proceso contra Francisco de Léon alias Garavito, por casado dos veces," 1575, AGN, Inq., vol. 104, exp. 10.

Chapter 4

Epigraph: "Carta del virey de la Nueva España, Don Martín Enríquez, al Rey Don Felipe II," *Cartas de Indias,* 300. "Pues, unininedo tanta suma cada año de negros, y los mulatos yendose multiplicando tanto, mire V.M., andando el tiempo, á qué número de gente aurá de llegar; y estos son señores de los indios, como nacidos entre ellos y criados."

1. "Proceso contra Francisco Jasso, mulato, esclavo de Martín de Jasso. Mexico," 1596, AGN, Inq., vol. 145, exp. 7, fs. 81–131.

2. "Proceso contra Juana Agustina, natural de Oaxacatlan de las minas," 1595, AGN, Inq., vol. 185, exp. 6, fs. 201–43.

3. López de Velasco, *Geografía y descripción universal*, 267.

4. Bakewell, *Silver Mining and Society*, 6–9; Bakewell, "Mining," 221–29.

5. Recent works adding to our understanding of Afro-indigenous ties across Spanish America include Brockington, *Blacks, Indians, and Spaniards*, 158–170; Bryant, *Rivers of Gold, Lives of Bondage*, 97–104; Proctor, *Damned Notions of Liberty*, 54–55; Rappaport, *The Disappearing Mestizo*, 61, 86–87; Restall, *The Black Middle*, 220–38, 257–65; Sierra Silva, "From Chains to Chiles."

6. Other *mulatos* appeared as witnesses but could not be included in this analysis because their testimony did not provide any personal details. The sample contained thirty-five women and twenty-five men.

7. Thirteen men and seventeen women were born in the Americas.

8. The Iberian-born sample included seven men and three women.

9. Some *indios* and *mestizos* did travel to Iberia during the sixteenth century. However, they represented a small fraction of the total population. Consequently, while African-indigenous unions could have happened in Iberia, the absolute and relative number of such cases would have been very small.

10. "Carta de Fray Nicolas de Witte a S. M.," AGI, Mexico 280, N. 57.

11. "Carta del virey de la Nueva España, Don Martín Enríquez, al Rey Don Felipe II . . . 9 de Enero de 1574," in *Cartas de Indias*, 298–99. Given the rhetorical complexity of the letter, I have included the Spanish transcription here:

> Solo vna cosa vá cada dia poniendose en peor estado, y si Dios y V.M. no lo remedian, temo que no uenga á ser la perdicion desta tierra, y es el creçimiento grande en que ván los mulatos, que de los mestizos no hago tanto caudal, aunque ay muchos entre ellos de muy ruyn biuienda y de ruynes costumbres; mas, al fin, son hijos despañoles y todos se crian con sus padres que, como pasen de quarto o çinco años, salen de poder de las indias y siempre an de seguir el vando de los spañoles, como parte de que ellos más se honrran; mas los mulatos, que son hijos de negros, crianse siempre con las madres y dellas ni de los padres no pueden tomar muy buenas costumbres, y como personas libres, hazen de sí lo que quieren y muy pocos se aplican á offiçios y casi ninguno á cultiuar la tierra, sino á guarder ganados y otros offiçios adonde anden con libertad. Y es cosas que no se dexa creer el havilidad y fuerças que todos tienen vniuersalmente; porque hazen tanta uentaja á los mestizos, como de hombres á munecas, con ser hijos despañoles los mestizos, que parece que naturaleza obra en esto con más fuerza, y siempre andan entre los indios por la parte que dellos tienen de que más se honrran, de lo qual los indios reziben artos daños.

12. "Carta del virey de la Nueva España, Don Martín Enríquez, al Rey Don Felipe II . . . 9 de Enero de 1574," in ibid., 299–300.

Hallará V.M. que cada año vienen gran cantidad de negros á esta tierra, y que forçoso an de uenir, porque no ay en ella otro seruicio, asi para minas como para todas las otras cosas, y los españoles no solamente se siruen acá, para neçesidades forzosas, de los sclavos, mas honrranse dellos, y tienen algunos más pajes y lacayos, que todos son negros, que en España; y las indias es gente muy flaca y muy perdidas por los negros, y asi se huelgan más de casar con ellos, que con indios, y ni más ni menos los negros se casan con ellas, antes que con otras negras por razon de dexar á sus hijos libres. Pues, uniniendo tanta suma cada año de negros, y los mulatos yendose multiplicando tanto, mire V.M., andando el tiempo, á qué número de gente aurá de llegar; y estos son señores de los indios, como nacidos entre ellos y criados, y son hombres que osan morir, tambien como quantos españoles ay en el mundo. Pues, si los indios uniniesen á malear y estos se juntasen con ellos, no se yo quien seria parte para resistillos.

13. "Carta del virey de la Nueva España, Don Martín Enríquez, al Rey Don Felipe II . . . 9 de Enero de 1574," in ibid., 300. "Aunque por esto no auian de dexar de nacer muchos mulatos, era muy differenty ser esclavos o ser libres y asi mismo la criança, porque se auian de criar con españoles, y no con libertad como agora entre los indios; y no podian dexar de ser muchos menos, aunque Su Santidad no prohibiese los casamientos, porque los negros, por solo dexar los hijos libres, pretenden casarse con las indias, y las indias, uisto que sus hijos no auian de ser libres, no se casarian tanto con los negros."

14. See chapter 5, tables 5.2–5.9. Studies of later periods identify similar trends, although by the seventeenth century *mestizas* joined *indias* and *mulatas* as common free spousal choices for *negros*. Cope, *The Limits of Racial Domination*, 81–82; Proctor, *Damned Notions of Liberty*, 58–60; Valdes, "Decline of the Sociedad de Castas," 35–37.

15. López de Velasco, *Geografía y descripción universal*, 43. "Demás de estos hay muchos mulatos, hijos de negros y de indias, que se llaman zambaigos, que vienen a ser la gente mas peor y vil que en aquellas partes hay; de los cuales y de los mestizos, por haber tantos, vienen a estar algunas partes en peligro de desasosiego y rebelión: mulatos hijos de españoles y de negras no hay tantos, por las muchas indias que hay ruines de sus personas."

16. Such fluency was not limited to *mulatos*. For a discussion of how *mulatos* and *mestizos* operated within and across cultural boundaries, see Robert C. Schwaller, "The Importance of *Mestizos* and *Mulatos*."

17. "Proceso contra María Ramírez, por otro nombre Joana ramírez, por casada dos veces," 1574, AGN, Inq., vol. 101, exp. 7, fs. 277.

18. Juana was likely born between 1545 and 1550. Even if Francisca gave birth to Juana as a teenager, Francisca could not have been born later than 1530.

19. During Francisca's formative years there were no widespread efforts to Hispanicize the indigenous population. Although she likely interacted with

members of the clergy, as long as she lived in Texcoco she probably did not have significant exposure to Spanish culture beyond Christianity.

20. Enciso Contreras, *Taxco*.

21. Gerhard, *A Guide to the Historical Geography of New Spain*, 170–71.

22. AGN, Inq., vol. 101, exp. 7, fs. 280v. "Dijo que cuando este vino de guinea la hallo en Taxco chiquita."

23. Berdan and Anawalt, *Essential Codex Mendoza*, 124–25.

24. One witness recalled that Francisca had used the punishment on Juana. While the witnesses attesting to Juana's scar disagreed as to who punished her, that disagreement does not negate the likely appropriation of indigenous cultural practices by Antón. Even if Francisca had been the one who punished Juana with chili smoke, the fact that one witness remembered Antón committing the act represents sufficient evidence that in their eyes Antón could have engaged in such a practice. If Antón had not manifested any familiarity with native cultural practice, no witness would have made such an attribution.

25. After 1580 the ethnolinguistic diversity of *bozales* diminished as more and more slaves were brought to Spanish America from central West Africa, a region with greater linguistic commonalities. Carroll, *Blacks in Colonial Veracruz*, 28–33, 158–61; Proctor, *Damned Notions of Liberty*, 46–50; Heywood and Thornton, *Central Africans, Atlantic Creoles*, 38–42; Thornton, *Africa and Africans*, 116–33, 187–91.

26. "Proceso contra Francisca de Acosta, por casada dos veces," 1559, AGN, Inq., vol. 91, exp. 2, fs. 5–16.

27. The canonical rules governing the sacrament of marriage changed in 1563. Prior to that date the sacrament of marriage was considered valid if a couple exchanged vows (ideally, but not necessarily, before witnesses) and later consummated those vows. Since at least the Fourth Lateran Council such unions incurred sin for occurring outside of clerical oversight and skipping the posting of the banns. Nevertheless, such clandestine marriages were considered sacramentally valid. Following the Decree Tametsi of 1563, clandestinity was added to the list of marital impediments that negated the conferral of the sacrament.

28. AGN, Inq., vol. 91, exp. 2, fs. 13v.

29. Ibid., fs. 14. "Dixo a la dicha Francisca mulata señora quereys os casar conmigo y ella callo y segunda vez lo ynterrogo y dixo señora days os por mi mugger y ella le respondio en la lengua mexicana quema que quire decir si."

30. "Proceso contra Luis Hernández por dos veces casado," AGN, Inq., vol. 95, exp. 4, fs. 200–17. This case file contains two separate cases against two different men named Luis Hernández.

31. Ibid., fs. 209.

32. Ibid., fs. 213.

33. "Tabla General en que van las Provincias del Arcobispado de Mexico con los Partidos," AGI, Mexico 112, R. 3, s/f.

34. Other defendants attempted to similarly obfuscate their pasts. Yet, if their attempts to evade investigation failed, the accused could throw themselves at

the mercy of the court. Often such reversals were accompanied by notations that the defendant had dropped to "their knees with tears in their eyes" (*hincado de rodillas con lagrimas*). For other examples, see AGN, Inq., vol. 1495, exp. 4; AGN, Inq., vol. 145, exp. 11.

35. "Proceso contra Isabel Díaz, mulata, por casada dos veces," 1574, AGN, Inq., vol. 101, exp. 8, fs. 309–42.

36. Ibid., fs. 317.

37. "Proceso contra Francisco Granados, mulato chapinero, por casado dos veces," 1574, AGN, Inq., vol. 102, exp. 2, fs. 48.

38. "Proceso contra Beatriz Ramírez, mulata, por casada dos veces," 1574, AGN, Inq., vol. 134, exp. 3, fs. 17.

39. Don Luis de Castilla was one of the wealthiest men in New Spain, a distant relative of the Habsburg monarchs, and a distant relative (by marriage) to Viceroy Don Luis de Velasco. John F. Schwaller, "Early Life of Luis de Velasco," 31.

40. The exchange of vows that occurred during a *desposorio* was considered sufficient for the sacrament of marriage. If followed by consummation, canon law considered the couple married.

41. AGN, Inq., vol. 134, exp. 3, fs. 13.

42. Ibid., fs. 8.

43. "Proceso contra Gonzalo Hernández, mulato libre, vecino de la Colonia obispado de Michoacan," 1586, AGN, Inq., vol. 137, exp. 6, fs. 142–86.

44. Presumably because the first marriage was considered valid, Gonzalo would have been ordered to resume married life with Francisca. It is possible that the bishop might have ordered him to provide some sort of support for Catalina.

45. Gerhard, *Historical Geography of New Spain*, 60, 156–57, 192–94. Although the location of Amatitlan cannot be determined, the communities of Maquilí and Içatlan were both located in western New Spain along the Pacific coast near the border with Nueva Galicia.

46. "Proceso contra Joan de Perales mulato libre natural de Mexico, casado dos vezes," 1575, AGN, Inq., vol. 103, exp. 5, fs. 191–253.

47. Ibid., fs. 233. The Inquisition normally opened questioning by asking witnesses to give general information that included their name, occupation, residence, and place of birth. Often *género* labels appear in these answers, suggesting that witnesses chose to self-identify when providing this information.

48. Ibid., fs. 196.

49. Rappaport, *The Disappearing Mestizo*, 196–98.

50. For other examples, see "Proceso contra Cristobal de Ayala, por casado dos veces," 1565, AGN, Inq., vol. 26, exp. 4, fs. 89, 109v; "Proceso contra Jeronimo Perez, flamenco, por casado dos veces," 1567, AGN, Inq., vol. 27, exp. 3, fs. 305, 306v; "Licencia a Juan Sardina de color mulato para traer una espada y daga," 1601, AGN, General de Parte, vol. 5, exp. 1319, fs. 291v.

51. Rappaport, *The Disappearing Mestizo*, 193–94.

52. "Proceso de la justicia eclesiastica contra Francisco Gutierrez, por casado dos veces," 1561, AGN, Inq., vol. 23, exp. 5, fs. 127; "Proceso contra Francisco de

Acosta, por haber hecho ciertas amonestaciones y ser casado dos veces," 1565, AGN, Inq., vol. 26, exp. 6, fs. 227v; "Nombre y señas de los hombres escapados de las árceles del S. Oficio," 1578, AGN, Inq., vol. 84, exp. 27, fs. 154.

53. "Proceso contra Francisca de Acosta, casado dos vezes," 1559, AGN, Inq., vol. 91, exp. 2, fs. 9, 13v–14; "Proceso Contra Beatriz Hernández residente en las minas de Tasco," 1572, AGN, Inq., vol. 95, exp. 3, fs. 120v–121; "Proceso contra Pero Hernández negro horro vecino de la ciudad de la Veracruz casado dos vezes," 1574, AGN, Inq., vol. 102, exp. 3, fs. 70, 72, 74.

54. "Proceso contra Mariana de la Cruz, mulata libre, natural de Mexico, residente en Acapulco, por bigamia," 1593, AGN, Inq., vol. 185, exp. 2, fs. 11–69.

55. Ibid., fs. 38.

56. Ibid., fs. 34.

57. The same notary, Pedro de los Ríos, recorded each interview. It is possible that the two descriptions reflect his influence. Certainly the description of Mariana as a *negra amulatada* reflects his or the Inquisitors' ascription. The appearance of *"mulata negra"* in Isabel's testimony may have resulted from Ríos accidentally inserting one or both of the labels. Yet Isabel ratified her statement as the trial progressed. When the court read back her testimony she did not correct that description. Consequently, the ascription of *"mulata negra"* should be taken as reflecting Isabel's perception of Mariana.

58. "Proceso contra Pedro Gonzales de León, por bigamo," 1590, AGN, Inq., vol. 184, exp. 9, fs 210–28.

59. Ibid., fs. 228.

60. The court typically used such accounts to solicit information from individuals who had arrived in Mexico from distant parts, especially Iberia or other parts of the Indies.

61. AGI, Mexico 109, R. 3, N.18, fs. 282–602.

62. This finding appears to represent a consistent trend over time. In the late seventeenth century, Cope noted that colonial subjects showed almost no variability in the labeling of *negros* and *mulatos*. Cope, *The Limits of Racial Domination*, 77, table 4.6.

CHAPTER 5

Epigraph: AGI, Mexico 72, N. 137. "Es necesario tener diputadas personas que acudan a la proteccion y amparo de los indios de la ciudad y sus alderedores y tienen bien que hazer en librar los y ampararlos de los negros mulatos y meztizos para que no los maten y les tomen sus haziendas que seria cien leguas de aqui en un pueblo donde no uviese corregidor que un solo mulato bastaria a rebolverlo y aun a saquearlo demas de que como el reino es tan grande todos los delinquentes y jente de mal bibir mestizos y mulatos se alojerian a los pueblos de los indios de donde resultarian dos grandes danos destruirlos totalmente y ampararse y esconderse ellos dondelas justicias no pudiesen prenderlos para castigar delitos y podria el numero crecer tanto que no oviese camino seguro."

1. "Proceso contra Marcos Ruiz, por casado dos veces. Oaxaca," 1575, AGN, Inq., vol. 104, exp. 8, fs. 212–79.

2. For a similar story of a muleteer forming social and marital bonds in the early seventeenth century, see Boyer, "Juan Vázquez."

3. Herrera, *Natives, Europeans, and Africans*, 68–71.

4. Boyer, *Lives of the Bigamists*, 64.

5. Morin, "Libros parroquiales."

6. The lack of *género* labels in early colonial parish documents may reflect the lack of importance such terms had within the sacramental life of parishioners. Eventually such terms would prove useful in differentiating individuals between individuals who shared the same name but were ascribed different *géneros*.

7. Cope, *The Limits of Racial Domination*, 69–70; Morin, "Libros parroquiales," 392–94; Restall, *The Black Middle*, 106–8.

8. Chance, *Race and Class*.

9. Seed, "Social Dimensions," 592; Cope, *The Limits of Racial Domination*, 76–78. In my examination of baptismal records in parishes with sixteenth-century marriage registers, I have found that even if priests were consistent in ascribing *género* labels to marrying couples, they frequently omitted the same labels for baptisms, failing to label parents and almost unanimously omitting an ascription for the child.

10. Boyer, *Lives of the Bigamists*, 32.

11. Such a trend can be seen in the sentences meted out by the tribunal as lower-ranking persons uniformly received greater punishment.

12. "Matrimonios de Españoles, 1576–1600" and "Matrimonios de Españoles, 1626–1641," film/fiche no. 35848 Mexico, Archivo de la Parroquía de la Santa Veracruz, vols. 2–3; "Matrimonios de Indios, 1576–1601," film/fiche no. 35855 Mexico, Archivo de la Parroquía de la Santa Veracruz; "Matrimonios de castas 1605–1688," film/fiche no. 668893, Mexico, Archivo de la Parroquía de Santa Fe, Guanajuato (Gto.) Mexico, vol. 1, Family History Library, Salt Lake City Utah. Although listed as "Matrimonios de Castas 1605–1688," the Guanajuato register also contains *españoles* and *indios*.

13. "Tabla General en que van las Provincias del Arcobispado de Mexico con los Partidos," AGI, Mexico 112, R. 3, s/f.

14. Ibid. Specifically, these *géneros* along with some *españoles* were omitted because they lacked fixed residences and wandered in vagabondage. "Ay otra muncha gente assi de españoles mestizos como negros mulatos e yndios que por andar vagando y no tener ciertos asientos y abitaciones no se puede hazer padron ni numero dellos."

15. Blanco, Parra, and Ruiz Medrano, *Breve historia de Guanajuato*, 42–46; García, *Los mineros mexicanos*, 160; Gerhard, *A Guide to the Historical Geography of New Spain*, 121.

16. Bakewell, "Mining," 221–29; Lane, "Africans and Natives in the Mines of Spanish America," 174–76.

17. Guevara Sanginés, "Guanajuato colonial," 153–56.

18. Bakewell, "Notes on the Mexican Silver Mining Industry," 189, table 1.

19. Guevara Sanginés, "Guanajuato colonial," 157; Tutino, *Making a New World*, 134–35.

20. Bakewell, "Notes on the Mexican Silver Mining Industry," 194, table 3(a).

21. The parish of Santa Veracruz was established in 1568; however, the area that it served had represented Mexico City's western boundary since its foundation in 1521.

22. The Santa Veracruz registers suggest that the *género* of the groom determined where a marriage was recorded, with registers mirroring the divisions established by the two-republic model. The *matrimonios de españoles* register contained *español* grooms as well as any *mestizo, mulato,* and *negro* grooms, while the *matrimonios de indios* register only recorded the marriages of *indio* grooms.

23. Cope, *The Limits of Racial Domination*, 79–80; Proctor, *Damned Notions of Liberty*, 64–67; Rust and Seed, "Equality of Endogamy."

24. Cope, *The Limits of Racial Domination*, 80–81.

25. Proctor, *Damned Notions of Liberty*, 56–57; Cope, *The Limits of Racial Domination*, 80.

26. Castro Rivas, Rangel López, and Tovar Rangel, *Desarrollo socio demográfico*, 49–50.

27. Proctor, *Damned Notions of Liberty*, 14–15; Carroll, *Blacks in Colonial Veracruz*, 28–37.

28. Proctor, *Damned Notions of Liberty*, 57–60.

29. Tutino, *Making a New World*, 133–36; Castro Rivas, Rangel López, and Tovar Rangel, *Desarrollo socio demográfico*, 27–45.

30. Cope, *The Limits of Racial Domination*, 27–38.

31. Ibid., 79, 81–82, tables 4.7, 4.8, 4.9.

32. "Proceso contra Bartolome Hernández, arriero, por casado dos veces," 1578, AGN, Inq., vol. 107, exp. 3, fs. 143–86.

33. AGN, Inq., vol. 107, exp. 3, fs. 173. There are several communities with the toponym Actopan. Bartolomé was referring to one that is located on the coast of the Gulf of Mexico, about halfway between Xalapa and Veracruz. Gerhard, *Historical Geography of New Spain*, 221.

34. Totomihuacan was an indigenous community located south of Puebla de los Angeles. At the time of this case it was part of an *encomienda* held by Alonso Dávila. It was later held by Alonso Galeote. Ibid.

35. Nazzari, "An Urgent Need to Conceal," 104–5.

36. "Proceso contra Pedro de Carranza, por casado dos veces," 1572, AGN, Inq., vol. 98, exp. 7, fs. 343–74.

37. Socolow, *Women of Colonial Latin America*, 116–18.

38. *Real Academia Española*, s.v. "camarero," http://lema.rae.es/drae/?val=camarero, accessed July, 21, 2015.

39. Boyd-Bowman, *Patterns of Spanish Emigration (1493–1580)*, 26.

40. *Recopilación de Leyes de las Indias,* Lib. VII, Tit. III, leyes i and viii.

41. See "Carta de don Luis de Velasco a S.M," 1550, AGI, Mexico 19, N. 3; "Carta de don Martín Enríquez a S.M," 1573, AGI, Mexico 19, N. 142; "Carta de don Luis de Velasco a S.M.," 1590 and 1594, AGI, Mexico 22, N. 16 and N. 128.

42. Boyd-Bowman, *Patterns of Spanish Emigration to the New World (1493–1580),* 49.

43. Ibid., 79.

44. Boyd-Bowman, "Patterns of Spanish Emigration to the Indies, 1579–1600," 84.

45. Socolow, *Women of Colonial Latin America,* 8–9.

46. "Proceso contra Francisco Gutiérrez por casado dos veces," 1561, AGN, Inq., vol. 23, exp. 5, fs. 59–134.

47. Early modern Catholic marriage rites occurred in two stages. The betrothal (*desposorio*) fulfilled the canonical requirement for the exchange of consent between partners. After the betrothal, often months or years later, came the blessing (*velación*). Prior to the Council of Trent, many couples never solemnized their marriage through a *velación*. The requirements for sacramental marriage only required an exchange of vows, before witnesses, and consummation. Although prior impediments might allow for subsequent annulments, the Church and society considered couples that had exchanged vows and consummated the union to be married. The Council of Trent modified this system to require the publication of the banns prior to the betrothal and to celebrate both the betrothal and the blessing in the same ceremony, among other changes. D'Avray, *Medieval Marriage,* 60, 144–48, 173–74; Donahue, *Law, Marriage, and Society,* 16.

48. "Proceso contra Pedro de Herrera Padilla escriviente vecino de Mexico, casado dos vezes," 1572, AGN, Inq., vol. 95, exp. 1, fs. 1–105. Mari's mother Juana Sánchez was never called an *india* in this investigation, but Mari was consistently called a *mestiza*.

49. Nazzari, "An Urgent Need to Conceal," 105.

50. Kuznesof, "Raza, clase y matrimonio," 382; John F. Schwaller, "Identidad sexual," 59–60; Nazzari, "An Urgent Need to Conceal," 104–7.

51. Boyer, *Lives of the Bigamists,* 66–79, 93.

52. Castañeda, "La formación de la pareja," 85–86.

53. Bennett, *Africans in Colonial Mexico,* 8–10; Bennett, *Colonial Blackness,* 86–113.

54. Bennett, *Colonial Blackness,* 21.

55. Proctor, *Damned Notions of Liberty,* 67.

56. "Proceso contra Mariana de la Cruz, mulata libre, natural de Mexico, residente en Acapulco, por bigamia, y contra Anton Hernández, que se caso con ella sabiendo que era casada," 1593, AGN, Inq., vol. 185, exp. 2, fs. 11–69.

57. Ibid., fs. 21v–22.

58. "Proceso contra Joan de Perales mulato libre natural de mexico, casado dos vezes," 1575, AGN, Inq., vol. 103, exp. 5, fs. 191–253.

59. Ibid., fs. 217.

60. John F. Schwaller, "Early Life of Luis de Velasco," 31, 43.

61. Proctor, *Damned Notions of Liberty,* 16–19.

62. "Proceso contra Diego de Hojeda, arriero, por casado dos veces," 1580, AGN, Inq., vol. 134, exp. 8, fs. 126–62.

Chapter 6

Epigraph: "Cedula dirigida al Arçobispo de Mexico . . . procurar que los mulatos de aquella tierra sean doctrinados como los indios," in Encinas, *Cedulario indiano,* vol. 4, 392–93. "Iuan de Peña en nombre de los mulatos de essa tierra me ha hecho relacion, que a causa de andar la mayor parte de tiempo ocupados en la labor de minas, y en guardas de las haziendas de estancias de ganados, y otras cosas fuera de poblado no son doctrinados ni industriados en las coas de nra Santa Fé Catolica, como seria justo lo fuessen, y padecen detrimento sus animas y conciencias en quanto a su salvacion, de que Dios nuestro Señor ha sido y es muy deservido."

1. "Proceso contra Juan Méndez, mestizo zapatero, por casado dos veces, Antequera," 1564, AGN, Inq., vol. 26, exp. 2, fs. 13–29.

2. Under Castilian law, a dowry remained the property of the woman after marriage. While husbands could manage the assets brought to the marriage by their wife, they were not considered communal property. Flint, *No Mere Shadows,* 7.

3. John F. Schwaller, *Church and Clergy,* 89; Parry, *Audiencia of New Galicia,* 122.

4. Flint, *No Mere Shadows,* 119.

5. Cope, *The Limits of Racial Domination,* 18; Chance, *Race and Class,* 99–101.

6. Seed, "Social Dimensions," 583.

7. Bennett, *Colonial Blackness;* Brading, *Miners and Merchants;* Carroll, *Blacks in Colonial Veracruz;* Chance, *Race and Class;* Chance and Taylor, "Estate and Class in a Colonial City"; Chance and Taylor, "Estate and Class: A Reply"; Cope, *The Limits of Racial Domination;* Herrera, *Natives, Europeans, and Africans;* McAlister, "Social Structure and Social Change"; McCaa, Schwartz, and Grubessich, "Race and Class"; Mörner, *Race Mixture;* Restall, *The Black Middle;* Seed, "Social Dimensions"; Valdes, "Decline of the Sociedad de Castas."

8. Brading, *Miners and Merchants,* 258; Chance and Taylor, "Estate and Class in a Colonial City," 472–73; Cope, *The Limits of Racial Domination,* 86–89; Seed, "Social Dimensions," 579–84.

9. Robert C. Schwaller, "For Honor and Defense."

10. "Proceso contra Alonso Ruiz, platero, por casado dos veces," 1564, AGN, Inq., vol. 26, exp. 3, fs. 31–83.

11. "Proceso contra Gabriel Carrasco, por casado dos veces," 1566, AGN, Inq., vol. 27, exp. 1, fs. 3–108.

12. "Proceso de oficio de la autoridad eclesiástica contra Pedro Sánchez de Reyna," 1569, AGN, Inq., vol. 10, exp. 4, fs. 110–49.

13. "Proceso contra Diego de Hojeda, arriero, por casado dos veces, Mexico," 1580, AGN, Inq., vol. 134, exp. 8, fs. 126–62.

14. The term *sedero* could apply to silk weavers or to silk merchants. Nothing in the case suggests that Diego or his relatives were merchants. The apprenticeship to his father and grandfather suggests that there was a long period of training in the delicate art of working with silk.

15. AGN, Inq., vol. 134, exp. 8, fs. 149. "Pide penitencia con misercordia porque el no lo hizo con malicia ni por hazer burla del sancto matrimonio y que en pago de su delito el estara en monasterio sirviendo en su oficio de sedero que lo save muy bien hazer." I have changed the tense from the notarial third person to the first-person tense Diego likely used.

16. "Proceso contra Josep de Molina, mestizo, alias Cristobal de Molina, por bigamo," 1600, AGN, Inq., vol. 262, exp. 3, fs. 32–82.

17. While the literature from later periods suggests that these organizations became increasingly discriminatory against non-Spaniards, none of the tradesmen discussed here mentioned guilds or their regulations. See Carrera Stampa, *Gremios Mexicanos*.

18. AGN, Inq., vol. 95, exp. 4, fs. 200–217. The case against Luis Hernández is included at the end of another case from 1563 that was brought against an Iberian-born *mulato* of the same name.

19. "Proceso contra Diego Jimenez por otro nombre Diego Piloto, mulato," 1575, AGN, Inq., vol. 104, exp. 2, fs. 16–31.

20. Ibid., fs. 23v.

21. These individuals did not always work with cattle. Many worked with sheep and horses. I will use the term "cowboy" as the generic term for someone involved in tending livestock.

22. While many tradesmen and artisans mention learning their trade, muleteers and cowboys simply noted that they started working in those professions. Although these occupations certainly required specialized knowledge and skills, the cases suggest that many men learned on the job.

23. Hassig, *Trade, Tribute, and Transportation*, 193; Calderón, *Historia económica*, 450.

24. Herrera, *Natives, Europeans, and Africans*, 176–77; Calderón, *Historia económica*, 452; Suárez, "Los arrieros novohispanos," 82–90.

25. Hassig, *Trade, Tribute, and Transportation*, 197–200; Calderón, *Historia económica*, 450.

26. Hassig, *Trade, Tribute, and Transportation*, 212–14. Such variation was common throughout the colonial period. Even in the eighteenth century, wages varied widely between men. Suárez, "Los arrieros novohispanos," 100.

27. The average unskilled laborer earned approximately one real (one-eighth of a peso) per day. If one worked 250 days per year (not working on Sundays or other mandatory religious feast days), one would earn roughly thirty pesos per year. Gibson, *The Aztecs under Spanish Rule*, 250–51. Contract laborers in the textile mills (*obrajes*) of seventeenth-century Queretaro earned between 28 and 36 pesos per year. Tutino, *Making a New World*, 502.

28. Arroyo Abad, Davies, and van Zanden, "Between Conquest and Independence," 155–58. During the first half of the sixteenth century, real wages for unskilled workers were depressed due to coercive labor arrangements and only represented between half and three-quarters of a living wage. By the early seventeenth century, increased wage labor and liberalization in employment led to a rise in real wages such that the averaged unskilled worker likely earned just over what was needed for subsistence.

29. "Proceso contra Mariana de la Cruz, mulata libre . . . y contra Antón Hernández mulato libre, que se caso con ella sabiendo que era casada. Acapulco," 1593, AGN, Inq., vol. 185, exp. 2, fs. 11–69.

30. "Proceso contra Juan de Perales mulato libre por casado dos veces, Mexico," 1575, AGN, Inq., vol. 103, exp. 5, fs. 191–254.

31. "Proceso contra Manuel Díaz vecino de Jalapa por casado dos veces," 1572, AGN, Inq., vol. 94, exp. 2, fs. 68–112.

32. He used the word *levante*.

33. He was born in Alvor, a port town of the Algarve region in southern Portugal.

34. AGN, Inq., vol. 94, exp. 2, fs. 99. "Primeramente un caballo rucio; una silla jineta con estribos estradiotes; un freno jinete viejo y una espuelas; una frazada vieja; un pabellón de manta de la tierra; una ballesta con su carcax; un herramental, tenazas, martillo, pujavante; un sayo pardo Viejo; unos zaragüelles azules viejos; una manta de la tierra; un capote negro traído; unos zaragüelles de manta de la tierra; un machete bracamarte; once reales en dineros."

35. Chevalier, *Land and Society*, 85, 104; Calderón, *Historia económica*, 338–39.

36. Chevalier, *Land and Society*, 106–7.

37. Ibid., 107.

38. Ibid., 40–41.

39. AGI, Mexico 109, Ramo 3, N. 18, fs. 282–602. See also Greenleaf, "Antonio de Espejo."

40. For more details about the interethnic relationships on this *estancia*, see Robert C. Schwaller, "The Importance of *Mestizos* and *Mulatos*," 718–20.

41. AGI, Mexico 109, Ramo 3, N. 18, fs. 382–84.

42. AGI, Mexico 105, s.f.

43. AGN, Inq., vol. 134, exp. 8, fs. 149v.

44. "Proceso contra Manuel Diaz vecino de Jalapa por casado dos veces," 1572, AGN, Inq., vol. 94, exp. 2, fs. 100.

45. "Proceso contra Antonio de Arenas, mulato portugues, por casado dos veces, Mexico," 1578, AGN, Inq., vol. 107, exp. 4, fs. 187–225.

46. *Grumete* can also be translated as "cabin boy" but represents a position for slightly older youths.

47. For a more detailed description of the commerce between Iberia and the Americas, see Sanz, *Comercio de Espana*. Volume 1 contains a detailed history of the slave trade, its regulation, and procedures.

48. AGN, General de Parte, vol. 5, exp. 1319, fs. 291v.

49. "Proceso Joaquin de Santa Ana, mulato esclavo de don Carlos Samano, residente en Xalapa, por blasfemo," 1599, AGN, Inq., vol. 148, exp. 6, fs. 202–41.

50. "Proceso contra Ysabel mulata esclava que vino de castilla en flota deste ano 1576," AGN, Inq., vol. 48, exp. 7, fs. 266–79.

51. Proctor, *Damned Notions of Liberty,* 98–109; Villa-Flores, *Dangerous Speech,* 130.

52. Socolow, *Women of Colonial Latin America,* 116–18.

53. "Proceso contra Pedro de Herrera Padilla escriviente vecino de Mexico, casado dos vezes," 1572, AGN, Inq., vol. 95, exp. 1, fs. 1–105.

54. "Proceso contra Martín Ochoa de Salvatierra, fraile Agustino, por haberse casado, por otro nombre Martín de Salvatierra," 1578, AGN, Inq., vol. 84, exp. 3, fs. 5–41.

55. The fact that authorities allowed the marriage to occur despite parental opposition is not surprising for the sixteenth century. In the early colonial period, most theologians placed the intent of the contracting parties above the concerns of family. Seed, *To Love, Honor, and Obey,* 37.

56. "Proceso contra Beatriz Martín alias Ana Martín por dos veces casada," 1572, AGN, Inq., vol. 94, exp. 1, fs. 1–67.

57. "Proceso contra Juan de Perales mulato libre por casado dos veces," 1575, AGN, Inq., vol. 103, exp. 5, fs. 191–253.

58. "Proceso contra Francisca Ramírez, mulata, por casada dos veces," 1577, AGN, Inq., vol. 107, exp. 1, fs. 1–37.

59. AGN, Inq., vol. 107, exp. 1, fs. fs. 27. The phrase she used was "la avia avido Pedro de la Peña."

60. Powers, *Women in the Crucible of Conquest,* 152.

61. "Proceso contra Juana Agustina, natural de Oaxacatlan de las minas," 1595, AGN, Inq., vol. 185, exp. 6, fs. 201–243.

62. Guaxacatlan is likely the modern municipality of Juanacatalán, located just southwest of Guadalajara.

63. AGN, Inq., vol. 185, exp. 6, fs. 241. "No se ande distraida."

64. Powers, *Women in the Crucible of Conquest,* 152–67; Socolow, *Women of Colonial Latin America,* 113–17.

65. "Proceso contra Barbola de Zamora, supersticiones," 1565, AGN, Inq., vol. 38, exp. 11, fs. 238–68; "Proceso contra Barbola de Zamora, Minas de San Martín Nuevo Galicia," 1570, AGN, Inq., vol. 39, exp. 4, fs. 311–63; "Proceso contra Ana Cavallero mulata vezina de mexico, proposiciones," 1574, AGN, Inq., vol. 116, exp. 6, fs. 252–66.

66. If a newborn was in danger of dying before he or she could be baptized by a priest, the child could be baptized by any layperson. In practice this duty often fell to midwives who were present at the birth. In this case, Barbola did not know the proper wording. Such confusion was not uncommon as other midwives underwent investigations for similarly heterodox activities. Socolow, *Women of Colonial Latin America,* 120.

67. Other scholars have investigated syncretism and folk practices. For longer descriptions of such practices, see Bristol, *Christians, Blasphemers, and Witches*; Lewis, *Hall of Mirrors*; Few, *Women Who Live Evil Lives*; Proctor, *Damned Notions of Liberty*. For a discussion of *mestizos* and *mulatos* as cultural intermediaries, see Robert C. Schwaller, "The Importance of *Mestizos* and *Mulatos*."

68. Socolow, *Women of Colonial Latin America*, 116.

69. AGN, Inq., vol. 116, exp. 6, fs. 257–70. "Más vale estar bien amancebada que mal casada." At this time the Mexican Holy Office was particularly concerned with moral vices, especially those concerning sex and marriage. Greenleaf, *Mexican Inquisition*, 160.

71. Encinas, *Cedulario indiano*, vol. 4, 349.

72. Herrera, *Natives, Europeans, and Africans*, 56–57; Cope, *The Limits of Racial Domination*, 110–12.

73. Robert C. Schwaller, "For Honor and Defense," 251.

74. "Proceso contra Francisco Rodríguez mulato portugues natural de Tavira vecino de Guaçaqualco, casado dos veces," 1579, AGN, Inq., vol. 108, exp. 4, fs. 121–22.

75. "Proceso contra Beatriz Martín alias Ana Martín por dos veces casada," 1572, AGN, Inq. 94, exp. 1, fs. 6.

76. *Pesos de tepuzque* were coins made of a copper and gold amalgam that were approximately equivalent to a silver peso or eight reales. John F. Schwaller, *Origins of Church Wealth*, 5.

77. Seeger, "Media of Exchange," 183–84.

78. Ibid., 172; Simpson, *The Encomienda in New Spain*, 188n1.

Conclusion

1. Rappaport, *The Disappearing Mestizo*, 11, 95. John Chance made a similar observation about *mestizos* living in seventeenth-century Oaxaca. Chance, *Race and Class*, 138.

2. Proctor, *Damned Notions of Liberty*, 61; Martínez, *Genealogical Fictions*, 164–67.

3. Vinson, *Bearing Arms for His Majesty*; Germeten, *Black Blood Brothers*.

4. O'Toole, *Bound Lives*; Restall, *The Black Middle*; Brockington, *Blacks, Indians, and Spaniards*.

5. Proctor, *Damned Notions of Liberty*, 37–67; Bennett, *Africans in Colonial Mexico*; Bennett, *Colonial Blackness*.

6. Cope, *The Limits of Racial Domination*, 80–84; Chance, *Race and Class*, 135–39; Chance and Taylor, "Estate and Class in a Colonial City," 477–81. In the Veracruz region, Patrick Carroll has found, *mestizos* tended to be more endogamous than *mulatos* and more similar to *españoles*, at least until the eighteenth century. Carroll, "Los Mexicanos negros: Anexo de cuadros," vii–x, tables 4–7.

7. For examples of such studies, see Althouse, "Contested Mestizos, Alleged Mulattos"; Frederick, "Without Impediment"; Sierra Silva, "From Chains to Chiles."

8. Chance, *Race and Class*, 139–42; Chance and Taylor, "Estate and Class in a Colonial City," 473; Cope, *The Limits of Racial Domination*, 87–89; McCaa, Schwartz, and Grubessich, "Race and Class," 432; Restall, "Ways of Work," chap. 4 in *The Black Middle*; Seed, "Social Dimensions," 580–83; Vinson, *Bearing Arms for His Majesty*, 105, tables 19–20; Vinson, "From Dawn 'til Dusk."

9. Hering Torres, "Purity of Blood," 30–31.

10. Such a finding parallels research into the indigenous experience of colonialism. The legal system provided an important venue where the incongruities between law and practice allowed for the negotiation of colonial relationships. For example, see Kellogg, *Law and the Transformation of Aztec Culture*; Owensby, *Empire of Law*; Yannakakis, *The Art of Being In-Between*.

Bibliography

Archival Sources

Archivo General de Indias (AGI), Seville, Spain
   Contratación
   Filipinas
   Indiferente General
   Mexico
   Panama
   Patronato
   Santa Fe
   Santo Domingo
Archivo General de la Nación, Mexico City
   General de Parte
   Inquisición
   Matrimonios
   Reales Cédulas Duplicadas

Published Primary Sources

Acosta, José de. *Historia natural y moral de las Indias: en que se tratan de las cosas notables del cielo, elementos, metales, plantas y animales dellas; y los ritos, y ceremonias, leyes y gobierno de los Indios.* 1590. Reprint. Mexico City: Fondo de Cultura Económica, 1962.

Altamira, Rafael. "El texto de las leyes de Burgos de 1512." *Revista de Historia de América*, no. 4 (1938): 5–79.

Ayala, Manuel Joseph de. *Diccionario de gobierno y legislacion de Indias.* 13 vols. Madrid: Ediciones de Cultura Hispanica, 1991.

Berdan, Frances, and Patricia Rieff Anawalt, eds. *The Essential Codex Mendoza*. Berkeley: University of California Press, 1997.

Cartas de Indias. Madrid: Imprenta de Manuel G. Hernández, 1877.

Colección de documentos inéditos relativos al descubrimiento, conquista y colonización de las posesiones españolas en America y Oceanía. First series. 42 vols. Madrid: Imprenta Española, 1864–84.

Colección de documentos inéditos relativos al descubrimiento conquista y organización de las antiguas posesiones españolas de ultramar. Second series. 27 vols. Madrid: Real Academia de Historia, 1885–1932.

Columbus, Christopher. *Los cuatro viajes del almirante y su testamento*. Edited by Ignacio B. Anzoátegui and Bartolomé de las Casas. Madrid: Espasa-Calpe, 1992.

Cortés, Hernán. *Cartas de relación*. Edited by Angel Delgado Gómez. Madrid: Editorial Castalia, 1993.

Covarrubias Orozco, Sebastián de, Ignacio Arellano, and Rafael Zafra. *Tesoro de la lengua castellana o española*. 1611. Reprint, Madrid: Universidad de Navarra; Iberoamericana, 2006.

De la Torre Villar, Ernesto, ed. *Instrucciones y memorias de los virreyes novohispanos*. 2 vols. Mexico: Editorial Porrúa, 1991.

De la Vega, Garcilaso. *Los comentarios reales de los Incas*. Lisboa: Officina de Pedro Crasbeeck, 1609.

Diccionario de Autoridades: Edición facsímil. 3 vols. 1726–39. Reprint, Madrid: Editorial Gredos, 1964.

Eannes de Azurara, Gomes. *Cronica do descobrimento e conquista de Guiné*. Paris: J. P. Aillaud, 1841.

Encinas, Diego de. *Cedulario indiano*. 4 vols. 1596. Reprint, Madrid: Ediciones Cultura Hispánica, 1945.

Ibn Khaldun and Franz Rosenthal. *The Muqaddimah: An Introduction to History*. 3 vols. Princeton: Princeton University Press, 1967.

Icazbalceta, Joaquín García. *Colección de documentos para la historia de México*. 2 vols. Mexico: Porrúa, 1980.

Levillier, Roberto, ed. *Gobernantes del Perú, cartas y papeles: Siglo XVI, documentos del Archivo de Indias*. 14 vols. Madrid: Sucesores de Rivadeneyra, 1921–26.

Konetzke, Richard. *Colección de documentos para la historia de la formación social de Hispano América, 1493–1810*. 3 vols. Madrid: Consejo Superior de Investigaciones Científicas, 1953.

López de Velasco, Juan. *Geografía y descripción universal de las Indias*. Madrid: Real Academia de la Historia, 1894.

Motolinía, Toribio. *Historia de los indios de la Nueva España*. Edited by Georges Baudot. Madrid: Castalia, 1985.

Recopilación de leyes de los Reynos de las Indias. 4 vols. 1681. Reprint, Madrid: Ediciones Cultura Hispánica, 1973.

SECONDARY SOURCES

Aguirre Beltrán, Gonzalo. *La población negra de México: Estudio etnohistórico.* 2nd ed. Mexico City: Fondo de Cultura Económica, 1972.
Alonso, Martín. *Enciclopedia del idioma,* vol. 3 (N–Z). Madrid: Aguilar, 1958.
Althouse, Aaron P. "Contested Mestizos, Alleged Mulattos: Racial Identity and Caste." *Americas* 62, no. 2 (2005): 151–75.
Altman, Ida. "Spanish Society in Mexico City after the Conquest." *Hispanic American Historical Review* 71, no. 3 (1991): 413–45.
Arrom, José Juan. "Criollo: Definición y matices de un concepto." *Hispania* 34, no. 2 (1951): 172–76.
Arroyo Abad, Leticia, Elwyn Davies, and Jan Luiten van Zanden. "Between Conquest and Independence: Real Wages and Demographic Change in Spanish America, 1530–1820." *Explorations in Economic History* 49, no. 2 (2012): 149–66.
Bakewell, Peter J. "Mining." In *Colonial Spanish America,* edited by Leslie Bethell, 203–49. Cambridge: Cambridge University Press, 1987.
———. "Notes on the Mexican Silver Mining Industry in the 1590's." In *Mines of Silver and Gold in the Americas,* edited by P. J. Bakewell, 75–94. Brookfield, Vt.: Variorum, 1997.
———. *Silver Mining and Society in Colonial Mexico: Zacatecas, 1546–1700.* Cambridge: Cambridge University Press, 1971.
Bartlett, Robert. "Medieval and Modern Concepts of Race and Ethnicity." *Journal of Medieval and Early Modern Studies* 31, no. 1 (2001): 39–56.
Baumer, Franklin Le Van. "The Conception of Christendom in Renaissance England." *Journal of the History of Ideas* 6, no. 2 (1945): 131–56.
Beatty-Medina, Charles. "Caught between Rivals: The Spanish-African Maroon Competition for Captive Indian Labor in the Region of Esmeraldas during the Late Sixteenth and Early Seventeenth Centuries." *Americas* 63, no. 1 (2006): 113–36.
Bennett, Herman L. *Africans in Colonial Mexico: Absolutism, Christianity, and Afro-Creole Consciousness, 1570–1640.* Bloomington: Indiana University Press, 2003.
———. *Colonial Blackness: A History of Afro-Mexico.* Bloomington: Indiana University Press, 2009.
Blackburn, Robin. "The Old World Background to European Colonial Slavery." *William and Mary Quarterly* 54, no. 1 (1997): 65–102.
Blanco, Mónica, Alma Parra, and Ethelia Ruiz Medrano. *Breve historia de Guanajuato.* Mexico City: Colegio de México Fondo de Cultura Económica, 2000.
Borah, Woodrow, and Sherburne F. Cook. "Sobre las posibilidades de hacer el estudio histórico del mestizaje sobre una base demográfica." *Revista de historia de América* 53/54 (1962).

Bowser, Frederick P. *The African Slave in Colonial Peru, 1524–1650.* Stanford: Stanford University Press, 1974.
Boyd-Bowman, Peter. *Léxico hispanoamericano del siglo XVI.* London: Tamesis, 1971.
———. "Negro Slaves in Early Colonial Mexico." *Americas* 26, no. 2 (1969): 134–51.
———. "Patterns of Spanish Emigration to the Indies, 1579–1600." *Americas* 33, no. 1 (1976): 78–95.
———. *Patterns of Spanish Emigration to the New World (1493–1580).* Special Studies, no. 34. Buffalo: SUNY Buffalo, Council on International Studies, 1973.
Boyer, Richard E. "Juan Vázquez, Muleteer of Seventeenth-Century Mexico." *Americas* 37, no. 4 (1981): 421–43.
———. *Lives of the Bigamists: Marriage, Family, and Community in Colonial Mexico.* Albuquerque: University of New Mexico Press, 1995.
———. "Negotiating *Calidad*: The Everday Struggle for Status in Mexico." *Historical Archaeology* 31, no. 1 (1997): 64–73.
Brading, D. A. *Miners and Merchants in Bourbon Mexico, 1763–1810.* Cambridge: Cambridge University Press, 1971.
Braude, Benjamin. "The Sons of Noah and the Construction of Ethnic and Geographical Identities in the Medieval and Early Modern Periods." *William and Mary Quarterly* 54, no. 1 (1997): 103–42.
Bristol, Joan Cameron. *Christians, Blasphemers, and Witches: Afro-Mexican Ritual Practice in the Seventeenth Century.* Albuquerque: University of New Mexico Press, 2007.
———. "From Curing to Witchcraft: Afro-Mexicans and the Mediation of Authority." *Journal of Colonialism and Colonial History* 7, no. 1 (2006).
Brockington, Lolita Gutiérrez. *Blacks, Indians, and Spaniards in the Eastern Andes: Reclaiming the Forgotten in Colonial Mizque, 1550–1782.* Lincoln: University of Nebraska Press, 2006.
Bryant, Sherwin K. *Rivers of Gold, Lives of Bondage: Governing through Slavery in Colonial Quito.* Chapel Hill: University of North Carolina Press, 2014.
Calderón, Francisco R. *Historia económica de la Nueva España en tiempo de los Austrias.* Mexico City: Fondo de Cultura Económica, 1988.
Cañizares-Esguerra, Jorge. *How to Write the History of the New World: Histories, Epistemologies, and Identities in the Eighteenth-Century Atlantic World.* Stanford: Stanford University Press, 2001.
———. "New World, New Stars: Patriotic Astrology and the Invention of Indian and Creole Bodies in Colonial Spanish America, 1600–1650." *American Historical Review* 104, no. 1 (1999): 33–68.
Carrera, Magali Marie. *Imagining Identity in New Spain: Race, Lineage, and the Colonial Body in Portraiture and Casta Paintings.* Austin: University of Texas Press, 2003.
Carrera Stampa, Miguel. *Los gremios mexicanos: La organización gremial en Nueva España, 1521–1861.* Mexico City: Iberio Americana Publicaciones, 1954.

Carroll, Patrick. *Blacks in Colonial Veracruz: Race, Ethnicity, and Regional Development.* 2nd ed. Austin: University of Texas Press, 2001.

———. "Los Mexicanos negros, el mestizaje y los fundamentos olvidados de la 'Raza Cosmica': Una perspective regional." *Historia Mexicana* 44, no. 3 (1995): 403–38.

———. "Los Mexicanos negros, el mestizaje y los fundamentos olvidados de la 'Raza Cosmica': Una perspective regional: Anexo de cuadros" *Historia Mexicana* 44, no. 3 (1995): i–xvi.

Castañeda, Carmen. "La formación de la pareja y el matrimonio." In *Familias novohispanas: Siglos XVI al XIX*, edited by Pilar Gonzalbo, 73–90. Mexico City: Colegio de México, 1991.

Castañeda Delgado, Paulino. "El colegio de San Juan de Létran de México (Apuntes para su historia)." *Anuario de Estudios Americanos* 37 (1980): 69–126.

Castro Rivas, Jorge A., Matilde Rangel López, and Rafael Tovar Rangel. *Desarrollo socio demográfico de la ciudad de Guanajuato durante el siglo XVII: Investigación histórica.* Guanajuato, Gto.: Universidad de Guanajuato, 1999.

Cervantes Saavedra, Miguel de. *El ingenioso hidalgo don Quijote de la Mancha.* Madrid: Editorial Gredos, 1987.

Chance, John K. *Race and Class in Colonial Oaxaca.* Stanford: Stanford University Press, 1978.

Chance, John K., and William B. Taylor. "The Ecology of Race and Class in Late Colonial Oaxaca." In *Studies in Spanish American Population History*, edited by David J. Robinson, 93–117. Boulder: Westview Press, 1981.

———. "Estate and Class: A Reply." *Comparative Studies in Society and History* 25 (1979): 434–42.

———. "Estate and Class in a Colonial City, Oaxaca in 1792." *Comparative Studies in Society and History* 19 (1977): 454–87.

Chevalier, François. *Land and Society in Colonial Mexico: The Great Hacienda.* Translated by Alvin Eustis. Berkeley: University of California Press, 1963.

Chipman, Donald E. *Moctezuma's Children: Aztec Royalty under Spanish Rule, 1520–1700.* Austin: University of Texas Press, 2005.

Chuchiak, John F. "The Sins of the Fathers: Franciscan Friars, Parish Priests, and the Sexual Conquest of the Yucatec Maya, 1545–1808." *Ethnohistory* 54, no. 1 (2007): 69–127.

Collantes de Teran, Antonio. *Sevilla en la baja edad media: La ciudad y sus hombres.* Seville, Spain: Seccion de Publicaciones del Excmo. Ayuntamiento, 1977.

Cope, R. Douglas. *The Limits of Racial Domination: Plebeian Society in Colonial Mexico City, 1660–1720.* Madison: University of Wisconsin Press, 1994.

Corominas, Joan. *Diccionario crítico etimológico de la lengua castellana.* 6 vols. Madrid: Editorial Gredos, 1980.

Cortes, Vicenta. *La esclavitud en Valencia durante el reinado de los Reyes Catolicos (1479–1516).* Valencia: Archivo Municipal de Valencia, 1964.

D'Avray, D. L. *Medieval Marriage: Symbolism and Society.* New York: Oxford University Press, 2005.

Deive, Carlos Esteban. *Los guerrilleros negros: Esclavos fugitivos y cimarrones en Santo Domingo.* Santo Domingo: Fundacion Cultural Dominicana, 1989.

Deutsch, Karl W. "Medieval Unity and the Economic Conditions for an International Civilization." *Canadian Journal of Economics and Political Science* 10, no. 1 (1944): 18–35.

Diggs, Irene. "Color in Colonial Spanish America." *Journal of Negro History* 38, no. 4 (1953): 403–27.

Domínguez Ortiz, Antonio. *Las clases privilegiadas en la Espana del antiguo régimen.* Madrid: Ediciones ISTMO, 1973.

Don, Patricia Lopes. *Bonfires of Culture: Franciscans, Indigenous Leaders, and the Inquisition in Early Mexico, 1524–1540.* Norman: University of Oklahoma Press, 2010.

Donahue, Charles. *Law, Marriage, and Society in the Later Middle Ages.* Cambridge: Cambridge University Press, 2007.

Enciso Contreras, José. *Taxco en el siglo XVI: Sociedad y normatividad en un real de minas novohispano.* Zacatecas, Zac.: Ayuntamiento de Zacatecas: Facultad de Derecho de la Universidad Autónoma de Zacatecas: Consejo Nacional para la Cultura y las Artes, 1999.

Few, Martha. *Women Who Live Evil Lives: Gender, Religion, and the Politics of Power in Colonial Guatemala.* Austin: University of Texas Press, 2002.

Flint, Shirley Cushing. *No Mere Shadows: Faces of Widowhood in Early Colonial Mexico.* Albuquerque: University of New Mexico Press, 2013.

———. "Treason or Travesty: The Marín Cortés Conspiracy Reexamined." *Sixteenth Century Journal* 39, no. 1 (2008): 23–44.

Forbes, Jack D. *Africans and Native Americans: The Language of Race and the Evolution of Red-Black Peoples.* Urbana: University of Illinois Press, 1993.

Franco Silva, Alfonso. *La esclavitud en Andalucia.* Granada: Universidad de Granada, 1992.

Frederick, Jake. "Without Impediment: Crossing Racial Boundaries in Colonial Mexico." *Americas* 67, no. 4 (2011): 495–515.

García, Trinidad. *Los mineros mexicanos.* 2nd ed. Mexico City: Ing. Jose Garcia, 1968.

Garofalo, Leo J. "The Shape of a Diaspora: The Movement of Afro-Iberians to Colonial Spanish America." In *Africans to Spanish America*, edited by Sherwin K. Bryant, Rachel Sarah O'Toole, and B. Vinson, III, 27–49. Urbana: University of Illinois Press, 2012.

Geertz, Clifford. *The Interpretation of Cultures: Selected Essays.* New York: Basic Books, 1973.

Gerbet, Marie-Claude. *La nobleza en la corona de Castilla: Sus estructuras sociales en Extremadura (1454–1516).* Salamanca: Institución Cultural "El Brocense," Excma. Diputación Provincial Caceres, 1989.

Gerhard, Peter. "A Black Conquistador in Mexico." *Hispanic American Historical Review* 58, no. 3 (1978): 451–59.

———. *A Guide to the Historical Geography of New Spain*. Norman: University of Oklahoma Press, 1993.

Germeten, Nicole von. *Black Blood Brothers: Confraternities and Social Mobility for Afro-Mexicans*. Gainesville: University Press of Florida, 2006.

Gibson, Charles. *The Aztecs under Spanish Rule: A History of the Indians of the Valley of Mexico, 1519–1810*. Stanford: Stanford University Press, 1964.

Góngora, Mario. *El estado en el derecho indiano: Época de fundación (1492–1570)*. Santiago, Chile: Instituto de Investigaciones Historio-Culturales: Facultad de Filosofía y Educación, Universidad de Chile, 1951.

———. "Institutions and Founding Ideas of the Spanish State in the Indies." Translated by Richard Southern. In *Studies in the Colonial History of Spanish America*, 67–126. Cambridge: Cambridge University Press, 1975.

———. *Studies in the Colonial History of Spanish America*. Translated by Richard Southern. Cambridge: Cambridge University Press, 1975.

Greenleaf, Richard E. "Antonio de Espejo and the Mexican Inquisition 1571–1586." *Americas* 27, no. 3 (1971): 271–92.

———. *The Mexican Inquisition of the Sixteenth Century*. Albuquerque: University of New Mexico Press, 1969.

Griffiths, Nicholas. *The Cross and the Serpent: Religious Repression and Resurgence in Colonial Peru*. Norman: University of Oklahoma Press, 1996.

Gruzinski, Serge. *Man-Gods in the Mexican Highlands: Indian Power and Colonial Society, 1520–1800*. Stanford: Stanford University Press, 1989.

Guevara Sanginés, María "Guanajuato colonial y los afroguanajuatenses." In *Memoria Del III Encuentro Nacional De Afromexicanistas*, edited by Luz María Martinez Montiel, 152–66. Colima, Mexico: Gobienro del Estado de Colima; Consejo Nacional Para la Cultura y las Artes, 1993.

Guillot, Carlos F. *Negros rebeldes y negros cimarrones: Perfil afroamericano en la historia del Nuevo Mundo durante el siglo XVI*. Buenos Aires: Librería y Editorial "El Ateneo," 1961.

Guitar, Lynne. "Boiling It Down: Slavery on the First Commercial Sugarcane Ingenios in the Americas (Hispaniola, 1530–45)." In *Slaves, Subjects, and Subversives: Blacks in Colonial Latin America*, edited by Jane G. Landers and Barry Robinson, 39–82. Albuquerque: University of New Mexico Press, 2006.

Haskett, Robert Stephen. *Indigenous Rulers: An Ethnohistory of Town Government in Colonial Cuernavaca*. Albuquerque: University of New Mexico Press, 1991.

Hassig, Ross. *Trade, Tribute, and Transportation: The Sixteenth-Century Political Economy of the Valley of Mexico*. Norman: University of Oklahoma Press, 1985.

———. "Xicotencatl: Rethinking an Indigenous Mexican Hero." *Estudios de Cultura Náhuatl* 38 (2001): 29–49.

Hering Torres, Max S. "The Purity of Blood: Problems of Interpretation." In *Race and Blood in the Iberian World*, edited by Max S. Hering Torres, María Elena Martínez and David Nirenberg, 11–38. Zurich: Lit Verlag, 2012.

Herrera, Robinson A. *Natives, Europeans, and Africans in Sixteenth-Century Santiago de Guatemala.* Austin: University of Texas Press, 2003.

Herzog, Tamar. *Defining Nations: Immigrants and Citizens in Early Modern Spain and Spanish America.* New Haven: Yale University Press, 2003.

Hesse, Barnor. "Racialized Modernity: An Analytics of White Mythologies." *Ethnic and Racial Studies* 30, no. 4 (2007): 643–63.

Heywood, Linda M., and John K. Thornton. *Central Africans, Atlantic Creoles, and the Foundation of the Americas, 1585–1660.* New York: Cambridge University Press, 2007.

Israel, Jonathan I. *Race, Class, and Politics in Colonial Mexico, 1610–1670.* London: Oxford University Press, 1975.

Jackson, Robert H. "Race/Caste and the Creation and Meaning of Identity in Colonial Spanish America." *Revista de Indias* 55, no. 203 (1995): 149–73.

Jones, W. R. "The Image of the Barbarian in Medieval Europe." *Comparative Studies in Society and History* 13, no. 4 (1971): 376–407.

Jordan, Winthrop D. *White over Black: American Attitudes toward the Negro, 1550–1812.* Chapel Hill: Published for the Institute of Early American History and Culture by the University of North Carolina Press, 1968.

Kamen, Henry. *Spain, 1469–1714: A Society of Conflict.* 3rd ed. New York: Pearson/Longman, 2005.

———. *The Spanish Inquisition: A Historical Revision.* New Haven: Yale University Press, 1997.

Katzew, Ilona. *Casta Painting: Images of Race in Eighteenth-Century Mexico.* New Haven: Yale University Press, 2004.

Kellogg, Susan. *Law and the Transformation of Aztec Culture, 1500–1700.* Norman: University of Oklahoma Press, 1995.

Konetzke, Richard. "El mestizaje y su importancia en el desarrollo de la población Hispanoamericana durante la época colonial." *Revista de Indias* 7, nos. 23, 24 (1946): 7–44, 215–37.

Kuznesof, Elizabeth A. "Ethnic and Gender Influences on 'Spanish' Creole Society in Colonial Spanish America." *Colonial Latin American Review* 4, no. 1 (1995): 153–76.

———. "Raza, clase y matrimonio en la Nueva España: Estado actual del debate." In *Familias novohispanas: Siglos XVI al XIX*, edited by Pilar Gonzalbo, 373–88. Mexico City: Colegio de México, 1991.

Lane, Kris E. "Africans and Natives in the Mines of Spanish America." In *Beyond Black and Red: African-Native Relations in Colonial Latin America*, edited by Matthew Restall, 159–84. Albuquerque: University of New Mexico Press, 2005.

Lanyon, Anna. *The New World of Martin Cortes.* Cambridge, Mass.: Da Capo Press, 2004.

Lewis, Laura A. *Hall of Mirrors: Power, Witchcraft, and Caste in Colonial Mexico.* Durham: Duke University Press, 2003.

Lockhart, James. *The Nahuas after the Conquest: A Social and Cultural History of the Indians of Central Mexico, Sixteenth through Eighteenth Centuries.* Stanford: Stanford University Press, 1992.

———. *Of Things of the Indies: Essays Old and New in Early Latin American History.* Stanford: Stanford University Press, 1999.

———. "Social Organization and Social Change in Colonial Spanish America." In *The Cambridge History of Latin America*, edited by Leslie Bethell, 265–320. Cambridge: Cambridge University Press, 1984.

———. *Spanish Peru, 1532–1560: A Colonial Society.* Madison: University of Wisconsin Press, 1968.

López Martínez, Héctor. "Un motín de mestizos en el Perú (1567)." *Revista de Indias* 24, no. 97–98 (1964): 367–82.

Lovejoy, Paul E. *Transformations in Slavery: A History of Slavery in Africa.* 2nd ed. Cambridge: Cambridge University Press, 2000.

MacCormack, Sabine. *Religion in the Andes: Vision and Imagination in Early Colonial Peru.* Princeton: Princeton University Press, 1991.

Mangan, Jane E. "Moving Mestizos in Sixteenth-Century Peru: Spanish Fathers, Indigenous Mothers, and the Children in Between." *William and Mary Quarterly* 70, no. 2 (2013): 273–94.

Marshall, C. E. "The Birth of the Mestizo in New Spain." *Hispanic American Historical Review* 19, no. 2 (1939): 161–84.

Martin, Norman Francis. *Los vagabundos en la Nueva España: Siglo XVI.* Mexico: Editorial Jus, 1957.

Martínez, María Elena. *Genealogical Fictions: Limpieza de Sangre, Religion, and Gender in Colonial Mexico.* Stanford: Stanford University Press, 2008.

McAlister, Lyle N. "Social Structure and Social Change in New Spain." *Hispanic American Historical Review* 43, no. 3 (1963): 349–70.

———. *Spain and Portugal in the New World, 1492–1700.* Minneapolis: University of Minnesota Press, 1984.

McCaa, Robert, Stuart B. Schwartz, and Arturo Grubessich. "Race and Class in Colonial America: A Critique." *Comparative Studies in Society and History* 25 (1979): 421–33.

Megged, Amos. "Magic, Popular Medicine and Gender in Seventeenth-Century Mexico: The Case of Isabel de Montoya." *Journal of Social History* 19, no. 2 (1994): 189–207.

Miers, Suzanne, and Igor Kopytoff. *Slavery in Africa: Historical and Anthropological Perspectives.* Madison: University of Wisconsin Press, 1977.

Miller, Mary E., and Barbara E. Mundy. *Painting a Map of Sixteenth-Century Mexico City: Land, Writing, and Native Rule.* New Haven: Beinecke Rare Book and Manuscript Library, Yale University, 2012.

Milton, C., and B. Vinson III. "Counting Heads: Race and Non-Native Tribute Policy in Colonial Spanish America." *Journal of Colonialism and Colonial History* 3, no. 3 (2002): 1–18.

Mira Caballos, Esteban. *Indios y mestizos Americanos en la España del siglo XVI.* Madrid: Iberoamericana, 2000.

Mondragón Barrios, Lourdes. *Esclavos africanos en la Ciudad de México: El servicio doméstico durante el siglo XVI.* Mexico City: Ediciones Euroamericanas: Conaculta, INAH, 1999.

Morin, C. "Los libros parroquiales como fuente para la historia demográfica y social novohispana." *Historia Mexicana* 21, no. 3 (1972): 389–418.

Mörner, Magnus. "Economic Factors and Stratification in Colonial Spanish America with Special Regard to Elites." *Hispanic American Historical Review* 63, no. 2 (1983): 335–69.

———. *Race Mixture in the History of Latin America.* Boston: Little, Brown, 1967.

Nazzari, Muriel. "An Urgent Need to Conceal: The System of Honor and Shame in Colonial Brazil." In *The Faces of Honor: Sex, Shame, and Violence in Colonial Latin America,* edited by Lyman L. Johnson and Sonya Lipsett-Rivera, 103–26. Albuquerque: University of New Mexico Press, 1998.

O'Toole, Rachel Sarah. *Bound Lives: Africans, Indians, and the Making of Race in Colonial Peru.* Pittsburgh: University of Pittsburgh Press, 2012.

Ots Capdequi, Jose Maria. *El estado Español en las Indias.* 2nd ed. Mexico City: Fondo de Cultura Economica, 1946.

Owensby, Brian P. *Empire of Law and Indian Justice in Colonial Mexico.* Stanford: Stanford University Press, 2008.

Palmer, Colin A. *Slaves of the White God: Blacks in Mexico, 1570–1650.* Cambridge, Mass.: Harvard University Press, 1976.

Parry, J. H. *The Audiencia of New Galicia in the Sixteenth Century: A Study in Spanish Colonial Government.* Cambridge: Cambridge University Press, 1948.

Peralta Rivera, Germán. *Mechanismos del comercio negrero.* Lima: Kuntur Editores, 1990.

Phillips, William D. *Slavery from Roman Times to the Early Transatlantic Trade.* Minneapolis: University of Minnesota Press, 1985.

Pike, Ruth. "Black Rebels: The Cimarrons of Sixteenth-Century Panama." *Americas* 64, no. 2 (2007): 243–66.

———. "Sevillian Society in the Sixteenth Century: Slaves and Freedmen." *Hispanic American Historical Review* 47, no. 3 (1967): 344–59.

Poole, Stafford. *Juan de Ovando: Governing the Spanish Empire in the Reign of Phillip II.* Norman: University of Oklahoma Press, 2004.

Powell, Phillip Wayne. *Spaniards, Indians, and Silver: The Northward Advance of New Spain, 1550–1600.* Berkeley: University of California Press, 1952.

Powers, Karen Vieira. *Women in the Crucible of Conquest: The Gendered Genesis of Spanish American Society, 1500–1600.* Albuquerque: University of New Mexico Press, 2005.

Price, Richard. *Maroon Societies: Rebel Slave Communities in the Americas.* 3rd ed. Baltimore: Johns Hopkins University Press, 1996.

Proctor, Frank T. *"Damned Notions of Liberty": Slavery, Culture, and Power in Colonial Mexico, 1640–1769*. Albuquerque: University of New Mexico Press, 2010.

Rappaport, Joanne. *The Disappearing Mestizo: Configuring Difference in the Colonial New Kingdom of Granada*. Durham: Duke University Press, 2014.

Restall, Matthew, ed. *Beyond Black and Red: African-Native Relations in Colonial Latin America*. Albuquerque: University of New Mexico Press, 2005.

———. "Black Conquistadors: Armed Africans in Early Spanish America." *Americas* 57, no. 2 (2000): 171–205.

———. *The Black Middle: Africans, Mayas, and Spaniards in Colonial Yucatan*. Stanford: Stanford University Press, 2009.

———. "A History of the New Philology and the New Philology in History." *Latin American Research Review* 38, no. 1 (2003): 113–34.

———. *Seven Myths of the Spanish Conquest*. New York: Oxford University Press, 2003.

Restall, Matthew, Lisa Sousa, and Kevin Terraciano. *Mesoamerican Voices: Native-Language Writings from Colonial Mexico, Oaxaca, Yucatan, and Guatemala*. Cambridge: Cambridge University Press, 2005.

Rípodas Ardanaz, Daisy. *El matrimonio en Indias: Realidad social y regulación jurídica*. Buenos Aires: Fundación para la Educación, la Ciencia y la Cultura, 1977.

Rodríguez-Salgado, M. J. "Christians, Civilised and Spanish: Multiple Identities in Sixteenth-Century Spain." *Transactions of the Royal Historical Society* 8 (1998): 233–51.

Rueda Novoa, Rocío. *Zambaje y autonomía: historia de la gente negra de la provincia de Esmeraldas: Siglos XVI–XVIII*. Esmeraldas, Ecuador: Municipalidad de Esmeraldas; Quito, Ecuador: Taller de Estudios Históricos, 2001.

Ruiz, Teofilo F. *Spain's Centuries of Crisis: 1300–1474*. Malden, Mass.: Blackwell, 2007.

———. *Spanish Society, 1400–1600*. Harlow, England: Longman, 2001.

Russell-Wood, A. J. R. "Iberian Expansion and the Issue of Black Slavery: Changing Portuguese Attitudes, 1440–1770." *American Historical Review* 83, no. 1 (1978): 16–42.

Rust, Philip F., and Patricia Seed. "Equality of Endogamy: Statistical Approaches." *Social Science Research* 14, no. 1 (1985): 57–79.

Sahlins, Marshall David. *Islands of History*. Chicago: University of Chicago Press, 1985.

Sanz, Eufemio Lorenzo. *Comercio de España con America en la época de Felipe II*. 2 vols. Valladolid: Diputación Provincial de Valladolid, 1979.

Schwaller, John F. *The Church and Clergy in Sixteenth-Century Mexico*. Albuquerque: University of New Mexico Press, 1987.

———. "Conversion, Engagement, and Extirpation: Three Phases of the Evangelization of New Spain, 1524–1650." In *Conversion to Christianity from Late Antiquity to the Modern Age: Considering the Process in Europe, Asia, and the Americas*, edited by Calvin B. Kendall, Oliver Nicholson, William D. Phillips, and Marguerite Ragnow, 259–92. Minneapolis: Center for Early Modern History and the University of Minnesota, 2009.

———. "The Early Life of Luis de Velasco, the Younger: The Future Viceroy as Boy and Young Man." *Estudios de Historia Novohispana* 29, no. 29 (2003): 17–47.

———. *The History of the Catholic Church in Latin America: From Conquest to Revolution and Beyond.* New York: New York University Press, 2011.

———. "La identidad sexual: Familia y mentalidades a fines del siglo XVI." In *Familias Novohispanas: Siglos XVI al XIX*, edited by Pilar Gonzalbo, 59–72. Mexico City: Colegio de México, 1991.

———. *Origins of Church Wealth in Mexico: Ecclesiastical Revenues and Church Finances, 1523–1600.* Albuquerque: University of New Mexico Press, 1985.

———. "The Private Correspondence of Don Luis de Velasco, the Younger, with the Court of Phillip II." Paper presented at Pennsylvania State University, March 18, 2009.

Schwaller, Robert C. "'For Honor and Defense': Race and the Right to Bear Arms in Early Colonial Mexico." *Colonial Latin American Review* 21, no. 2 (2012): 239–66.

———. "The Importance of *Mestizos* and *Mulatos* as Bilingual Intermediaries in Sixteenth Century New Spain." *Ethnohistory* 59, no. 4 (2012): 713–38.

———. "'Mulata, Hija de Negro y India': Afro-Indigenous *Mulatos* in Early Colonial Mexico." *Journal of Social History* 44, no. 3 (2011): 885–910.

Schwartz, Stuart B. "Spaniards, '*Pardos*', and the Missing *Mestizos*: Identities and Racial Categories in the Early Hispanic Caribbean." *New West Indian Guide* 71, no. 1–2 (1997): 5–19.

Seed, Patricia. "The Social Dimensions of Race: Mexico City 1753." *Hispanic American Historical Review* 62, no. 4 (1982): 569–606.

———. *To Love, Honor, and Obey in Colonial Mexico: Conflicts over Marriage Choice, 1574–1821.* Stanford: Stanford University Press, 1988.

Seeger, Martin L. "Media of Exchange in 16th Century New Spain and the Spanish Response." *Americas* 35, no. 2 (1978): 168–84.

Sierra Silva, Pablo Miguel. "From Chains to Chiles: An Elite Afro-Indigenous Couple in Colonial Mexico, 1641–1688." *Ethnohistory* 62, no. 2 (2015): 361–84.

Silverblatt, Irene Marsha. *Modern Inquisitions: Peru and the Colonial Origins of the Civilized World.* Latin America Otherwise. Durham: Duke University Press, 2004.

Simpson, Lesley Byrd. *The Encomienda in New Spain: The Beginning of Spanish Mexico.* Berkeley: University of California Press, 1966.

Socolow, Susan Migden. *The Women of Colonial Latin America.* Cambridge: Cambridge University Press, 2000.

Suárez, Clara Elena. "Los arrieros novohispanos." In *Trabajo y sociedad en la historia de México*, edited by Gloria Artís Espiru, Brígida von Mentz, Luz María Mohar Betancourt, Beatriz Scharrer Tamm, and Suárez Argüello, 77–158. Mexico City: Centro de Invesigaciones y Estudios Superiores de Antropología Social; Ediciones de la Casa Chata, 1992.

Sweet, James H. "The Iberian Roots of American Racist Thought." *William and Mary Quarterly* 54, no. 1 (1997): 143–66.
Tardieu, Jean-Pierre. *Cimarrones de Panamá: La forja de una identidad afroamericana en el siglo XVI.* Madrid: Iberoamericana Editorial, 2009.
Tavárez, David. "Legally Indian: Inquisitorial Readings of Indigenous Identity in New Spain." In *Imperial Subjects: Race and Identity in Colonial Latin America*, edited by Andrew B. Fisher and Matthew D. O'Hara. Durham: Duke University Press, 2009.
Thornton, John K. *Africa and Africans in the Making of the Atlantic World, 1400–1800.* 2nd ed. Cambridge: Cambridge University Press, 1998.
Tutino, John. *Making a New World: Founding Capitalism in the Bajío and Spanish North America.* Durham: Duke University Press, 2011.
Valdes, Dennis Nodin. "Decline of the Sociedad de Castas in Mexico City." PhD diss., University of Michigan, 1978.
Vega Boyrie, Wenceslao. "El cimarronaje y la manumisión en el Santo Domingo Colonial. Dos extremos de una misma búsqueda de libertad." *CLÍO* 174 (2005): 65–102.
Villa-Flores, Javier. *Dangerous Speech: A Social History of Blasphemy in Colonial Mexico.* Tucson: University of Arizona Press, 2006.
Villella, Peter B. "Native Elites and the Discourse of Blood Purity in Late Colonial Mexico." *Hispanic American Historical Review* 91, no. 4 (2011): 633–63.
Vinson, Ben, III. *Bearing Arms for His Majesty: The Free-Colored Militia in Colonial Mexico.* Stanford: Stanford University Press, 2001.
———. "From Dawn 'til Dusk: Black Labor in Late Colonial Mexico." In *Black Mexico: Race and Society from Colonial to Modern Times*, 96–135. Albuquerque: University of New Mexico, 2009.
———. "Introduction: African (Black) Diaspora History, Latin American History." *Americas* 63, no. 1 (2006): 1–18.
———. "Race and Badge: Free-colored Soldiers in the Colonial Mexican Militia." *Americas* 56, no. 4 (2000): 471–96.
———. "Studying Race from the Margins: The 'Forgotten Castes'—*Lobos, Moriscos, Coyotes, Moros,* and *Chinos* in the Colonial Mexican Caste System." Paper delivered at the International Seminar on the History of the Atlantic World, Harvard University, 2002.
Vinson, Ben, III, and Matthew Restall. "Black Soldiers, Native Soldiers: Meanings of Military Service in the Spanish American Colonies." In *Beyond Black and Red: African-Native Relations in Colonial Latin America*, edited by Matthew Restall, 15–52. Albuquerque: University of New Mexico Press, 2005.
Whitehead, Neil L. *Lords of the Tiger Spirit: A History of the Caribs in Colonial Venezuela and Guyana, 1498–1820.* Dordrecht, Holland: Foris, 1988.
Yannakakis, Yanna. *The Art of Being In-Between: Native Intermediaries, Indian Identity, and Local Rule in Colonial Oaxaca.* Durham: Duke University Press, 2008.
Zavala, Silvio A. *Las instituciones jurídicas en la conquista de América.* 2nd ed. Mexico City: Editorial Porrúa, 1971.

INDEX

References to illustrations appear in italic type.

Acapulco, Mex., 175–76, 199
Acosta, Francisca de, 129, 251n27
Actopan, Mex., 164, 255n33
Afro-indigenous marriage pairings (Santa Veracruz and Guanajuato), 120–23
Afro-indigenous *mulatos*. See *mulatos*, Afro-indigenous
Afro-Mexicans: acculturation to local indigenous languages, 130, 137; attention given to, 7, 8; and interconnections between social networks, 178–79, 226; marriage patterns, 182; "racial consciousness" lacking in, 174
AGI (Archivo General de Indias), 10
AGN (Archivo General de la Nación), 10
Aguas Calientes, 142
Agustina, Juana, 111–14, 141–42, 210–11, 250n60
Algarve of Portugal, 205, 259
Alonso, Catalina, 186
Alonso, Martín, 171, 179
Altamirano, Doña Agustina, 175
Altamirano, Hernando, 174–75, 176
Alvares Sardina, Juan (captain), 206
amancebaday, defined, 125
amancebamiento, 175, 177, 191–92
amulatado, 140, 142
Ana, *negra* slave, 179–80
Ana, Veronica, 164
Angulo, Geronima de, 111
Antequera (Oaxaca), 128, 135, 140–41, 147, 185–86, 192–93

António Saco, José, 46
Archivo General de Indias (AGI), 10
Archivo General de la Nación (AGN), 10
Arena, Gaspar de, 205
Arenas, Antonio de, 205–6
artisans and tradesmen, 189–97, 220–21; case of Alonso Ruiz (silversmith), 98, 189, 191; case of Diego de Hojeda (*sedero*), 158n15, 193–94, 195, 258n14; case of Diego Ximénez (muleteer), 196–97, 199; case of Graviel Carrasco (locksmith), 191–92; case of Jusepe de Molina (low-skill occupations), 194–95; case of Luis Hernández (tailor), 195–96, 258n18; case of Pedro Sánchez de Reyna (tailor), 192–93; and diversity of employment, 220–21, 222, 223–24; *género* not impediment to training, 195, 221, 258n17; *mestizo* and *mulato* tradesmen, 197
asiento system, 61, 206
Asunción Sagrario cathedral, 152, *153* (map), 254n14
Audiencia of New Spain, 64, 78
audiencias (high courts), 52
Augustina, *mulata*, 130–32
Avalos, Alonso, 135–37
Avalos, Licenciado, 178, 179

Balderas, Urbán de, 212
bearing arms, 62–65, 72–73, 75, 78, 104–5, 242nn73

Beatriz, Doña, 96
Bennett, Herman, 173–74
Biafara, Juan, 210
Bonilla, Juan Carlos de, 93
bozales, 41, 60–61, 62, 125
Bravo, Juan, 166–67

cacao beans, 219–20
caciques y gobernadores, 102–5; case of María García Pareja, 106; and familial ties, 103; and *género* ascription, 105; and indigenous elites, 103–4; subsets of those of Spanish-indigenous ancestry, 102; tacit *indios* versus tacit *españoles*, 105, 248n48; and Zarate's request to bear arms, 104–5
calidad and *casta*, usage of, 5–6, 8, 229n6
calidades (qualities), 27, 233nn33–35
Cañizares-Esguerra, Jorge, 44
Cano, Mariana, 113
Cano, Martín, 113
Çarate, Don Francisco de, 147–48
Cardona, Juan Bautista de, 77–78
Carranza, Ana, 166
Carranza, Pedro de, 165–68
Carrasco, Graviel, 191–92
Carrasco, Pedro, 191
Casa de Contratación (House of Trade), 168
casta (ethno-religious concept), 21–22, 27, 232n31, 233n32
casta and *calidad*, usage of, 5–6, 229n6
Castañeda, Juana de, 134
Castañeda, Leonor de, 147–49
Castañeda, Luis de, 164
Castilian language, 10, 230n21
Castilla, Don Luis de, 134, 177, 178, 252n39
Castillo, Diego del, 179
castizo, defined, 48
casuist legislation, 53–54, 55, 63, 65, 78
Catalina *india*, 179
Cavallero, Ana, 212–13, 221, 261n69

Cedulario Indiano (aka Cedulario de Encinas), 55
Cerda, Cristóbal de la, 178, 179
Cerrezo, Gonzalo, 166
Cervantes, Miguel de, 29
Charles V of Spain, 3–4, 35, 66, 99, 236n84
Chichimec raiders, 194, 202–4
children of *conquistadores*. See *hijos de los conquistadores*
children of *españoles* and *indias*. See *hijos de españoles y indias*
children of *negros, indias, españoles*, and *negras*. See *hijos de negros y indias y españoles y negras*
chili smoke as punishment for *mulatos*, 126–27, *128*
Cisneros, Hernando de, 210
Codex Mendoza, 127, *128*
cofradia records, 7
Cohen's kappa values (statistical measures), 156
colegio de niños, 194
Collacos, Agustina de, 164
Collacos, Pedro de, 164
Colón, Diego, 59
Columbus, Christopher, 34, 35, 235n60
concubinage. See *amancebamiento*
conquistador-settlers in New Spain, documentation by, 87, 245n1
Contreras, García de, 210
Cope, Douglas, 157, 254n9, 255nn23–24
Cordina, Francisco de, 97
Correa, Isabel de, 205
Cortés, Don Martín, 72
Cortés, Hernan, 35–36, 51
Council of the Indies, 55
Covarrubias Horozco, Sebastián de, 22, 30, 46–47
cowboys and muleteers, 197–204; case of Antón Hernández (muleteer), 199–200; case of Antonio de Espejo, 202–3; case of Domingo Pérez, 200–201; case of Juan de

INDEX 279

Perales (carter), 200; case of Manuel Díaz (muleteer), 200; cowboy as second most common profession, 201–2; danger and difficulty of these professions, 204, 221; and Don Lope de Sosa's account of Chichimec raid, 203–4; as most commonly held jobs, 198, 258n21; muleteer most commonly held profession, 198–99; wages of, 199, 221, 258nn26–27, 259n28
criada (or *criado*), defined, 207
criollo (creole), defined, 41–42, 43
cristianos nuevos (New Christians), 231n9
cristianos viejos (Old Christians), 21, 231n9
Cruz, Madalena de la, 130–32
Cruz, Mariana de la, 139–40, 174, 199

defining difference in Iberia and the Americas, 17–49, 230n1; overview of search for difference, 11, 17–19; Castilian semantic domains of difference, *19*; early Spanish American overview, 26–27; and Ferdinand and Isabel marriage, 18; and *género* category *español*, 39–44; and *género* category *indio*, 34–39; and *género* category *negro*, 31–34; Iberian ethno-geographic terms, 23–25; Iberian ethno-religious terms, 21–23; Iberian socioeconomic terms, 19–21; new categories, 223; new *géneros* categories *loro, mulato, zambaigo, mestizo*, 44–49; Spanish American *géneros de gente*, 27–31. *See also* mixed-ancestry groups; *specific terms and categories*
derecho indiano, 51–55, 78; Spanish colonial law, 51–52, 55
D'Espinosa, Doña Mariana, 194
Díaz, Diego (alias Rodríguez), 216
Díaz, Isabel, 133–34, 215

Díaz, Manuel: birth of, 204–5, 259n33; clothing owned by, 215, 217; currency declared by, 219; horse owned by, 215, 218; as man of the sea, 204–5; property declared by, 200–201, 214, 215
Díaz, Miguel, 170
dowries, 186

Ehinger, Heinrich, 61
El ingenioso hidalgo don Quijote de la Mancha (Cervantes), 29–30
Elvira (free *mulata*), 179, 193
Enríquez, Don Martín (viceroy), 117–19, 249n11
Escobar, María de, 180
español category, 41; and contrasting theories of difference, 44; lengthy development of, 39–40; as privileged class, 223; purposes served by, 41, 236n83; and term *criollo* (creole), 41–42; and terms *chapetón* and *peninsular*, 42, 43, 237n91
Espejo, Antonio de, 142, 202–3
Espina, Juana de, 210
Espinosa, Antonio de, 166
Espinosa, María de, 166
ethno-religious terms, 21–23

Ferdinand of Aragon and Isabel of Castile, marriage of, 18
Flores, Juan, 209–10
Francisca *india*, 125–26
Fuente, Isabel de la, 165–68

Gallegos, Juan Bautista, 213
Gama, Inés de la, 166–67
García, Andrés and Luisa, 91, 92, 94, 102
García, Catalina, 135–37
García, Hipólito, 185–86
García, Pedro, 111
García Pareja, María, 91, 92, 93–94, 96, 106, 245n23

Gasca, Pedro de la (viceroy), 99
géneros, new (people in middle), 44–45
géneros de gente (roughly, types of people): complex origin of, 13; concept of, 6; in describing social diversity in colonial documentation, 28, 226–27; and Iberian concepts, 8; legal codification of, 223–24; usage of phrase, 27, 28, 29–30, 233n36
Gentil, Cristóbal, 92, 95
Gentil, Melchior, 95
Gómez, Francisca, 94, 106
Gómez, Juan, 197
Gómez, Pedro, 200
Gómez de Almaçan, Juan, 91, 93, 94, 106, 107, 246n18
Gómez de Valverde, Hernán, 187
Gonzáles, Pedro, 140
Granados, Francisco, 133–34
Guadalajara, Mex., 113, *155* (map)
Guanajuato mines, 152, 154
Guaxacatlan, 113
Guillén, Madalena, 209
Gutiérrez, Francisco, 170, 193

Ham (Noah's son), 33
Haskett, Robert, 102
Heredia, Francisco de, 185–87
Hermoso, Diego, 96
Hernández, Antón, 199–200
Hernández, Antonio, 174
Hernández, Bartolomé (elder), 164
Hernández, Bartolomé (younger), 163–65, 216, 218
Hernández, Beatriz, 216, 219–20, 221
Hernández, Cristobal, 177
Hernández, Diego, 93, 112
Hernández, Gonzalo, 135–37
Hernández, Juana, 93, 139, 177, 210
Hernández, Luis, 130–32, 195–96
Hernández, María, 177
Hernández Coyote, Pedro, 216, 220
Herrera, Robinson, 148
Herzog, Tamar, 23

hijos de españoles y indias, 69–75; and adultery policy against *españoles,* 73–74; changing royal policy toward, 69; marriage mandatory for *encomenderos,* 71; perceived illegitimacy of, 69–70, 242n68; plots involving, 72; and right to bear arms, 72–73, 242n73; and school for young, 70, 242n67; shift against in 1560s, 74–75; and Toledo's letter to crown, 72–73

hijos de los conquistadores, 91–102; and Alonso Rieros's *probanza,* 97–98, 247nn28–29; Alonso not called a *mestizo,* 98, 247n35; and Antonio de Leyba's petition, 99–100; Antonio not called a *mestizo,* 100; and Antonio's recommendation, 100; and Francisca's petition for services of Almaçan, 94, 246n18; and gender and familial support, 96–97; and Isabel's relationship to Montejo, 96, 247n26; and key roles of tacit *españoles,* 101–2; and María's poverty, 94, 246n17; and marriage of Andrés García and Doña Luisa, 94, 246n19; and *probanza* of Isabel de Montejo by husband, 95–96; and *probanza* of Maria García Pareja, 91, 92, 93–94, 245n23; and status marker of *doña* absent from Isabel's *probanza,* 96, 247n27; and tacit *españoles* as offspring of first settlers, 91, 245n11; and timing of Alonzo's petition, 98–99

hijos de negros y indias y españoles y negras, 75–79; arms restrictions on *mulatos,* 75; economic success of, 79; increasing numbers of, 75–76; and Juan Bautista's petition, 77–78, 244n100; and Quesada's petition, 78; and restrictions on *mulatos* and *negros,* 79; royal policy toward, 75; tribute burdens of, 76–77, 243n95

hijos naturales, defined, 89
Hinojosa family, 102–3
Hispaniola, 59, 60–61, 66, 67, 99
Hojeda, Diego de, 179, 193, 204
Hojeda, Francisco de, 179, 193
Hojeda, Juan de, 179–80, 193

Iberian antecedents: socioeconomic terms, overview of, 231nn7–8
india principal, defined, 93
"indigenous," defined, 113–14
indios: branded as cannibals, 37, 235n67; branded as weak, 37–38; Christian faith of, 38–39; and Columbus, 34, 35, 235n60; enslavement of banned, 38, 235n70; failings of cataloged, 39; inhabitants of India, 54; positive accounts of, 35–37; in sixteenth-century Iberia, 45, 237n105; subjugation of, 56
interethnic unions and marriage, 65–69; and African marriage policy, 66–68; and clerics' opposition to crown policy, 69; crown's approach to, 66; Friar Nicholas's opposition to, 4–5; legislation on (1501), 65–66; prevalence of, 65; tensions resulting from regulation of, 68–69; and two-republic system, 68–69
Isabel, *india*, 131

Japheth (Noah's son), 33
Jasso, Francisco, 111–13, 115
Jasso, Juan de, 99–100
Juárez, Francisco, 177

Khaldun, Ibn, 33–34

labels, national, 25
Las Casas, Bartolomé de, 38
Laws of Burgos (1512), 56
legislation, casuist. *See* casuist legislation
Leyba, Antonio de, 99–100

limpieza de sangre (purity of blood), 22–23, 231n14
Lockhart, James, 10
López, Diego, 134–35, 252n40
Lopez, Gerónimo, 203
López, Mari, 194
López de Velasco, Juan, 113, 237n88, 237n96; on *criollos*, 42, 43; on *indios*' failings, 39; reduction of slave trade urged by, 62; on rise of *mulatos* in Americas, 119, 250n15; on term *zambaigo*, 46–47
loros, 45, 64, 237n102
Luisa, *mulata*, 177
Luna y Arellano, Don Tristán de, 191

Madalena, *india*, 131
Manuel, *negro* slave, 180
María (*criada* of Carasco), 192
María, Juana, 93
María Inés, *india*, 196
Márques, Pedro, 209–10
marriage: overview of marriage patterns, 12, 147–49, 227; beyond exogamy and endogamy, 181–84; sources, 149–51, 254n6, 254n11. *See also* interethnic unions and marriage; marriageable *mestizas*; *mestizo* marriages; *mulato* social networks; parish marriages (1576–1641)
marriageable *mestizas*, 168–73; case of Ana Melgarejo, 170, 171, 256n47; case of Mari Sánchez, 171–73; and increase in number of female emigrants, 169; and *mestiza-españole* marriages, 169; *mestiza* kin treated as *española*, 169–71; and new emigration policy, 168–69; and shortage of women (*españolas*), 168, 184; value of, 173
Marroquín, Catalina, 148
Martín, Ana (alias Beatriz), 209–10, 216, 218–19, 220, 221
Martín, Juan, 210

Martínez, Diego, 29, 30, 234n42
Martínez, María Elena, 23, 231n9
Matias, Juan, 164
Maxixcatzin, 93, 246n15
Medina, Juan de, 134
Melgarejo, Ana, 170, 171, 256n47
Méndez, Juan, 104, 185–87, 221–22
Mendoza, Antonio de, 52, 63, 98
mestizo marriages, 163–68; and Bartolomé Hernández case, 163–65; and multiethnic membership of households, 168; and Pedro de Carranza case, 165–68; and shared residence in spouse selection, 165, 167–68, 183
mestizos: ascription of, 137–38; category defined, 47–48, 88; diversity among, 225–26; and Spanish laws, 103. See also *hijos de españoles y indias*; marriageable *mestizas*; Méndez, Juan; *mestizo* marriages; Pareja, Maria García
Mexía, Andrés, 95
mines, 152, 154
Miranda, Gaspar de, 177, 178
mixed-ancestry groups: diversity of, 11–12, 13, 223–24; policy to expel (1589), 58; rise of, 9. See also defining difference in Iberia and the Americas
Molina, Guiomar de, 93
Molina, Juan de, 194
Molina, Jusepe de, 194–95, 217, 218
Montaño, Francisco, 93
Montaño, Juan, 93
Montejo, Diego, 95–96, 246n23
Montejo, Doña Catalina, 95
Montejo, Don Francisco de, 95, 246n21
Montejo, Isabel de, 92, 95
Montesinos, Antonio, 38
Morales, Don Pedro de, 164
Morales, Gonzalo de, 189
Morales, María de, 189
Moreno, Andrés, 171–72, 208

morenos, 129, 135, 138–39, 144, 148, 177, 196
moriscos, 63–64, 77
moros, 21, 31–32, 60
Motolinía. *See* Toribio de Benavente (Motolinía)
mulato ascription variability, 137–45; application of label *mulato*, 137, 145; blurred line between *mulato* and *indio*, 140; case of Antonio de Espejo, 142; case of Juana as *mulata esclava*, 138–39, 252n47; case of Juana Augustina as *mestiza mulata*, 141–42, 253n60; case of Juana's use of *moreno*, 138–39; case of Madalena Osorio *india*, 140–41; case of Mariana de la Cruz as *mulata libre*, 139–40; colonial consensus on term, 45–56, 47, 110, 143–45, 226, 253n62; diversity of ascriptions for Andrés Vásquez, 142–43; and *mestizo* label, 137–38; varying descriptions of Mariana, 140, 253n57. *See also entries beginning with* mulato(s)
mulatos, 12, 111–15, 145–46; American-born, 115–16; in colonial society, 123–37; diversity of lived experiences, 114–15, 145, 223–24; Fray Nicolas de Witte's characterization of, 116; Jasso and Agustina, 111–14, 112–13; and marriage pairings in Santa Veracruz and Guanajuato, 120–23; and Mexican Inquisition cases, 115, 249nn6–9; and use of term "indigenous," 113–14; variability in ascription of, 137–45; Viceroy Martín Enríquez on growth of, 117–19, 249nn11–12, 250n13
mulatos, Afro-indigenous, 123–24; and acquisition of indigenous culture, 132; Antón's knowledge of native culture, 126–27; case of Beatriz Ramírez, 134–35, 252n38; case

of Francisca de Acosta and Antón
  Sanchez, 129, 251n27; case of Isobel
  Díaz, 133–34, 215; case of Juana
  Ramírez, 124–27, 215, 219, 250nn18–19;
  case of Luis Hernández, 130–32,
  195–96, 251n34; chili smoke as
  punishment for, 126–27, *128*; and
  cross-cultural awareness, 124,
  250n16; and Gonzalo Hernández's
  marriages, 135–37, 252n44; language
  acculturation by, 130; moving
  between cultures, 132–33; and
  multigenerational ties, 133–37;
  Nahuatl used in vows, 129–30; ties
  between natives illustrated by
  Gonzalo, 137. *See also entries
  beginning with* mulato(s)
mulato social networks, 173–81; case
  of Francisco de Hojeda, 179–80,
  193; case of Juan de Perales, 177–79,
  200, 210; case of Mariana de la
  Cruz and Antonio Hernández,
  174–76; endogamy as diachronic
  trend, 173; *mulato* endogamy
  facilitated by, 180–81, 182; racial
  consciousness absent from, 174
muleteers and cowboys. *See* cowboys
  and muleteers
multigenerational ties of
  Afro-indigenous *mulatos*, 133–37
Muñoz, Bartolomé, 96
Muñoz, Francisco, 203

nación (nation) of origin, 24–25
Nahua disciplinary techniques, *128*
Nahuatl (language), 129–30, 131, 142,
  164, 196
Najera, Francisca (*india principal*), 92,
  99–100
Najera, Juan de, 92, 99
Narváez, Pánfilo de, 91
naturaleza (place of birth), 23–24
naturalezas, non-Castilian, 24–25
negros: and color basis for
  differentiation, 32; historical basis
  of social meaning of term, 31;
  prejudice against, 32–33, 34,
  234n55; prohibitions against (1541),
  57; and servitude, 33, 234n55; and
  "Sons of Noah," 33, 234n53; as
  sub-Saharan African slaves, 23, 24,
  31, 32, 232n26
New Laws (1542): effect of, 56;
  and *encomiendas*, 98; and
  increased royal control, 87; in
  Peru, 102
New Philology, 10
New Spain: and arms licenses, 75;
  colonial order after Spanish
  conquest, 3–4; defining difference
  in, 26–27, 232n30; and Don Martín
  Cortés, 72; and Fray Nicolas's
  warning, 4–5; and initial
  conquistador-settlers, 87; northern,
  155 (map); and semantic domains, 10
Nicolás, *moreno*, 177, 178
northern New Spain, *155* (map)
Nuevo Reino de Granada, 81,
  244n110
Núñez, Hernan, 167
Núñez, Pascual, 177

Oaxaca, Mex. *See* Antequera (Oaxaca)
occupations: case against Juan
  Méndez, 185–87; Juan's flight with
  Catalina's dowry, 186, 257n2;
  Juan's ownership of shoe store,
  185–86, 221–22; of *mestizas* and
  mulatas (1555–1657), 190; of *mestizas*
  and *mulatas* (1564–98), 191; and
  range of occupations held by
  mulatos and *mestizos*, 12–13, 187–88,
  221–22, 223–24; and testimony
  presented, 186–87. *See also* artisans
  and tradesmen; cowboys and
  muleteers; personal property;
  transatlantic crossings and slave
  trade; working women
Ocelotepec, Mex., 97, 98, 247n31
Oñate, Bernardo de, 166

Ovando, Nicolás de, 40, 65
Owensby, Brian, 9

Pacheco, Diego, 148
Padilla, Pedro de, 171–72, 208
parish marriages (1576–1641):
  endogamy prevalent in, 156–57,
  181; Guanajuato marriages
  (1631–41), 160–61, 161; Guanajuato
  mines, 152, 154; Guanajuato parish
  records, 151–52, 156, 157t, 158, 161;
  marriage patterns, 157–59, 157–58,
  227; *mestizo* marriages from early
  Santa Veracruz, 159–60, 160, 183;
  periods for each parish, 154–55,
  255n21; preservation of *indio*
  marriages, 155–56; random pairing
  in Guanajuato, 159; Santa Veracruz
  mestizo marriages, 160–62; Santa
  Veracruz parish records, 151–52,
  156, 157, 160, 255n22; statistical
  measures used, 156; trends
  revealed in, 163. *See also* marriage
Parroquía de la Santa Veracruz
  (Mexico City) parish, 151–52, 254n12
Pastrana, Cristóbal de, 179–80
Pedro Brizeño, Gaytán, 210
Peña, Pedro de, 210
peninsular, defined, 42
Perales, Juan (aka Juan de Ayala),
  177–79, 200, 210, 252n47
Pérez, Alonso, 93
Pérez, Domingo, 200
Pérez, Juan, 177
Pérez, Madalena, 208–9, 260n55
Pérez, Manuel, 208–9
Pérez Calvillo, Juan, 170
Pérez de Arza, Alonso, 28, 30
Pérez de Padilla, Luis, 93
Pérez Negrón Gordillo, Don
  Diego, 170
personal property, 214–20; animals,
  218–19; cacao beans as currency,
  219–20; clothing, 214, 217; currency,
  219; declared in Inquisition, 214,
  215, 216; as modest, 220; men versus
  women, 214; weapons, 218
Peru, 57, 62, 64, 67–68, 72, 73, 81–82
Portugal, 200, 204–6
Proctor, Frank, 174, 181, 182, 207
property. *See* personal property
publica voz y fama (public reputation),
  23, 232n16

Quesada, Rodrigo, 135
Quesada de Figueroa, Juan, 78
Quiroga, Vasco de, 97, 98

racialization, process of, 6, 7–8,
  227–28, 262n10
Ramírez, Beatriz, 134–35, 252n38
Ramírez, Francisca, 210
Ramírez, Juana, 124–27, 215, 219,
  250nn18–19
Ramírez de Cartagena, Cristóbal, 28–29
Rangel, Francisca, 135–37
Rappaport, Joanne, 90, 226–27, 245n9
raza (ethno-religious concept), 22
Real y Minas de Santa Fe de Guana-
  juato parish, 151, 254n12
Real y Supremo Consejo de Indias
  (Royal and Supreme Council of the
  Indies), 52
Recopilación de Leyes de Las Indias, 55
Republica de españoles. See
  two-republic system
Republica de indios. See two-republic
  system
Reyes, Baltasar de los, 175
Reyes, Mariana de los, 214, 215
Ribera, Diego de, 210
Rieros, Alonso, 92, 97–99, 247nn28–29
Rieros, Alonso Martín, 92, 97–98
Rieros, Luisa, *india*, 92, 97
Roças, Andrés, 99
Rodríguez, Francisco, 167, 194, 215,
  218, 220, 221
Rodríguez, Sebastián, 63
Rodríguez del Pozo, Diego, 214,
  217, 218

Rodríguez de Robles, António, 29
Rojas family, 103
Rubio de Cardona, Gaspar, 77
Ruiz, Alonso, 98, 189, 191
Ruiz, Bartolomé, 189
Ruiz, Catalina, *india*, 189
Ruiz, Juan, 207
Ruiz, Marcos, 147–49
Ruiz, Pedro, 147
Ruiz, Teofilo, 18

Saavedra, Juan de, 135
Salas, Sebastian de, 193
Salazar, Hernando, 175
Salvatierra, Martín de, 208–9
Sámano, Don Carlos de, 207
Sámano, Juan de, 177
Sanchez, Antón, 129, 251n27
Sánchez, Catalina, 185–87, 208
Sánchez, Doña Juana, 104
Sánchez, Juana, 171, 256n48
Sánchez, Mari, 171–73, 208
Sánchez, Miguel, 135
Sánchez de Reyna, Bartolomé (cleric), 193
Sánchez de Reyna, Pedro, 192–93
San Juan de los Naturales (Mexico City), 141, 152
San Miguel, Martín de, 129, 130
San Miguel de Chichimecas (mod. de Allende), 152
San Pablo (Mexico City), 131–32
Santa Ana, Joaquín de, 207
Santa Veracruz parish. *See under* parish marriages (1576–1641)
Sarpara, Ana, 209
Sedeño, Dr., 179
Seed, Patricia, 69, 150
Seiller, Hieronymus, 61
Selada, Catalina de, 147–48
Selada, Juan de and Isabel (*india*), 148
Serna, Juan de la, 199
shaping society, 11–12, 50–51; creating two republics, 55–58; features of Spanish jurisprudence, 51–55. *See also* interethnic unions and marriage; slave policy, of sixteenth century; vagabond problem
Shem (Noah's son), 33
sistema de castas (sociedad de castas), 5, 7
slave policy, sixteenth century, 58–65; African slaves outnumber Spanish residents, 60–62; arming of slaves, 62–63, 240n45, 241nn47–48; *asiento* system, 61; and fears of rebellion, 58–59, 62; and insurrection of 1521, 59; laws regulating *negros*, 63–64; licensing of slaves, 61, 224–25; *negro* rebellion of 1537, 63–64; paradoxes of, 65; regulations of 1522, 59–60. *See also* Mendoza, Antonio de
sociedad de castas (sistema de castas), 5–6
socioeconomic terms, 19–21
"Sons of Noah," 33, 234n53
Sosa, Don Lope de, 203–4
Sosa, Gonzalo de, 94, 106

tacit *españoles* and colonial society, 12, 105–10; *criollo* population growth, 108–9; gradual diminution in number of tacit *españoles*, 106, 109; *mestizo* category avoided, 107, 108; "passing" in the socio-racial hierarchy, 107–8; and *probanza* of Francisca Gómez, 106–7, 248n50; and social positioning, 109–10; unique position of tacit *españoles*, 105–6, 110
tacit *españoles*, 87–91; documentation produced by, 87, 245n1; and *indios*, 90–91; and *mestizos*, 88, 90, 245nn9–10; and phrase "tacit *españoles*," 88–89; and Spanish-indigenous relationships, 89, 245n5, 245n8; and threats to new life, 87–88; upwardly mobile drive of, 90. See also *caciques y gobernadores*; *hijos de los conquistadores*; tacit *españoles* and colonial society
Tarrique, Manuel, 177, 178, 191, 210

Taxco, Mex., 124–27, 134, 154
Tello, Don Francisco, 174, 176
Tenochtitlan, city council of (1554), 3–4
Tepi, María, 93
Tlatelolco, Mex., 94
Tlaxcala, Mex., 91–93, 95, 164, 165
Toledo, Don Francisco de, 72, 75
Toribio de Benavente (Motolinía), on *indios*, 36–37, 38
Totomihuacan, Mex., 164, 255n34
transatlantic crossings and slave trade, 204–7; case of Antonio de Arenas, 205–6; case of Manuel Díaz, 204–5; and Juan Sardina's request for arms, 206; and *mulato* slaves, 206–7
translation and language note, 13–14
tribute, 38, 76–77
two-republic system, 56–57, 68–69

vagabond problem, 79–83; *género* categories transcended by, 82; and local enforcement of new laws, 83; new legislation addressing, 82–83; and new plans, 81, 244n108; resettling of vagabonds, 80–81; and travel made easy, 79–80; and Viceroy Velasco's complaint on, 80; and younger Velasco's task, 82
Vargas, Bernaldo de, 164
Vargas, Catalina de, 170
Vásquez, Andrés, 142–43
Vásquez, Juana, 134
vecinidad (citizenship), 23–24, 25
Vega, Agustín de, 210
Velasco, Don Francisco, 124
Velasco, Don Luis de (the elder): and recommendation of "protectors" (1554), 3; reduction in African slave imports urged by, 62; and relationship with Castilla, 178; as slaveholder, 177; and vagabond problem, 80; value of cacao beans ordered by, 219
Velasco, Don Luis de (the younger), 82
Velázquez, Francisca, 170
Velázquez, Licenciado, 170
Villa-Flores, Javier, 207
Villalobos, Doña Luisa de, 213
Vinson, Ben, 10–11

Witte, Fray Nicolas de, 4–5, 116
women, working. *See* working women
working women, 207–14; case of Ana Cavallero, 212–13; case of Ana Martín, 209–10; case of Barbola de Zamora, 211–12, 213, 260n66; case of Catalina Sánchez as *mestiza criada*, 208; case of Francisca Ramírez, 210; case of Juana Agustina, 210–11; case of Juana Hernández, 210; case of Madalena Pérez, 208–9, 260n55; case of Mari Sánchez, 208; and distinction in *criada* (or *criado*), 207–8; domestic service most common among, 207, 221; and powerlessness of *criadas*, 211, 221; work other than domestic, 211–14

Ximénez, Antón, 174–75
Ximénez, Diego, 196–97, 199
Ximénez, Juan, 196, 197
Ximénez, Martín, 129–30

Yaruniga, Antón, 124, 126

Zacatecas, 152–54, 193, 194, 199, 205
zambaigos, 46–47, 119
zambo, 46–47
Zamora, Barbola de, 211–12, 213, 260n66
Zarate, Don Juan de, 104–5

www.ingramcontent.com/pod-product-compliance
Ingram Content Group UK Ltd.
Pitfield, Milton Keynes, MK11 3LW, UK
UKHW041450180426
11946UKWH00013B/142/J